LAW AT THE CUTTING EDGE

This collection celebrates the immense contribution of Sarah Worthington to the field of private law. Defining the subject broadly, experts from the judiciary and the academy address contemporary challenges arising in the fields of agency, company law and insolvency, contract law, equity and trusts, the law of money, personal property, restitution and unjust enrichment. The breadth of the contributors' expertise and their willingness to offer innovative and insightful solutions to difficult problems perfectly mirror Sarah Worthington's rigorous and inspirational approach to private law scholarship.

Law at the Cutting Edge

Essays in Honour of Professor Dame Sarah Worthington DBE KC (Hon) FBA

Edited by
Sinéad Agnew
and
Sir Marcus Smith

• HART •
OXFORD • LONDON • NEW YORK • NEW DELHI • SYDNEY

HART PUBLISHING

Bloomsbury Publishing Plc

Kemp House, Chawley Park, Cumnor Hill, Oxford, OX2 9PH, UK

1385 Broadway, New York, NY 10018, USA

29 Earlsfort Terrace, Dublin 2, Ireland

HART PUBLISHING, the Hart/Stag logo, BLOOMSBURY and the Diana logo are trademarks of Bloomsbury Publishing Plc

First published in Great Britain 2024

A catalogue record for this book is available from the British Library.

A catalogue record for this book is available from the Library of Congress.

Library of Congress Control Number: 2023950521

ISBN: HB: 978-1-50996-515-1
ePDF: 978-1-50996-517-5
ePub: 978-1-50996-516-8

Typeset by Compuscript Ltd, Shannon

for Sarah

Preface

SARAH WORTHINGTON IS a remarkable person who has made – and continues to make[1] – a remarkable contribution to legal scholarship. The essays in this *Festschrift* are written in her honour. When conceiving of how we might try to do justice to Sarah and her career, we had two ambitions. We wished to gather as many of Sarah's friends and colleagues together in one place for a day of stimulating debate about legal problems and ideas that would be of interest to her, followed by a party. And we were particularly keen to ensure that the topics for discussion would reflect the extraordinary breadth of Sarah's career, both as an academic and (more recently) a judge (sitting as a deputy High Court Judge in the Chancery Division of the High Court). In 2021, together with Stelios Tofaris and Louise Merrett, we set about trying to bring these ambitions to fruition. Eventually, in the summer of 2022, Sarah's friends and colleagues from all over the world gathered in person in Cambridge and remotely for a memorable and packed day of intellectual endeavour and celebration. This collection of essays is the result.

Of course, none of this would have happened without the support of various people and institutions. We are very grateful to the conference, IT and catering teams at Newnham College for ensuring that the daytime conference passed off smoothly across several time zones, to Trinity College and its catering team for providing us with a wonderful drinks reception and dinner, and to the Cambridge Private Law Centre for its financial support. We owe a debt of thanks to Sinéad Moloney and Sasha Jawed at Hart Publishing for being so supportive of this book and making the production process so easy. And finally, we are enormously grateful to Mark Phillips KC, Will McKinlay and all at South Square for their unwavering enthusiasm for this project and their incredible generosity in helping us to make it happen.

When deciding on a title and themes for the collection, we tried to reflect Sarah's varied interests: the subject-matter spans property and insolvency, obligations and remedies, persons and agency, equity and the common law. We were also conscious of the fact that Sarah has never been content with simply reciting what the law is or what the cases say, invaluable though such efforts are, and significant as her contribution has been, even in this regard. As Sarah would routinely ask her PhD students, 'So what?' and 'Why does it matter?' She has always been acutely concerned with the way in which the law in our common law system evolves to remain relevant and grapple with new practical problems, and how it manages through incremental change and reaction to remain both predictable and adaptable, particularly in the light of social and technological development. That is why this *Festschrift* is entitled 'Law at the Cutting Edge', for that is where Sarah stood, and that is where these essays find their

[1] Officially, Sarah 'retired' in 2022, but a year later she is still as busy as ever ....

focus. They are intentionally controversial, and the aim has been to create a dialogue between authors who see difficult things differently.

Our objective, when seeking contributors was to ensure that those who had played a part in Sarah's career (academic and professional mentors, colleagues, former students, fellow judges and practitioners, intellectual sparring partners, and friends) were well represented at the conference and in this collection. So many people were eager to participate that we found ourselves putting coauthors together and asking others to comment on papers and chair sessions. We are very grateful to all the participants and contributors, some of whom were gamely writing together for the first time, for their generosity of spirit: it made the occasion truly memorable.

This collaborative approach had a secondary, and hugely important, purpose and effect, which was to draw out and debate areas of controversy and disagreement in the best traditions of the quest for the better or right answer. The 'right' answer is an objective that will never, truly, be attained (due to differing values and changing circumstances) but the process of debate and discussion is the only way that ambition can be approached. So, the reader will see imaginative ways of respectful disagreement running throughout this *Festschrift* and that is as it should be. A cutting edge involves the sharp drawing of distinctions which will have a certain quality of violence to them. It is in formulating and debating these distinctions that we think Sarah will – in her remarkable career – most be remembered, and we have sought to promulgate essays that at least try to achieve the same thing.

The essays seek to reflect Sarah's career and contributions in other respects too. First, Sarah's body of work has not only covered an extraordinary range in terms of subject-matter: it has also sought to articulate both important detail in the law, and (although not necessarily at the same time) the broader picture. One only needs to consider Sarah's analogy explaining the interaction between the common law and equity in terms of children playing the same game, but by different rules, to appreciate the latter point. The former point can be made by reference to much of Sarah's writing. The essays seek to reflect this, and it is this shift (from the broad to the specific) that informed our ordering of the essays in this *Festschrift*.

This volume begins with a biographical introduction about Sarah and her work, penned by Sir Ross Cranston and Lord Leggatt (chapter 1). The introduction is followed by Sir Marcus Smith's careful examination of the role played by the rule of law in arguments opposing the return of cultural property to its place of origin (chapter 2). In keeping with the innovative theme of this collection, his chapter involves an entertaining and illuminating imagined dialogue between heritage and law about the case for the return of the Elgin Marbles. Sir William Trower, Mark Phillips KC and Madeleine Jones then offer a fascinating account of how financial and other crises have informed the development of company and insolvency law (chapter 3). This chapter could, of course, have been pigeon-holed under insolvency – and the chapter is a hugely valuable contribution in that area – but (as with Sarah's career) it is so much more, spanning two centuries of legal history and ending with a discussion of the impact of the coronavirus pandemic and the invasion of Ukraine.

The subject-matter then moves to a series of essays (chapters 4–7) which touch on a wide range of practical problems that arise in the context of the law of persons. In chapter 4 Rachel Leow engages directly with Sarah's work on three long-standing questions in the law of attribution and agency, before offering a fresh perspective and new and different solutions to these old problems. Paul Davies then grapples with the difficult question of when parent companies should be liable for wrongdoing committed within their foreign subsidiaries (chapter 5). He argues that an expansion in parent liability has been caused by a doctrinal shift, whereby tort – rather than corporate – law now forms the paradigm for analysis of the question, but that a more regulatory approach may tie parental liability back to company law in the future. Hugh Collins puts forward a positive case for recognising networks as a new legal concept that refers to a particular kind of business organisation, on the ground that this would obviate the need to resort to legal fictions and improve the law's ability to deliver both coherence and commercially sensible results (chapter 6). Finally, Sir Antony Zacaroli discusses the importance of classes in insolvency and restructuring (chapter 7). He offers insights as to how the courts' role in insolvency schemes and restructuring plans has developed in response to the tensions that may arise between the rights and interests of different groups of stakeholders in a single class. It is pleasing to see an enormously underrepresented part of the common law (the law of persons) featuring – if only by accident, not design – so prominently in a set of essays intended to be forward and not backward looking.

Next, and ever more specific, we have a series of essays grappling with claims to property, both personal and in rem, thus engaging both the law of obligations and the law of property (chapters 8–15). Michael Bryan evaluates Sarah's argument that the function of the law of unjust enrichment is to restore the economic benefit of an asset to the party entitled to that benefit, and concludes that it is compelling (chapter 8). Ultimately, however, he takes the view that practical and doctrinal difficulties will preclude the trust from becoming the primary mechanism for reversing unjust enrichment. Next, Simone Degeling and Lionel Smith engage in conversation on a topic close to Sarah's heart: fiduciary obligations (chapter 9). They reflect on the extent to which equitable notions of loyalty and stewardship inform other areas of law, considering specifically the application of the law of fiduciary relationships to advisors. They conclude that advisory relationships can be fiduciary and that powers over non-financial interests can also be held in a fiduciary capacity. In chapter 10, Jessica Hudson and Pauline Ridge heed Sarah's call to pay attention to the risk of incoherence in a dualist system of law by identifying and addressing incoherence in equity's responses to breach of trust. Using the equitable proprietary claim and knowing receipt as examples, they make the important point that achieving coherence in this area of law requires us to engage more precisely with the content and operation of these rules and the normative values that underpin them. James Penner then argues that the standard explanation of a beneficiary's ability to trace misapplied trust assets through payment systems, employing a kind of 'exchange analysis', is founded upon an error, but one easily corrected. The correct analysis turns on understanding the legal concept of 'payment' as it was developed in the laws of contract and agency (chapter 11). This leads him to conclude that we do not need the concept of 'backwards tracing' to explain why a beneficiary can trace through an overdrawn account. Ultimately, the only question we need to ask is whether the payer's power to pay money into the account was wholly or partially *funded* with trust assets: if so, then the beneficiary is able to trace into assets acquired by expenditures from that account.

The law relating to security interests is always developing, and Michael Bridge considers the different ways in which quasi-security and true security are treated in English law (chapter 12). He argues that so long as freedom of contract is preserved in relation to remedies, the English law of security should be codified in a manner which would focus less on ownership and instead assimilate security and quasi-security for the purposes of notice and priority. Charles Mitchell then takes us to the cutting edge of the English law of unjust enrichment (chapter 13). He explores the implications of *Test Claimants in the FII Group Litigation v Revenue and Customs Commissioners* [2021] UKSC 31, [2021] 1 WLR 4354, in which the Supreme Court accepted the proposition that in appropriate cases the extent of a defendant's enrichment should be determined by netting off her gains against losses caused by receipt of the gains. The content of such a 'netting off' rule has yet to be worked out by the courts, and the chapter offers some observations as to what such a rule might look like, and whether the issues such a rule might seek to address could be better resolved through the change of position defence.

The cutting edge of property law forms the focus of the final two essays in this collection. Peter Watts and Kelvin Low consider the arguments for and against the recognition of cryptoassets as property (chapter 14). They conclude that in light of how laypersons generally regard and treat cryptoassets, it is expedient to recognise them as property, and the courts should do so unless and until they are banned by the legislature. Julius Grower takes a different view (chapter 15): he argues that the judiciary does not have the competence to answer the question whether cryptoassets should be treated as property, and that this is a question which only the legislature can decide.

In addition to the essays in this volume, two other papers were presented and discussed on the day. Robert Stevens argued that there was no coherent understanding of what constitutes a 'proprietary base' for a proprietary claim, roping in Sir William Trower as a participant in his examples, which prompted a lively debate (and wry smiles from Sir William). Louise Gullifer and Ben McFarlane's paper offered some fascinating insights on dematerialised securities and the nature of trusts and equity. A full list of contributors, commentators and chairs from the *Festschrift* conference can be found at page xiii below.

This volume endeavours to state the law as at December 2022, with some minor additions at proof stage.

Sinéad Agnew
Sir Marcus Smith
August 2023

Contents

List of Contributors

Editors

Sinéad Agnew is Catherine Seville Associate Professor of Law at the University of Cambridge and a fellow of Newnham College.

Sir Marcus Smith is a judge of the High Court of England and Wales and President of the Competition Appeal Tribunal.

Authors

Michael Bridge KC (Hon) FBA is Professor of Law at the National University of Singapore, Cassel Professor of Commercial Law Emeritus at the London School of Economics, and Senior Research Fellow at Harris Manchester College, Oxford.

Michael Bryan is Professor of Law Emeritus at the University of Melbourne.

Hugh Collins FBA is Cassel Professor of Commercial Law at the London School of Economics and Vinerian Professor of English Law Emeritus at All Souls College, Oxford.

Sir Ross Cranston FBA is Professor of Law at the London School of Economics.

Paul Davies KC (Hon) FBA is Allen & Overy Professor of Corporate Law Emeritus at the University of Oxford, Cassel Professor of Commercial Law Emeritus at the London School of Economics, and Senior Research Fellow at the Commercial Law Centre, Harris Manchester College, Oxford.

Simone Degeling is Professor of Law at the University of New South Wales.

Julius Grower is an Associate Professor of Law at the University of Oxford and a Fellow of St Hugh's College.

Jessica Hudson is an Associate Professor of Law at the University of New South Wales.

Madeleine Jones is a barrister who practises from South Square.

The Right Honourable Lord Leggatt is a Justice of the United Kingdom Supreme Court.

Rachel Leow is an Assistant Professor of Law at the London School of Economics.

Kelvin FK Low is Professor of Law at the National University of Singapore.

Charles Mitchell KC (Hon) FBA is Professor of Law at University College London.

James Penner is Kwa Geok Choo Professor of Property Law at the National University of Singapore.

Mark Phillips KC is a barrister who practises from South Square.

Pauline Ridge is Professor of Law at the Australian National University.

Lionel Smith is Downing Professor of the Laws of England at the University of Cambridge and a Fellow of Gonville and Caius College.

Sir Marcus Smith is a judge of the High Court of England and Wales and President of the Competition Appeals Tribunal.

Sir William Trower is a judge of the High Court of England and Wales.

Peter Watts KC is a barrister who practises from Bankside Chambers, Auckland, and Fountain Court, London. He is also Visiting Professor of Law at the University of Oxford, Professor of Law Emeritus at the University of Auckland, and Senior Research Fellow at Harris Manchester College, Oxford.

Sir Antony Zacaroli is a judge of the High Court of England and Wales.

Other Conference Contributors, Commentators and Chairs

Elise Bant is Professor of Private Law and Commercial Regulation at the University of Western Australia.

The Right Honourable Lord Briggs of Westbourne is a Justice of the United Kingdom Supreme Court.

The Right Honourable Lord Burrows is a Justice of the United Kingdom Supreme Court.

William Day is a barrister who practises from 3 Verulam Buildings and is a Fellow of Downing College, Cambridge.

The Honourable Justice Edelman is a Justice of the High Court of Australia.

David Fox is Professor of Common Law at the University of Edinburgh.

Amy Goymour is an Associate Professor of Law at the University of Cambridge and a Fellow of Jesus College.

Louise Gullifer KC (Hon) FBA is Rouse Ball Professor of English Law at the University of Cambridge and a Fellow of Gonville and Caius College.

Lusina Ho is Harold Hsiao-Wo Lee Professor in Trusts and Equity at the University of Hong Kong.

Ben McFarlane is Professor of English Law at the University of Oxford and a Fellow of St John's College.

Louise Merrett is Professor of International Commercial Law at the University of Cambridge, Vice-Master of Trinity College, and a barrister who practises from Fountain Court.

Eva Micheler is Professor of Law at the London School of Economics.

The Right Honourable Lord Justice Newey is a Lord Justice of Appeal.

The Right Honourable Lord Justice Snowden is a Lord Justice of Appeal.

Robert Stevens is Herbert Smith Freehills Professor of English Private Law at the University of Oxford and a Fellow of Lady Margaret Hall.

Stelios Tofaris is an Associate Professor of Law at the University of Cambridge and a Fellow of Girton College.

Ryan James Turner is a barrister who practises from Maitland Chambers.

Graham Virgo KC (Hon) is Professor of English Private Law at the University of Cambridge and Master of Downing College.

Stephen Watterson is Professor of Private Law at the University of Cambridge and a Fellow of Trinity Hall.

Table of Cases

Australia

Canada

Hong Kong

New Zealand

Singapore

United Kingdom

European Court of Human Rights

United States of America

Table of Legislation

Statutes

Australia

Bankruptcy Act 1966 (Cth)
s 116(2)(a) 199, 200
Charitable Trusts Act 1993 (NSW)
s 6 204
Corporations Act 2001 (Cth) 200
Personal Property Securities Act 2009 (Cth)
s 8(1)(h) 162
Probate and Administration Act 1898 (NSW)
s 45 199
Succession Act 2006 (NSW)
s 4(5) 199

Canada

Personal Property Security Act 1993
s 2(1)(jj)(i) 259
s 2(1)(jj)(ii) 259
s 34(5) 259

France

Law no 2017-399 of 27 March 2017 97

Japan

Japanese Civil Code 293
Payment Services Act 2010 295

New Zealand

Crimes Act 1961 (NZ) 290
Companies Act 1993 (NZ)
s 2 ....303, 309

Singapore

Singaporean Contributory Negligence and Personal Injuries Act (Cap 54, 2002) 66

United Kingdom

Table of International Conventions, Treaties and Agreements

1

Sarah Worthington: A Biographical Sketch

ROSS CRANSTON AND GEORGE LEGGATT

SARAH WORTHINGTON (NÉE Monks) was born in Yorkshire, although both of her parents were Lancastrians. Her father was a civil engineer, her mother a passionate gardener who eventually built ten acres of garden at their home in Tasmania. Shortly after Sarah's birth, the family moved first to Uganda, followed by Kenya, where Sarah's father worked on water projects. School was mornings only (8.00am–1.00pm), then home for lunch and the swimming pool in the afternoon. Her parents gave her a sense of independence and adventure, but also of working hard and 'using your talents'. Education was valued because it opened new worlds, opportunities and challenges. Growing up in Africa meant she had seen other cultures at close hand. These early years inevitably moulded her view of life.

After a short period in England during her father's long-service leave – with the novelty of multistorey terrace houses, winter clothes and stiff shoes – the family resettled in Tasmania, Australia's smallest state. Its first hydroelectric power station was opened in 1916, and until dam construction came to an end in the early 1980s the state's Hydro-Electric Commission built a web of hydropower schemes, roads and towns.[1] Like many others, Sarah's father relocated to work on these.[2]

For Sarah it was first a private Catholic school in the state's capital, Hobart (hats, gloves and blazers). That was followed by the coeducational state high school in Devonport on the north coast (still hats, gloves and blazers) because the Catholic high school there did not teach science or mathematics, or have matriculation classes. Sarah's was a generation in Australia when, if one could do science, one did it: science was the country's future. Consequently, she studied chemistry, physics, geology and maths, along with English and French. There was a great deal more besides – Duke of Edinburgh bush walks, the freedom to roam with friends, and time on the beach.

[1] www.hydro.com.au/about-us/our-story (accessed 25 September 2023).

[2] See C Price, 'Post-War Immigration: 1947–98' (1998) 15 *Journal of the Australian Population Association* 115; ER Woolmington, 'Post-War Immigration and Industrial Development in Australia' (1958) 30 *Australian Quarterly* 77, 83.

Then it was an escape from Tasmania with the goal of a career in cancer research – a science degree at the Australian National University (ANU), established as a federal government funded research university, with separate teaching for undergraduates.[3] In her second year she met her husband to be, Peter Worthington, a law student, and a constant in her life ever since; in her fourth, her honours year, she discovered a completely unexpected passion for teaching – it was a mandatory requirement for honours students to tutor those in the earlier years and she loved it.

Two years into a PhD at the University of Queensland, with more science teaching to medical students, she finally realised that despite the inspiring professor leading the research programme, Professor Cheviot (Chev) Kidson, she did not like laboratory work, with its constant repetition. Against all advice she undertook a year's teaching qualification and began teaching science at an all-girls Catholic school in Brisbane. She attributes her later focus on logic and principle to her time in science. She also looks back with some pride on how with her as a role model many of her high-school pupils became radiographers, science teachers and pharmacists, when their professed ambitions beforehand were to be secretaries and nurses.

In her second year of high-school teaching she began a law degree, part-time, at the University of Queensland. Since childcare was limited and timetables fixed, she mostly went to tutorials, not lectures. Four children later, and now in her early thirties, she graduated with a first-class degree and some prizes in 1986. Notable during her time at the Law School were the courses taught by Dr Jim O'Donovan on equity, where she discovered Paul Finn's *Fiduciary Obligations*,[4] and company and insolvency law. O'Donovan, she says, provided memorable lessons on good teaching and is probably the reason she became an academic.[5]

When the family moved to Melbourne – Peter had transferred from private practice as a law firm partner to work as legal counsel with BHP, headquartered there[6] – she obtained a lectureship in the University of Melbourne Business School for a year, teaching contract and company law to accountants, and began the Law School's LLM on a part-time basis (two years full time), during which she became a lecturer there, teaching what for her was her dream list of subjects – equity, company law and contract. Melbourne Law School was an ideal place to begin her academic career, since young academics were well supported, and her colleagues were smart and enthusiastic. The Law School allowed academics to work one day a week in practice

[3] SG Foster and M Varghese, *The Making of The Australian National University 1946–1996* (Canberra, ANU Press, 2009) 198–200, 364.

[4] S Worthington, 'Fiduciaries: Following Finn' in T Bonyhady (ed), *Finn's Law. An Australian Justice* (Sydney, Federation Press, 2016) 34. See P Finn, *Fiduciary Obligations. 40th Anniversary Republication with Additional Essays* (Sydney, Federation Press, 2016). Finn graduated and taught at the University of Queensland, was research professor of law at ANU, and a judge of the Federal Court of Australia.

[5] Dr James O'Donovan became professor of law at the Law School at the University of Western Australia and was the author, inter alia, of *Company Receivers and Administrators*, 2nd edn (Sydney, LBC Information Services, 1992) (with J Phillips and W Courtney), *The Modern Contract of Guarantee*, 4th English edn (London, Sweet & Maxwell, 2020), *Personal Property Securities Law in Australia* (Sydney, Thomson Reuters, 2009).

[6] G Blainey, 'A Brief History of BHP Billiton' (2010) 8 *Journal of Australasian Mining History* 23.

or in similar positions, and she began to qualify for practice at Arthur Robinson & Hedderwicks, now part of Allens.[7]

A flourishing career at Melbourne Law School and completion of her qualification to practice were unexpectedly cut short by the family's uprooting to Moscow in 1992–1994 through Peter's employment. The Soviet Union had collapsed and foreign mining companies like BHP needed to be there.[8] Sarah offers an insight into the economic and social implications for life in post-Soviet Moscow:

> When we arrived in early 1992 there was nothing we were used to, no English communications, no maps (in any language), no western style shops or Russian equivalents – so no milk, cereal etc for four primary school children. Things changed rapidly, but in the beginning we shipped food and as well shopped in the local markets. The pollution was terrible especially in summer; the water, even after filtering and boiling, still odd; and the rule of law non-existent. But the people were wonderful, the buildings and countryside remarkable, the adventures unbelievable.[9]

For a few months she was with a US law firm, teaching Russian lawyers to communicate with Western clients, and in particular that research notes for the firm needed to be full and frank, not simply what one outside (Russian) party would prefer.

But doctoral studies beckoned, and she soon began her PhD at Wolfson College, Cambridge. Her supervisor was Dr Len Sealy, a New Zealander, who spent his academic life at Gonville & Caius College, and whose *Cases and Materials in Company Law* Sarah subsequently coauthored with Sealy, before authoring several editions on her own and, more recently, bringing in new collaborators.[10] It was a tricky exercise meeting the Cambridge residence requirements, but with Sealy's help the pattern in term was six weeks in Cambridge and two weeks in Moscow on rotation for the first academic year, and in the second year six weeks at home in Moscow and two weeks reading and photocopying in the Squire Law Library. Then submission, with Professor Sir Roy Goode as an examiner. The PhD thesis became a book, *Proprietary Interests in Commercial Transactions*,[11] which was widely and favourably reviewed.

The BHP plan was now for Peter to be based in London, so the family moved there and Sarah obtained a lectureship (later senior lectureship) in 1994 in the newly established Department of Law at Birkbeck College, the college of the University of London providing evening higher education. (In fact, changes in BHP's management in Melbourne meant Peter commuted for a year before his transfer to London was

[7] *Allens. The First 200 Years* (Sydney, Allens, 2022) 240.

[8] For example, see A Shleifer and D Treisman, *Without a Map: Political Tactics and Economic Reform in Russia* (Cambridge, MA, MIT Press, 2000) 19ff; A Åslund, *How Russia Became a Market Economy* (Washington, DC, Brookings Institution Press, 1995) 364.

[9] For life from the viewpoint of ordinary Muscovites: C Humphrey, *The Unmaking of Soviet Life: Everyday Economies after Socialism* (Ithaca, NY and London, Cornell University Press, 2002) 44–52, 178–80.

[10] S Worthington and S Agnew, *Sealy & Worthington's Text, Cases, and Materials in Company Law*, 12th edn (Oxford, Oxford University Press, 2022). On Sealy, see www.squire.law.cam.ac.uk/eminent-scholars-archive/professor-len-sealy (accessed 25 September 2023).

[11] S Worthington, *Proprietary Interests in Commercial Transactions* (Oxford, Oxford University Press, 1996).

confirmed.) The Law Department had a heavy theoretical bent.[12] Sarah was largely isolated from this in teaching company law and equity to students in their final year. She was not the first Antipodean lawyer to marvel that company law was not compulsory for lawyers intending to practise, and that the hours of face-to-face contact in subjects like those she taught were far less than what she had experienced at the University of Queensland and the University of Melbourne. Nonetheless she notes that the Birkbeck students were committed, clever and with fascinating hinterlands. At Birkbeck Sarah was the lone commercial lawyer so that when the opportunity came to move to the London School of Economics and Political Science (LSE) she took it.

At the LSE from 1997 to 2011 there was a blossoming of Sarah's research, with major publications such as the book of which she is most proud, *Equity*,[13] along with much else in the way of books and articles. *Equity* epitomises Sarah's intellectual approach. Most unusually for a book about law, the first edition cited no cases and named no commentators.[14] The book is, as she wrote in the preface, 'about legal ideas and their rigorous and principled analysis'. Not for her equity as an esoteric system, accessible only to Chancery initiates; nor as a source of uniquely conscience-based discretion, measured by the length of the Chancellor's foot. It is a well-developed body of law, no different in principle from the common law but which for historical reasons evolved as a separate set of rules. This historical accident provides no justification for retaining two distinct, and therefore inevitably disjointed, jurisdictions, coexisting uneasily with each other. The aim of *Equity* is nothing less than to indicate how the integration of equity and the common law can be achieved. The prize of such integration is coherence in the law. In Sarah's exacting world view, the quest for such coherence can be seen as the driving force and ultimate goal of all legal scholarship.

As well as teaching in equity and company law at the LSE, there were excursions into classes on commercial contracts and restitution. Outside the LSE, she began with visiting professorial appointments to teach on a regular basis at the universities of Melbourne and Hong Kong, as well as elsewhere on an episodic basis. In 2007–2008 she was the president of the Society of Legal Scholars, the learned society for law teachers and, as is customary, hosted the Society's annual conference.

Two years after her promotion to professor in 2003, Sarah was appointed as LSE's Pro-Director (Deputy Vice-Chancellor) for Research and External Relations. The research aspect included taking the lead for LSE's 2008 entry for the REF (the research assessment programme for the UK's higher-education funding bodies) as well as successfully proposing an internal seed-funding grants scheme. External relations involved much travel abroad, including various trips to China and India to forge academic partnerships, raise funds and wave the LSE flag. Sarah also proposed that students at the LSE should have some insight into disciplines other than their own, which led to lunchtime sessions over the academic year called 'Thinking Like a Social

[12] There is a short history of the department in the early years at www.bbk.ac.uk/schools/law/our-history (accessed 25 September 2023), although it omits the instrumental role of the College's Master, Baroness Blackstone, in its foundation.

[13] S Worthington, *Equity* (Oxford, Oxford University Press, 2003).

[14] A second edition, replete with footnotes, was published in 2006.

Scientist', which became LSE100, a compulsory course for all LSE undergraduates in their first year.[15]

Despite her unbounded enthusiasm for the LSE – to which she returned in 2022 – Sarah unsurprisingly applied for and was appointed to the Downing Professorship of the Laws of England at Cambridge in 2011, the chair previously occupied by luminaires such as FW Maitland, Sir Ivor Jennings, Stanley de Smith and, most recently, Sir John Baker. At Cambridge she continued to publish and teach, including a new and popular LLM course in advanced private law. She set up the Cambridge Private Law Centre, with its regular seminars, public lectures and edited collections. And she revived the Cambridge Law Club, originally established by Maitland to pursue the 'social study of law', and turned it into a flourishing and fruitful focus of intellectual exchange and social contact between faculty members and senior judges.

Her two previous attempts to qualify for legal practice having been cut short, Sarah was finally called to the bar at Middle Temple in 2005 under the special route for senior academics. She undertook pupillage at South Square – a leading set of barristers specialising in insolvency, restructuring and other commercial matters – and stayed on as an academic member of those chambers. She was elected a Bencher of Middle Temple in 2010, the same year she was made a Queen's Counsel (honoris causa). Professional qualification enabled her to be appointed in 2017 as a Deputy High Court judge, authorised to sit in the Chancery Division. That led to judgments in familiar areas such as *Quistclose* trusts, shareholders' rights and insolvency.[16] But there were also adventures in other areas such as local government law, summary judgment and the dispute resolution rules of the Financial Conduct Authority.[17]

Sarah's public activities have not been confined to law. Elected a member of the British Academy in 2009, she served on its council and also as its treasurer from 2015 to 2020. She became a trustee of the British Museum in 2020.

Much-deserved public recognition of her services to English private law came when Sarah was appointed Dame Commander of the Order of the British Empire (DBE) in the 2020 Birthday Honours. In July 2022 her extraordinary achievements were celebrated at an event held at Cambridge to mark her retirement from the Downing Chair. Many distinguished legal scholars from opposite ends (geographically) of the common law world took part, all of whom have been inspired by Sarah and her work whether as colleagues, students or friends (or in some cases as all three). It was a day of intense discussion of a remarkable range of papers paying tribute to the breadth and depth of Sarah's legal scholarship. Those papers have now been refined into this collection of essays which we are proud to introduce. They constitute a book, as she would wish, about legal ideas and their rigorous and principled analysis; and they have much to say and show about the fundamental value of coherence in the law.

[15] see https://info.lse.ac.uk/current-students/lse100 (accessed 25 September 2023).

[16] *Ali v Dinc* [2020] EWHC 3055 (Ch); *Prince Marwaha v Entertainment One Ltd* [2023] EWHC 480 (Ch); *Hikari Miso (UK) Ltd v Knibbs* [2023] EWHC 1340 (Ch); *Qureshi v Association of Conservative Clubs Ltd* [2019] EWHC 1165 (Ch) respectively. An appeal in *Ali v Dinc* was dismissed: [2022] EWCA Civ 34; Sarah's judgment was cited favourably by Fancourt J in *Byers v Samba Financial Group* [2021] EWHC 60 (Ch).

[17] *Ramsgate Town Council v Thanet DC* [2018] EWHC 3042 (Ch); *Raja v McMillan* [2020] EWHC 951 (Ch); *Davis v Lloyds Bank Plc* [2020] EWHC 1758 (Ch), respectively.

2

*Cultural Property and the 'Dark Side' of the Rule of Law**

SIR MARCUS SMITH

I. INTRODUCTION

THIS CHAPTER BEGAN as an attempt to understand the different arguments that arise in relation to the return of cultural property. I should state, at the outset, that I have no ambition to try to resolve these arguments. My conclusion, which also formed my starting point, and which has been amply justified by the work done between starting point and conclusion, is that resolution of these arguments involves the consideration and balancing of non-legal judgemental factors that have no place in an essay such as this, written by a judge.

Accordingly, they find no place here.

But that does not mean that an attempt to understand why these arguments are so difficult to resolve is not worthwhile. My conclusion is that the reason these arguments are so difficult is because they involve the interplay of, and conflict between, two sets of values which lie in opposition to one another. The first is the desire to return cultural property to its place of origin (a value I am going to *assume* as valid[1]); the second is the rule of law (a value whose relevance I *am* going to try to explain and unpack).

I am going to suggest that the reason these questions are so fraught – when, on their face, they really should not be – is because the values in play are to a very considerable extent operating on different planes, which makes even agreement of common terms of reference hard.

So much by way of 'content warning'. I will begin with the relatively safe ground of how, as a matter of law, disputes concerning moveable property are resolved.

* A copy of this chapter first appeared as an article in the South Square Digest, www.southsquare.com.

[1] I am, therefore, not going to justify it. That is for others. This means that I spend more time on the areas that I *am* qualified to consider, which are the legal questions. That means that this essay is inevitably somewhat one-sided in terms of words devoted to cultural property as opposed to the rule of law. I hope that any reader will appreciate that that is *not* because I am discounting the importance of the return of cultural property: I am merely discounting my ability to comment meaningfully on this value.

II. RESOLVING DISPUTES ABOUT MOVEABLE PROPERTY

A. The 'Domestic' Case

Laying on one side, for a moment, international questions,[2] even a *domestic* dispute (by which I mean a case where all disputants and the property in question are, and at all material times were, in the same jurisdiction) regarding moveable property can give rise to difficult questions of fact and law. The problem with moveable property is that it is intrinsically transferable[3] and so – if there is a dispute about ownership – typically a series of transactions transferring the moveable in question, going back in time (sometimes quite far back), will have to be examined. Title is tricky, even in the domestic case: but we have rules (albeit rules that are too perhaps complex) to resolve such cases in a prospective and (ideally) clear and predictable manner. I am not going to go into such rules any further.[4]

B. The 'International' Case

The international case is even more problematic. Two complications arise: (i) Which courts have jurisdiction? (ii) What law or laws do they apply, where the court does have jurisdiction?

Jurisdiction is the more straightforward case. The basic rule is that the courts where the property in question is located have primary – and sometimes exclusive – jurisdiction. There are good reasons for such a rule. It is consistent with the general rule that a claimant should seek out their defendant and sue in the defendant's courts. The defendant is involuntarily a party to the suit, and ought (prima facie, at least) to have the home advantage. Litigating where the property is situated also pays due regard to the importance of property rights being protected locally. That is particularly important in the case of immovable property, but remains important in cases of other types of property, including moveable and intangible property.[5] Finally, litigating abroad in relation to domestic property carries with it a dash of interference with rights that ought to be protected or abrogated by the domestic courts; and more than a hint of an affront to international comity between jurisdictions. Why should a domestic jurisdiction enforce a foreign judgment depriving a defendant of property they hold within that very jurisdiction?

[2] By which I mean questions of private international law or the conflict of laws. Issues relating to public international law are considered later in this chapter.

[3] That is one of the 'bundle of rights' that the owner of property has by virtue of his or her ownership. In an essay published in 1961, Honoré sought to enumerate the various rights that might comprise the highest possible interest in a thing – ie the 'bundle' of rights in a thing or in property that represents the highest level of interest that can be. This was an interest that he termed 'ownership': A Honoré in A Guest (ed), *Oxford Essays in Jurisprudence*, (Oxford, Oxford University Press, 1961) ch V; M Smith and N Leslie, *The Law of Assignment*, 3rd edn (Oxford, Oxford University Press, 2018) paras 2.39 and 2.41.

[4] But see, generally, Smith and Leslie (n 3).

[5] Thus, intellectual property rights tend to be locally protected (see *Lucasfilm Limited v Ainsworth* [2011] UKSC 39), but also moveable property, as we shall see.

The jurisdictional question thus resolves itself relatively straightforwardly. Matters are very different when choice of law questions arise. A choice of law rule indicates the legal system that is to supply the answer to a particular legal question. There is an immediate tension between the framing of the question and the resultant answer. That is because the question or issue can often be framed in different ways, and not necessarily in accordance with 'objective' factors. The way in which the question is framed may well suggest the answer, which is never satisfactory. This is the problem or 'art' of characterisation, which involves working out whether an issue in dispute is – or is not – subsumed within the abstract proposition that is the particular choice of law rule.

Assuming that an English court properly has jurisdiction, the law that will be chosen to determine, for example, the lawfulness of any transfer, is the law of the country where the moveables are situated at the time of the transfer in question (ie the applicable law is the *lex situs*).[6] This reflects the important fact that moveable property is … moveable. Why should the law of the jurisdiction where the moveable thing is presently held determine the validity of a transaction that took place previously in another jurisdiction, where that thing was then located? A choice of law rule indicating the applicable law as the law of present location would be a bad rule.[7] A rule based on present location would impose on the parties to the foreign transaction a law that they cannot have expected to have applied, in place of the law that (probably) they did expect to apply, namely the *lex situs*. A rule based on present location would also be open to abuse: it is possible, in the case of moveable property (as opposed to immovable property), for the party holding the property to relocate it to a jurisdiction favourable to them.

Whilst the rule that the applicable law is the *lex situs* might be hard to apply – and less easy to justify – in the case of intangible property, I venture to suggest that it makes good sense in the case of moveable (tangible) property. But let us not fool ourselves that the rule is easy to apply. Any rule that can be so shortly stated inevitably has hidden complexities. In this case, difficulties are likely to arise on the following points: (i) whether the property in question is, in fact, moveable property at all;[8] (ii) whether the property, albeit moveable, is inalienable by its nature;[9] (iii) whether questions of capacity to transfer are governed by an altogether different law;[10] and (iv) which law applies in the case of successive transfers where there are competing claims of different priority.[11]

All of these points may suggest different applicable laws. The subjective or policy problems that 'characterisation' must deal with are evident. Even if the

[6] J Carruthers, *The Transfer of Property in the Conflict of Laws*, (Oxford, Oxford University Press, 2010) para 3.07. Prior to the decision in *Cammell v Sewell* (1858) 3 H&N 617, 157 ER 615 and (1860) 5 H&N 728, 157 ER 1371, there are a number of rival choice of law rules: see, further, Carruthers, ibid, ch 3.

[7] In contrast to the determining of jurisdiction, which turns on the present location of the thing.

[8] There may be an issue as to whether the property is, in fact, immovable (eg a fixture) or indeed intangible (eg as in the case of documentary intangibles).

[9] As, under some rules, is the case with objects of cultural significance: Carruthers (n 6) paras 3.13–3.18.

[10] ibid paras 3.17–3.18.

[11] ibid para 3.22.

lex situs rule were monolithic, which it is not,[12] and even if it were of straightforward application, which it is also not,[13] these problems would continue to bedevil lawyers.

It is clear that international cases concerning moveable property are going to be hard to resolve, even at the legal, conflict of laws, level, and leaving out of account the resolution of the difficult factual questions that will likely arise where ownership is contested, and application of the substantive rules of whichever jurisdiction is found to apply.

I am not going to go further into the detail of the law. Time and space do not permit, and an exposition of the detail is not the point of this essay. Rather, my point is that we have evolved sophisticated rules for dealing with disputes as regards property, including where the interests of foreign nations and persons of foreign nationality or domicile are engaged. By 'we' I include the courts of this jurisdiction but also those of many other jurisdictions, who apply similar (although not identical) rules and principles. These courts and jurisdictions are all seeking to resolve, in accordance with prospective and (ideally[14]) clear and predictable rules, difficult legal questions.

III. CLAIMS TO PROPERTY NOT LEGALLY RECOGNISED AND THE RULE OF LAW

A. The Framing of the Claim: Difficulties

So far as I am aware, no proceedings have been brought before the English courts seeking the return to Greece of the Elgin Marbles aka the Parthenon Stones.[15,16] That is entirely unsurprising, given the formidable legal difficulties that lie in the path of succeeding, which may be set out (on a non-exclusive basis) as follows:[17]

1. *Standing*. There is a question of standing or the identity of the true claimant. The Marbles were acquired (I am attempting to use a neutral term: others, depending on their views, might use the term 'stolen'; or insert before 'acquired' the word 'lawfully' or 'unlawfully') in 1801[18] at a time when the relevant government of

[12] Carruthers (n 6) lists various exceptions to the rule at paras 3.23ff.

[13] As Curruthers, ibid, notes at para 3.07 fn 14: 'Inherent in the deceptively simple *situs* rule are complex questions of definition and interpretation: what is the *situs*, and in turn, what is meant by the law of the *situs*? By whom, and according to what law, is the connecting factor to be defined?'.

[14] I appreciate that the preceding paragraphs indicate how far short of the ideal our rules are. But that is more a reflection of the complexity of the interests involved than any suggestion that we are not, bona fide, trying to grapple with these issues.

[15] Even the terms 'Elgin Marbles' versus 'Parthenon Stones' show the controversies into which I am quite deliberately *not* trying to wade. I shall generally use the term 'Marbles'.

[16] There was an attempt in the European Court of Human Rights, *Syllogos Ton Athinaion v The United Kingdom*, Case No 48259/15 (31 May 2016) but the Court held that it lacked temporal jurisdiction (ie the Convention rights relied upon were not retrospective in effect).

[17] Jenkins notes that '[f]ew doubt the legal right of the British Museum to keep the Elgin Marbles. Many, however, openly and vocally dispute the moral right': T Jenkins, *Keeping Their Marbles*, (Oxford, Oxford University Press, 2016) 2. I shall return to both the question of the extent to which the legal rights of the British Museum are questioned and to the question of morality in due course. For the present, I simply seek to articulate (some of) the legal difficulties that arise.

[18] ibid 93, 94.

the relevant territory was the Ottoman Empire. It was only decades later, after the Greek Wars of Independence, that Greece was recognised as an independent nation.[19] Who, now, is the appropriate claimant?

2. *Authority to take.* Assuming that the Marbles were state property and that acts by the relevant officials of the Ottoman Empire were valid (themselves open questions that would have to be determined), the question arises as to whether Lord Elgin had any authority physically to remove the Marbles. Initially, the thinking appears to have been simply to access the site and draw the artefacts there, rather than take them. Two firmans (a form of authority) were granted, but there are questions as to whether they are lawful and – even if they are lawful – whether they permitted Lord Elgin to remove sculptures from the site.[20]
3. *Subsequent transfer, free of prior claim.* The journey of both the Marbles and Lord Elgin to England was fraught. Lord Elgin was taken prisoner by the French (he was released in 1806), and the sculptures arrived over the course of a decade or so in London.[21] They went on show in 1807.[22] It was at this point that controversy regarding their legal status and their acquisition ignited, never to be put out between then and now.[23] Lord Elgin – now broke and also wanting rid of a controversial acquisition – 'petitioned the House of Commons to appoint a Select Committee to investigate the circumstances of acquisition and to recommend on what terms, if any, they should be sold to the government'.[24] The matter was debated over the years, and the question of Lord Elgin's title was squarely raised, as well as the question of their acquisition for the nation.[25] On 25 March 1816, the Select Committee recommended purchase;[26] the matter was then debated in Parliament and it was resolved (82 for, 30 against) to purchase the Marbles for £35,000 (rather less than Lord Elgin was hoping to get).[27] An Act of Parliament, which I shall refer to as the 'Elgin Marbles Act 1816',[28] was passed to sanction the purchase. The Act provides:

> That the Lord High Treasurer of Great Britain, or the Lords Commissioners of His Majesty's Treasury, or any Three or more of them, shall and he or they is and are hereby authorised and empowered, out of any of the Aids or Supplies granted in this Session of Parliament for the Service of Great Britain for the Year one thousand eight hundred and sixteen, immediately after the passing of this Act, to issue and advance the Sum of thirty five thousand pounds to the Trustees of the British Museum, or any person to be appointed by the said Trustees to receive the same, which Money shall be paid without any Fee or other Deduction whatever, and shall be applied in the

[19] ibid 99–100.
[20] ibid 94–95.
[21] ibid 102.
[22] ibid 102.
[23] ibid 102–05.
[24] ibid 105.
[25] ibid 105.
[26] ibid 107.
[27] ibid 109. Lord Elgin wanted £73,600: ibid 105.
[28] This was before the introduction of short titles to Acts of Parliament. The name of the Act is 'An Act to vest the Elgin Collection of ancient Marbles and Sculpture in the Trustees of the British Museum for the Use of the Public'.

> Purchase of the said Collection; and that the Trustees of the British Museum shall, on or before the First Day of September one thousand eight hundred and sixteen, require the Delivery of the said Collection; and if the same shall be then delivered to them, and they shall be satisfied that the several Statues and other Articles forming the said Collection are then conformable to the Catalogue thereof delivered in to a Committee of the House of Commons, they the said Trustees shall, on delivery of the same into their Custody, pay the said sum of thirty five thousand pounds to the said Thomas Earl of Elgin, his Executors, Administrators and Assigns.

So there has been a transfer of title from Lord Elgin to the trustees of the British Museum. The question arises as to whether, as a result, the British Museum takes free of any taints or deficiencies (to the extent that any exist, again an open question[29]) in Lord Elgin's title. One interesting question – not, as far as I know, resolved – is whether the Elgin Marbles Act 1816 removes the application of the *nemo dat quod non habet* rule. Normally, as regards legal property,[30] no one can give better title than they have. The original owner, having better title, can reclaim from a later holder, even if that later holder acquired for value and in good faith.[31] The question is whether the statutory transfer of property contained in the Elgin Marbles Act 1816 has abrogated this rule. The Act seems to have been very carefully drafted to say nothing about this, which may, in itself, speak volumes.[32]

4. *Limitation*. Finally, there would – if an action were commenced now – be a question of limitation.

B. The Marbles as a Good (if Dangerous[33]) Example to Debate

I have selected the Marbles as the case to discuss because there is a considerable body of opinion today advocating for the return of the Marbles to Greece. Such opinions are not merely held by the Greek state, but by many others with no particular links with Greece or to the Marbles. What such persons share is an acute moral sense that the Marbles are not where they belong. As I have already indicated, it is no part of this chapter to debate the moral rights and wrongs of Lord Elgin's acquisition. Any view that I might express (and I am seeking to express no view) is no better than anybody else's. Judges have no more finely tuned moral compass than any other right-minded person, and it would be both presumptuous and wrong to seek to foist any views I might have on an innocent readership looking for legal, and not moral, elucidation.

[29] By which I mean a question as yet undetermined by a court of competent jurisdiction.

[30] In contradistinction to equitable property, where altogether different questions arise: the various rules regarding priority are comprehensively set out in Smith and Leslie (n 3) ch 27.

[31] In the case of legal property – which this is – equity's darling is not protected. Where equitable rules of priority are in play, the bona fide purchaser for value without notice of the prior claim will take free of that prior claim. But this only applies in the case of equitable title and property.

[32] I have not, to be clear, considered the legislative history of the 1816 Act.

[33] The controversy surrounding the Marbles makes them both a good and dangerous example.

C. Putting a Moral Case in Legal Terms: The Problems

My interest is engaged because a number of advocates favouring the return of the Marbles to their place of origin put their case in legal terms.[34] Often, this is no more than the moral case dressed up to look like a legal case, but from time to time a legal argument is sought to be made.[35] It is at this point that my interest becomes engaged, because these arguments tend to have a number of characteristics which differentiate them from the normal process of vindicating a legal right. Specifically:

1. *Polemic, not analysis.* They are long on polemic, and short on analysis. Geoffrey Robertson's interesting and entertaining book,[36] for instance, has a 'puff' from Stephen Fry:

   > A book that proves beyond any reasonable doubt that the Parthenon Marbles belong back in Athens.

   I appreciate that this is a 'mere puff' to sell the book, but the 'puff' betrays a mind-set, and in this case it begs a serious question. There are, as I have described, ways of vindicating a right to ownership – and those rights are vindicated in this jurisdiction not by proving a fact 'beyond reasonable doubt' but on the 'balance of probabilities'. What one really needs to do, before questions of standard of proof become engaged, is state the legal remedy that is being (or is sought to be) enforced. Then, perhaps, in considering these questions, one can say that something is proved or established to the requisite standard.
2. *Deployment of international law.* International law is usually deployed to 'come to the rescue'.[37] That is convenient, because international law is, inherently, much more vague than municipal or national law.[38] Even here, there are stark – and probably impossible to overcome – problems. Thus, public international law, as I am going to call it, is (generally speaking) not retrospective.[39] Of course, it is possible to circumvent these problems by asserting that there is a prospective

[34] As I have noted (n 16), there was an attempt, in 2016, to engage the jurisdiction of the European Court of Human Rights. This failed.

[35] For instance: https://reuniteparthenon.org/the-legal-case/ (accessed 24 June 2022); Z Small, 'Prominent Lawyer Suggests that Officials Committed Fraud to Keep Elgin Marbles in England During 19th Century', *ARTnews*, 26 February 2020, available at www.artnews.com/news/david-rudenstine-elgin-marbles-fraud-claims-1202679058/ (accessed 24 June 2022); G Robertson, *Who Owns History: Elgin's Loot and the Case for Returning Plundered Treasure*, (London, Biteback Publishing, 2019) xviii–xix, ch 6.

[36] Robertson (n 35).

[37] ibid, ch 6 is, indeed, entitled 'International Law to the Rescue?'.

[38] As Robertson himself notes: ibid 137.

[39] The main sources of public international law – there are others – are 'international custom' and 'treaties'. Neither is retrospective in operation. On international custom, see J Crawford, *Brownlie's Principles of International Law*, 9th edn (Oxford, Oxford University Press, 2019) 21–22, 26 (where the concept of the 'persistent objector' makes the point clearly). On treaties, see A McNair, *The Law of Treaties*, (Oxford, Oxford University Press, 1961) ch XI. A possible exception is the concept of international human rights. That depends on whether one adopts a 'natural law analysis' (these were always rights, always effective and in force) or 'retrospective analysis' (even though the law not always been thus, these rights are so important that they should, in breach of the norm, be given retrospective effect).

right to have returned previously acquired objects of cultural heritage.[40] But that is simply sleight of hand and does not diminish the retrospectivity of what is being contended for.

3. *Use of 'jury' points.* 'Jury' points are prevalent. Self-evidently, the manner in which Lord Elgin acquired title will be of enormous significance in any attempt, by a prior owner, to assert priority of title. But it is not the *only* significant point. In the case of the Marbles, the subsequent transfer to the British Museum by Act of Parliament is obviously key,[41] as are other points standing in the way of a claimant (as described above). There is no point in an advocate of a prior legal claim highlighting one aspect of that claim (where particular strength may be shown), without also at least mentioning, and dealing with, the weak points that may serve to defeat the claim.

   Undoubtedly, there are points that can be made about Lord Elgin's acquisition of the Marbles. Put more objectively, the point is this:

> In removing the Marbles from the Acropolis, Lord Elgin did not act, as is often forgotten, entirely without official sanction; the antiquities were removed only after the issue of a 'firman', a formal grant of authority, from the Ottoman authorities in Constantinople to the Ottoman authorities in Athens. Lord Elgin's displacement of the Marbles bore a stamp of local assent. Quite legitimately, therefore, it was asserted during United Kingdom parliamentary proceedings in 1984 that 'The collection secured by Lord Elgin, as a result of the transactions conducted withy the recognised legitimate authorities of the time, was subsequently purchased from him and vested by an Act of Parliament in the trustees of the British Museum in perpetuity'. The United Kingdom has maintained this stance since 1816 when Lord Elgin was exonerated by the House of Commons Select Committee responsible for investigating his acquisition of the collection and subsequent sale therefore to the British Government for a sum of £35,000.[42]

Of course, fragilities in Lord Elgin's claim to title appear to exist. The facts (hard to ascertain after all these years), the documents (many have disappeared, if they

[40] That is the approach of Robertson (n 35) 162–63:

> The sources of international law that have been surveyed in this chapter indicate that a norm requiring the restitution of wrongfully extracted high-value cultural heritage to states of origin has by now crystallised: analogous conventions, state practice, principles shared by civilised nations and decisions of domestic courts cohere to a point in that direction.

Yet the UNESCO Convention 1970 on the Means of Prohibiting and Preventing the Illicit Import, Export and Transfer of Ownership of Cultural Property (relied upon by Robertson (n 35) 141, 143) is *expressly* prospective in effect. See, for instance, Art 3, which provides: 'The import, export or transfer of ownership of cultural property effected contrary to the provisions adopted under this Convention … shall be illicit.' The United Kingdom acceded to the UNESCO Convention 1970 on 31 October 2002. Quite how the UNESCO Convention can affect the acquisition of the Elgin Marbles in the early 1800s and their transfer to the British Museum in 1816 is not understood. The law on the treatment of cultural property is helpfully described in Carruthers (n 6) ch 5. At no point is it asserted that any of the law there set out is of retrospective effect and – given the general dislike of retrospectivity – a presumption of retrospectivity could not properly be asserted. (And, to be clear, Carruthers does not assert this.)

[41] An advocate for the return of the Elgin Marbles might, properly, ask why an Act of Parliament at all? Was it because of concern about the manner of Lord Elgin's acquisition and potential effect of the *nemo dat quod non habet* rule. I am not sufficiently versed in the history to even venture a view, even as to whether this was an unusual way of doing things. But the point is certainly one of interest.

[42] Carruthers (n 6) para 5.05.

ever existed) and the relevant law (see above) are all not straightforward. They are all illustrative of a 'weak' case, for the burden will rest on the claimant, the party seeking to remove the Marbles from the British Museum's grasp. Clearly, weaknesses in the British Museum's case should be articulated. But they must be relevantly articulated and articulated in context if a legal argument is properly to be made. It is one thing to say: 'There is a strong moral obligation on the British Museum to return the Marbles because the person they were purchased from acquired them in circumstances tantamount to (or actually amounting to) theft and fraud.' It is quite another thing to say that there is a *legal* obligation to return the Marbles, because that proposition requires an impartial evaluation of and adjudiciation upon all material points that go to establishing that claim (here, of prior title).

The problem with the debate is that there is a 'cherry-picking' approach, intended not to make a *legal* argument but to advance a point of prejudice under the guise of a legal argument. Robertson, for example, correctly says that '[t]he lawfulness of Elgin's behaviour must be judged by the rules that applied in Athens in 1801',[43] and that is a (broadly correct) formulation of the rules of applicable law under the English conflict of law rules articulated above. And I fully respect the argument that if Lord Elgin were to be categorised as either 'thief or saviour',[44] the former may well be more probable than the latter. But simply establishing the fact that Lord Elgin's title may be invalid – which may be difficult enough – does not establish the other elements of a sustainable claim.

4. *'Play the man, not the ball.'* The proponents 'play the man, not the ball'. *Ad hominem* attacks are made, which have no relevance to the point, but which are deployed as part of a non-legal argument. Thus, in referring to the Natural History Museum's proposed retention and analysis of certain Aboriginal skulls and bones from Tasmania, and of the Museum's resistance to returning them, Robertson says:

> That did not, at first, attract the museum, whose scientists held the view (as did Dr Mengele) that the pursuit of knowledge is an overriding good in itself.[45]

Mr Jeremy Wright – sometime Attorney General and sometime Culture Secretary – is described as 'a nondescript criminal barrister', and his expressed opposition to the Marbles as 'incoherent'.[46] Lord Elgin is 'an under-bright but over ambitious Tory', amongst other attributes, none of them good.[47]

My reason in raising criticisms of this sort of analysis is not to prevent them from being made – arguments can and should be made, and in the appropriate context, anything goes. Arguments, however, framed, should not be thrown out without being heard. In short, arguments are better for being heard, and then rejected as bad, rather than dismissed out of hand.

[43] Robertson (n 35) 63.
[44] The title of ch 3 in Robertson (n 35).
[45] ibid xix. Unpacking it, the analogy to Dr Mengele is regrettable.
[46] ibid 21.
[47] ibid 59.

D. Why Frame a Moral Case in Legal Terms? Enter the Rule of Law

The arguments I am talking about and have described are not 'just' arguments, they are moral arguments framed as *legal* claims, suggesting that a claimant can vindicate a legal right. The question immediately arises: why frame these matters as a legal claim at all, when – in order to make that legal argument – irrelevant, bad and/or meretricious points end up having to be taken? Why not simply assert a moral claim, without 'dressing it up'?

The answer to this question – why frame moral arguments as legal claims? – I am going to suggest, is that we regard legal arguments as being of peculiar force and so better capable of justifying certain conduct or outcomes. It is better – in the sense that the assertion has more force – to frame something as 'lawful' than to frame something as 'I have a moral right' or 'This is something I think should be done' or even 'I want to do this'. It is far more powerful to say, not 'I want to do this', but 'This must be done, for various reasons, and the law allows me to do so'. That is why – from Hitler to Putin – the indefensible is wrapped up in legal justification. That is particularly the case in Western democracies, with their (broadly speaking) common understanding of the rule of law.

In short, there is particular force in advancing a *legal* justification for a claim, and that is the *moral* force arising out of the rule of law.

Lord Bingham, in his book on the rule of law, sought to define the rule of law as follows:

> The core of the existing principle is, I suggest, that all persons and authorities within the state, whether public or private, should be bound by and entitled to the benefit of laws publicly made, taking effect (generally) in the future and publicly administered in the courts … generally speaking and departure from the rule I have stated calls for close consideration and clear justification. My formulation owes much to Dicey, but I think it also captures the fundamental truth propounded by the great English philosopher John Locke in 1690 that 'Wherever law ends, tyranny begins'. The same point was made by Tom Paine in 1776 when he stated 'that in America THE LAW IS KING. For as in absolute government the King is law, so in free countries the law ought to be King; and there ought to be no other.'[48]

I appreciate that the 'rule of law', whilst containing a core where there is broad agreement as to its content, is murky or penumbral around the fringes. In particular, there is a dispute as to whether basic human rights fall within or without the rule of law.[49] The wider one draws the content of the rule of law, the greater the fragmentation of

[48] T Bingham, *The Rule of Law*, (London, Allen Lane, 2010) 8.

[49] A debate described by Bingham, ibid 66–68. At one extreme lies Professor Raz, who sees the rule of law as a more or less technical doctrine concerned with effectiveness more than anything else. Thus, Professor Raz says: '[C]onformity to the rule of law is one among many moral virtues which the law should possess. The present consideration shows that the rule of law is not merely a moral virtue – it is a necessary condition for the law to be serving directly any good purpose at all. Of course, conformity to the rule of law also enables the law to serve bad purposes …': J Raz, *The Authority of Law: Essays on Law and Morality*, 1st (paperback) edn (Oxford, Oxford University Press, 1983) 225. Lord Bingham himself is a proponent of a wider view of the rule of law, but see also: F Neumann, *The Rule of Law: Political Theory and the Legal System in Modern Society*, (Leamington Spa, Berg, 1986); A Babington, *The Rule of Law in Britain*, (Chichester, Barry Rose, 1985); F Pirie, *The Rule of Laws*, (London, Profile Books, 2021).

acceptance[50] and the greater the risk of internal inconsistency. For the purposes of this chapter, and without prejudice to any wider formulation that I might attempt on another occasions, I am going to concentrate on the *procedural* side of the rule of law.

I doubt if it could be contended that the right to the return of cultural property forms a part of the rule of law, and (given my thesis that this undoubted value stands in opposition to the rule of law) adopting a really wide definition of the rule of law runs the risk of making this chapter incoherent. So the version of the rule of law that I propose to adopt for the purposes of this essay is a hard, 'due process', formulation, that bears some resemblance to the hard procedural due process protection espoused by Justice Jackson in the US Supreme Court's decision in *Shaughnessy v United States ex rel Mezei*:

> Procedural fairness, if not all that originally was meant by due process, is at least what it most uncompromisingly requires. Procedural due process is more elemental and less flexible than substantive due process. It yields less to the times, varies less with conditions, and defers much less to legislative judgment. Insofar as it is a technical law, it must be a specialised responsibility within the competence of the judiciary on which they do not bend before political branches of the Government, as they should on matters of policy which comprise substantive law. If it be conceded that in some way [the agency in the case could act as it did], does it matter what the procedure is? Only the untaught layman or the charlatan lawyer can answer that procedure matters not. Procedural fairness and regularity are of the indispensable essence of liberty. Severe substantive laws can be endured if they are fairly and impartially applied. Indeed, if put to the choice, one might well prefer to live under Soviet substantive law applied in good faith by our common-law procedures, than under our substantive law enforced by Soviet procedural practices. Let it not be overlooked that due process of law is not for the sole benefit of an accused. It is the best insurance for the Government itself against those blunders which leave lasting stains on a system of justice but which are bound to occur on *ex parte* consideration.[51]

This formulation – to the extent it is a formulation of the rule of law at all – captures the essence of what I, at least, am talking about in this chapter. I am not denying the existence of other values, but I am framing the peculiar value of the rule of law in a relatively narrow way, because it is thus that the opposition of the rule of law to other values (such as the restoration of cultural property) can best be understood. I hope that what I mean by the rule of law will become clearer in what follows.

My point, for the present, is that, at least and particularly in Western democracies, deployment of *legal* argument adds lustre to what would otherwise be a purely moral argument precisely *because* of the rule of law. The pseudo-legal arguments that I have been describing regarding the Marbles – and other points to which I will come – seek to appropriate that lustre and deploy it, illegitimately, to advance what are otherwise

[50] Taking the approach of Professor Raz is likely to engender the greatest common ground. On this basis, where effectiveness is essentially the essence of the rule, one might be able to achieve a formulation acceptable on a worldwide basis. See eg Y Wang, *Tying the Autocrat's Hands: The Rise of the Rule of Law in China*, (Cambridge, Cambridge University Press, 2015).

[51] *Shaughnessy v United States ex rel Mezei* 345 US 206 (1953), 224–25. On the extent to which procedural due process can appropriate soften substantive evil, see D Dyzenhaus, *Hard Cases in Wicked Legal Systems: South African Law in the Perspective of Legal Philosophy*, (Oxford, Oxford University Press, 1991).

perfectly proper moral arguments, deserving of respect and attention on that basis (but not any other).

In doing so, those advancing such moral claims or values do themselves – and, more particularly, their cause – no service at all. Instead of articulating what is on the face of it a legal claim in support of a particular cause – for instance, the return of the Marbles to Greece – thereby impliedly appropriating the moral force of the rule of law, it needs to be recognised, in order to understand the implications of the assertion of such moral values, that what is being proposed actually goes *against* the rule of law, but is (in the particular case) nevertheless justified.

In other words, persons advancing a moral claim of this sort are endorsing a <u>breach</u> or infringement of the rule of law when they advocate for the enactment of a new law (here, enforcing the return of the Marbles) in place of the old (whereby the present holder is justified in retaining the Marbles). It is necessary to expand upon this proposition:

1. *A competition between two moral values.* What we are confronted with is a competition between two moral values. No one – least of all Bingham – is suggesting that the rule of law *is* a rule of law. It is an ideal, a value, to which we all – and particularly legislators, judges and the legal profession – should aspire to and seek to promulgate. As such, it is a value that is opposed to the return (to stick to the Marbles) of past-acquired objects of cultural significance. The rule of law, in short, stands in opposition to and seeks to prevent such return. Recognition of this fact is critical to understanding some of the reluctance to accede to what might otherwise be a far less controversial assertion of moral rightness.
2. *The rule of law is not an absolute value.* When I say that the rule of law stands in opposition to other values, I am not saying that the rule of law is an absolute 'road block'. To assume the rule of law exists as an absolute would be wrong. For example, in breach of the rule of law, retrospective legislation is quite often enacted in this jurisdiction and others, and the courts will (through slightly to moderately gritted teeth) uphold such legislation, although they may construe such legislation narrowly. Thus, in *Lauri v Renad*, Lindley LJ stated:

   > It is a fundamental rule of English law that no statute shall be construed so as to have a retrospective operation, unless its language is such as plainly to require such a construction. And the same rule involves another and subordinate rule, to the effect that a statute is not to be construed so as to have a greater retrospective operation than its language renders necessary.[52]

   This, then, is the accommodation English law has reached with the values contained within the rule of law. Not no retrospective legislation, but a presumption against such legislation, capable of being overridden.

   Whether the rule of law should be overridden is left to our legislators, not to the courts.[53] A complex balancing exercise is thus undertaken: it is for the legislator to determine what the substance of the law should be, including as to

[52] *Lauri v Renad* [1892] 3 Ch 402 (CA) 421.

[53] As to the law in this area, see D Greenberg (ed), *Craies on Legislation*, 11th edn (London, Sweet & Maxwell, 2017) paras 10.3.1ff.

whether it should be retrospective or backward looking. When the law has been enacted by our legislators, there will be no judicial quibbles as to its substantive content. The law, properly construed, will be applied.[54] This is as it should be in our constitutional settlement.[55] If the decision to enact a retrospective law is made, then – provided it is clearly enough expressed – the courts will give force to it. But the legislators will, themselves, have regard to the rule of law, and will or ought to appreciate that (because of that rule) there are prudential or moral fetters not on what they can do, but on what they should do. That involves balancing the values of the rule of law against the interests (whatever they may be) that actuate the need for the legislation in question.

3. *The 'dark side' of the rule of law.* That is why I am calling this conflict between moral values the 'dark side' of the rule of law. Not because the rule of law is 'dark' – it has enormous positive value – but because it acts as a restraint and constraint in relation to other things which, for perfectly sound (and usually moral) reasons, we would like to do but which the rule of law may prevent or obstruct us from doing.

IV. A DIALOGUE BETWEEN HERITAGE AND LAW

So, to return to the Marbles, the question for debate becomes: does the moral force impelling the return of the Marbles outweigh the moral force, embodied by the rule of law, in preventing or inhibiting that very outcome? I cannot possibly answer that question in this chapter or at all; and I am not even going to begin to try for reasons that I have given.

What I *am* going to do is imagine the sort of dialogue that might arise between a well-informed proponent of the Marbles' return, a person open to other values and a person not-unsympathetic to that position,[56] but also a robust respecter of the rule of law (understood as I have described it), is a fruitful dialogue worth imagining.[57] I call the protagonists 'Heritage' and 'Law' for obvious reasons, and I extend my apologies to Andrew Marvell:[58]

[54] As to this, see Lord Burrows, 'Statutory Interpretation in the Courts Today', Sir Christopher Staughton Memorial Lecture 2022 (University of Hertfordshire, 24 March 2022), published at https://www.supreme-courtuk/docs/sir-christopher-staughton-memorial-lecture-2022.pdf (accessed 12 November 2022).

[55] We do not, in this jurisdiction, since departing the European Union, and subject to an unarticulated reservation to act in extremis, have any kind of entrenched higher law whereby a judge can strike down primary legislation.

[56] ie, someone who – but for the moral force they attribute to the rule of law – would rather the Marbles be returned than remain with the British Museum.

[57] Thanks are due to Lionel Smith and Simone Degeling for coming up with this idea, which I have adopted. I am formulating both sides of the debate, which inevitably means a high level of subjectivity in the points taken and not taken. I hope I have captured both sides' best points but am well aware that I may not have done. During the conference at which an earlier version of this chapter was presented, it was suggested that I have given Law the best lines. I fear that may be right, largely because I have assumed and not advocated for the value of the return of cultural property. I can only stress that I have tried to give Heritage a fair shake of the dice. Nevertheless, my dialogue betrays where my true interests lie, which is in understanding the role of the rule of law. I have numbered the dialogue ('[X]') to facilitate later reference.

[58] See, for something sublime rather than pedestrian, A Marvell, 'A Dialogue Between the Soul and Body' (1681).

[1] Heritage Okay, let me accept (without prejudice to making any such point in the future) that I don't have a legal leg to stand on.

You surely would accept – for your part – *first*, that the return of objects of cultural heritage is a good thing to do; and, *secondly*, that there is no absolute reason why the Marbles can't be returned?

[2] Law I'll make a lawyer out of you yet, Heritage! And yes, I will stipulate that the return of objects of cultural heritage is a worthy thing to do; and that – provided an appropriately framed Act of Parliament was passed – there is no lawful reason why the Marbles could not be returned to Greece.

But you do understand why an Act of Parliament is required? The Marbles vested in the British Museum by virtue of the 1816 Act,[59] now repealed.[60] In place of the various obligations imposed on the Trustees of the British Museum by that Act, we now have a statutory obligation to keep the British Museum's collection whole.[61]

[3] Heritage Fine, let's get the Act passed, repealing this obligation, and obliging the Trustees to return the Marbles. I know you're going to say this is retrospective legislation, but is it? Really? All it's doing is saying *prospectively* that the British Museum should divest itself? (See, the lawyer stuff isn't that hard!)

[4] Law You're right! Retrospectivity is really tricky.

Of course, you are right: telling the Trustees to return the Marbles to Greece is in that sense purely prospective. Even Parliament cannot turn back the clock, and wish Lord Elgin had never been. The transfer back has to take place in the future.

But the point is that since 1816, the Trustees have been obliged – under a statutory duty – to preserve the Marbles for the British people. You are varying a regime that has operated for a long time, by telling the Trustees to do something different; you are thereby depriving future viewers of the Marbles of that opportunity; and you are *expropriating* the 'true' owner of the Marbles, the Trustees of the Museum, who hold these artefacts on terms.

However you dress it up, you are changing past-created and presently subsisting rights and obligations.

[5] Heritage Hang on a minute. What do you mean by expropriation?

[6] Law Well, what I will call the 'ownership question' is disguised by the fact that the British Museum is a public body. Suppose, though, Lord Elgin had sold the Marbles to a very rich private individual instead, who had kept the Marbles on their property and bequeathed them, over the generations, to other private individuals.

[59] The terms of which were described above.

[60] But the transfer would remain effective. Repeals of Acts are prospective in effect only. This is not a point I am going to develop. It may very well be that Heritage – if it came to litigation – could make all kinds of points in relation to the legislative history that I do not anticipate.

[61] See British Museum Act 1963, s3.

And I'll make it easy for you – let's suppose this individual is quite selfish (and their predecessors in title were also), so that no one ever even got to look at the Marbles. The fact is that this inheritor, the present holder – I'll call them X – would 'own' the Marbles. And the right to property is an important right – protected by the European Convention on Human Rights (ECHR), no less.[62]

I'm not saying that property rights are part of the rule of law. But taking away property rights without a hearing *is* an affront to the rule of law; and doing so by changing the existing legal rules of ownership is expropriation – which is another way of saying that existing legal rights are retrospectively overridden.

So there are two (linked) infringements of the rule of law that you are contemplating when returning the Marbles: retrospective legislation *and* doing something nasty to someone without a proper hearing. And, of course, a hearing can only really be proper when you've framed – in advance – what you are arguing about.[63]

Even if you are going to deprive X of their rights retrospectively, you've got to articulate the (retrospective) basis on which you're doing that.

So – on what basis are you going to deprive X of their property rights? Are you going to give X compensation? And if you are, how much is that going to be? I'm not sure what the going rate for the Marbles is …

I'm not even going to go into the importance of stable property rights for ongoing economic prosperity![64]

[7] **Heritage** Hmmm … I think there is some sleight of hand going on here. The point is that X doesn't own the Marbles – the British Museum does.

[8] **Law** So you're saying that a body that is preserving an object for the nation should be treated *less well* than selfish old X? That can't be right! Even if the British Museum isn't a private body with public functions, why should a public body that can hold private property be treated any differently from a private body holding private property? Tell me that!

[62] Art 1 of the Protocol to the Convention for the Protection of Human Rights and Fundamental Freedoms provides:

> Every natural or legal person is entitled to the peaceful enjoyment of his possessions. No one shall be deprived of his possessions except in the public interest and subject to the conditions provided for by law and by the general principles of international law.
>
> The preceding provisions shall not, however, in any way impair the right of a State to enforce such laws as it deems necessary to control the use of property in accordance with the general interest or to secure the payment of taxes or other contributions or penalties.

This protection is a part of English law as a result of the Human Rights Act 1998. To be clear, Law is neither saying that this right is absolute (it clearly is not) nor that it forms part of the rule of law (which is consistent with the definition I have articulated). However, the rule of law *does* require existing rights to be regarded and only abrogated under specific conditions.

[63] On retrospectivity, see Bingham (n 48) ch 3 (which ranges rather more widely than simply retrospectivity, but includes it). This chapter also deals with the broader, but no less important, point concerning the proper framing of laws, so that those subject to them know what is expected of them. On the right to a fair hearing, see Bingham (n 48) ch 8.

[64] Although Law does not go into detail, this is a reference to Hernando de Soto's work: H De Soto, *The Mystery of Capital*, (Cambridge, Black Swan, 2000). De Soto's thesis is that one needs respect for property rights in order to build wealth for everyone. By way of example, if a bank considers that it will not safely be able to secure its loan over a borrower's property, it will likely not lend at all, depriving the borrower of immediate capital necessary to develop their business.

[9] Heritage Well, don't you think that public bodies *ought* to be held to a higher standard? And do the right thing? Look at the Holocaust (Return of Cultural Objects) Act 2009.[65] That obliges public bodies to look at the moral case for the return of looted property, not the legal case you are advocating.

[10] Law I think you are making my point for me. The 2009 Act and the advisory body it establishes is an exception to the norm, and one can see why. Let me give you four reasons.

First, the return of such objects *is* morally imperative,[66] because of the awfulness of the Nazi regime.

Secondly, the events are in the relatively recent past, so one can identify the persons who have been wronged or their immediate descendants/successors in title, and so right an *individual* wrong.

Thirdly, the chain of title by way of which the museums may have got such objects may be such that no right-thinking person would want to rely on it; and no person not sharing this thinking ought not to be entitled to rely on this 'legal' chain of title.[67]

[65] This Act establishes a spoliation advisory panel (s 3) which can help resolve claims in respect of cultural objects looted during the Nazi era (1933–45) (s 2). Although 'advisory', provided the Secretary of State approves the panel's advice, the museum in question (which includes the British Museum) will return the object in question, and the panel will consider not merely questions of law, but also moral values. That is important, because one of the hallmarks of the Nazi regime was the fact that it did awful things under the cloak of legality. In short, the rule of law (in the Raz sense) *was not very much disregarded*. Bad things were written into horribly effective law. It would do no credit to our society to have arguments about the validity of horrible laws debated in our courts in an effort to resist the return of a looted artefact. But, equally significantly, the binding nature of the regime does not extent to private persons. As to this regime generally, see Carruthers (n 6) paras 5.35ff.

[66] Although even here not everyone agrees. See N O'Donnell, *A Tragic Fate*, (Chicago, Ankerwycke, 2017) on the private law battles regarding Nazi-looted art. His book begins with this example (at ix):

> *Rue Saint-Honoré, apres-midi, effet de pluie (Rue St Honoré, Afternoon, Rain Effect)* was painted by Camille Pissarro in 1892. It shows the new Paris of Georges-Eugène Haussmann's design, with a sharp angular perspective rushing to the top left. The soft focus and muted colours mirror the subject: the wide boulevards on a rainy day. Carriages and pedestrians tread the cobblestones amidst leafless trees. It is a depicition of an ordinary day that would normally merit no commemoration. In this way, Pissarro's technique also reflects the history of the painting since World War II. On the surface, the dispute is similar to many others, but digging deeper one finds a multi-layered puzzle that embodies the competing narratives often at play in restitution cases: persecution, obfuscation, the murky environment of the art market after the war, and the basic tension between legal systems and those who bear the burden of resolving the competing claims.
>
> The painting once belonged to Fritz and Lilly Cassirer, members of a family that achieved monetary success in electrical component manufacturing and later in the collection and sale of art. The Cassirers were second-generation Jews, integrated members of the Germany of which they were citizens and supporters. They assembled a collection including numerous great works of Western art.
>
> However, the Pissarro is no longer in their collection. Lilly Cassirer was targeted by a Nazi opportunist, and she sold the painting for a fraction of its value before escaping her home country. After a series of sales and donations, the painting hangs today in the Thyssen-Bornemisza Museum in Madrid, a state-run institution that exhibits a world-class collection.

Go to the Museum's website, and one can find a note describing the state of play of proceedings in the United States regarding the ownership of this picture, where the Museum expresses confidence that the position of the 'Fundacion' as the legitimate owner will in due course be affirmed: www.museothyssen.org/sites/default/files/document/2022-04/Nota_Pissarro_22.04.22_ING.pdf (accessed 4 July 2022).

[67] The Nazi regime was and is famous for doing awful things lawfully, and a right-thinking society might not even want to sully itself considering the technical validity of immoral laws.

Fourthly, this is a case where we would be prepared to treat like cases alike. In short, every case falling within defined parameters would be treated similarly.

And that brings me back, in a different way, to a key question here. Supposing I agree that public bodies are different from private bodies: is whatever principle that you are framing for the Marbles one you are prepared to apply generally, to like cases? Or is your position on the Marbles that they are unique – and, if so, why is that?[68]

[11] Heritage Why does that matter? I'm not interested in anything but the return of the Marbles! Everything else can stay where presently located in England.

[12] Law How can that be right? You haven't – yet – framed the justification for the return of the Marbles, but (basically) it involves the return of objects of cultural significance to their 'true origin' by whoever now holds that object (even if there has been a subsequent transfer or transfers after the original acquisition), when the original acquisition was somehow 'tainted'.

If I've got that right, then surely you've got to treat all similar cases in the same way? You can't discriminate between similarly placed claimants, and you can't – without being arbitrary – impose the outcome on a single special case.

Let's take it as a fact that most museums – including those in the UK – obtained their collections from private collectors, who gifted them, or obtained them in purchase from what appeared to be respectable third parties.[69] I suspect that many of these were acquired in 'tainted' circumstances. Are you going to reverse all of these dealings, and strip our museums bare?[70]

[13] Heritage Well, I think – and most people in this country think – the Marbles should go back. Are you really saying that is wrong?

[14] Law No, I'm not. But I do think you need to understand the price you are paying – or the price you are asking other people to pay. Basically:

(1) If this was a private person, you would be expropriating them (without compensation) for a reason that you have not precisely framed. Inevitably that involves a degree of *retrospectivity*.

(2) You consider that a public body should be in a different position, and I am sure that a case could be made out for that. But you need to articulate the basis upon which something set up for the public good should now be lost. In other words, the principle on which you are operating by repurposing public property needs to be stated as a *general precept*.

[68] The importance of general propositions of law being made legislatively and (in the specific case) then being applied by a court underlies most of the rule-of-law doctrine I am considering. See, generally, Bingham (n 48).

[69] Jenkins (n 17) ch 1 – but the whole of part I of the book pays reading on this point, which includes discussion of looted property.

[70] Robertson (n 35) considers this to be a terrible point, for (I think) two reasons. First, that not as many objects would be affected as might be thought (120–21), but secondly because the proposition that museums

> (3) You need to be willing – or explain why that is unnecessary – to *apply that general precept to like cases.*
>
> So, I'm not even saying there should be compensation for the loss of the Marbles – although that would be a point to discuss, it doesn't arise out of (my formulation of) the rule of law. What I am saying is that what you are proposing looks pretty arbitrary to me – and the only way to overcome that, is to ensure proper (by which I think I mean voluntary) consent (informed by the appropriate values).
>
> I know that begs an awful lot of questions …

V. SYNTHESIS

A. The Starting Point

Taking the Marbles as an appropriate – if controversial – example of why the debate between Law and Heritage is so difficult, the starting point to understanding the difficulty (without resolving it: that is beyond this paper) is to recognize that: (i) there is no rule of law mandating the return of the Marbles (ie no right to insist on their return); but that (ii) there is no absolute bar to a law, mandating their return, from being enacted.

In a different state, with entrenched constitutional rights, there might be such a bar, but not in this jurisdiction.[71] At most, in the United Kingdom, one could say that such a law might infringe the ECHR (ie the right to property, described above) but – to be clear – I do not regard that right as an element of the rule of law, and I will proceed on the basis (as I think must be right) that it could be overridden. Since this chapter is interested in the interplay between the demands of morality (in the shape of the moral desirability to make cultural restitution) and the moral quality of the rule of law, I am going to take the ECHR out of the equation.

B. The Value of the Rule of Law

I have been speaking a great deal about the intrinsic *moral* value of the rule of law, and do not propose to say more than has already been said. The rule of law's great virtue embraces Raz's point that law is a tool which, in order to be effective, must have certain

should show original artefacts to the world, away from their cultural origin, is flawed (8–11). He may well be right on both points, and he makes the argument with verve and force. The point Law is making is that the debate needs to be articulated and set against other (countervailing) values (which also need to be defined).

[71] The United Kingdom famously has 'no constitution'. That is incorrect: the United Kingdom has no *codified* constitution, and that is because of our doctrine of parliamentary sovereignty. The will of Parliament, expressed in an Act of Parliament, is supreme and that is in essence inconsistent with a codified constitution, which tends to place itself at the apex with the courts and judges as 'gatekeepers' or protectors of the constitutions. Where the codified constitution is at the apex, someone has to decide what is constitutional and what is not, and that (usually) is the judiciary, which immediately changes the power balance between the three functions of the state that are defined by the separation of powers (ie the legislature, the judiciary and the executive).

attributes. Like most commentators, I consider that the rule of law goes well beyond this, to embrace the sort of hard-edged procedural due process enunciated by Justice Jackson. Almost certainly, this is also too limited a formulation, and I suspect that the rule of law goes beyond even this. The problem with wider formulations is that the essence of the value of the rule of law merges into other (also extremely important) values, resulting in confusion, and not analytical clarity. As Professor Raz puts it:

> If the rule of law is the rule of the good law, then to explain its nature is to propound a complete social philosophy. But if so, the term lacks any useful function.[72]

Lord Bingham agreed with this, but considered the effort worth the while, even at the price of controversy and disagreement:

> [T]his is a difficult area since there is no universal consensus on the rights and freedoms which are fundamental, even among civilised nations. In some developing countries a higher premium is put on economic growth than on protection of individual rights, and in some Islamic countries little or no protection is given to some rights that are cherished elsewhere. It must be accepted that the outer edges of some fundamental human rights are not clear-cut. But within a given society there is ordinarily a large measure of agreement on where the lines are to be drawn at any particular time, even though standards change over time, and in the last resort the courts are there to draw them. It is, I think, possible to identify the rights and freedoms which, in the UK and developed Western or Westernised countries elsewhere, are seen as fundamental, and the rule of law requires that those rights should be protected.[73]

It may be that the time has come to separate out the procedural aspects of the rule of law from its substantive aspects. There is insufficient room even to begin to address this question in this chapter. However, simply for clarity, my principal concern is with the procedural aspects of the rule of law – whatever else the rule of law may embrace – and the very specific virtues that these aspects have.

The point can be made more pragmatically. As I have described, the municipal laws of states have evolved extremely sophisticated rules, including as to the ownership of property. Those rules incorporate due regard for the laws of other states, where there is an 'international' element. We change these laws – even prospectively – at our peril. As Hernando de Soto has made clear,[74] one of the key factors in enabling economic development is the stability and predictability of property rights. If I am going to invest in a given state or advance money on a security in a given state, I am going to want to be assured that the rules of the game are not going to change, and that if my investment fails, it will not be because the rules that informed my expectations and judgement *at the time of the investment* have changed. This is, of course, a kind of argument against retrospectivity, but in fact underlines just how slippery the question of retrospectivity is. What I am focusing on here is the need for prospective stability, and I am underlining the seriously adverse consequences of not having a stable legal base in which or on which to transact.

[72] Raz (n 49) 211.
[73] Bingham (n 48) 68.
[74] De Soto (n 64).

Take, for example, entrepreneur A who structures their business on the basis of hiring extremely capable employees in a particular field. Suppose the rules change (either the tax system changes prospectively, rendering A's offers of work less attractive; or the rules for the hiring of foreign nationals change, so that it is harder to hire new workers). Neither of these instances is a retrospective change; but they both go to the viability of A's *established* business, and – if there are frequent such changes – the effect will be to make A and entrepreneurs like A much more cautious *in the future* about investing.

Put in the context of museums, if we want to continue to augment our collections through the gifts of donors or the deployment of public/privately gifted funds in the augmentation of collections, we need to protect past acquisitions, and divest with care. Preserving or not preserving the past has an effect on future conduct, whether we like it or not.

C. The Irrelevance, in this Case at Least, of Public International Law

For the reasons given, this chapter proceeds on the basis that there is no *existing* claim in law mandating the return of the Marbles. The arguments for their return involve not the formulation of an existing rule of law that has hitherto been overlooked or not understood, but the creation of a new rule. There is nothing wrong with this. Indeed, it is entirely right to say that the law in this area has been and is developing, both domestically (eg the Ancient Monuments Protection Act 1882; the Dealing in Cultural Objects (Offences) Act 2003) and internationally (eg the 1970 UNESCO Convention). If the proposition is that the direction of travel of the law in this area is changing, then that is clearly right. If Lord Elgin were to try to do today what he did do in the late 1700s and early 1800s, he would not get away with it, and would probably commit a whole series of legal violations.

But this evolution of legal norms to a different and better goal is, of course, prospective. That is the nature of moral evolution: society begins to understand better that certain values matter more, and the law, ever behind the curve in responding to change, in due course follows.

International law is often deployed as a means of advancing the arguments in favour of developing moral values, and is a useful tool for this purpose. That is because – unlike a municipal legal system, where it is easy to separate what *is* law from what the law *should be* – the 'is' and the 'should' are much less distinguishable on the international plane. For this reason – because the rule of law is essentially concerned with the 'is' and its proper application – it is important to stress the fundamental irrelevance of public international in cases such as the present. Although the role of international agencies as actors on the stage of public international law and the increased importance of human rights law have both served to erode the distinction between public international law as the law that regulates relations between nations, and municipal law, which concerns the relationship between state and persons (natural or legal) and between persons *inter se*, that distinction still matters. The fate of the Marbles depends in the first and last instance on the private law, because the rights of individual persons are engaged, and such persons have no standing on the international stage. Of course, international law may – often does – cause consequential changes to municipal law. But it is trite that the mere entry, by the Government of the United Kingdom, into an international treaty affects no municipal rights at all.

The short point is that international law is *not* a law higher than private law, but a *different* law regulating different entities. It should not be deployed in what is a question of private law.

D. Aspects of the Rule of Law that are Engaged

The dialogue between Heritage and Law identified a number of facets of the rule of law that are engaged by the case of the Marbles. In particular, these are the need to avoid retrospective laws; the importance of treating like cases alike, and avoiding arbitrariness and discretion; and the importance of individual adjudication, with due process, according to a general rule of law that has already been promulgated.

1. *Retrospection.* I am only going to touch lightly upon this aspect of the rule of law, because I am conscious that a great deal has already been written on the subject, and what I say is going to add little, if anything. Clearly, the creation of a new rule regarding cultural property only assists the repatriation of the Marbles if it is made retrospective.[75] The law frowns upon retrospectivity, but does not preclude it. In fact, I would suggest that the presumption against retrospectivity is a relatively light one, particularly in the case of evolving moral norms. How, one might ask rhetorically, can one right a past wrong without retrospection?
2. *Treating like cases alike.* One of the points that arose out of the dialogue between Heritage and Law was the extent to which there exists a distinction between public bodies (or private bodies exercising public functions) and private bodies *stricto sensu*.[76] In the latter case, the interests are quite clear: there is a vested property interest. In the former case, there may be higher values in play, as reflected (in this jurisdiction at least) in the spoliation rules that I have described.[77] There may even be a worthwhile distinction to be drawn between the natural person (who was only born and so came on the scene after the events in question) and the legal person that has always been in place. In a sense, this continuous presence dulls still further the objection to retrospectivity. Suppose Corporation X had obtained the Marbles (through the agency of Lord Elgin) and remained in being, and in ownership of the Marbles, to this day? My sense is that this might very well make a difference, although I confess to finding it difficult to articulate that difference.[78]

[75] See the dialogue between Heritage and Law ('Dialogue') at [3]–[4].

[76] See Dialogue at [6]–[9].

[77] See Dialogue at [9].

[78] The point emerges most clearly in D de Jong, *Nazi Billionires*, (London, William Collins, 2022), which describes the enrichment (during the Nazi era) of various companies, still in being today, and still very wealthy. Of course, on one level, retrospectively expropriating these corporations damages the interests of the shareholders, who may very well have come on the scene later. So it may be that the distinction between natural and legal persons is, ultimately, not a good one. But it is certainly one worth very careful consideration (not undertaken here).

Interesting though these distinctions are, and important though it might be that they be drawn, these specific questions are nothing to do with the rule of law. These are matters of policy for legislators to consider. The rule of law, I suggest, is not concerned with these policy questions, but with the manner in which they are framed. The rule of law does not care, when it comes to cultural heritage, whether the regime for restoration proposed applies differently to public bodies, legal persons or natural persons provided that an arbitrary regime is avoided. The rule of law opposes the arbitrary, where things are done inconsistently, with like cases not treated alike, and different cases not treated appropriately differently, according to general precepts. The passage of legislation involves the articulation of a general norm by the legislature, which norm is then applied, with all due process, by the courts in the specific case.

In the first instance, that involves the framing of general propositions. I do not say that those general propositions need to be 'just' or 'right' or 'in accordance with some higher law'. I am a legal positivist (with perhaps a hint of natural law in the most extreme of cases[79]). So the rule of law says nothing about the *content* of these propositions. But I do say they need to be generally framed, and that what goes for the Marbles ought also to go for, for example, the Benin Bronzes. In this regard, it is interesting to note that our parliamentary processes recognise this. Acts of Parliament ought not, without more, be deployed in the specific case. It is the role of the legislature to frame general propositions (ie laws), which are then applied in the specific case by courts.[80]

So it seems to me that the advocate for the Marbles' return needs to have answers to at least the following questions: (i) How do you define an object of cultural heritage? (ii) In the case of a past acquired object, are there any limits on how far back you go when making restitution? (iii) To whom is restitution to be made, and are there any obligations on the claimant as to public display of the object and the costs of removal? (iv) Does the rule apply to private owners? (v) Is there to be any compensation to the present owner of the object?

[79] Bingham (n 48) ch 10.

[80] See A Dismore, *The Parthenon Sculpures: A Legal Perspective*, published online only at www.andrewdismore.org.uk/home/2012/06/25/the-parthenon-sculptures-legal-perspective-by-andrew-dismore/ (accessed 30 September 2023). The "Parthenon Sculptures" are, of course, the Elgin Marbles by another name, and Mr Dismore says this about the general and the specific:

> If a Bill is seen to be very specific and referring only to a particular private interest, for example referring only to the [Parthenon Sculptures] and their repatriation, there is a risk the Bill could be deemed to be hybrid.
>
> A hybrid bill is a public Bill which affects the private interests of a particular person or organisation. It is generally initiated by the Government on behalf of non-Parliamentary bodies such as local authorities and is treated like a private Bill for the beginning of its passage through Parliament. This gives individuals and bodies an opportunity to oppose the bill or seek its amendment before a select committee in either or in both Houses. This procedure is long drawn out and very problematic, so it is important that any Bill cannot be seen as hybrid, so it needs to be as broadly drawn as possible, and certainly not just referring to the [Parthenon Sculptures] alone.

This then creates a political problem: the 'floodgates' argument. One of the main arguments deployed against the [Parthenon Sculptures'] return is that if the [Parthenon Sculptures] are returned, this will feed demands for other cultural objects to be repatriated too. The most obvious case is that of the Benin Bronzes, but no doubt we can all think of others.

3. *A fair hearing*. This is a flip side to the point just discussed. Lawmakers make the laws, in accordance with established procedures – hopefully reflecting the democratic will of the people electing the legislature.[81] Once general propositions have been made into law, any dispute about their specific application falls to the courts. But the law, articulated as a general proposition, needs to be stated before the specific act of adjudication can take place.[82]
4. *'Stare decisis'*. 'To stand by things decided' is the foundation of our law of precedent, but here I am referring to matters that have not, quite, been decided, and certainly cannot be regarded as precedent in any legal sense. Instead, I am asking what we are to make of matters that have been debated in the past, and decided, seemingly on a 'once and for all' basis. For instance, in the case of the Marbles, it is quite clear that there was a great deal of debate about the propriety of Lord Elgin's conduct, the lawfulness of his title and the strength of the claims of the country from which the Marbles had been taken.[83] Similarly, in the case of Nazi looting, and Nazi wrongdoing generally, when one reads the history, it is clear that the questions of enrichment and restitution have been dealt with, time and again, as a final resolution sought to be achieved.[84]

   Although predictability – and so a respect for precedent – is an important part of the rule of law, the notion of constraining the repeated raising of the same question must, surely, be inimical to the rule of law. The point is that we, as a society, evolve in our values, and the repeated putting of the same question should not be suppressed, but encouraged. Our progression to newer, and hopefully better, values is not a matter that the rule of law ought to constrain, and is perhaps a good indicator that the rule of law is more important as a rule of process than as a rule of substance.

VI. THE 'DARK SIDE' OF THE RULE OF LAW

A. The Problem of Inertia

I have mentioned the 'dark side' of the rule of law already, but it is now possible to be a little clearer about the nature of this 'darkness'. It is, obviously, a provocative term, and not one that I really mean. The rule of law is an ideal – of uncertain ambit, admittedly – but which, at least on its procedural side, contains real merit.

[81] Again, although a trite part of the thinking of Western democracies, this is not (as I see it) a part of the rule of law.

[82] That gives rise to another interesting question – also not addressed here – as to the role of the common law and its interplay with the rule of law. Long gone are the days when the theory was that judges did no more than articulate or find law already laid down. Judges do make law, but they do so without framing general propositions and retrospectively. See eg J Stapleton, *Three Essays on Torts*, (Oxford, Oxford University Press, 2021) 4ff.

[83] I refer to the debates that lead to the Elgin Marbles Act 1816.

[84] See, generally, de Jong (n 78). The question really, boils down to 'Was what was done in the past enough? Should a prior settlement, reached after due consideration, be revised after the event?'.

But the concomitant of a system compliant with the rule of law is a system that inevitably contains within it a high degree of inertia or preservation of the status quo. This is the perhaps inevitable consequence of the virtues or precepts of the rule of law. General laws must be passed, and they must be applied in impartial courts, where reasons must be given. Like cases must be treated alike. There is a view that discretion is a 'bad' thing. All of this has an inhibitory effect on change.

This may explain some of the bitterness and violence of words between – to continue using the Marbles as an example – advocates of return and advocates of retention. I am sure that in many cases, battle is joined on the simple issue of 'return' or 'retention', and here the issues, although not simple, are at least qualitatively the same. One side will value cultural heritage over retention and display; and the other side will have the opposite view. But the debate, at least, is one of equivalent arguments – 'apples and apples', if you like, not 'apples and oranges'.

The values of the rule of law have nothing to do with this debate: they lie on a different plane and engage different interests. But those values nevertheless frame the debate, and should at least give it structure. It is, or at least ought to be, quite possible for a person entirely neutral on the question of return – or even for someone in principle favouring return on the basis that they wish that the expropriation had never taken place[85] – to be against return for no other reason than because of the rule of law. The rule of law – because of the inertia it creates – results in opposition to an otherwise sound moral proposal created not out any disagreement with the moral value that is under discussion, but by reason of the manner in which the change by way of which the moral value is to be brought about is being effected.

Put another way, a one-line Act of Parliament saying 'The British Museum shall facilitate the return to Greece of the artifacts known by it as the Elgin Marbles' contains within it sufficient problems – viewed purely from the rule of law point of view – as to at least make the lawyer subscribing to the rule of law uneasy. I am not saying that such a law would be unlawful, and that this could not be done.[86] What I *am* saying is that I would very much hope that there would be debate not merely about the substantive question of return (about which I have nothing to say in this chapter at all) but also the process by which such a rule is put into law and thereafter applied and (as appropriate) challenged by any interested person affected.

Interestingly, it is precisely this unease about process – and so this inertia – that provokes the most heated debate, because the side that does not get what it wants substantively ends up saying 'I don't care about the law'. The problem is that that is – I think – a profoundly immoral response in its own right, and a threat to the rule of law. We should always know the price we are paying for end we want to achieve, before we pay it. So, it seems to me that the advocate of the return of cultural property needs to recognise two things: first, that it is important to make the case for the return of such property – the positive case, as it were. But secondly, to recognise, respect and

[85] I have in mind a kind of wishful thinker who ducks the questions the rule of law gives rise to by wishing the problem had never occurred – wishing, in this case, Lord Elgin away.

[86] We are so far away from the notion that an Act of Parliament can be set aside for breach of some fundamental rule that I am not going to even discuss this. But this is where 'natural law' fits – for me – as a legal positivist.

seek to minimise the damage done to the values of the rule of law, even if those values inhibit what is sought, for good reason, to be achieved.

As I have stressed, the rule of law is neither an absolute value nor is it a rule of law. It is perfectly possible, lawfully, to achieve the return of the Marbles, but unless and until the competing values for and against this outcome are untangled, there will be debate that creates more heat than light.[87]

B. Moving Forward

The nature of the debate that I have been considering sheds valuable light on aspects of the rule of law that have either not sufficiently been articulated or else have been hidden by the more prominent features of the rule of law that are more often discussed. There are three aspects that I want to touch upon, less as a conclusion, and more an an invitation for further consideration and debate in addition to this principal point:

1. *The danger of inertia.* The inertia inherent within the rule of law is undoubtedly a problem. The law needs to be appropriately responsive to changing values in society. This is not – at any level – a question for the judiciary. It is a question

[87] The means to resolving competing values in the public arena are almost always laid down in advance in general terms, obliging the court to determine – according to the applicable test – the outcome. Simply wanting something to happen – even if there is good reason – will rarely be enough. Take, for example, the removal of the memorial of Tobias Rustat from the chapel in Jesus College, Cambridge. It will be recalled that Mr Rustat was said to have such involvement in the slave trade that the removal of the memorial was sought by a number of persons. In *Re The Rustat Memorial* [2022] ECC Ely 2, the Deputy Chancellor (David Hodge, QC) ruled that the memorial could not be removed. In reaching this conclusion, he was – to the doubtless dismay of those petitioning – simply applying the rule of law. As he noted at [5]:

> Those coming to this petition with no knowledge of planning and ecclesiastical law may wonder why the College itself cannot simply implement the decision its governing body has already made and remove the memorial to a safe, secular space elsewhere within the College itself. The answer is that the chapel is a Grade I listed building, which means that the chapel is of exceptional interest in a national context. That listing extends to any object or structure fixed to the building, and that includes the Rustat memorial. If the Rustat memorial were within a secular space, its removal would require listed building consent from the local authority or the Secretary of State. Because the chapel is included in the list of places maintained by the Church Buildings Council …, it is subject to the faculty jurisdiction of the diocese of Ely, exercised through its consistory court. It therefore benefits from the 'ecclesiastical exemption' from the need for listed building consent. This means that a faculty (or permission) from the consistory court of the diocese takes the place of listed building consent. But it is important to understand that it only does so because the state regards the faculty jurisdiction as equivalent to secular listed building consent, in terms of due process, rigour, consultation, openness, transparency and accountability; although this does not mean that the consistory court is required to apply precisely the same approach to listed buildings as is followed in the secular system.

I am not going to unpack the value that Mr Hodge applied, nor seek to approve or defend his conclusion. The point I am making is that Mr Hodge was applying the rule of law, in that he was looking not just to the 'right' outcome in the given case (although that is, clearly, important) but to the 'right' outcome given all of the procedural values inherent in the rule of law, including the law laid down as regards listed building consent. That is not because listed building consent is part of the rule of law: it is because the law laid down needs to be applied in accordance with the rule of law. The danger is that when faced with an apparently righteous claim, the rule of law's inevitably conservative stance runs the danger of sounding like the Little Britain comedic catchphrase 'Computer says no'. Of course, when it is the state seeking to enforce unjust laws (as in Nazi Germany or apartheid South Africa), 'Computer says no' becomes rather important as a bulwark. See, further, Dyzenhaus (n 51).

for our legislators and politicians. One can see – in the debates that surrounded the Marbles themselves – how Parliament acted as a sounding board for a debate that continues to this day; and polemicists such as Geoffrey Robertson perform a critical function in informing and stirring such debate. But one does wonder, in this age of the digital platform and information exchange, whether more cannot be done to ensure that the competing values that our society holds continue to be reflected in the laws that the courts enforce. I suspect that this is not, actually, a facet of the rule of law: but it is a critical determinant of the extent to which the rule of law actually serves its true purpose.[88] If the laws do not appropriately keep up with society, then the rule of law serves as the protector of interests that have passed their day, and a mismatch arises between substantive content and enforcement.

2. *Does discretion have too much of a bad name?* In a society as complex as ours, where legislative time (and I include in relation to delegated legislation) is so limited, I wonder whether the dangers of overregulation and the virtues of discretion are not being overlooked. There are two issues here: first, the extent to which discretion is actually a 'bad thing'. And secondly, if discretion is a 'bad thing', how one can constrain the excesses of overregulation.
3. *To what extent is there a proper correlation between law and its enforcement?* Professor Raz identifies a number of principles that can be derived from his – admittedly very narrow – conception of the rule of law.[89] One attribute missing from his list is the (to my mind) important attribute that law needs to be effective in the sense that the rights it confers and the obligations it imposes are easily capable of enforcement, so that there is a correlation between, let us say, entitlement (as in a state benefit) or infringed right (as in a breach of contract or tort) and the receipt of that entitlement or the effective enforcement of the infringed right. It may be that this is less an attribute of the rule of law and more a measure of how far a given society is compliant with the ideal that is the rule of law.

[88] Take, for instance, the damage inflicted on the Colston statue in Bristol. Leaving entirely on one side the lawfulness of such conduct (a matter that certainly troubled the courts), it is on any view undesirable for a large and heavy statue to be forcibly taken down in an unplanned way, by unskilled actors. The risk of injury is too great, and perils of self-help are obvious. What is troubling about the case is less whether a criminal offence had been committed, but more why – over the years – articulated concerns about what the statue stood for were sidelined and disregarded.

[89] Raz (n 49) 214ff.

3

*Insolvency and Economic Disaster**

SIR WILLIAM TROWER, MARK PHILLIPS KC AND MADELEINE JONES

I. INTRODUCTION

INSOLVENCY LAW HAS developed to deal with crises – at least in the sense that insolvency is a crisis in the life of a company or individual. As befits a form of crisis management, in the extraordinary circumstances of an insolvency, extraordinary rules apply: property rights, contractual rights, even (to some extent) human rights are suspended and varied. Certain insolvencies are not only a crisis for the debtor and its creditors, but may give rise to aftershocks that ripple far outside this immediate context. A bank failure is the paradigm of such a crisis. The banking system depends on credit, both in the technical meaning of moneylending and in the more fundamental sense of trust. When a bank defaults on a liability, financiers fear that the sudden loss of liquidity will cause knock-on defaults in other entities (a failure of the system of credit in the technical sense); they also fear that consumers and market players alike will lose confidence – credit – in the bank (or perhaps in the banking sector in general) and withdraw funds en masse out of fear there will be insufficient funds for future withdrawals, thereby precipitating the catastrophe they fear.[1]

This chapter examines the development of English company, insolvency and banking law in the context of past financial and economic crises. We suggest that, whereas in the nineteenth and into the twentieth century such crises were treated as commercial issues to be solved in the marketplace rather than the courts, over time the law has developed principles and tools to handle insolvencies and economic disasters.

II. COMPANY LAW BEFORE THE NINETEENTH CENTURY[2]

Although there are earlier antecedents, modern company law has its origins in the seventeenth century. From this period, merchant adventurers engaged in overseas

* A copy of this chapter first appeared as an article in the South Square Digest, www.southsquare.com.

[1] Recent examples of the impact of loss of confidence in banks include Silicon Valley Bank and Credit Suisse. In the age of smartphones one concern is that a run on a bank can now occur almost instantly. It does not depend on customers queuing to recover their funds.

[2] For the development of company law, see LCB Gower, *Principles of Modern Company Law*, 6th edn (London, Sweet & Maxwell, 1997), chs 2 and 3 (the historical material is omitted from later editions).

trade formed companies under royal charter (the East India Company is the best-known example). By the end of the seventeenth century, companies in something closer to their modern sense had emerged: joint stock companies, operating a joint account, sometimes with transferable shares, established and governed by statutory or royal charter, and enjoying legal personality at least in the sense that they might sue and be sued.

The Bank of England was one such company, incorporated by statute in 1694[3] as a lender to the government, to finance the Nine Years War against France. On its incorporation it was not a state body but a deposit-taking commercial enterprise. However, it was able to leverage its closeness to government into a series of statutory privileges which gave it a superior position in the English financial system.

Before the nineteenth century there was no developed company law to govern these new legal entities. The courts applied partnership law as modified by the provisions of the particular company's charter. Although joint stock companies had legal personality, their charters tended to empower them to make calls on their members. Such calls may have been possible even in the absence of an express power.[4] As members' liability was unlimited, there was no pressing need for a corporate insolvency regime to wind up companies' affairs.

III. EARLY SPECULATION IN COMPANIES

At the start of the eighteenth century the company appeared a novel and exciting prospect – a model under which ordinary people could share in the returns of overseas trade or burgeoning domestic industries by an investment as large or modest as their means allowed. Companies advertised investment opportunities in handbills and as the country was swept up in the excitement, investment schemes became more and more ambitious, until one enterprise, the South Sea Company,[5] proposed to buy up the country's entire national debt in the hope of raising vast sums to expand its activities – principally slave trading in South America. In fact, the South Sea Company's trade was nowhere near developed enough to produce a return on the vast sums that flowed into its accounts. It was reduced to using investors' funds to bribe officials to allow it to acquire national debt, which it purchased at unfavourable prices compared to its competitor, the Bank of England. In 1720 the South Sea Company's share price collapsed when these shortcomings became apparent.[6] Many of its investors were ruined and the magnitude of the failure combined with the involvement of public funds caused a national scandal.

[3] The Bank of England Act 1694.

[4] Direct liability for contributories, independent of any provision in the corporate charter, was upheld in the seventeenth century: *Edmunds v Brown & Tilliard* (1667) 1 Lev 237, 83 ER 385 and *Salmon v Hamborough Co* (1671) 1 Ch Cas 204, 22 ER 763. By the nineteenth century, deeds of settlement included express provisions for liability of members where this was intended.

[5] Incorporated by Act of Parliament in 1711.

[6] On the South Sea Bubble, see eg H Paul *The South Sea Bubble: An Economic History of its Origins and Consequences* (Abingdon, Routledge, 2013) and W Quinn and JD Turner, *Boom and Bust: A Global History of Financial Bubbles* (Cambridge, Cambridge University Press, 2020).

IV. THE FALLOUT FROM THE SOUTH SEA BUBBLE

The South Sea Bubble was the first major financial crisis in England. It arose due to rising demand for investment opportunities. This demand, and the fact that the South Sea Company's collapse discredited stocks and shares in investors' eyes, impacted the development of company law and the finance industry over the rest of the eighteenth century. The South Sea Bubble and the associated overhyping and subsequent collapse of various other dubious share offerings in the same period[7] became indelibly associated with the notion of a company itself. It was clear that investors needed protection that they did not then have.

In response to the crisis, Parliament passed the Bubble Act 1720.[8] This rambling piece of legislation, which Maitland said 'seems to scream at us from the Statute Book',[9] banned unincorporated companies (formed otherwise than by Royal Charter or Private Act of Parliament), though specifying that this should do nothing 'to prohibit or restrain the carrying on of any home or foreign trade in partnership in such manner as hath hitherto usually and may be lawfully done according to the Laws of this Realm now in force'.[10] This proved an unhelpful provision, given the contemporary lack of legal clarity as to the difference between a partnership and an unincorporated company. The Bubble Act distorted the development of the company as a vehicle for business for a hundred years. The Act attempted to deal with the perceived cause of the financial disaster but did little to assist in developing structures responsive to the growing demand for investment opportunities.

The South Sea Bubble also bolstered the Bank of England's position by warning officials off from placing government funds in private investment vehicles, securing the Bank's place as a quasi-official body tasked with keeping and lending government money. Amidst the furore surrounding share investment, even before the final crash, the Bank was appointed by the government to manage its debts.[11] Over the next hundred years, its bills became the dominant form of currency and it emerged as the central bank in England and Wales, with which other banks placed their surplus funds and from whom they took loans.

By the nineteenth century, England had a strong central bank, but a financial market populated by a mixture of partnerships, unincorporated associations (held together by partnership agreements and/or trust deeds) and companies established by Act of Parliament and Royal Charter, with no coherent legal regime and no certainty as to what would happen if these entities failed.

[7] See J Hoppit, *A Land of Liberty? England 1689–1727* (Oxford, Oxford University Press, 2000).

[8] This ill-thought-out legislation was passed before the Bubble reached its peak to stop capital being attracted away from the South Sea Company and was apparently supported by the South Sea Company's directors: see R Harris, 'The Bubble Act: Its Passage and its Effects on Business Organization' (1994) 54(3) *Journal of Economic History*.

[9] FW Maitland, 'Trust and Corporation' in *The Collected Papers of Frederic William Maitland*, vol 3 (Cambridge, Cambridge University Press, 2013) 390.

[10] s 25.

[11] Under the National Debt Act 1715 (1 Geo I Stat 2, c19).

V. BANKRUPTCY UP TO THE START OF THE NINETEENTH CENTURY

Corporate insolvency developed initially in the nineteenth century by reference to bankruptcy law. Bankruptcy was first formally regulated by the Statute of Bankrupts 1542 – 'An Acte against suche persones as doo make Bankrupte'. Its preamble paints a vivid picture of the main preoccupation of the draftsman (absconding debtors) but also introduces the legal concept of *pari passu* distribution, which remains one of the principles fundamental to insolvency law to this day.[12]

A 1571 Act[13] limited the bankruptcy procedure to 'any Merchant or other Person, using or exercising the Trade of Merchandise by way of Bargaining, Exchange, Recharge, Bartry, Chevisance, or otherwise in Gross or by Retail, … or seeking his or her Trade by buying or selling'.[14] Until the nineteenth century, debts incurred otherwise did not fall within the bankruptcy regime.[15] This restriction gave rise to a body of case law on whether various moneymaking activities counted as 'trades' so that attendant debts fell within the bankruptcy process upon an 'act of bankruptcy' (another concept introduced by this Act, which persisted until the Insolvency Act 1985). This made the bankruptcy process particularly arbitrary: if a man lost money through 'trade' he could surrender his estate to creditors and make a fresh start, his debts discharged. If he lost it through some other endeavour, he could lose everything to one creditor by enforcement, and not be free of the others, whose only recompense would be the vindictive satisfaction (to modern eyes) of having him consigned to debtor's prison.

The bankruptcy regime was only tangentially relevant to financial services at the beginning of the nineteenth century, in that if an entity failed, creditors might seek to make the individuals behind it liable. Even in the case of companies this was generally possible due to the near ubiquity of terms in companies' charters providing for members' liability.

Discharge for bankrupts was introduced by the Bankruptcy Act 1705.[16] This Act incentivised cooperation by allowing bankrupts a 5 percent share of their estate (capped at £200) where realisations exceeded 8 shillings. Discharge encouraged enterprise by enabling tradesmen to continue in business free from historic trading debt. On one view the 1705 Act reflected a crude and embryonic form of the 'rescue culture'.

VI. MODERNISATION OF THE LAW IN THE NINETEENTH CENTURY

Over the eighteenth century, neither company nor bankruptcy law kept pace with the increasing sophistication of the business community and money markets. The

[12] The Preamble concludes that the property of the bankrupt (referred to as the 'Offender') should be granted to pay his creditors, 'That is to say, to every of the said Creditors, a Portion Rate and Rate like, according to the Quantity of their Debts.'

[13] 13 Eliz I, c 7.

[14] It also introduced commissioners for the administration of bankrupts, replacing members of the judiciary.

[15] M Lester, *Victorian Insolvency* (Oxford, Clarendon Press, 1995) 15–17, 88–89.

[16] 4 Anne c 17.

concept of incorporation was still relatively undeveloped (companies could still only be incorporated by Royal Charter or by Private Act of Parliament); incorporation with limited liability was effectively unavailable. However, there was an increasing appetite for risk and demand for different forms of corporate trading vehicle. The Bubble Act, outlawing unincorporated companies save as allowed by partnership law, was in force but widely disregarded. Common law had developed such that in practice unincorporated companies were permissible (as a form of partnership) so long as their shares were not freely transferrable, though participating tradesmen remained personally liable for the debts of the unincorporated entity, and subject to bankruptcy law, in the event of failure.

In the second quarter of the nineteenth century a flurry of legislation dramatically modernised English corporate, insolvency and banking law. The Bankruptcy Act 1831[17] brought administration of a bankrupt's estate under the control of the courts rather than the creditors' assignees, and established a specialist Bankruptcy Court in London. This would later result in trustees, liquidators and other office-holders being officers of the court.

The money markets were by this time populated by dozens of banking 'companies' – unregistered and operating (so far as legal analysis of their activity was undertaken) under partnership law.[18] The Country Bankers Act 1826[19] and the Bank of England Act 1833[20] provided that banking companies could sue or be sued in the names of their officers and required them to register certain particulars. The Duties of Offices Act 1825[21] repealed the Bubble Act and enabled corporations to declare the extent of members' liability in their charters. In 1845 the courts confirmed that companies with shares freely transferable at the will of the holder were legal at common law, even if unincorporated.[22] In 1834, the Trading Companies Act empowered the crown to confer the privileges of incorporation by letters patent without granting a charter.

The Chartered Companies Act of 1837 provided that members' personal liability might be limited by letters patent and therefore incentivised enforcement against an insolvent company. This in turn necessitated a winding-up regime – instituted for joint stock companies seven years later. The Joint Stock Companies Act 1844[23] provided for the registration (by the Registrar of Companies, a newly created post) of all new associations with more than twenty-five members or shares transferable without members' consent. For the first time, incorporation was available by registration, as opposed to by Private Act, charter or letters patent. Existing unincorporated companies could obtain the benefits of incorporation by registration. Under the first Companies Winding Up Act 1844[24] companies were made subject to bankruptcy law

[17] 1 & 2 Will 4, c 56.

[18] Their numbers had been dramatically reduced by a crash in December 1825 when forty-three country banks failed on the collapse of Pole, Thornton & Co, with eighty more failing during the early months of 1826. See B Hilton, *A Mad, Bad, Dangerous People? England 1783–1846* (Oxford, Oxford University Press, 2006) 300ff.

[19] 7 Geo 4, c 46.

[20] 3 & 4 Wm 4, c 98.

[21] 6 Geo 4, c 9.

[22] *Harrison v Heathorn* (1843) 6 Man & G 81, 134 ER 817.

[23] 7 & 8 Vict c 110.

[24] 7 & 8 Vict c 111.

with the proviso that the company's insolvency did not entail the insolvency of its shareholders. Corporate insolvency law was born.

The 1844 legislation left members liable for corporate losses (normally by an express provision to this effect in the company's charter). This changed with the enactment of the Limited Liability Act of 1855,[25] subsequently repealed and incorporated into the Joint Stock Companies Act 1856,[26] which finally introduced the defining feature of modern company law and business practice – limited liability – and for the first time introduced detailed provisions on winding up. It also included several safeguards to protect creditors. The Companies Act 1862 removed many of these, although not the mandatory inclusion of the word 'Limited' in the company's name, which continues to this day.

As for banks, the Joint Stock Banks Act 1844[27] provided for registration of all joint enterprises engaged in banking with more than six members and introduced requirements for minimum nominal and paid-up capital. Limited liability for banks (like insurers, initially excluded from the scope of the 1855 and 1856 Acts) was introduced by the Joint Stock Banks Act 1858,[28] three years after it had been introduced for companies.

By the mid-nineteenth century, a legal framework for incorporation, insolvency and the financial sector was in place. Companies, including banks, could incorporate with limited liability and be subject to the newly established corporate insolvency regime. The model was not universally adopted, however, as the collapse of City of Glasgow Bank in 1878 bears witness. This caused the bankruptcy of several hundred of its contributories and had a major adverse impact on the Scottish economy.[29] It was the last nail in the coffin of banks with unlimited liability, at least those with shares held by members of the public. However, there have remained certain tax and other advantages for banks to trade with unlimited liability and some have continued to do so with protection higher up the corporate chain (the English Lehman entity, Lehman Brothers International (Europe), is one modern example).

VII. NINETEENTH-CENTURY BOOMS AND BUSTS

Also in the mid-nineteenth century came a recognition that the loss of one cog in the City of London's financial machinery could cause a breakdown of the entire engine. The money markets were jittery, with panics in 1825, 1837–39, 1847 and 1857. Each time the Bank of England stepped in to provide liquidity to the market, its role as the custodian of the markets became entrenched. It continued to be a privately owned customer bank, although in recognition of the potential conflict between its roles as central bank and market participant, restraints were placed on its activities. The Bank Charter Act 1844 limited the value of Bank notes in issuance to the value of its gold

[25] 18 & 19 Vict c 133.
[26] 19 & 20 Vict c 47.
[27] 7 & 8 Vict c 113.
[28] 21 & 22 Vict c 91.
[29] *Houldsworth v City of Glasgow Bank* (1880) 5 App Cas 317 (HL) is the best-known example of the widespread litigation that ensued.

reserves,[30] but did not prescribe any particular level of reserve; there were no capital or liquidity requirements for any bank until the twentieth century.[31]

The reality of systemic risk was highlighted in 1865 by the failure of Overend, Gurney and Company, a 'discount house', or trader in discounted bills of exchange, the sort of securities trading that is still carried out by investment banks and hedge funds. By 1850, Overend Gurney was larger than the next three bill brokers combined and turning over bills equal to half the national debt each year. In 1856, Overend Gurney changed its investment model by taking long-term as well as short-term positions, tying up its funds in illiquid positions. In 1857, there was a panic when it – and other financial houses – could not honour their obligations. The Bank, as was by this time expected of it, assisted by purchasing distressed lenders' debt-based assets in exchange for Bank notes and deposits. The 'bail-out' gave rise to concern among the Bank's governors that the availability of emergency liquidity disincentivised discount houses from keeping their own reserves. Therefore, in 1858 the Bank restricted brokers' access to its discount window (the framework for providing emergency liquidity).[32] In 1860, a peevish consortium of bill brokers, including Overend Gurney, organised a mass withdrawal of deposits from the Bank apparently to bring home their power over it in protest at these restrictions.[33] The Bank's reserve was about £7.7 million at the time.[34] The Bank won the power struggle with the brokers, who realised that they would indeed need to hold higher levels of (unprofitable) reserves to weather storms without access to the Bank's discount window. When this dawned on Overend Gurney, it redeposited its funds and apologised. It also sought to protect its profits by continuing its expansion into higher-risk investments outside its core business – inter alia in railways and foreign plantations.

In 1865, Overend Gurney transferred its business to a new joint stock company with limited liability. It thereby became – unintentionally – a test for the robustness of the corporate model for banks in insolvency. Already at the time of its incorporation, the house was hopelessly mired in difficulty. It had been losing an average £0.5 million

[30] This provision was suspended in 1847, a year of financial crisis precipitated by a major harvest failure in Ireland and England in 1846 and the 'railway mania' which commenced in 1845. See R Dornbusch and JA Frenkel, 'The Gold Standard and the Bank of England in the Crisis of 1847' in MD Bordo and AJ Schwartz (eds), *A Retrospective on the Classical Gold Standard, 1821–1931* (Chicago, University of Chicago Press, 1984).

[31] In the conclusion (chapter 13) of *Lombard Street: A Description of the Money Market*, 6th edn (London, HS King, 1875), Walter Bagehot argued against the introduction of a law requiring the Bank to keep a reserve fixed in proportion to its liabilities, on the basis that this would give the Bank's directors insufficient flexibility having regard to the nature of the Bank's liabilities from time to time. In 1891, following the Barings crisis, the Chancellor of the Exchequer argued for more robust reserve requirements, but no legislation followed: see D Kynaston *Till Time's Last Sand: A History of the Bank of England 1694–2013* (London, Bloomsbury, 2020) 233–36.

[32] See R Sowerbutts, M Schneebalg and F Hubert, 'The Demise of Overend Gurney' [2016] Q2 *Bank of England Quarterly Bulletin* and Kynaston (n 31) 168–72.

[33] The Governor of the Bank found an anonymous note on his desk one morning: 'Overends can pull out every note you have, from actual knowledge the writer can inform you that with their own family assistance they can nurse seven millions!!': Kynaston (n 31) 169.

[34] A Hauser, Head of Sterling Markets Division, Bank of England, 'The Five Ages of (Sterling Man): Prospects for the UK Money Market', speech given to the London Money Market Association, 13 June 2013; available at www.bankofengland.co.uk/-/media/boe/files/speech/2013/the-five-ages-of-sterling-man-prospects-for-the-uk-money-market.pdf (accessed 3 October 2023).

per year for five years. It was later established that at the time of the equity fundraising, Overend Gurney had a shortfall of £4–5 million against assets of £20 million.

In 1866, rumours about the company's liabilities came to a head when the Court of Common Pleas ruled that the Mid-Wales Railway Company's acceptance of bills of exchange by the company and others as indorsees was unenforceable.[35] This sparked a run on its deposits as the market correctly surmised that many other of the company's debts would suffer from the same defect. The Bank of England, on inspecting the company's books, refused to intervene: it was hopelessly insolvent. Overend Gurney suspended payment and on the following day, 11 May 1866, called by *The Times* 'Black Friday', panic set in as depositors withdrew funds from banks across England. The Governor of the Bank wrote to the Chancellor of the Exchequer explaining that the Bank started the day with a reserve of £5.7 million and, under a policy of not refusing 'any legitimate application for assistance', expected to end it with less than £3 million. The Chancellor responded to what he called – with a shade of reproach – 'the liberal answer of the Bank to the demands of commerce' by suggesting that such assistance should be provided at an interest rate of not less than 10 percent.

Walter Bagehot gave a description of the Bank of England's operations as lender of last resort and a manifesto for its role in future in his essay *Lombard Street*, first published in 1873 and revised several times in new editions. On last-resort lending, which he regarded as crucial to the successful functioning of the City, Bagehot set out two rules: first, that loans should be made to distressed institutions at a very high interest rate; and secondly, that these loans should be available to all comers, to ensure continued public confidence in the banking system.[36]

Bagehot was less interested in the legal mechanisms by which banks operated than the macroeconomic environment they inhabited. He argued that the Bank's position as lender of last resort should be acknowledged to increase public confidence in the financial system and decrease the likelihood of panics. It is today clear that market confidence is also assured by predictability as to how creditors will fare in an insolvency, something which has only been achieved by the introduction of a coherent corporate insolvency regime.

The interplay of pragmatic reaction and legalistic response is illustrated by the responses to Overend Gurney's collapse: the immediate making available of cash to the market by the Bank and the orderly treatment of creditors in due course in the house's liquidation, which vindicated the limited liability corporation as a vehicle for business. Despite criticism in the press of the principle of limited liability given the company's conduct,[37] there was no legislative initiative or demand from business to cement prudential requirements for banks or roll back limited liability.

The outline of the Bank's response to banking crises was set. As Bagehot had recommended, the Bank would facilitate funding to banks in a crisis. When Barings Bank reached the brink of collapse in 1890, a consortium of investors assembled by the Bank's Governor created a fund to guarantee its debts and avert systemic crisis.

[35] *Bateman v The Mid Wales Railway Company* (1865–66) LR 1 CP 499 (CP).

[36] Bagehot (n 31) 197.

[37] C Hunt, *The Development of the Business Corporation in England 1800–1862* (Cambridge, MA, Harvard University Press, 1936), 153.

Barings' salvageable business was hived off as a 'good bank' (Baring Brothers Ltd) and its toxic assets taken over by the Bank in return for a loan, backed by a 'Guarantee Fund' raised from market participants and repayable by Baring Brothers Ltd. The restructuring was successful. Panic on the market was contained and Baring Brothers Ltd survived until 1995.

By the end of the nineteenth century, when the House of Lords in *Salomon v Salomon*[38] unanimously held that even the shareholder-director of a one-man company was not liable for company debts, company law and insolvency law were a sophisticated and reliable system. However, there was no understanding of the law as a tool in managing financial crises. Insolvency law facilitated distribution of available assets: it was a terminal procedure.[39] Bank insolvency was still considered a business matter, to be managed by the Bank of England, whose dual role as market participant and central bank masked the fact that the conditions for its assistance were the start of a de facto system of bank regulation.

VIII. BANKS IN THE EARLY PART OF THE TWENTIETH CENTURY

After the First World War, with a growing trend towards state oversight of public life, the Bank of England was subordinated to the Government in setting monetary policy.[40] However, there was no formalisation of its role as protector of the banking system or move towards bank regulation. This lack of barriers to institutions behaving like banks left the financial sector vulnerable. The only legislation akin to banking regulation was the Moneylenders Act 1900. This required the registration of moneylenders, but expressly made exempt from its provisions 'any person bona fide carrying on the business of banking'. The 1900 Act did not explain the meaning of this exemption, and there were several cases dealing with its interpretation,[41] until section 123 of the Companies Act 1967 empowered the Board of Trade to grant certificates providing that a company was 'carrying on the business of banking' for the purpose of the 1900 Act.

In the 1940s, Parliament showed more interest in bank regulation. Section 4 of the Bank of England Act 1946 enabled the Bank to 'request information from and make recommendations to bankers' and made provision for the Treasury to direct the Bank to 'issue directions to any banker for the purpose of securing that effect is given to any such request or recommendation'. However, the definition of banker in the section was 'any such person carrying on a banking undertaking as may be declared by order of the Treasury to be a banker for the purposes of this section'. As the Treasury never made any such order, the Bank could never exercise these powers. Further authorisations for banks were established for narrow purposes. The Exchange Control Act 1947 required the Treasury and the Bank of England to establish a list

[38] *Salomon v Salomon* [1897] AC 22 (HL).

[39] Although see Sir Antony Zacaroli on schemes in 'The Importance of Classes in Insolvency and Restructuring' in ch 7 of this volume.

[40] See CAE Goodheart, 'Bank of England' in SN Durlauf and LE Blume (eds), *The New Palgrave Dictionary of Economics*, 2nd edn (London, Palgrave Macmillan, 2008).

[41] See eg *Litchfield v Dreyfus* [1906] 1 KB 584 (KB) and *Edgelow v Macelwee* [1918] 1 KB 205 (KB).

of banks authorised to deal in foreign exchange and exercise delegated powers under the Act ('authorised banks'). The Companies Act 1948, and later section 127 of the Companies Act 1967, required the Board of Trade and the Bank to establish a list of banks which were permitted accounting privileges relating to their maintenance of inner reserves. Failures of non-bank deposit-taking institutions[42] inspired the Protection of Depositors Act 1963, which required institutions to make available certain information if they advertised to take deposits. However, these initiatives did nothing more than generate official lists of banking or banking-adjacent institutions. It did not grant any body oversight over them.

The banking industry grew up with the Bank of England at its centre. The trust placed in Bank of England bills, its unrivalled ability routinely to provide high levels of liquidity through the discount window and the sophistication of its clearing house system meant that, at the turn of the twentieth century, there were almost no participants in the banking sector which did not keep their reserves at the Bank and make use of its clearing house. However, over the mid-twentieth century, the financial services industry changed. Institutions no longer depended on the discount market and could operate without regular dealings with the Bank, and therefore without the development of personal relationships with Bank personnel and de facto daily provision of information. The informality of the Bank of England's role fitted the market in which it had developed but was not sufficiently flexible to deal with changes in that market.

IX. THE SECONDARY BANKING CRISIS 1973–1975[43]

In the 1950s and 1960s London was regaining its role as an international financial centre, which had fallen away during the war years. The City's financial ecosystem became increasingly complex and was no longer concentrated on a single discount market. New, so-called secondary, markets were established – the Local Authority Market, the Certificate of Deposit Market, the Corporate Debt Market and the Inter-Bank Market to name a few. On these markets, particularly the Inter-Bank Market, institutions could access short-term funding limited only by their market standing. There was a growth in lending by small fringe banks, which held deposits from players on the money markets, to property developers in the booming UK residential market. These banks tended to offer slightly better rates than mainstream banks.

These secondary banks were able to obtain certificates from the Board of Trade under section 123 of the Companies Act 1967, providing that they were carrying on the business of banking for the purpose of the Moneylenders Act 1900 and therefore exempt from the registration requirements in that Act. This may have given the impression that they had a more general 'official' recognition as banks, though no such formal recognition existed.

[42] An example is Mortgage Investment (Albert Square) Ltd, a property investment company reputed to have attracted deposits of over £750,000 from small-scale investors. See JS Fforde, *The Bank of England and Public Policy, 1941–1958* (Cambridge, Cambridge University Press, 1992) 761–71.

[43] The fullest account of the crisis is given in M Reid *The Secondary Banking Crisis, 1973–1975* (London, Hindsight Books, 2003).

In the early 1970s, the country experienced a storm of economic disasters: inflation was high, the pound weakened severely, the oil price soared and at the end of 1973 and into 1974 the stock market crashed. In 1973, the Bank of England raised its lending rate to an unprecedented 13 percent. A fall in house prices in 1973 was the final straw for several secondary banks. The first to find itself in difficulties was London and County Securities Group – a well-known entity on whose board the then-Liberal Party leader Jeremy Thorpe sat. London and Counties was unable to renew deposits taken through the money markets. It later emerged that it was beset by fraud. The Bank of England mounted a hasty rescue operation. However, problems spread to similar banks, as depositors lost confidence. Three weeks after the collapse of London and Counties, the Bank of England also had to rescue Cedar Holdings.

In response, in the last days of 1973 the Bank established the Control Committee of the Bank of England and English and Scottish Clearing Banks, or the 'Lifeboat'. This was tasked with identifying fringe banks in difficulty and – where appropriate – providing support. The conventional bank with the closest connection to each struggling institution was appointed its 'related bank'. The related bank reviewed the struggling institution's affairs and reported back to the committee. The committee then decided whether to offer support in the form of secured lending. The banks all shared risk in relation to these funds (the Bank itself put forward 10 percent), but support was coordinated by the related bank. Twenty-six companies were given Lifeboat support. Eight were subsequently placed in receivership or liquidation.[44] The Bank also supported two institutions on its own account: Slater Walker Limited and Edward Bates & Sons Limited. Although these institutions were not banks in the traditional sense, the Bank recognised that their collapse would have 'threatened the well-being of some recognised banks'.[45] The total support committed by the Lifeboat approached £1,200 million by August 1974, about 40 percent of the estimated aggregate capital reserves of English and Scottish banks.[46]

The Lifeboat's modus operandi was essentially what Bagehot had proposed in *Lombard Street*: the extension of credit to struggling institutions to protect confidence in the system as a whole. Bagehot had not anticipated the scrutiny which the Lifeboat committee gave to institutions before handing over cash. Recognising that pouring money into an institution beyond rescue was not proportionate or necessary, the Lifeboat exercised an analytical role in deciding which institutions should be funded and directing how funds should be used. The Bank's essentially improvised reaction led to it adopting a proactive supervisory role over banks (considering their balance sheets and recommending interventions accordingly) which laid out a blueprint for what more formal bank regulation might look like.[47]

[44] DS Trust, 'The Secondary Banking Crisis and the Bank of England's Support Operations' [1978] Q2 *Bank of England Quarterly Bulletin*.

[45] ibid.

[46] ibid para 38.

[47] ibid.

X. THE BANKING ACTS 1979 AND 1987

The Banking Act 1979 was a direct response to the secondary banking crisis and an attempt to formalise the ersatz supervisory position adopted by the Bank during the crisis. The 1979 Act required the Bank of England to issue licences to banks and deposit-takers, following an assessment of their capital adequacy. The Bank was also required to monitor and supervise institutions, controlling and where appropriate withdrawing authorisation.[48] The Act focused solely on microprudential supervision – supervision of individual entities – and did not require the Bank to take a macro-prudential view of the systemic health of the banking system. It also introduced the Deposit Protection Scheme.

After the enactment of the 1979 Act, several years passed without any bank failures. Then, in 1984, auditors of Johnson Matthey Bankers, the banking subsidiary of Johnson Matthey PLC, identified that a number of its commercial borrowers were likely to default and that this would wipe out the bank's capital. Johnson Matthey was a leading gold trader and one of five London Gold Market members which provided daily price fixings. The bad debts were unrelated to its role in the gold market, but its failure would disrupt this internationally important exchange. The Bank of England intervened with a rescue package – the bank's parent agreed to inject $62 million into the bank and to sell it to the Bank for a nominal sum. Other banks were found to take stakes and a separate consortium of banks and members of the gold market provided it with credit lines.[49] The Bank undertook this rescue not in a supervisory capacity but in its traditional, non-statutory role as central bank, to prevent disruption to the gold market and the banking system.

The Banking Act 1987 established the Bank of England's Board of Banking Supervision, strengthening the Bank's supervisory function.[50] The Act restricted deposit-taking to authorised institutions and required authorised institutions to report 'large exposures' to the Bank,[51] in an acknowledgement that systemic risk was greater the greater the degree of exposure a particular institution had. The 1987 Act also expanded the Bank's supervisory powers: it could require an authorised institution to provide information or documents or to commission a report by an accountant[52] and appoint persons to investigate the authorised institution.[53] It relaxed the duty of confidentiality of auditors so that this was not contravened by a report to the Bank in good faith on any matter relevant to the Bank's supervisory function.[54] These enhanced powers made banking regulation more of a force to be reckoned with.

[48] Banking Act 1979, s 3 and see the criteria for authorisation in part 2 of schedule 2. Licensed deposit-taker status was intended to catch the secondary banks.

[49] See the Bank of England's Annual Report for 1985 at 33ff, available at www.bankofengland.co.uk/-/media/boe/files/annual-report/1985/boe-1985.pdf (accessed 3 October 2023).

[50] Banking Act 1987, ss 1 and 2.

[51] ibid s 38.

[52] ibid s 39.

[53] ibid s 41.

[54] ibid s 48.

XI. THE INSOLVENCY ACT 1986

In 1977 the Labour government commissioned a review into insolvency law and practice, chaired by Kenneth Cork, head of a well-known firm of insolvency practitioners, Cork Gully, and a key figure in the meetings at the Bank of England during the secondary banking crisis. In 1982, the committee published its Report of the Review Committee on Insolvency Law and Practice,[55] known as the Cork Report. Following the Cork Report's recommendations, insolvency statute was completely overhauled in the Insolvency Act 1985, which was consolidated into the Insolvency Act 1986.

The 1986 Act represented a sea change in English insolvency law. For the first time, a rescue culture – the potential for insolvency law to act not only to sweep up the remains of failed businesses but to promote salvage and regeneration – was formally recognised in English law. This philosophy had been adopted elsewhere, notably with the introduction of Chapter 11 in the US Bankruptcy Code in 1979.

In the context of corporate insolvency, the 1986 Act introduced administration.[56] This introduced rescue culture into English law, despite having been loosely based on receivership, a form of secured creditor enforcement.[57] The company could be protected from its creditors while the administrator sought to achieve one of four purposes: the survival of the company, the approval of a creditors' voluntary arrangement, the approval of a scheme of arrangement, or a better realisation of the company's assets than would be achieved in liquidation.[58] Administration proved an effective tool. In the first decade after its introduction, Canary Wharf was restructured through administration,[59] the *Daily Mirror* was saved, administration was used to rescue what was viable in the Maxwell Group,[60] and both Drexel Burnham Lambert and Barings Bank were sold through administration.[61] Under the Enterprise Act 2002, the appointment of an administrative receiver by the holder of a floating charge created on or after 15 September 2003 was prohibited, eliminating the anomaly of administrative

[55] Department of Trade and Industry, *Report of the Review Committee on Insolvency Law and Practice* (1982) Cmnd 8558 (Cork Report).

[56] See *Bristol Airport Plc v Powdrill* [1990] Ch 744 (Ch) 756–57 (Sir Nicolas Browne-Wilkinson V-C) for a classic description of the procedure.

[57] Receivership is unusual among insolvency procedures in that it derives from the bipartisan relationship between a secured creditor and debtor created and governed by contract. Administration is notable as a *collective* process, introduced by Parliament, although it derived from the *bipartisan* relationship which enabled receivership.

[58] Insolvency Act 1986 s 8, as enacted. Section 8 as amended implements Schedule B1 to the 1986 Act. Paragraph 3(1) of Schedule B1 lists the following purposes of administration: (a) rescuing the company as a going concern, (b) achieving a better result for the company's creditors as a whole than would be likely if the company were wound up (without first being in administration), or (c) realising property in order to make a distribution to one or more secured or preferential creditors.

[59] The administration of its holding company, Olympia and York (Canary Wharf) Ltd, produced several reported judgments: [1993] BCC 154 (Ch), [1993] BCC 159 (Ch), (1994) 68 P&CR 451 (Ch), [1993] BCC 866 (Ch), [1995] 69 P&CR 43 (CA).

[60] See eg *Re Maxwell Communications Corp plc* [1992] BCC 372 (Ch) (appointment of administrators), *Re Maxwell Communications Corp plc* [1993] BCC 369 (Ch) (an important case which established the validity in principle of debt subordination agreements in insolvency).

[61] See eg *Re Drexel Burnham Lambert UK Pension Plan* [1995] 1 WLR 32 (Ch), an application by DBL's administrators which produced a significant judgment on trustees' duties and powers. Barings was sold to ING for £1 in administration.

receivership as a non-collective insolvency procedure. It also became possible to file for administration on paper without a court hearing,[62] a development that facilitated the rise of the pre-pack administration sale.[63] The Insolvency Act 1986 also introduced individual and company voluntary arrangements – which enabled creditors to enter into a compact with a debtor in what was intended to be a more straightforward and affordable procedure.

XII. BANK FAILURES IN THE 1990s

The financial system's continued stability after the enactment of the Banking Act 1987 may be partly attributable to the relatively favourable economic conditions that prevailed after the difficulties of the 1970s. However, it is likely that the regulatory regime introduced by the 1979 Act and strengthened in the 1989 Act also played its part. The period of stability was interrupted in the 1990s – Bank of Credit and Commerce International (BCCI) collapsed in 1991, as did Barings Bank in 1995. Both collapses were precipitated by fraud: in BCCI's case, money laundering and other financial crimes had been committed on a massive scale across many jurisdictions and executives had covered up the fact that the bank had been insolvent since the 1970s; in Barings' case, fraudulent gambling by the head derivatives trader in Singapore brought down the whole bank. The collapses did not cause any larger systemic shock but did highlight flaws in the regulatory regime. BCCI's collapse demonstrated the challenge that the cross-border nature of modern banking and finance poses to effective regulation. No single regulator took responsibility for cross-border transactions and conduct by BCCI which should have raised red flags.

Both BCCI and Barings were dealt with under existing insolvency procedures, stretched to their limits by the complexity of modern cross-border banking. On the first hearing of the Bank of England's petition to wind up BCCI,[64] Sir Nicolas Browne-Wilkinson V-C, lamented that, in considering a creditor's application for an adjournment, he had to choose between the interests of depositors, whose accounts were frozen while the petition was ongoing, and the possibility of negotiating a rescue plan which might provide a better outcome for stakeholders, but which would take time. He stood over the petition, unhappy with the compromise. The court was confronted with the fact that, with limited cross-border recognition, an international entity had to be wound up in each of the countries it operated in. The judge could not see a 'better way' without statutory reform.

Following BCCI's collapse, Lord Justice Bingham (as he then was) chaired an inquiry into its failure. The subsequent Report[65] focused on the Bank of England's

[62] See paras 22–34 of Schedule B1 to the Insolvency Act 1986.

[63] This has not been without its problems, some of which are sought to be dealt with by the Administration (Restrictions on Disposal etc to Connected Persons) Regulations 2021/47, in force since 30 April 2021.

[64] *Re BCCI (Bank of Credit and Commerce International)* [1991] Lexis Citation 2512 (Ch).

[65] The Right Honourable Lord Justice Bingham, *Inquiry into the Supervision of the Bank of Credit and Commerce International* (HC 1992, 198) (Bingham Report); available at https://assets.publishing.service.gov.uk/government/uploads/system/uploads/attachment_data/file/235718/0198.pdf (accessed 3 October 2023).

supervision of BCCI and largely endorsed the current regulatory systems[66] and the EC Regime.[67] It recommended that the Bank should have the power to refuse or revoke authorisation on the basis that an entity cannot be supervised, whether on structural or other grounds,[68] where an entity's business comprises 'a tangled web of domestic companies', 'a complex and fragmented group such as BCCI', 'the involvement of any centre where secrecy or commercial practice precludes a clear view of a group's affairs' or 'a structure which makes a group incapable of being effectively supervised'.[69] These proposals were reflected in the renewed regulatory regime implemented under the Financial Services and Markets Act 2000 (FSMA 2000) (the ability of the Financial Conduct Authority (FCA) or the Prudential Regulation Authority (PRA) to be able to 'effectively supervise' a person is a threshold condition for authorisation under amendments to Schedule 6 to FSMA[70]). The Report also recommended that administration under the 1986 Act should be extended to UK branches of overseas banks.[71] Several UK branches have indeed been subject to the 1986 Act in this way, eg Iraq's Rafidain Bank.

The move to international recognition of insolvency procedures has gained traction with the UNCITRAL Model Law on Cross-Border Insolvency, which was published in 1995 and has the force of law in England and Wales pursuant to the Cross-Border Insolvency Regulations 2006,[72] and the EU Insolvency Regulation, which was introduced in 2000, recast in 2015 and which is retained (for the time being) in amended form post-Brexit.[73] Both the UNCITRAL Model Law and the EU Insolvency Regulation aim to deal with the territoriality of national insolvency laws and pre-empt the consequences of financial crisis in a globalised world.

Insolvency practitioners and their advisers have played a role in brokering arrangements that go beyond what was anticipated by existing insolvency procedures. They are pragmatic responses to the difficult problems arising. Examples include a scheme by the liquidators of BCCI for the pooling of the assets and liabilities of two companies within the BCCI group rather than dealing with these in separate liquidations,[74] and an incident in the insolvency of Maxwell Communication Corporation (MCC), which collapsed the same year as BCCI. MCC was subject to insolvency proceedings in both the Southern District of New York and London. Hoffmann J in England and Judge Tina Brosman in New York discussed by telephone how to deal with the joint estate, an innovative approach to cross-border judicial cooperation necessitated by the absence of legislation equipped to deal with the increasingly complex demands of major cross-border insolvencies. This led to the American Law Institute's Guidelines

[66] ibid paras 3.1–3.10.
[67] ibid paras 3.19–24.
[68] ibid paras 3.14–16.
[69] ibid para 3.23.
[70] Financial Services and Markets 2000 (Threshold Conditions) Order, SI 2013/555 paras 2C, 3B, 4F and 5F.
[71] The Bingham Report (n 65) para 3.58.
[72] SI 2006/1030.
[73] Pursuant to the Insolvency (Amendment) EU Exit Regulations 2019 and 2020, SI 2019/146, SI 2020/647.
[74] See the Court of Appeal's ruling in *Re Bank of Credit and Commerce International SA (No 3)* [1993] BCLC 1490 (CA), affirming the decision at first instance of Sir Donald Nicholls V-C [1993] BCLC 106 (Ch).

Applicable to Court-to-Court Communications in Cross-Border cases, adopted and promulgated on 16 May 2000.[75]

XIII. FINANCIAL SERVICES AND MARKETS ACT 2000

The recommendations of the Bingham Report and other lessons from BCCI provided impetus for the enactment of FSMA 2000. This overhaul of financial services regulation replaced the FSA 1986. It reconciled the regulation of banks and other financial service providers in a single regime, so that regulation focused on the nature of the activity undertaken rather than of the institution undertaking it. This purposive approach was designed to avoid a repeat of crises like the secondary banking crisis, when fringe entities were able to undertake bank-like activities free of scrutiny. Initially, FSMA 2000 installed the Financial Services Authority (FSA) as the main regulator, with certain functions in relation to banks retained by the Bank of England and the Treasury. Subsequently, responsibility for bank regulation was transferred to the PRA and conduct of business regulation to the FCA (replacing the FSA).[76] FSMA 2000 is extremely broad. At its heart is the 'general prohibition' under section 19, which prohibits persons from carrying out regulated activities (defined in the Act) unless they are authorised or exempt from the need to obtain authorisation. The Act also sets out powers of investigation and enforcement and grants express powers to the FCA and the PRA to initiate and participate in insolvency proceedings of regulated entities (under Part 24 of the Act), further cementing the insolvency regime as a tool in the service of maintaining the health of the financial system.

XIV. THE 2007–2009 FINANCIAL CRISIS

In 2007 the finance system suffered a global crisis. Like the secondary banking crisis, the 2007 crash was rooted in overexposure to the property market. This time, investments were made via sophisticated financial products that appear not to have been fully understood by some bankers who used them. The popularity of bonds backed by pooled residential and commercial mortgage liabilities meant that lenders, overenthused by the secondary market value of their debts, made risky loans to customers whose situations would formerly have been undesirable. Inevitably, many of these 'subprime' loans defaulted, and the knock-on defaults on the corresponding mortgage-backed securities – and the attendant massive loss of investor confidence – caused huge losses on the part of financial institutions. The secondary banking crises was managed outside the statutory framework because winding up was the only available option. By 2007 the Insolvency Act 1986 had been in force for twenty years.

[75] The use in England of court-to-court communication was considered by David Richards J in *Re T&N Ltd and others* [2004] All ER (D) 146 (Dec) (Ch) [29].

[76] Pursuant to the Financial Services Act 2012.

Although preceded by the collapse of Northern Rock in the United Kingdom and a bail-out of Bear Stearns in the United States, the largest and best-known bank collapse of this era was Lehman Brothers, the venerable US investment bank. The bank's UK subsidiary, Lehman Brothers International (Europe), an unlimited liability company, was placed in administration in England before the start of business on Monday 15 September 2008, after the collapse of the US business made clear that it would be unable to settle its obligations that day. However, once amounts due to the bank were netted off, it was left with a surplus of several billion US dollars as regards unsecured creditors and has now even paid much of its subordinated debt in full. Over the administration, the courts were faced with a number of applications raising novel points and they responded by a combination of pragmatic responses and adapting established principles and applying them to the novel situation. An example is the application of the long-established contributory rule, first applied in a corporate insolvency in *Re Overend, Gurney and Co; Grissell's Case*,[77] to a distributing administration by the Supreme Court in *Re Lehman Bros International (Europe) (No 4)*.[78]

The Lehman administration also threw up a series of cases, the Waterfall applications, in which the ranking of creditor claims and issues of priority fell to be decided. Their resolution, together with a large number of other disputes which arose (for example, on the construction of the ISDA (International Swaps and Derivatives Association) master agreement and on the close-out of derivative positions) led to a number of innovative solutions and procedures for the resolution and efficient management of those disputes, including the use of position papers,[79] which proved invaluable for narrowing the issues and ensuring that the many disputes were triable.

Although the courts were proactive and imaginative, the management of the administration would not have been possible if it had not been combined with deal-making by the administrators. Its apogee was the court's approval of a remarkable settlement between the English and US insolvent estates, which reflected a commercial compromise reached within the parameters of a formal insolvency process.[80]

In 2010, UK financial regulation was again overhauled, in response to the financial crisis. Under the Financial Services Act 2010 oversight is split between the FCA, PRA (a subsidiary organisation of the Bank of England) and the Treasury. While the FCA and PRA retain a focus on microprudential supervision (the activities and risk of individual institutions), a newly created Financial Policy Committee (another Bank of England body) is now obliged to report to the PRA on macroprudential matters (assessment and limitation of risk on a systemic level), and the PRA is obliged to act on its concerns. This focus on macroprudential risk was adopted pursuant to the review into the causes of the financial crisis conducted by Lord Turner, who took over as chairman of the FSA as Lehman went into administration. The Turner Review concluded that macroprudential oversight 'fell between the gaps in the UK

[77] *Re Overend, Gurney and Co; Grissell's Case* (1865-66) LR 1 Ch App 528 (CA).

[78] *Re Lehman Bros International (Europe) (No 4)* [2017] UKSC 38, [2018] AC 465.

[79] Introduced by Briggs J in his role as judge supervising the administration.

[80] See the comments of David Richards J in a judgment delivered after direct communication with Judge Peck in the US Bankruptcy Court: *Re Lehman Brothers International Europe* [2013] EWHC 1664 (Ch), [2014] BCC 132 [14]–[15].

supervisory system' (with the Bank of England focusing on monetary policy analysis, and its macroprudential analysis not resulting in policy, and the FSA focusing on individual institutions in isolation) and that this 'was one of the crucial failures of the years running up to the crisis'.[81]

XV. THE BANKING ACT 2009

A major legislative response to the Lehman insolvency came with the Banking (Special Provisions) Act 2008, the Banking Act 2009 and the Investment Bank Special Administration Regulations 2011. Like the Acts of 1979 and 1989, the 2008 Act (a piece of emergency legislation with a sunset clause after one year) and the 2009 Act updated the banking regulatory regime in the wake of a specific financial crisis. For the first time, a full statutory framework was provided for managing bank failures. Administration was a significant step forward compared to the ad hoc rescue mission of the Lifeboat Committee in the 1970s, but Lehman demonstrated that provisions intended to make administration available to all companies could not deal comprehensively with a bank administration. The post-Lehman legislative approach was in part due to the renewed confidence in the insolvency profession which the 1986 Act had brought about. Insolvency practitioners, previously seen in some quarters as cowboys, were now respected as professionals, capable of dealing with the intricacies of a major bank insolvency.

The shift in approach also resulted from a changed political climate. The rescues of Slater Gordon and Johnson Matthey were arranged by the Bank of England in late-night meetings behind closed doors with figures from the British finance industry. This was typical of a time when the Governor's eyebrows carried great significance, but also reflected the lack of a statutory framework for bank rescue. In 1991, and certainly by 2007, such an approach would not have been publicly acceptable. The failure of a bank was recognised as a national problem, its solution would need to be subject to scrutiny and those involved in its implementation would have to be accountable for it. This is illustrated by the failures of Northern Rock and Bradford & Bingley, both of which were dealt with in economic terms in broadly the same way as previous bank failures – with an influx of public funds to cover short-term liabilities and avert shock to the banking system, while for the long-term their profitable assets were sold off and their toxic liabilities assumed by the state. However, decisions in respect of the future of these institutions were not made in the depths of the Bank of England but by the legislature.

The Banking (Special Provisions) Act 2008 (BSPA) was produced in very short order after the failure of Northern Rock. The government announced it had acquired all the shares in Northern Rock the day after the BSPA received Royal Assent (under the Northern Rock plc Transfer Order 2008). Later in 2008, the FSA determined that the Bradford & Bingley building society no longer met the threshold conditions to operate as a deposit-taker under FSMA 2000. Again, the government acquired its shares

[81] FSA, *The Turner Review: A Regulatory Response to the Global Banking Crisis* (London, 2009) 84.

under secondary legislation enacted under the BSPA (in this case the Bradford & Bingley plc Compensation Scheme Order 2008). Following these initiatives, the Banking Act 2009 received Royal Assent on 12 February 2009, shortly before the temporary provisions under the BSPA ceased to have effect. Its main provisions are as follows. Part 1 gives the regulatory authorities tools to deal with banking institutions in financial difficulties and replaces the regime under the BSPA with a permanent Special Resolution Regime (SRR) for banks. Part 2 introduces the Bank Insolvency Procedure (BIP) – a winding-up procedure tailored to failed or failing banks. Part 3 introduces a Bank Administration Procedure for use where part of a failing bank's business has been transferred, by means of the SRR, to a private or bridge bank.

The BSPA and the 2009 Act are the first legislation to deal specifically with bank failure. They constitute a recognition that the collapse of a bank requires a discrete set of tools – ones which allow those in charge of a failed bank to act very quickly to shore up its position, protect depositors and provide certainty to counterparties, to prevent repercussions from rippling across the market. However, both Acts rely on other market players coming forward to acquire failed banks' salvageable assets, implementing a practical rather than legalistic strategy developed within the banking industry and familiar from nineteenth-century rescues, such as that of Barings Bank in 1890, and from the secondary banking crisis. The willingness of Parliament, the courts and practitioners to adopt a practical approach has been key to the successful containment of crises over the years. However, a legislative response was required to deal with the complexity of twenty-first-century bank restructurings. Absent the 1986 Act, it would have been impossible to mitigate market disruption and to avoid systemic collapse in 2007–2009. Although the courts can be flexible, there are limitations set by the available statutory framework.

XVI. THE INVESTMENT BANK SPECIAL ADMINISTRATION REGULATIONS 2011

The Investment Bank Special Administration Regulations 2011 is an industry-specific special administration procedure. An investment bank enters special administration by court order[82] and the administrator is to pursue the special administration objectives, which differ from the purposes in schedule B1.[83] Those objectives, which do not stand in a fixed hierarchy,[84] are: the return of client assets, to ensure timely engagement with market infrastructure bodies and relevant Authorities, and to either rescue the investment bank as a going concern or to wind it up in the interests of the creditors.[85] One reason for the introduction of special administration was to avoid market disruption and speed up the administration of a bank's insolvency. Those were lessons learnt from the collapse of Lehman Brothers. MF Global was the first institution placed in special administration, in 2011.[86]

[82] Investment Bank Special Administration Regulations 2011, SI 2011/245, reg3(2)(a).
[83] ibid reg 3(2)(c).
[84] ibid regs 10–13; for the lack of hierarchy see reg 10(3), although the appropriate regulator can direct prioritisation (reg 19).
[85] ibid reg 10(1).
[86] *Re MF Global Overseas Ltd (in administration)* [2012] EWHC 1091 (Ch), [2012] BCC 490.

XVII. THE RESPONSE TO THE CORONAVIRUS PANDEMIC

COVID-19 resulted in another unexpected financial challenge (which coincided in the United Kingdom with Brexit). This crisis is unlike the others discussed in this chapter in that it was a major economic shock which did not originate in the financial system. To combat the effects of the pandemic, many countries, including the United Kingdom, imposed lockdowns that caused large parts of the economy to be shut down or severely curtailed. Many perfectly healthy businesses, especially in the retail and leisure sectors, suffered sudden and unexpected cashflow insolvency, caused simply by being forced to shut their doors, while still accruing liabilities on rent, utilities and other fixed costs.

The response to the pandemic was unprecedented. Parliament, the courts and the insolvency profession reacted quickly to help businesses across all sectors of the economy affected.

One of the first responses came from the insolvency profession. In March 2020 the Insolvency Lawyers Association published a 'Consent Protocol' to facilitate so-called 'light touch' administrations.[87] Paragraph 64 of Schedule B1 to the Insolvency Act 1986 prohibits a company in administration or its directors from exercising management powers without the administrators' consent. In the pandemic, administrators used the Consent Protocol to grant permission to directors to continue their management in 'light touch' administrations, similar to US Chapter 11 bankruptcy proceedings. Given that the issues suffered by many companies were not their directors' fault, this sharing of responsibility was appropriate. It also kept the costs of administrations to a minimum.

The government's legislative response fell into two parts. First, there were the government's initial pragmatic responses, such as the furlough scheme and the temporary moratoria relating to winding-up petitions and landlords' ability to evict for breach of a covenant to pay rent. Secondly, the opportunity was seized to introduce permanent innovations that had been under discussion built on insolvency principles. In this category we may now count many provisions in the Corporate Governance and Insolvency Act 2020 (CIGA 2020).

The furlough scheme, introduced in March 2020, enabled employers to reclaim from HMRC up to 80 percent of the salaries of employees who were not working due to the restrictions placed on businesses by coronavirus legislation. The scheme's guidance made clear it was intended to be available to administrators as well as solvent employers, although no guidance was given as to how this would work under existing insolvency legislation. In *Re Carluccio's Limited (in administration)*[88] and *Re Debenhams Retail Limited (in administration)*,[89] the courts set out a practical way forward for administrators to make furlough payments to company employees: by adopting the employment contract (in the meaning of paragraph 99(5) of Schedule

[87] Available at www.ilauk.com/docs/ILA.consent_.protocol_.17.April_.2020.V2_.pdf (accessed 3 October 2023).

[88] *Re Carluccio's Limited (in administration)* [2020] EWHC 886 (Ch), [2020] 3 All ER 291.

[89] *Re Debenhams Retail Limited (in administration)* [2020] EWHC 921 (Ch), [2020] 3 All ER 319; [2020] EWCA Civ 600; [2020] 3 All ER 319.

B1 to the 1986 Act) or making a payment otherwise than in accordance with the statutory payment waterfall on the grounds the administrator thinks it likely to assist achievement of the purpose of administration (under paragraph 66 of Schedule B1). The courts were willing to work with administrators to achieve an outcome in the public interest and in the spirit of the scheme.

As to CIGA 2020, this introduced both provisions that had been under discussion for some time and temporary measures to combat the financial impact of the pandemic. Among the latter was a moratorium on winding-up petitions where the company would not be insolvent but for the financial effect of the pandemic.[90] CIGA 2020 also suspended a director's potential liability for wrongful trading during the coronavirus period[91] and landlords' ability to evict tenants who fell into arrears on rent falling due during the coronavirus crisis.[92] These measures dealt with the immediate risk to businesses, but more permanent solutions were needed to restructure their liabilities. Two new procedures were introduced: the moratorium[93] and the restructuring plan.[94] Under the first, the company is given a temporary moratorium intended to enable it to reach agreement with its creditors, with oversight by a monitor. CIGA 2020 introduced temporary provisions intended to make the moratorium more widely available.[95] Whilst evidence is limited, anecdotally the moratorium has not been used as much as had been hoped.[96] The second new procedure, the restructuring plan, had been under discussion before COVID-19. Unlike in schemes under Part 26 of the Companies Act 2006, the court in the new restructuring plan may grant a cross-class cramdown, provided one class of creditors with an interest in the outcome votes in favour of the plan and that other classes are not worse off than they would have been in the relevant alternative.[97] Several companies in various sectors had restructuring plans sanctioned during pandemic.[98] It is noteworthy that these were largely companies which would otherwise have used the Part 26 scheme process (which is comparable in complexity and cost to the restructuring plan) and few, if any, were small to medium-sized firms.

[90] See CIGA 2020, sch 10, para 2. This provision was given effect by the court even before CIGA 2020 had passed into law: see *Re A Company* [2020] EWHC 1406 (Ch), [2021] 1 All ER (Comm) 181 and *Re A Company* [2020] EWHC 1551 (Ch), [2020] BCC 773, where injunctions restraining advertisement of petitions were granted on the strength of the likelihood that the CIGA Bill, as it was at the time, would pass into law and prevent the relevant companies being wound up.

[91] CIGA 2020, s 12.

[92] ibid s 82.

[93] ibid ss 1–3 and schs 1–3.

[94] ibid s 7 and schedule 9 that introduced Part 26A to the Companies Act 2006.

[95] ibid sch 4; the moratorium rules expired on 30 September 2021.

[96] The moratorium regime was considered by Norris J in *Re Corbin & King Holdings Ltd* [2022] EWHC 340 (Ch), [2023] 1 All ER (Comm) 51.

[97] 'Condition A' under Companies Act 2006, s 901G.

[98] eg *Re Virgin Active Holdings Ltd* [2021] EWHC 814 (Ch) and [2021] EWHC 911 (Ch); *Re Amicus Finance plc* [2021] EWHC 2340 (Ch) and [2021] EWHC 3036 (Ch), [2022] Bus LR 86; *Re DeepOcean 1 UK Ltd* [2020] EWHC 3549 (Ch), [2021] Bus LR 632 and [2021] EWHC 138 (Ch), [2021] BCC 483; *Virgin Active* [2021] EWHC 814 (Ch), [2021] EWHC 911 (Ch) and [2021] EWHC 1246 (Ch), [2022] 1 All ER (Comm) 1023. The court refused sanction of Hurricane Energy plc's Part 26A scheme: *Re Hurricane Energy plc* [2021] EWHC 1759 (Ch), [2021] BCC 989.

Notwithstanding CIGA 2020, thousands of businesses remained unable to pay their rent. Meanwhile, landlords were prevented from enforcing their rights. There was a political and social imperative to achieve a compromise between the upholding of landlords' rights and the avoidance of the mass insolvency of otherwise viable businesses that were unable to pay lockdown rent arrears. Parliament's attempt at a solution to this dilemma came in the form of the Commercial Rent (Coronavirus) Act 2022 (CRCA 2022).[99] This introduced an arbitration procedure, under which the arbitrator determines not legal rights, but which of the competing proposals from landlord and tenant should be implemented having regard to their impact on the viability and solvency of the landlord and tenant.[100] This unique approach stands apart from other insolvency procedures in that it is not a collective process, although it does incorporate principles familiar from a post-1986 insolvency context, notably the aim of saving viable businesses and the idea that discharge from debt is a tool which may be used to achieve this. Anecdotally, however, this procedure has not been much used, and instead the post-pandemic moratorium period has seen a significant increase in winding-up petitions.

The final initiative was a pragmatic response of the insolvency profession to deal with the consequences of the pandemic. In June 2021, the trade body for insolvency professionals, R3, launched its 'Back to Business' initiative,[101] an information service for businesses about the options available to them to deal with coronavirus debt. The Back to Business website also lists insolvency practitioners who will give free initial consultation.[102] The initiative has been rolled out in over fifty-two countries in which businesses are receiving advice and help (usually free).

XVIII. THE INVASION OF UKRAINE AND SANCTIONS

Russia's invasion of Ukraine in February 2022 disrupted global economic stability, largely because of disruption to energy and food supplies, but also through the impact of sanctions, including against financial institutions and the Russian Central Bank, and Russian countermeasures against 'hostile countries' of which the United Kingdom is one. The problem for the insolvency profession was exacerbated by the concern that professionals advising entities that were, or might be sanctioned, might themselves breach sanctions.

The flexibility of the United Kingdom's insolvency processes meant entities that were, or were likely to become, insolvent as a result of sanctions could be placed under the control of a special manager or special administrator, under Schedule B1 or (in the case of banks) under the Investment Bank Special Administration Regulations 2011. As Michael Green J commented on an application by a sanctioned bank, Sberbank

[99] The Act applies to Protected Rent Debt as defined in CRCA 2022, s 3. CRCA 2022, ss 11 and 12 provide that each party produces one or two proposals and written statements.

[100] The principles by which he does that are set out in CRCA 2022, s 15.

[101] Available at www.r3.org.uk/press-policy-and-research/r3-blog/more/29932/back-to-business-campaign-preparing-directors-for-the-future/ (accessed 3 October 2023).

[102] At the time of writing over 230,000 companies have made use of this resource.

CIB (UK) Ltd, for the appointment of special administrators, this special administration regime provides a prudent and practical way forward.[103] This is an example of existing statutory provisions being used to deal with financial distress caused by circumstances not contemplated by the drafters of the legislation. Insolvency practitioners were faced with unprecedented problems. Following directions from the court they were able to effect novel solutions. First, in *Re Petropavlovsk plc* the court directed that the administrators were able to effect the sale of three Russian goldmines in circumstances where there were Russian countermeasures that restricted the persons to whom such strategic assets could be sold.[104] In *Re Sova Capital Ltd*, the estate held assets tradable by Russians on the Moscow stock exchange, but not tradable by the administrators. A Russian creditor took assignments of four claims and then bid those unsecured claims to purchase the shares. In exchange for the shares the creditor waived their unsecured claim.[105] These responses to unprecedented circumstances were both pragmatic and based upon fundamental insolvency principles.

XIX. CONCLUDING THOUGHTS

History shows that most, if not all, major insolvency crises give rise to problems that were not predicted (and often not predictable). The question then arising is whether the responses to those crises are pragmatic or principled. The answer is that they are both. The courts and practitioners have responded to the different crises over time with pragmatic responses but those responses have always been grounded in, and applications of, the core principles of insolvency law. Often, after a particular problem has emerged, Parliament has then made changes to insolvency law to better facilitate dealing with the new scenario (perhaps by introducing a tailor-made type of administration).

Insolvency law derives its force from statute, but the principles running through it are not ahistorical. Insolvency proceedings are a collective process that responds to financial distress by recognising existing rights but restricting their enforcement and exercise. As Professor Goode has pointed out, the principles underpinning this procedure derive from equity, in particular the maxim that 'equality is equity'.[106] These principles have been developed by a series of legislative and judicial responses to distinct historical circumstances and often in response to an economic catastrophe.

Although the balance between jurisprudential principle and statute is delicate, the law's success in dealing with recent crises – the collapses which ushered in the 2007–8 financial crisis, the coronavirus crisis and the failure of sanctioned Russian financial institutions – shows that English insolvency law is well placed to see institutions

[103] *Re Sberbank CIB (UK) Ltd* [2022] EWHC 1059 (Ch), [2022] All ER (D) 108 [29].

[104] *Re Petropavlovsk plc* [2022] EWHC 3448 (Ch).

[105] *Re Sova Capital Ltd (in special administration)* [2023] EWHC 452 (Ch), [2023] Bus LR 779. Miles J held that this was neither a breach of the *pari passu* rule, nor was it a distribution *in specie*. The administrators had power to sell the assets and the sale was for the best price reasonably obtainable in the circumstances.

[106] R Goode *Principles of Corporate Insolvency Law*, 5th edn (London, Sweet & Maxwell, 2018) ch 3.

and society through economic storms. However, the key role that well-framed statute plays in any novel situation means it would be foolhardy to be complacent about the law's ability to deal with new kinds of crisis. While practitioners and judges will continue to adapt existing procedures to unforeseen circumstances, it is to be hoped that academics will continue to set out forward-looking proposals for reform to mitigate the consequences of the next financial crisis for the economy and for society as a whole.

4

Attribution and Agency: Back to Basics Again

RACHEL LEOW*

I. INTRODUCTION

No shortage of literature on corporate attribution and agency exists.[1] Many topics within the broad field can be canvassed, ranging from general accounts of corporate attribution to specific applications in a narrow area. This chapter falls into the latter category.

In 2017, Sarah Worthington tackled three long-standing questions in the law of attribution and agency law in her *Law Quarterly Review* article, 'Corporate Attribution and Agency: Back to Basics'.[2] They were:

1. The '*Stone & Rolls*' problem: should acts and states of mind of a person acting for a company be attributed to the company when the company is bringing a claim against another, such that the company's claim fails for illegality?[3]
2. Can an agent have actual authority to act contrary to the interests of his principal?[4]

* I am grateful to Sarah Worthington for discussing many of the ideas in this chapter with me over the course of my doctorate, and to participants at the conference for their helpful comments. I am especially grateful to Sir William Trower for agreeing to act as commentator for my paper at short notice.

[1] E Ferran, 'Corporate Attribution and the Directing Mind and Will' (2011) 127 *LQR* 239; P Watts, 'Illegality and Agency Law: Authorising Illegal Action' [2011] *JBL* 213; P Watts, 'Principals' Tortious Liability for Agents' Negligent Statements – Is "Authority" Necessary?' (2012) 128 *LQR* 260; E Lim, 'A Critique of Corporate Attribution: "Directing Mind and Will" and Corporate Objectives' (2013) *JBL* 333; E Lim, 'Attribution in Company Law' (2014) 77 *MLR* 794; J Payne, 'Corporate Attribution and the Lessons of Meridian' in PS Davies and J Pila (eds), *The Jurisprudence of Lord Hoffmann: A Festschrift for Leonard Hoffmann* (Oxford, Hart Publishing, 2015); S Worthington, 'Corporate Attribution and Agency: Back to Basics' (2017) 133 *LQR* 118 (hereinafter 'Back to Basics'); P Watts, 'The Acts and State of Knowledge of Agents as Factors in Principals' Restitutionary Liability' [2017] *LMCLQ* 386; P Watts, 'Attribution and Limitation' (2018) 134 *LQR* 350; E Lim, 'Attribution' in W Day and S Worthington (eds), *Challenging Private Law: Lord Sumption on the Supreme Court* (Oxford, Hart Publishing, 2020); R Leow, *Corporate Attribution in Private Law* (Oxford, Hart Publishing 2022).

[2] Worthington, 'Back to Basics' (n 1).

[3] Named after *Stone & Rolls v Moore Stephens (a firm)* [2009] UKHL 39, [2009] 1 AC 1391. See Worthington, 'Back to Basics' (n 1) 118–31.

[4] Worthington, 'Back to Basics' (n 1) 131–39.

3. The *First Energy* problem: can an agent have apparent authority to communicate approval of a transaction even though he has no authority to approve it himself, so that the principal is bound by the transaction?[5]

The aim of this paper is to critically examine the solutions offered by that article to each of the three problems. It ultimately disagrees with the solutions, but for different reasons than those offered in the current literature.

II. *STONE & ROLLS*

Discussed by numerous ultimate appellate courts across the Commonwealth in the last decade, the *Stone & Rolls* problem is undisputedly one of the most significant attribution problems of modern times. Before the problem can be set out, some background context to attribution is necessary. The problem and the solutions in 'Back to Basics' and the recent case law are then explained. These solutions rely on the idea that it may be possible to attribute an act for one purpose but not another. They therefore subscribe to a conception of attribution where attribution is seen as a fictional deeming rule. Drawing on previous writing, I suggest an alternative conception of attribution, showing how it sheds light on the *Stone & Rolls* problem and how the latter should be resolved.

A. Corporate Attribution

As Lord Walker NPJ explained in *Moulin Global Eyecare Trading Ltd v Commissioner of Inland Revenue*:

> Attribution means, in this context, the process of legal reasoning by which the conduct or state of mind of one or more natural persons (that is, human beings) is treated as that of a non-natural person (that is, a company) for the purpose of determining the company's legal liability or rights in civil proceedings (in particular, its liability or rights in contract, in tort or for unjust enrichment) or its criminal liability.[6]

The leading decision on attribution is *Meridian Global Funds Management Asia Ltd v Securities Commission*.[7] Lord Hoffmann said that:

> A company exists because there is a rule (usually in a statute) which says that a persona ficta shall be deemed to exist and to have certain of the powers, rights and duties of a natural person. But there would be little sense in deeming such a persona ficta to exist unless there were also rules to tell one what acts were to count as acts of the company. It is therefore a necessary part of corporate personality that there should be

[5] Named after *First Energy (UK) Ltd v Hungarian International Bank Ltd* [1993] 2 Lloyd's LR 194 (CA). See Worthington, 'Back to Basics' (n 1) 139–42.

[6] *Moulin Global Eyecare Trading Ltd v CIR* [2014] HKCFA 22, (2014) 17 HKCFAR 218 [61].

[7] *Meridian Global Funds Management Asia Ltd v Securities Commission* [1995] 2 AC 500 (PC).

> rules by which acts are attributed to the company. These may be called 'the rules of attribution'.[8]

Lord Hoffmann then identified three categories of attribution rules: primary rules, general rules and special rules of attribution.[9] Primary rules of attribution are generally found in the company's constitution or in general company law.[10] An example includes the rule that 'for the purpose of appointing members of the board, a majority vote of the shareholders shall be a decision of the company'.[11,12] These are supplemented with general rules of attribution – the rules of agency.[13] They are 'general' rules because they also apply equally to human persons, while the primary rules do not. In some exceptional cases, neither of these two categories provide an answer, but the court may conclude that the substantive rule of law ought to apply to companies.[14] The court must then formulate a special rule of attribution, asking, '[w]hose act (or knowledge, or state of mind) was *for this purpose* intended to count as the act etc of the company?'[15] In doing so, the court has to take into account the language of the rule (if it is a statute), its content, and policy.[16]

Over time, *Meridian* eventually became closely associated with a highly context-specific approach to attribution. A key reason for this change was the *Stone & Rolls* problem.

B. The *Stone & Rolls* Problem

The *Stone & Rolls* problem, so named for the case in which it rose to prominence, occurs at the intersection of attribution and illegality. In *Stone & Rolls Ltd (in liquidation) v Moore Stephens*,[17] a company had been used by its controller, a Mr Stojevic, to perpetuate frauds on banks, inducing them to lend the company funds.[18] Stojevic then perpetuated a fraud on the company, dissipating those funds. The company, Stone & Rolls, went into liquidation. Its liquidators sued the company's auditors for breach of duty in negligently failing to detect the fraud perpetrated on the company. In response, the auditors argued that as the company's directing mind and will, Stojevic's acts and states of mind should be attributed to the company. As the company would then be party to illegal conduct, its claim against the auditors would fail under the illegality doctrine.

[8] ibid 506.
[9] ibid 506–07.
[10] ibid.
[11] See eg Model Articles for Public Companies, Model Art 20; Model Articles for Private Companies Limited by Shares, Model Art 17, which will apply to limited companies unless the company registers its own articles of association: Companies Act 2006, s 18.
[12] *Multinational Gas and Petrochemical Co v Multinational Gas and Petrochemical Services Ltd* [1983] Ch 258 (CA), cited at *Meridian* (n 7) 506.
[13] *Meridian* (n 7) 506–07.
[14] ibid.
[15] ibid 507.
[16] ibid.
[17] *Stone & Rolls* (n 3).
[18] See *Komercni Banka AS v Stone & Rolls Ltd* [2002] EWHC 2263 (Comm), [2003] 1 Lloyd's Rep 383.

This argument succeeded by a bare majority before the House of Lords, but each member of the majority gave different reasons for this conclusion. Diverse positions were taken on contested issues. One was whether attribution turned on the company being a 'one-person' company.[19] The scope and purpose of the illegality doctrine was another contested pressure point;[20] the scope of the auditors' duties yet another.[21] The Law Commission eventually regarded *Stone & Rolls* as a decision with 'no majority reasoning':[22] distilling a coherent ratio from it was seen as impossible by some.[23] Unsurprisingly, lower courts faced difficulty in applying *Stone & Rolls*. The key question remained: when and why could the acts and states of mind of a misbehaving director, employee or agent be attributed to the company when the company was suing that individual or a third party, whether for illegality or otherwise?[24]

C. Back to Basics

In *Stone & Rolls*, several members of the House of Lords relied on an exception to attribution in cases of fraud or breach of duty (sometimes called the *Hampshire Land* principle).[25] Under it, where the director or agent is acting to defraud the company or in breach of duty to it, his acts and states of mind cannot be attributed to the company.

Worthington argued in 'Back to Basics' that the key to solving the *Stone & Rolls* problem was to focus on corporate attribution. As she explains:

> An individual within the corporate structure may act, or intend or know a wide variety of things, but these will not count as the company's actions, intentions or knowledge for all purposes. Generalisations are impossible; context is all. And the context which matters is the legal claim in issue, not the parties' identities, the company's solvency, or the state of the market.[26]

Thus, the key question is 'whose act counts "for this purpose"?' To this, Worthington explains:

> The only context in which 'the Hampshire Land principle' finds traction is when *the company sues or is sued by its insiders*. Again, describing the principle as 'defensive' does

[19] See eg in favour of attribution, Lord Phillips at [48]–[56], Lord Walker at [168], but against, Lord Scott [117] (relying on the company being a victim of the frauds).

[20] Prior to *Patel v Mirza* [2016] UKSC 42, [2017] AC 467, compare eg *Tinsley v Milligan* [1994] 1 AC 340 (HL); *Gray v Thames Trains Ltd* [2009] UKHL 33, [2009] 1 AC 1339; *Hounga v Allen* [2014] UKSC 47, [2014] 1 WLR 2889; *Les Laboratoires Servier v Apotex Inc* [2014] UKSC 55, [2015] AC 430.

[21] In favour of attribution, see eg Lord Phillips [86], but against, contrast Lord Mance [256], [263], [265]–[270].

[22] Law Commission, *The Illegality Defence* (Law Com No 320, 2010) para 3.32.

[23] eg Worthington, 'Back to Basics' (n 1) 120.

[24] eg *Safeway Stores Ltd & Ors v Twigger* [2010] EWCA Civ 1472, [2011] 1 CLC 80; *Bilta (UK) Ltd (in liquidation) v Nazir (No 2)* [2012] EWHC 2163 (Ch) and [2013] EWCA Civ 968.

[25] Named after *Re Hampshire Land Company* [1896] 2 Ch 743 (Ch).

[26] Worthington, 'Back to Basics' (n 1) 124.

> not illuminate. The essential focus is not on the company, but on the corporate insider. Wrongdoing insiders who are sued by, or are suing, their companies cannot escape or limit liability by the ruse of claiming that *their own* acts, intentions, or knowledge, attributed to the company, deliver the result that the company has waived, or shared, or conspired in the insider's liability. Such assertions seem so contrary to common sense that, whatever our attribution rules, they cannot lead to this end.[27]

In short:

> [T]he rule can be stated very simply: no individual can claim against a company, or resist a claim by a company, if that individual's claim or defence can be made out only by attributing to the company the individual's own acts, intentions or knowledge.[28]

D. The Post-*Stone & Rolls* Case Law

However, post-*Stone & Rolls* case law has not adopted this reasoning. In three important cases, the Supreme Court stressed attribution's context-specificity, but with a different emphasis. In *Bilta (UK) Ltd (in liquidation) v Nazir*,[29] *Singularis Holdings Ltd (in official liquidation) v Daiwa Capital Markets Europe Ltd*[30] and *Crown Prosecution Service v Aquila Advisory Ltd*,[31] the Supreme Court concluded that an act or state of mind could be attributed to the company for one purpose but not for another. Even if that misbehaving director, employee or agent's acts or states of mind could be attributed to the company to establish its breach of duty or liability, it did not follow that those acts or states of mind could be attributed for other purposes, such as to defeat the company's claim for illegality. Attribution depended on the context, which might be such that attribution is unavailable.

In *Bilta*, directors used the company, Bilta, to perpetuate VAT frauds, leaving it obliged to account to the tax authorities for millions but with no assets to so account.[32] The fraud was discovered; Bilta went into liquidation. Its liquidators sued Bilta's former directors for breach of fiduciary duty. In response, the directors raised the same argument as in *Stone & Rolls*: their wrongful acts or knowledge should be attributed to Bilta, so Bilta's claim would fail for illegality. All five members of the Supreme Court unanimously agreed that Bilta's claim did not fail for illegality, but they took different routes in reaching this outcome. The majority, comprising Lords Neuberger (with whom Lords Clarke and Carnwath agreed), Mance, and Sumption, based their judgment primarily on attribution. They focused on the purpose of the relevant rule. Illustrative is Lord Mance's speech:

> As Lord Hoffmann made clear in *Meridian Global*, the key to any question of attribution is ultimately always to be found in considerations of context and purpose.

[27] ibid 126.
[28] ibid 127.
[29] *Bilta (UK) Ltd (in liquidation) v Nazir* [2015] UKSC 23, [2015] 2 WLR 1168.
[30] *Singularis Holdings Ltd (in official liquidation) v Daiwa Capital Markets Europe Ltd* [2019] UKSC 50, [2019] 3 WLR 997.
[31] *Crown Prosecution Service v Aquila Advisory Ltd* [2021] UKSC 49, [2021] 1 WLR 5666.
[32] For details of the type of fraud conducted, see *Bilta (UK) Ltd (in liquidation) v Natwest Markets plc* [2020] EWHC 546 (Ch), [1]–[30].

> The question is: whose act or knowledge or state of mind is for the purpose of the relevant rule to count as the act, knowledge or state of mind of the company?[33]

Lord Mance thus concluded that attribution might be available for one purpose, though not another. Where the company was enforcing duties owed by its directors to the company, it was 'self-evidently impossible'[34] for the directors' acts and states of mind to be attributed. As Lord Mance explained, 'Any other conclusion would ignore the separate legal identity of the company, empty the concept of duty of content and enable the company's affairs to be conducted in fraud of creditors.'[35] Broadly similar conclusions were reached by Lord Neuberger and, to a lesser extent, by Lord Sumption.[36] An alternative approach was taken by Lords Toulson and Hodge, who based their decision primarily on illegality, not attribution,[37] but they thought attribution would lead to the same result.[38]

Likewise, attribution was also unavailable in *Singularis*. Singularis's controller, a Saudi Arabian businessman named Al Sanea, instructed Daiwa, a bank and brokerage firm with which Singularis had an account, to make payments to entities controlled by Al Sanea. Daiwa did so; the money was lost. After Singularis went into liquidation, its liquidators sued Daiwa for dishonest assistance and breach of the *Quincecare* duty.[39] The latter obliges banks to refrain from executing orders made by its customer where it has reasonable grounds to believe that the order is an attempt to misappropriate the customer's funds.[40] In response, Daiwa argued that Al Sanea's acts and states of mind should be attributed to Singularis, so that Singularis's claims against Daiwa would fail, whether for illegality or other reasons.

Before the Supreme Court, the key issue was whether Al Sanea's conduct and states of mind were attributable to Singularis in its claims against Daiwa. Lady Hale, delivering the sole judgment of the court, affirmed the context-specific approach in *Bilta*. Thus, 'where the purpose was to attribute responsibility between the company and its agents so as to determine their rights and liabilities to one another, the answer might not be the same as where the purpose was to apportion responsibility between

[33] *Bilta* (n 29) [41].

[34] ibid [42].

[35] ibid [42].

[36] Lord Sumption initially reached his conclusion on the basis that the breach of duty exception applied, since the duty being enforced existed to protect the company from the directors ([86]–[89]) although he later accepted that '[a]nother way of putting the same point is to treat it as illustrating the broader point made by Lord Hoffmann in *Meridian Global* that the attribution of legal responsibility for the act of an agent depends on the purpose for which attribution is relevant' ([92]).

[37] ibid [130]–[131].

[38] ibid [206], [209].

[39] Named after *Barclays Bank plc v Quincecare Ltd* [1992] 4 All ER 363 (QB), see also *Lipkin Gorman v Karpnale Ltd* [1989] 1 WLR 1340 (CA).

[40] For more recent cases on the scope of the Quincecare duty, see *Federal Republic of Nigeria v JP Morgan Chase Bank NA* [2019] EWHC 347 (Comm) (Andrew Burrows QC); *Singularis Holdings Ltd v Daiwa Capital Markets Europe Ltd* [2018] EWCA Civ 84; [2018] 1 WLR 2777 and on appeal (n 30); *RBS International v JP SPC 4* [2022] UKPC 18, [2023] AC 461; *Philipp v Barclays Bank UK plc* [2022] EWCA Civ 318, [2022] 2 WLR 872; *Federal Republic of Nigeria v JP Morgan Chase Bank NA* [2022] EWHC 1447 [145]–[163] (Cockerill J). For criticism of the duty, see P Watts, 'The Quincecare Duty: Misconceived and Misdelivered' [2020] *JBL* 403.

the company and a third party'.[41] In *Singularis* itself, the relevant 'context' of the case was Daiwa's breach of its *Quincecare* duty, the purpose of which was to protect the company against the very kind of misappropriation of its funds that happened in this case.[42] Thus, attribution was not possible: 'To attribute the fraud of that person to the company would be … to "denude the duty of any value in cases where it is most needed".'[43]

Most recently, *Bilta* was reaffirmed in *CPS v Aquila Advisory*,[44] where the directors of a company, VTL, acted in breach of fiduciary duty to make a secret profit. The Supreme Court unanimously refused to attribute the directors' acts and states of mind to VTL for the latter's claim that the profits were held on constructive trust. It affirmed *Bilta*, reiterating that 'the unlawful acts or dishonest state of mind of a director cannot be attributed to the company so as to afford the director an illegality defence to the company's claim against him for breach of fiduciary duty'.[45] The purpose of the relevant rule – the duty owed by the directors to their company – meant that the company could not be identified with its officers.[46] Lord Stephens explained that holding otherwise would establish an exception to *Bilta*'s reasoning, which would undermine 'the clarity and simplicity of the law in relation to attribution'.[47] The 'protective', 'prophylactic way in which the director's fiduciary duties operate' would also be undermined.[48]

This trio of cases focused on the purpose of the cause of action relied on by the company, asking whether to attribute the misbehaving agent or employee's acts to the company under illegality would be inconsistent with that purpose. In all cases it was.

E. Attribution, Inconsistency and Self-contradiction

It is never easy resolving problems at the intersection of multiple issues. Which lever should one pull to solve the puzzle? Both 'Back to Basics' and the Supreme Court chose attribution as the solution.[49] Fundamental to both is the idea that acts and states of mind may be attributed for some purposes but not another; though exactly which purposes fall into which category is still unsettled.

These approaches are easiest to justify if one views attribution as no more than a fictional deeming process, necessitated by the legal fiction of the company itself. The company, an artificial legal person, has been created to achieve various goals, but those goals could not have been achieved unless there were means by which

[41] *Singularis* (n 30) [30].
[42] ibid [35].
[43] ibid [35].
[44] *Aquila* (n 31).
[45] ibid [81] and see also [79].
[46] ibid [71].
[47] ibid [72].
[48] ibid [75]. See also [74].
[49] See the majority in *Bilta* (n 29), and *Aquila* (n 31) [79] and [81].

the company could act, hence necessitating further extensions of that fiction – attribution rules.[50] As I have explained elsewhere, the difficulty with this approach is that it leaves attribution adrift, lacking justification.[51] As Robert Stevens once memorably described in the context of tort law:

> [W]hilst some sort of rules for the attribution of acts are essential, this does not tell us what the detailed content of those rules ought to be. ... What is the correct approach? How many players should a team of footballers contain? Five? Eight? Eleven? Twenty? It is important to know who counts as a member of the team, but there are different ways in which rational rules can be formulated. Whilst some answers may be demonstrably wrong (eg one-a-side, 90-a-side), there may be no single demonstrably right answer.[52]

If only a deeming rule, it would be perfectly possible in principle to attribute the acts of a stranger to the company, to attribute an employee's acts of getting married to the company, or to attribute the knowledge of a director's tooth-brushing habits to the company. Yet, this does not seem to be how judges, lawyers, and ordinary people think about attribution, which is remarkably consistent across jurisdictions.

Resolving the *Stone & Rolls* problem in this way thus generates other problems. Elsewhere, I have suggested that a better account of attribution focuses on the powers allocated and delegated to persons acting for the company.[53] Although companies are legal persons, legal personality in English law does not convey a fixed set of rights, duties and powers.[54] Companies incorporated by registration under general incorporation statutes will derive their powers either directly from statute or expressly or implicitly from the company's constitution. Through its constitution, the company allocates its powers to different groups or persons, typically dividing them between the board of directors and the shareholders in general meeting. Those bodies in turn can then delegate these powers to others. Where those who are allocated or delegated the company's powers exercise them, the company itself acts.

On this account, attribution is not merely fictional, but has a deeper significance. It identifies the intentional acts of the company done by the company as a 'group agent'[55] – an actor in its own right. These acts can truly be said to be those of the company's, as opposed to something being done to it. Consider a simple example involving a human person. The volitional bodily movement of A when he moves his arm, motivated by the aim of grasping an object is, standardly, an intentional act of A: a doing by A. By contrast, where B grasps A's hand and moves it against

[50] Most clearly, see *Meridian* (n 7) 506.

[51] Leow (n 1) ch 2.

[52] R Stevens, *Torts and Rights* (Oxford, Oxford University Press, 2007) 267.

[53] Leow (n 1).

[54] J Armour, 'Companies and Other Associations' in A Burrows (ed), *English Private Law* (Oxford, Oxford University Press, 2013).

[55] 'Agency' is used here in the sense in the philosophy of action, referring to a being with the capacity for action. On group agency generally, see further C List and P Pettit, *Group Agency: The Possibility, Design, and Status of Corporate Agents* (Oxford, Oxford University Press, 2011). See also PA French, *Collective and Corporate Responsibility* (Columbia, Columbia University Press, 1984); R Tuomela, *Social Ontology: Collective Intentionality and Group Agents* (Oxford, Oxford University Press, 2013).

A's protests, this is not an intentional act: there is no doing *by* A, only a doing *to* A by B. In the latter case A can simply say: this is no act of mine. It is not an act authored by A, only an event that occurred to him.

Some of these same ideas are embedded in the law outside attribution. In tort law, A does no act and thus commits no trespass where A is thrown onto land by B or enters the land 'in an effective state of automatism'.[56] Automatism in the criminal law is likewise a denial that the actus reus has been committed where the alleged offender's arm hits another as a result of reflex or muscular spasm[57] or stabs another while sleepwalking.[58] Likewise, in attribution, acts that can be attributed to the company truly belong to it, but acts that cannot be attributed do not.

On this account of attribution, an act either is or is not the company's. The same is true of states of mind. Attribution is binary. It would be inconsistent, even self-contradictory, to say, as the post-*Bilta* case law and 'Back to Basics' do, that an act or state of mind is the company's for one purpose but not another. This is true regardless of how the dividing line is formulated.

The better test, as I have suggested elsewhere, is the 'both ways' test used in contributory negligence.[59] If an act or state of mind is attributable to determine the company's duties or liability for breach, then it should also be attributable in situations in which the company is bringing claims against others. If so, resolving the *Stone & Rolls* problem simply requires applying the general approach to attribution. It poses no special difficulty.

Space precludes extensive discussion of all the problems with orthodox approaches to attribution. A detailed account can be found elsewhere.[60] It suffices to point out an important practical advantage of adopting the 'both ways' test. It avoids the need to identify when and why acts and states of mind are, exceptionally, unattributable. Recall the distinction between 'insiders' and 'outsiders' drawn on in 'Back to Basics'. Even in the 'insiders' cases such as *Bilta* and *Aquila*, in which directors, agents or employees are sued for breach of duty by the company, their acts and states of mind are clearly still attributable to the company for some purposes. For example, in *Bilta*, the objection was that the directors had, in breach of duty, committed Bilta to transactions they knew would make Bilta incur tax liabilities that it would be unable to discharge. At least for purposes of showing that Bilta had (i) suffered loss that was (ii) caused by the breach of duty, it must have been possible to attribute the directors' acts in committing Bilta to those transactions to Bilta. For some purposes their acts clearly are attributable. The difficulty is then to explain why they are not attributable for other purposes, and here little justification is often found beyond appeals to common sense,[61] references to the company's separate legal

[56] *Network Rail Infrastructure Ltd v Conarken Group Ltd* [2010] EWHC 1852 (TCC) [65], and see generally J Goudkamp, *Tort Law Defences* (Oxford, Hart Publishing 2013) 48–49.

[57] *Bratty v AG for Northern Ireland* [1963] AC 386 (HL) 409.

[58] *R v Hughes*, reported in *The Times*, 3 May 1978, p 5. See also *Bratty*, ibid 409, *R v Carter* [1959] VR 105, *Fain v Commonwealth* (1879) 39 Am Rep 213.

[59] After the passing of the Law Reform (Contributory Negligence) Act 1945.

[60] Leow (n 1) ch 7.

[61] Referencing 'absurdity', see *HKSAR v Luk Kin Peter Joseph* [2016] HKCFA 81, (2016) HKCFAR 619 [41] (Lord Hoffmann NPJ); 'self-evidently impossible' in *Bilta* (n 29) [42] (Lord Mance).

personality being ignored,[62] or the duty the company is enforcing being 'emptied of content'[63] or 'denuded'.[64]

F. The 'Both Ways' Test

If the 'both ways' test to attribution is adopted, two questions must be asked. First, are the relevant acts or states of mind attributable to the company to determine the company's breach of duty or liability? If so, under the 'both ways' test, it should also be attributable where the company is bringing an action to enforce its rights. Second, even if those acts and states of mind can be attributed, will the company's claim fail? This turns on the substantive doctrine of private law relied on.

I have advanced a full account of the answer to the first question elsewhere. In this essay, I focus on the second question to show that even if acts and states of mind are attributed to the company, the company's claim will not necessarily fail.

Let us first consider the simpler cases where the company is suing third parties ('outsiders'). In some cases, the effect of the doctrine will be such that the claim does not automatically fail. In contributory negligence, the effect of attributing the wrongdoing individuals' acts to the company is that damages recoverable by the company may be reduced due to the acts of wrongdoing individuals attributed to it,[65] rather than the claim failing altogether. Indeed, it has been argued that it is impossible for contributory negligence to result in the company's claim failing entirely.[66] Likewise, even if acts or states of mind were attributed to the company under illegality after *Patel v Mirza*,[67] the claim may not fail. Whether it does, turns on a range of considerations, including the purpose of the prohibition transgressed, other relevant public policies which might be rendered ineffective or less effective by denying the claim, and proportionality.[68] Even if Al Sanea's acts and states of mind were attributed to Singularis, the latter's claim against Daiwa would not have failed: it would be contrary to the purpose of the duty being enforced by Singularis.

Other requirements of the doctrine may also not be met. For example, even if the wrongdoing individual's knowledge of the wrongful act being done was attributed to the company, this would not necessarily mean that the company consented

[62] *Bilta* (n 29) [42] (Lord Mance).
[63] *Bilta* (n 29) [42] (Lord Mance).
[64] *Singularis* (n 30) [35] (Lady Hale).
[65] *Daniels v Anderson* (1995) 15 ACSR 607, [1995] PNLR 727 (NSWCA); *Barings plc v Coopers & Lybrand (No 7)* [2003] EWHC 1319 (Ch), [2003] ONLR 34, [961]–[964] (decided under the Singaporean Contributory Negligence and Personal Injuries Act (Cap 54, 2002 rev edn), which was materially identical to the 1945 Act). See also *Duke Group v Pilmer* [1998] SASC 6529 where contributory negligence failed because those individuals' conduct could not be attributed to the company.
[66] J Goudkamp, 'Rethinking Contributory Negligence' in SA Pitel, JW Neyers and E Chamberlain (eds), *Tort Law: Challenging Orthodoxy* (Oxford, Hart Publishing, 2013) 344–45.
[67] *Patel v Mirza* [2016] UKSC 42, [2017] AC 467.
[68] ibid [120] (Lord Toulson). Reaffirmed in *Stoffel & Co v Grondona* [2020] UKSC 42, [2021] AC 540; *Henderson v Dorset Healthcare University NHS Foundation Trust* [2020] UKSC 43, [2021] AC 563.

to or waived the breach. Knowledge alone does not amount to consent or waiver. Something more is required.

Similar points can be made where the company's claims are against 'insiders'. Even if the wrongdoing directors' acts or states of mind are attributed to the company, the company's claims will not *necessarily* fail for consent, conspiracy and so on.

First, some private law doctrines may not apply where the company is suing its directors or other agents for breach of duty. For instance, some English cases doubt that a company director can conspire with the company.[69] If so, then conspiracy is simply not relevant at all for these kinds of claims. Contributory negligence too may not always apply. It is probably simply unavailable where the directors' acts are intentional.[70] For example, it is not available as a defence to claims in deceit,[71] intentional torts to the person[72] and intentional trespass to goods,[73] although it ought to be available if the directors' acts were merely negligent.

Even if the doctrine does apply, its requirements may not be met. For instance, even if conspiracy is possible between company and director, something more is required beyond the company being attributed with the director's acts and states of mind. Some combination or agreement between the two seems necessary, as does an intention to injure.[74] Likewise, attributing a director's knowledge to the company does not itself establish consent.[75] The same point is also true for waiver.

Even if the problems above are not present, attribution may be much less key to the private law doctrine than assumed. Even if contributory negligence is available, whether the directors' acts are attributed to the company for contributory negligence is essentially irrelevant, because the key question for contributory negligence is not who did what or with what state of mind, but rather the relative blameworthiness between the two. Similarly, the availability of contribution[76] or indemnities as between company and 'insider' turns on their relative responsibility for the liability incurred to the third party, involving considerations of both blameworthiness and causative potency.[77] If, as between the individual and the company, the fault lay solely with the individual, then the company can obtain a full indemnity.[78] If, as between the two, the fault did not lie solely with the individual, then liability

[69] The position may be different in other jurisdictions, see eg in Singapore, *Lim Leong Huat v Chip Hup Hup Kee Construction Pte Ltd* [2009] SGHC 2, [2009] 2 SLR(R) 318; *Nagase Singapore Pte Ltd v Ching Kai Huat* [2007] SGHC 169, [2008] 1 SLR(R) 80; *PT Sandipala Arthaputra v ST Micorelectronics Asia Pacific Pte Ltd* [2018] SGCA 17, [2018] 1 SLR 818 (conspiracy by unlawful means). See also C Witting, 'Intra-corporate Conspiracy: An Intriguing Prospect' (2013) 72 *CLJ* 178.

[70] See also PS Davies, *Accessory Liability* (Oxford, Hart Publishing, 2015) 264. See eg *Nationwide Building Society v Balmer Redmore* [1999] PNLR 606 (Ch) 672–77 (Blackburn J).

[71] *Standard Chartered Bank v Pakistan National Shipping* [2002] UKHL 43, [2003] 1 AC 959.

[72] *Co-operative Group (CWS) Ltd v Pritchard* [2011] EWCA Civ 329.

[73] Torts (Interference with Goods) Act 1977, s 11(1).

[74] In both lawful means conspiracy and unlawful means conspiracy, combination or agreement between two or more individuals is necessary. See generally *Total Network SL v HMRC* [2008] UKHL 19, [2008] 2 All ER 413.

[75] *Multinational Gas and Petrochemical Co v Multinational Gas and Petrochemical Services* [1983] Ch 258 (CA).

[76] Under the Civil Liability (Contribution) Act 1978, s 2(1).

[77] *Madden v Quirk* [1989] 1 WLR 702 (QB), 707.

[78] As in *Lister v Romford Ice & Cold Storage Co* [1957] AC 555 (HL).

might be apportioned differently.[79] Finally, as contributory negligence shows, even if acts can be attributed, they may not lead to the company's claim failing in its entirety.

This account suggests that the *Stone & Rolls* problem is not always solely a problem about attribution. Not all these questions as to whether the company's claim will fail or be reduced can be answered solely by focusing on attribution of the 'insider's' acts and states of mind to the company. Doing so pushes all the problems into the law of attribution when some of them rightly belong elsewhere. Whether attribution is in fact available and the specific doctrine of private law in question both require careful consideration. It is not possible here to give a definitive account of all possibilities, but a longer discussion can be found elsewhere.[80]

III. ACTUAL AUTHORITY

This section then turns to another question: when do we attribute acts? One facet of this question appears as an agency law issue: can an agent have actual authority to act contrary to their principal's interests? The orthodox view today is that an agent cannot: their actual authority only exists to the extent that the agent is acting honestly and in the best interests of the principal. If the agent is acting otherwise, third parties must rely on the agent's apparent authority to establish that the act is binding on the principal. 'Back to Basics' argues against orthodoxy. This section concludes that the orthodoxy should prevail, as the Supreme Court has now accepted,[81] but for different reasons than those commonly given.

A. Orthodoxy

Perhaps surprisingly, today's orthodoxy is relatively modern. The leading case is *Hopkins v TL Dallas Group*, where Lightman J explained that:

> The grant of actual authority to an agent will not normally include authority to act for the agent's benefit rather than that of his principal and therefore, without agreement, the scope of actual authority will not include this. The grant of actual authority should be implied as being subject to a condition that it is to be exercised honestly and on behalf of the principal: *Lysaght Bros & Co Ltd v Falk* (1905) 2 CLR 421.[82]

In reaching this conclusion, Lightman J followed the 17th edition of *Bowstead & Reynolds*, which emphasised that:

> [T]he agent is simply not authorised to act contrary to his principal's interests: and hence that an act contrary to those interests is outside his actual authority. The transaction is therefore void unless the third party can rely on the doctrine of apparent authority.[83]

[79] eg *Jones v Manchester Corporation* [1952] 2 QB 852 (CA).
[80] Leow (n 1) ch 7.
[81] *Philipp v Barclays Bank UK plc* [2023] UKSC 25 [72]–[74].
[82] *Hopkins v TL Dallas Group* [2004] EWHC 1379 (Ch).
[83] ibid [88] (Lightman J).

Article 23 of the 17th edition provides that: 'Unless otherwise agreed, authority to act as agent includes only authority to act for the benefit of the principal.'[84] Editions after this have likewise maintained that no agent can have actual authority to act contrary to the principal's interests unless such authority is expressly conferred.[85] There is now a considerable body of case law following *Hopkins*.[86]

It is therefore striking to note that the views in the 17th edition of *Bowstead & Reynolds* represented a departure from previous editions. Earlier editions instead provided that:

> [A]n act of an agent within the scope of his actual or apparent authority does not cease to bind his principal merely because the agent was acting fraudulently and in furtherance of his own interests.[87]

This difference in views mirrors a similar equivocation in the case law before 2001. Important cases indicated that an agent could have actual authority even if he was acting other than for the principal's interests, with two examples being *Hambro v Burnand*[88] and *Macmillan Inc v Bishopsgate Investment Trust plc (No 3)*.[89] In *Hambro*, Collins MR dealt explicitly with the issue, holding that:

> It has been contended for the appellants that, although express authority was given in writing, as in the present case, authorizing an agent to make such a contract as he has made, it is open to the principal to say that, nevertheless, if it appears, on inquiring into the motives which existed in the agent's mind, that he intended, in making the contract, to misuse for his own ends the opportunity given to him by his authority, and apply it to a purpose, which, if the principal had known of it, he would not have sanctioned, then, because the agent was so influenced by improper motives, the principal is not liable upon the contract made by him. I should have said myself, apart from authority on the subject, that such a proposition could not hold water.[90]

Likewise, in *Macmillan*, Millett J (as he was then) followed the 15th edition of *Bowstead & Reynolds*, holding that:

> I am satisfied that under Delaware law as under English law: 'an act of an agent within the scope of his actual or apparent authority does not cease to bind his principal merely

[84] FMB Reynolds, *Bowstead & Reynolds on Agency*, 17th edn (London, Sweet & Maxwell, 2001) para 3-008.

[85] FMB Reynolds, *Bowstead & Reynolds on Agency*, 18th edn (London, Sweet & Maxwell, 2006) para 3-008; P Watts and FMB Reynolds, *Bowstead & Reynolds on Agency*, 19th edn (London, Sweet & Maxwell, 2010) para 3-007; P Watts and FMB Reynolds, *Bowstead & Reynolds on Agency*, 20th edn (London, Sweet & Maxwell, 2014) para 3-008; P Watts and FMB Reynolds, *Bowstead & Reynolds on Agency*, 21st edn (London, Sweet & Maxwell, 2017) paras 3-010 and 3-011; P Watts and FMB Reynolds, *Bowstead & Reynolds on Agency*, 22nd edn (London, Sweet & Maxwell, 2022) paras 3-011 and 3-012.

[86] *Lexi Holdings (in administration) v Pannone & Partners* [2009] EWHC 2590 (Ch) [75]; *Credit Agricole Corporate and Investment Bank v Ahmad* [2010] EWHC 3968 (QB) [33], [35]; *Re Capitol Films Ltd (in administration)* [2010] EWHC 2240 (Ch) [54]; *GHLM Trading Ltd v Maroo* [2012] EWHC 61 (Ch) [171]; *Relfo Ltd (in liquidation) v Varsani* [2012] EWHC 2168 (Ch) [86]; *Newcastle International Airport Ltd v Eversheds LLP* [2012] EWHC 2648 (Ch) [91].

[87] Art 74, 16th edn. Citing the equivalent article in the 15th edn, see *Macmillan Inc v Bishopsgate Investment Trust plc (No 3)* [1995] 1 WLR 978 (Ch).

[88] *Hambro v Burnand* [1904] 2 KB 10 (CA).

[89] *Macmillan Inc v Bishopsgate Investment Trust plc (No 3)* [1995] 1 WLR 978 (Ch).

[90] *Hambro* (n 88) 19–20.

> because the agent was acting fraudulently and in furtherance of his own interests:' see *Bowstead on Agency*, 15th ed (1985), p 279, art 74.[91]

Of course, authorities to the contrary existed. One line of cases is typified by *Midland Bank v Reckitt*,[92] best known today for establishing that powers of attorney are to be strictly construed. A solicitor was authorised by power of attorney to draw cheques on his client's bank account 'without restriction'.[93] The solicitor had repeatedly fraudulently drawn cheques on the account to pay the debts of his own firm to the same bank. In the House of Lords, Lord Atkin stressed that 'Lord Terrington had no actual authority to draw these cheques at all or to receive the proceeds. His only actual authority was to draw cheques for the principal's purposes.'[94] The agent's actual authority was limited to acting for the principal's purposes, even if the words conferring the authority are wide enough to encompass the acts which the agent did.

B. The Argument in 'Back to Basics'

'Back to Basics' argued against the modern orthodoxy. Its central claim is that there is, and should be, a distinction between actual authority's existence and its abuse.[95] Its existence appears to turn on the interpretation of the words conferring that authority. If the class of acts done by the agent falls within the words of the authority, the agent has actual authority, even if there is some other flaw with the agent's acts (eg if the agent is seeking to defraud the principal, acting in breach of fiduciary duty, or negligently). That flaw amounts at best to an abuse of authority.

Worthington raises five arguments for this conclusion. She argues that orthodoxy 'muddles two quite different contexts': that between principal and agent and those between principal and third party (or outsiders).[96] It also relies on apparent authority in a way that 'does not make sense'.[97] If the agent has no actual authority to act other than in the principal's interests, then the principal can only be bound to the transaction if the agent's apparent authority to enter it can be proven. However, it is argued, it is impossible to establish the agent's apparent authority as no one has actual authority to make the necessary representation that the agent has authority to act contrary to the principal's interests.[98] Third, the analysis cannot explain equitable cases where the agent enters self-dealing transactions,[99] makes contracts

[91] *Macmillan* (n 89) 984.
[92] *Midland Bank v Reckitt* [1933] AC 1 (HL).
[93] ibid 10.
[94] ibid 14.
[95] Worthington, 'Back to Basics' (n 1) 134–35.
[96] ibid 135.
[97] ibid 136.
[98] ibid.
[99] Citing *Hely-Hutchinson v Brayhead Ltd* [1968] 1 QB 549 (CA) 589–91; *Guinness plc v Saunders* [1990] 2 AC 663 (HL) 692–93.

for improper purposes[100] or cases where the agent is bribed.[101,102] In these cases, the transaction is only voidable, although the orthodoxy on actual authority suggests that it should be void. Fourth, the test is difficult to apply.[103] When is a transaction not in the interests of the company? Does this turn only on what the agent believes, or does it turn on what a reasonable person in the position of the agent would believe? Fifth, it is doubted that the orthodox approach is more protective of the principal, since it leads to the conclusion that the relevant transactions are void, which delivers poorer remedies (by way of constructive trusts) compared to transactions that are only voidable.[104] Worthington argues that treating flaws in the agent's acts as only abuses, not absences, of the agent's authority would avoid these difficulties.

C. Against 'Back to Basics'

'Back to Basics' provoked a swift response by Professor Watts in the *Journal of Business Law*,[105] which defended the modern orthodoxy and clarified the relevant provision in *Bowstead & Reynolds*. Article 23 previously stated that: 'Unless otherwise agreed, authority to act as agent includes only authority to act for the benefit of the principal.' This formulation was refined to read as follows: 'authority to act as agent includes only authority to act *for the purpose* of benefiting the principal'. As Watts explained, once refined, the second and fourth of Worthington's arguments fall away.[106] Three arguments remain. Watts rejects all, for reasons I think are sound.

First, I agree with Watts that the modern orthodoxy does not muddle the principal–agent context from the principal–third-party context.[107] The existence of actual authority is purely an internal matter between principal and agent, but its exercise has external effects.[108] This just is a feature of how actual authority

[100] Citing *Hogg v Cramphorn* [1967] Ch 254 (Ch); *Bamford v Bamford* [1970] Ch 212 (Ch); *Richard Brady Franks v Price* (1937) 58 CLR 112 (HCA); *Harlowe's Nominees Pty Ltd v Woodside (Lakes Entrance) Oil Company NL* (1968) 121 CLR 483 (HCA) 500 (Barwick CJ, McTiernan J and Kitto J); *Winthrop Investments Ltd v Winns Ltd* [1975] 2 NSWLR 666 (NSWCA) 697; *Whitehouse v Carlton Hotel Pty Ltd* (1987) 162 CLR 285 (HCA).

[101] Citing eg *Parker v McKenna* (1874–75) LR 10 Ch App 96 (CA) 118 (Lord Cairns LC), 124–25 (James LJ); *Panama and South Pacific Telegraph Co v India Rubber, Gutta Percha, and Telegraph Works Co* (1874–75) LR 10 Ch App 515 (CA), 528–29; *Armagas Ltd v Mundogas SA (The Ocean Frost)* [1986] AC 717 (HL), 742–45 (Goff LJ); *Shipway v Broadwood* [1899] 1 QB 369 (CA); *Logicrose Ltd v Southend United Football Club Ltd (No 2)* [1988] 1 WLR 1256 (Ch) 1260–62 (Millett J); *Hurstanger Ltd v Wilson* [2007] EWCA Civ 299, [2007] 1 WLR 2351 (CA) [39]; *Tigris International NV v China Southern Airlines Co Ltd* [2014] EWCA Civ 1649 [143].

[102] Worthington, 'Back to Basics' (n 1) 136–37.

[103] ibid 137.

[104] ibid.

[105] P Watts, 'Actual Authority: The Requirement for an Agent Honestly to Believe that an Exercise of Power is in the Principal's interests' [2017] *JBL* 269.

[106] ibid 273–74.

[107] ibid 271–73.

[108] ibid 272.

works. By contrast, it is apparent authority which concerns the external agency relationship between principal and third party.[109] Apparent authority today is widely understood as a species of estoppel by representation, established where the principal represents to third parties that the agent has authority.[110] Where the third party relies on the representation, the principal is estopped from denying the truth of his statement. As Watts points out, it is 'Back to Basics' that blurs the two.[111]

Furthermore, there is no dichotomy between inefficacy and breach of duty: a flaw can make a purported act both ineffective and a breach of duty.[112] Trustees exercising dispositive powers may fail to successfully exercise those powers where they act for improper purposes, but their attempt to do so may simultaneously amount to a breach of trust.[113] Fiduciaries entering self-dealing transactions for their principals with themselves may fail to successfully do so,[114] but whether they do or not, they are in breach of duty.

Second, on the authorities concerning equitable flaws being inconsistent with the orthodoxy, it has already been noted that the case law before *Hopkins* was hardly unanimous, even at common law. The support of the equitable cases is also doubtful since many of them are arguably consistent with orthodoxy. Arguably, in many, the agent was acting for the principal's interests, although an equitable flaw was also present. It is trite that an agent can contravene the no-conflict rule innocently and without fault.[115] An agent might honestly believe that he is acting in the principal's interests although he is acting in conflict of interest or contrary to the no-profit rule.[116] The same is true of the requirement to act for proper purposes. *Howard Smith v Ampol Petroleum* illustrates.[117] Company directors, honestly believing that they were acting in the company's interests, acted for improper purposes where they issued shares to a third party to dilute the existing shareholdings of potential takeover. The outcome – that the transaction was validly executed but could be set aside – is still consistent with orthodoxy. The agent has actual authority, though he is in breach of duty.

Third, it was suggested that the orthodox approach may not be as protective of principals as commonly suggested because of remedial differences between void and voidable transactions. This does not quite meet the mark either. Leaving aside those remedial differences, the orthodox approach is still more protective of principals. It only reaches the same outcome as the abuse-of-authority approach where the third

[109] ibid 272, citing the well-known case of *Freeman & Lockyer v Buckhurst Park Properties (Mangal) Ltd* [1964] 2 QB 480 (CA).

[110] *Freeman & Lockyer*, ibid 503–04.

[111] Watts (n 105) 272.

[112] ibid 272.

[113] eg *Re Pauling's Settlement Trusts* [1964] Ch 303 (CA).

[114] For what Conaglen refers to as the 'two party rule', which requires that any contract or conveyance involves more than one party: M Conaglen, *Fiduciary Loyalty* (Oxford, Hart Publishing, 2010) 78–79. See eg *Ingram v Inland Revenue Commissioners* [2001] 1 AC 293 (HL) 305 and 310.

[115] Famously *Keech v Sandford* (1726) Sel Cas T King 61, 25 ER 223 (Ch); *Boardman v Phipps* [1967] 2 AC 46 (HL).

[116] For well-known examples, see *Keech v Sandford* (n 115) (trustees); *Regal (Hastings) Ltd v Gulliver* [1967] 2 AC 134 (HL); *Boardman v Phipps* (n 115).

[117] *Howard Smith v Ampol Petroleum* [1974] AC 821 (PC).

party to the transaction at least knows of the flaw in the transaction.[118] Consider this problem, concerning a fraudulent agent:

> A, an agent, has actual authority to contract on behalf of their principal P. A dishonestly enters a contract highly disadvantageous to P with a third party, TP. TP knows that A is acting dishonestly.

Orthodoxy presents a simple answer to this problem. A has no actual authority, since he does not intend to act in the interests of P. Nor does A have apparent authority, since TP's knowledge of A's dishonesty means she knows that A has no actual authority, thereby negating any possible reasonable reliance by TP on representations as to A's authority.

By contrast, Worthington's approach seems to generate the wrong answer, one less protective of principals. A has no apparent authority but has actual authority since A does an act that falls within the scope of his authority. A's dishonesty only amounts to an abuse of his authority. Thus, P is bound by the contract unless he sets it aside. This conclusion is less protective of principals than the orthodoxy. It is, I suggest, also intuitively unappealing.

Since this chapter was first written, the orthodoxy has been resoundingly reaffirmed by the Supreme Court. In *Philipp v Barclays Bank UK plc*, Lord Leggatt said:

> 'The principle is now clearly, and in my opinion correctly, stated in Bowstead & Reynolds on Agency, 22nd ed (2021) at article 23 as follows:
>
> > "Authority to act as agent includes only authority to act honestly in pursuit of the interests of the principal."'[119]

D. Justifications

I agree with Watts that the orthodoxy should prevail but am less sure about the justification he offers.

For Watts, the agent cannot have actual authority to act otherwise than for the purposes of benefitting the principal because of actual authority's justification: consent. Watts explains:

> Principle holds that actual authority turns on a principal's willingness to be bound to what the agent does on the principal's behalf. … No principal can be taken to have consented (or assented) to an agent deliberately acting against the principal's interests, or even acting recklessly as to the principal's interests. … *To treat only the express terms of the power, or the type of power and not what the power is being used for, as all that matters, is to detach actual authority from its roots in consent. Actual authority becomes a construct and the resulting liability imposed rather than willed.*[120]

[118] See similarly ibid 274. For further evidence, see *Logicrose Ltd v Southend United Football Club Ltd* [1988] 1 WLR 1256 (Ch) 1261 (Millett J).

[119] *Philipp* (n 81) [72].

[120] Watts (n 105) 267–70 (emphasis added).

Hints of this explanation had appeared earlier in *Hopkins*, where Lightman J cited the 17th edition of *Bowstead and Reynolds*, explaining that the authority of an agent is

> actual (express or implied) where it results from a manifestation of consent that he should represent or act for the principal expressly or impliedly made by the principal to the agent himself.[121]

If actual authority's consensual nature is stressed, then it is a relatively small step to conclude that an agent cannot have actual authority to act other than in the principal's interests because the principal would not have consented to him so acting. This analysis sees actual authority's scope as subject to a carve-out where the agent is not acting in the principal's interests.

This type of consent-based justification appears to have been substantially endorsed by the Supreme Court in *Philipp*, where Lord Leggatt accepted that:

> In principle, the scope of an agent's authority is a matter of agreement between the agent and the principal. Where that agreement is recorded in writing, the question is one of interpretation of the document. *No doubt it would be possible in theory for a principal in appointing an agent to agree that the agent may bind the principal even if and when the agent is acting dishonestly with the aim of defrauding the principal. But it seems inconceivable that any sane person would ever agree, or could reasonably be presumed to have agreed, to confer such authority on an agent.* As is generally the case in commerce, parties to an agency relationship naturally deal with each other on an unspoken common assumption that each will act honestly in relation to the other. It goes without saying that authority conferred on an agent does not encompass acting dishonestly to further the agent's own interests in opposition to the interests of the principal.[122]

This type of consensual analysis is persuasive, especially given consent's prevalence in modern agency thinking. It is commonplace for agency lawyers to define agency by reference to the mutual consent of principal and agent.[123] However, not all agency relationships are consensual in this way. Perhaps best known is the example of agency of necessity, used in its strict sense to refer to cases where the agent has 'authority to create contractual rights and obligations between [its principal] and a third party that are directly enforceable by each against the other'.[124] The clearest example of agency of necessity is that which a master of a ship has to act on behalf of the cargo-owners in respect of the cargo, for example to sell it where the ship is damaged and the goods are at risk of deterioration.[125] As there is no prior agency relationship between the shipmaster and the cargo-owners, it is difficult to explain the master's authority as an extension of his pre-existing, consensually granted authority.[126]

[121] *Hopkins* (n 82) [87].
[122] *Philipp* (n 81) [73].
[123] See eg *Bowstead & Reynolds*, 22nd edn (n 85) para 1-001.
[124] *China Pacific SA v Food Corp of India (The Winson)* [1982] AC 939 (HL) 958 (Lord Diplock).
[125] See also *The Winson*, ibid (authority of master to enter salvage agreement on behalf of cargo-owners).
[126] Unlike the shipmaster's authority to sell with or deal with the ship on behalf of the shipowners.

Just as in actual authority, an agent of necessity will only have authority to act for the principal where the agent is acting bona fide in the interests of the principal.[127] However, the consent-based explanation cannot explain the existence of this parallel rule in cases where the authority is non-consensual. If consent is no longer the justification for the authority, then consent's absence likewise cannot justify the absence of that authority.

Although a more marginal case, the same objection might be made about agency created by statute. For instance, the Mental Capacity Act 2005 confers authority to do acts for the benefit of another person lacking or believed to be lacking capacity in certain circumstances. The person so authorised must reasonably believe that the acts will be in the interests of the incapacitated person.[128] Again, as this authority is clearly not consensual, this limitation cannot be explained by the absence of consent for acts done other than in the interests of the principal.

A consent-based justification comes very close to the mark, but not quite. If not consent, how then can orthodoxy be justified? In a different context, Lionel Smith explained that 'it is part of the logic of acting for another person that there is only one right way to do it: you must do it in the way that you think is best for that other person'.[129] Happily, this is also true of the agency relationship. It is part of the logic of acting as agent for another person that one must do it in the principal's interests. Here Watts is entirely right in observing that:

> This idea does in practice rest on an implication, since it is not in the nature of human relations for one proposing to employ the services of another to spell out that the purpose of the conferral of powers is that they should be exercised for the benefit of the former. But that purpose goes without saying.[130]

Orthodoxy, I suggest, appears best conceptualised as part of a 'proper purposes' requirement. One must act for another for proper purposes. In this context, for an agent to act for a proper purpose is to act bona fide in what he honestly believes to be the interests of the principal.

IV. APPARENT AUTHORITY: *FIRST ENERGY*

This final section turns to another agency law question, here concerning the familiar chestnut of *First Energy*, a favourite of examiners of undergraduate commercial law courses.[131] 'Back to Basics' presented a novel argument here too. It suggested that the problem was not with the Court of Appeal's conclusion that the senior manager

[127] *Prager v Blatspiel, Stamp & Heacock Ltd* [1924] 1 KB 566 (KB) 570; *Tronson v Dent* (1853) 8 Moo PC 419 (PC) 442–52; 14 ER 159, 168–172; *Re F (Mental Patient: Sterilisation)* [1990] 2 AC 1 (HL) 75.

[128] See eg Mental Capacity Act 2005, s 5 (acts in connection with care and treatment) and s 8 (authorising the agent to pledge the incapacitated person's credit and apply money in that person's possession for meeting the expenditure).

[129] L Smith, 'Fiduciary Relationships: Ensuring the Loyal Exercise of Judgement on Behalf of Another' (2014) 130 *LQR* 608, 613.

[130] Watts (n 105) 270.

[131] *First Energy* (n 5).

had apparent authority, but with the remedial consequences of this conclusion. It is argued here that, though intriguing, this argument does not work. Apparent authority operates as a form of estoppel by representation – a common law estoppel which operates as a rule of evidence. Thus, it has an 'all or nothing' character, delivering only a fixed remedy.

A. The *First Energy* Problem

First Energy needed credit facilities. It entered negotiations with the defendant bank for a long-term facility. Pending approval of that facility, the parties entered into an ad hoc financing agreement. The senior manager of the bank's Manchester branch, Mr Jamison, wrote and signed a letter which was interpreted as an offer of a loan, and hence as indicating approval of the transaction internally. In fact, the transaction had not been approved. The bank later argued that it was not bound. First Energy knew that the manager did not have actual or apparent authority to approve the facility agreement.[132] Could he nonetheless have apparent authority to communicate that approval had been received, so that the bank was bound to the facility agreement? Despite the somewhat unfavourable state of the authorities, most of which suggested the argument would fail,[133] the Court of Appeal held otherwise. The bank was bound.

Steyn LJ started his decision with the sentence: 'A theme that runs through our law of contract is that the reasonable expectations of honest men must be protected.'[134] If so, it is not so difficult to see why First Energy succeeded. It had honestly and reasonably relied on the appearance of Mr Jamison's authority to communicate that approval had been received, even though it had not.

This raises a familiar difficulty. There are two main approaches to apparent authority.[135] On one, the principal is bound because of something they have done which enables the agent to appear authorised. The other focuses on the third party's good faith and reasonable belief in the agent's authority. Although many systems hint at the latter, nearly all effectively use the former.[136] As Professor Francis Reynolds points out, it does not seem practical to use the latter, and one typically expects at least something basic that links the principal with what has happened.[137]

Some English cases clearly take the former approach, robustly insisting on a strong link connecting the principal with the agent's acts.[138] Thus, agents cannot 'self-authorise' because to do so would allow a principal to be bound without

[132] ibid 535.

[133] eg *Egyptian International Foreign Trade Co v Soplex Wholesale Supplies Ltd & anor (The Raffaella)* [1985] 2 Lloyd's Rep 36 (CA) 43 (Browne-Wilkinson LJ); *Armagas Ltd v Mundogas SA* [1986] AC 717 (CA) 730–33 (Goff LJ).

[134] *First Energy* (n 5) 533. See also 534, and later, Lord Steyn, 'Contract Law: Fulfilling the Reasonable Expectations of Honest Men' (1997) 113 *LQR* 433.

[135] F Reynolds, 'Apparent Authority' (2009) 17 *European Review of Private Law* 975, 976–77.

[136] ibid 976–77.

[137] ibid 976.

[138] eg *British Bank of the Middle East v Sun Life Assurance* [1983] 2 Lloyd's Rep 9 (HL).

any link between the principal and those acts done by the agent pursuant to the 'self-authorisation'.[139] On the other hand, *First Energy* points more towards the latter approach.

There is no real trouble with the doctrinal analysis that just as an agent can have apparent authority to enter contracts or transfer title to goods, they can also have apparent authority to represent that approval of a transaction had been received.[140] A classic example of such a person is the company secretary.[141] The difficulty is that very slender facts seem to generate the polar opposite outcome from the normal case of a self-authorising agent – in one case, the agent says 'I approved the deal', and the principal is not bound; and in the other, the agent says 'I got approval for the deal', and the principal is bound.

B. The Argument in 'Back to Basics'

'Back to Basics' advances a novel argument. As Worthington explains:

> The context is typically that a junior employee has incorrectly told a third party that there is a contract between the company and the third party, or that a deal has been done. Legal analysis must then answer the 'So what?' question. The slippage is typically to move too quickly from 'the corporate agent said there is a contract' to 'so there should be one'. This is not necessarily the right answer.[142]

She continues to say that, if apparent authority's requirements are met,

> then the court must consider the appropriate remedy; it must assess the losses suffered as a result of reasonable reliance on the representation made. … What should follow from reliance on that representation? Of course, knowing the precise facts in the case is essential to answering this question properly, but the reliance losses incurred when a bank incorrectly informs a customer that a financing deal has been agreed can often, it seems, be remedied by more limited awards than delivery of the exact deal inaccurately indicated to third parties.[143]

The problem with *First Energy* is thus not seen as the conclusion that there was apparent authority, but with the remedies that followed. The most appropriate remedy may be something other than holding the principal to the truth of whatever the agent had said. This solution has since been approved of in *Stavrinides v Bank of Cyprus Public Company Ltd*,[144] where John Kimbell QC (sitting as a Deputy Judge of the High Court) said that:

> It is important to distinguish between representations of transactional authority and conduit authority because the remedy may be very different (assuming reliance can be

[139] *AG for Ceylon v Silva* [1953] AC 461 (PC) 479; *Armagas* (n133) 749 (Goff LJ); *East Asia Company Ltd v PT Satria Tirtatama Energindo (Bermuda)* [2019] UKPC 30, [2020] 2 All ER 294 [61].

[140] See now *Lovett v Carson Country Homes Ltd* [2009] EWHC 1143 (Ch), [2011] BCC 789 [94]; *Kelly v Fraser* [2012] UKPC 25, [2013] 1 AC 450, [12]–[15]; *East Asia* (n 139) [61].

[141] *Lovett*, ibid [13].

[142] Worthington, 'Back to Basics' (n 1) 139.

[143] ibid 142.

[144] *Stavrinides v Bank of Cyprus Public Company Ltd* [2019] EWHC 1328 (Ch).

proved). A person who relies on a representation of a transactional authority will *prima facie* be able to enforce the contract against the principal or claim expectation losses for breach. A person who relies on a representation of conduit authority will generally be limited to claiming reliance losses only. As Prof Worthington points out in her article *Corporate Attribution and Agency: Back to Basics*, (2017) LQR 118 at 140, the 'authorised' conveyance of information that an offer has been accepted is not the same as the "authorised" conveyance of a binding offer. I agree.[145]

C. Refuting the Argument

Worthington's argument appears to rest on apparent authority's nature as a flexible estoppel. But estoppels are varied. Some estoppels, such as proprietary estoppel, permit significant remedial flexibility. Once proprietary estoppel is made out, the court must then award the minimum remedy necessary to satisfy the equity. This may be to award the representee what was represented,[146] or it may be something else.[147]

If apparent authority is an estoppel at all, it is not of this type.[148] It is an estoppel by representation.[149] Unlike proprietary estoppel, which seems to operate as a cause of action generating new rights,[150] an estoppel by representation is a rule of evidence.[151] Where one person makes a representation to another, intending the other to rely on it, and the representee reasonably relies on it to his detriment, the representor will be estopped from adducing evidence contrary to the representation he has made. He is thus barred from denying the truth of the statement against the representee.[152] Estoppel by representation thus operates in an 'all or nothing' way. Where A pays B £500 by mistake and represents to B that the money is his to do what he wishes with it, B has a defence to a claim to restitution of the full sum even if he has only spent £50 of it in reliance on the representation.[153]

If apparent authority is an estoppel by representation, as most accept that it is, then it is difficult to see how the most appropriate remedy in *First Energy*-type cases can be anything other than holding the principal to the truth of what the agent has said. Estoppel by representation generates no remedial flexibility. As a rule of

[145] ibid [100] (emphasis removed).

[146] eg *Thorner v Major* [2009] UKHL 1, [2009] 1 WLR 776.

[147] See eg *Jennings v Rice* [2002] EWCA Civ 159, 1 P & CR 100 [50].

[148] For discussion of the difficulties with an estoppel analysis, see *Bowstead & Reynolds*, 22nd edn (n 85) para 8-027.

[149] *Freeman* (n 109) 503 (Diplock LJ); *Akai Holdings Ltd v Thanakharn Kasikorn Thai Chamkat (Mahachon)* [2010] HKCFA 64, [2011] 1 HKC 357 [52] (Lord Neuberger NPJ); *East Asia* (n 139) [41]–[43], [84].

[150] On the difference between the two, see eg *Shortland v Hill* [2018] 1 P & CR 16 (Bristol County Court) [84] (HHJ Paul Matthews).

[151] *Low v Bouverie* [1891] 3 Ch 82 (CA) 105 (Bowen LJ); *London Joint Stock Bank Ltd v Macmillan* [1918] AC 777 (HL) 817–18 (Viscount Haldane); *Evans v Bartlam* [1937] AC 473 (HL) 484 (Lord Wright). Contrast attempts to identify a unified notion of estoppel as a substantive doctrine based on unconscionability, eg *Moorgate Mercantile Co Ltd v Twitchings* [1976] QB 225 (CA) 241–42 (Lord Denning MR).

[152] Compare *Eastern Distributors Ltd v Goldring* [1957] 2 QB 600 (CA) 611 (Devlin J), where for purposes of s 21(1) of the Sale of Goods Act 1979, apparent authority bound third parties other than the representee.

[153] *Avon CC v Howlett* [1983] 1 WLR 606 (CA) 620–25 (Slade LJ).

evidence, it bars the representor from adducing evidence contrary to the truth of his statement, whatever the content of that statement. If the statement is 'I approved the deal', then the agent's apparent authority to make the statement entitles the third party to hold the principal to the truth of the statement. The same is true if the statement is 'My superiors authorised the deal'; the principal is likewise bound to the truth of the statement. This is a feature, not a bug.

There is a different possibility which may lead to 'reliance losses' being remedied, but this option is in addition to rather than in substitution for the analysis above. The principal may be liable to the third-party representee for misstatements made by the agent in two ways. First, the principal can be held directly liable for authorising the making of the statement by the agent.[154] Certainly, cases where the agent had actual authority to make those statements will count; apparent authority probably will as well.[155] Second, the principal can be held vicariously liable for the tort of its agent. Here the principal is being held liable not for their own wrong, but for the wrong of another – their agent.[156] The agent must thus have committed a tort,[157] and the requirements for vicarious liability – a qualifying relationship[158] and a 'close connection' between the acts done and those the agent was employed to do[159] – must be met. In either possibility the principal may be liable for losses caused by reliance on the agent's misrepresentation to the principal; the precise measure may depend on whether the misrepresentation was fraudulent or negligent. However, even if the principal may be held liable for their agent's misstatements, that action would be an alternative to the third party seeking to hold the principal to the truth of the statement. There is no good justification why the former should trump the latter.

Worthington's argument might be seen as a call of a different kind, for changing apparent authority's nature as an estoppel by representation into some other kind of estoppel. This new estoppel might offer discretion in fashioning appropriate remedies or might be limited to remedying reliance losses. Either way, it would not operate as a rule of evidence. There is some support for this. In *National Westminster Bank plc v Somer International (UK) Ltd*, the Court of Appeal departed from the orthodox understanding of estoppel by representation by concluding 'there yet remained scope for the operation of equity to

[154] How this type of liability ought to be categorised is controversial. One view might be that the principal commits the tort himself (personally), albeit through the body of another. See eg R Stevens, *Torts and Rights* (Oxford, Oxford University Press, 2007) 245–48; R Leow, 'Understanding Agency: A Proxy Power Definition' (2019) 78 *CLJ* 99, 108. Another view is that it is a form of accessory or participatory liability, eg Davies (n 70) 191–92.

[155] eg *Colonial Mutual Life Assurance Society Ltd v Producers and Citizens Co-operative Assurance Co of Australia Ltd* (1931) 46 CLR 41, 48 (Dixon CJ). See Leow (n 1) 113–20 (in the context of corporate principals/employers).

[156] eg *Cox v Ministry of Justice* [2016] UKSC 10, [2016] AC 660 [15] (Lord Reed).

[157] eg *Axon v Ministry of Defence* [2016] EWHC 787 (QB), [2016] FSR 32 [68], [94] (Nicol J).

[158] See now *Claimants v Catholic Child Welfare Society* [2012] UKSC 56, [2013] 2 AC 1; *Barclays Bank v Claimants* [2020] UKSC 13, [2020] AC 97.

[159] Generally, see *Lister v Hesley Hall* [2001] UKHL 22, [2022] 1 AC 215; *Mohamud v WM Morrison Supermarkets plc* [2016] UKSC 11, [2016] 2 WLR 821. For misrepresentation torts, there is a difficult question of whether the 'close connection' test is limited by the existence of actual or apparent authority to make the statement, as suggested in *Armagas* (n 133) 737–40 (Goff LJ), on appeal, 782 (Lord Keith).

alleviate the position on grounds of unfairness or unconscionability ... whatever the appropriate judicial classification of estoppel by representation'.[160] In that case the bank paid approximately US$76,000 to the defendant Somer, which acted to their detriment by forwarding goods worth approximately £13,000 to their customer in the belief that the latter had paid them. Applying this unconscionability-based exception, the Court of Appeal concluded that Somer could only rely on the defence of estoppel by representation to the extent of their detriment.

Somer's conclusion is difficult to defend if estoppel by representation is a rule of evidence. But it is not so easy to see why apparent authority should develop into something else. One of the key functions of apparent authority is to protect the reasonable reliance of third parties on the appearance of authority which the principal has created. As said in *Morris v Kanssen*, 'the wheels of business will not go smoothly round unless it may be assumed that that is in order which appears to be in order'.[161] If remedies for apparent authority were subject to judicial discretion or limited only to remedying reliance losses, the ability of third parties to rely on the appearances of authority would be much more limited. In many apparent authority cases where the third party relies on the agent's authority to approve a transaction, the third party suffers very little detriment, perhaps only losing an opportunity to take some alternative course of action.[162]

Despite recent judicial support, the argument in 'Back to Basics' is incompatible with the underlying basis for apparent authority. As an estoppel by representation, apparent authority operates as a rule of evidence. There is only one possible result if apparent authority is established: against the third party, the principal is estopped from adducing evidence contrary to the truth of the statement he made. This conclusion does leave the *First Energy* problem intact; its resolution (if one exists) must be left for another day.

V. CONCLUSION

This chapter critically evaluates the three solutions offered in 'Back to Basics'. For the *Stone & Rolls* problem, it argues that the problem both with 'Back to Basics' and the recent analysis offered by the Supreme Court is that it wrongly identifies a context-specific approach attribution as the solution. The better view is that the resolution of the problem turns on a more careful approach to attribution and the effect of any private law rule in question. The chapter also disagrees with the analysis of the scope of an agent's authority, instead preferring the view that an agent does not have actual authority to act otherwise than for the principal's benefit, but for different reasons than those commonly stated. Finally, the innovative solution to the *First Energy* problem does not quite meet the mark; it is incompatible with the orthodox underlying basis for apparent authority as an estoppel by representation.

[160] *National Westminster Bank plc v Somer International (UK) Ltd* [2001] EWCA Civ 970, [2002] QB 1286 [40] (Potter LJ).

[161] *Morris v Kanssen* [1946] AC 459 (HL) 475 (Lord Simonds).

[162] eg *Kelly v Fraser* (n 140) [17].

Evident in 'Back to Basics' are some familiar themes of Sarah Worthington's work. The solution to the *Stone & Rolls* problem focuses on the need for the law to deliver predictable, commercially sensible outcomes. The discussion of the *First Energy* problem demonstrates a persistent focus on remedial issues,[163] while analysis of the scope of an agent's actual authority draws on efforts to show how the common law and equity can be coherently integrated into a single system, with different flaws generating different remedies.[164] Its innovative arguments are well worth considering, as this chapter has done.

[163] eg S Worthington, *Proprietary Interests in Commercial Transactions* (Oxford, Oxford University Press, 1996).

[164] S Worthington, *Equity*, 2nd edn (Oxford, Clarendon Press, 2006).

5

Corporate Liability for Wrongdoing within (Foreign) Subsidiaries: Mechanisms from Corporate Law, Tort and Regulation

PAUL DAVIES

I. INTRODUCTION

THE EXTENT TO which parent companies should be liable for wrongdoing committed within their subsidiaries is a question to which much attention has been devoted within academic scholarship over the years, although, so far, with relatively little outcome in terms of the law on the books. The dominant rule is one of non-liability: victims of wrongdoing are confined to remedies against the particular company within which the wrongdoing occurred. However, there have always been exceptions to this position of non-liability of the parent, and in recent years these exceptional cases have expanded their scope somewhat; and there are developments on foot which, if continued, would make the exceptions even more important. The purpose of this chapter is to analyse the scope and rationale for the exceptions, predominantly in UK and EU law. The chapter suggests that, doctrinally, the expanded scope of parent liability has involved a shift away from a corporate law analysis of the issue (the long-standing and intellectually unsatisfactory doctrine of piercing the corporate veil) to a tort analysis (now seen as a standard application of the tort of negligence) and, perhaps in the future, to a regulatory analysis, which requires companies to carry out a 'due-diligence' assessment of the more egregious risks associated with its businesses and makes them liable for harms resulting from inadequate due-diligence exercises. Thus both the tort and, to an even greater extent, the regulatory approach tie parental liability back to company law, since they rely on a core corporate governance mechanism – the board of the parent company – as the basis for corporate liability (tort theory) or to discharge an expanded monitoring role (regulatory theory). Even the tort approach generates incentives for the board to define more precisely its monitoring role in relation to unlawful conduct by subsidiaries, as we shall see below.

II. THE ISSUE IN CORPORATE LAW

There is probably no developed jurisdiction that does not attach separate legal personality to a business which incorporates under its general company law. The same statement may be made about limited liability, at least as a default rule. In the law and economics school of company law analysis, these two features are seen as together providing a core feature of the company form, namely asset partitioning.[1] Under this view, it is a central feature of the company (and of some, but not all, other forms of business organisation provided by the law) that the business assets of the shareholders are strictly demarcated from their personal assets. This is achieved by allocating the business assets to the company (via its separate personality) and then hindering both the creditors of the company from attaching the shareholders' personal assets and the shareholders' creditors from attaching the assets of the company. Limited liability clearly hinders the company's creditors vis-à-vis the shareholders' assets, while the separate legal personality of the company hinders the shareholders' creditors vis-à-vis the company's assets. The advantages and disadvantages of limited liability are much debated in corporate law scholarship, but the majority view is that its advantages outweigh its disadvantages. Less often noticed, however, is the benefit of asset partitioning to corporate creditors (and others involved in the company). The shareholders' creditors may attach their debtors' shares, of course, but the company's assets cannot be touched, even in the case of a controlling shareholder, to the clear benefit of those (other shareholders, employees, consumers) who benefit from the company's continuation as an operating business.[2]

However, within the asset partitioning analysis, there is room for qualification of the conclusion that strict separation is always the most efficient position. Indeed, the very authors who are most closely associated with the asset partitioning analysis have suggested two cases where qualification would be beneficial: (a) where the creditors are tort victims (and, possibly, other 'non-adjusting' creditors);[3] and (b) where it is sought to apply asset partitioning within groups of companies.[4] The first qualification is driven by a desire to control 'externalities', ie costs of production which the company does not bear because those costs have been thrown onto others (without any explicit or implicit agreement that this transfer should occur). The consequence of externalities is that the company's goods or services are produced 'too cheaply' and so 'too much' of them is consumed. The classic case of an externality is environmental harm for which the company is not liable, either contractually or under regulation; but tort victims whose claims exceed value of the company's assets fall into the same category.

[1] H Hansmann and R Kraakman, 'The Essential Role of Organizational Law' (2000–01) 110 *Yale Law Journal* 387.

[2] P Davies, *Introduction to Company Law*, 3rd edn (Oxford, Oxford University Press, 2020) 6–9.

[3] H Hansmann and R Kraakman, 'Towards Unlimited Shareholder Liability for Corporate Torts' (1991) 100 *Yale Law Journal* 1879.

[4] H Hansmann and R Squires, 'External and Internal Asset Partitioning: Corporations and their Subsidiaries' in J Gordon and W-G Ringe (eds), *Oxford Handbook of Corporate Law and Governance* (Oxford, Oxford University Press, 2018).

Despite the support for this first qualification from the authors of the asset partitioning analysis, it has gained little traction in doctrinal reform in any jurisdiction I am aware of. Most probably this is due to the availability of a range of alternative, and arguably more effective, techniques for addressing this issue. Most prominent, perhaps, is mandatory insurance for those engaging in hazardous activities, a technique capable of embracing all those whose assets are likely to be insufficient to meet their liabilities. It is a mistake to think that the only tortfeasors at risk of being unable to meet in full a judgment against them are limited companies.

The second qualification stems from the broader view that most of the advantages claimed for asset partitioning do not exist within groups, either as a matter of logic or of intra-group practice.[5] For example, the benefits in terms of reduced monitoring of the wealth of fellow shareholders which shareholders of the parent company gain from the limited liability of that company are not enhanced by the limited liability of subsidiaries (at least where the subsidiaries are wholly owned), while other benefits are undermined in fact by the widespread practice of offering major creditors cross-company guarantees, ie limited liability is contracted out of *pro tanto*. Consequently, in relation to groups it is arguable that the costs of asset partitioning exceed its benefits. Perhaps for these reasons, the second qualification to strict asset partitioning has encountered a somewhat warmer welcome across jurisdictions. In courts, this has normally taken the form of a greater willingness to apply the doctrine of veil piercing,[6] whilst at a legislative level some jurisdictions have adopted (or there have been proposed) more elaborate arrangements, normally involving some trade-off of parent company liability for subsidiaries' debts in exchange for greater formal control over the subsidiaries' decisions by the parent board.[7]

The UK legislature has joined in the general reluctance to impose liability upon shareholders for corporate torts where the company's assets are insufficient, but the courts have also rejected any special rule for qualifying limited liability within corporate groups. In *Adams v Cape Industries plc*,[8] the Court of Appeal rejected a

[5] ibid.

[6] Which is in fact the principal doctrinal recommendation of Hansmann and Squires (n 4). Nevertheless, as a matter of current court practice, even in the United States (generally regarded as more open to veil piercing than most others), veil piercing is not often used: R Thompson, 'Piercing the Corporate Veil: An Empirical Study' (1991) 76 *Cornell Law Review* 1036; and 'Piercing the Corporate Veil within Corporate Groups: Corporate Shareholders as Mere Investors' (1999) 13 *Connecticut Journal of International Law* 379. For other jurisdictions see Tan Cheng Han, J Wang and C Hofmann, 'Piercing the Corporate Veil: Historical, Theoretical, and Comparative Perspectives' (2019) 16 *Berkeley Business Law Journal* 140.

[7] These arrangements have been reviewed, recently and somewhat sceptically, by L Enriques and S Gilotta, 'The Case against a Special Regime for Intragroup Transactions', Part IV (ECGI Law Working Paper 641/2022, May 2022). The best-known example of this approach is German 'group law', under which the parent is granted the freedom to direct the subsidiary's actions in exchange for indemnification of the subsidiary against losses thereby incurred. In the case of wholly owned subsidiaries, it is not clear that the parent obtains much benefit from such an arrangement, so long as the subsidiary is a going concern, and even when the subsidiary is in the vicinity of insolvency, doing what the parent requires is not always contrary to the interests of the subsidiary. See *Charterbridge Corporation v Lloyds Bank* [1970] Ch 62 (Ch).

[8] *Adams v Cape Industries plc* [1990] Ch 433 (CA). In this case, a federal court in Texas had given judgement against, inter alia, the UK-incorporated parent. The parent had not defended the proceedings

whole raft of arguments that might have led to the opposite result. There was 'no general principle that all companies in a group of companies are to be regarded as one'. The court had no jurisdiction to pierce the corporate veil within groups where the interests of justice so required. The fact that the parent had overall control of the subsidiary was not a basis for ignoring the separate legal personalities of the two companies. There was no presumption that the subsidiary was to be regarded as the agent of the parent/principal. Overall, 'if a company chooses to arrange the affairs of its group in such a way that the business carried on in a particular foreign country is the business of its subsidiary and not its own, it is, in our judgement, entitled to do so'.[9]

III. THE ISSUE IN TORT LAW

Adams was by no means the end of the story. In a series of later decisions, sometimes involving the same company as in the *Adams* case, the courts made use of the law of tort to create a duty of care owed directly by the parent company to those harmed by the actions of its subsidiary, provided the parent exercised the required degree of managerial control over the subsidiary. These 'parent control' cases are capable of generating a broad set of circumstances in which the parent will be liable for tortious conduct occurring within the subsidiary. Second, in a doctrinally separate development, the courts have expanded the exceptions to the general principle that there is no liability in tort for harm caused to others as a result of the intervention of a third party. In a corporate context, this is a narrower basis of liability than the managerial control theory, but it has the capacity to operate not only in relation to harm caused by subsidiaries and contractors but also more widely.

A. The Managerial Control Theory

(i) The Parent's Duty of Care Accepted in Principle

In *Chandler v Cape plc*,[10] the Court of Appeal upheld Wyn Williams J's finding of liability in tort after a trial. Unlike the arguments for piercing the veil, which focus exclusively on the relationship between the parent and the subsidiary, the tort theory concentrates on the relationship between the parent and those who suffered harm. Indeed, it seems possible that the tort theory could result in liability for the parent,

or otherwise submitted to the jurisdiction of the Texas court. The successful plaintiffs sought to enforce the Texas judgment against the parent in the United Kingdom. The enforceability of the judgment in the English courts turned on whether the parent was 'present' in Texas, something which could be shown only by treating the parent as present via its US subsidiaries and affiliates, since the group had arranged its affairs so that the parent did not operate in the United States.

[9] Subsequent decisions about veil piercing in free-standing companies have evinced no greater fondness for making exceptions to the general rule: *Prest v Petrodel Resources Ltd* [2013] UKSC 34, [2013] 2 AC 415.

[10] *Chandler v Cape plc* [2012] EWCA Civ 525, [2012] 1 WLR 3111.

even when the subsidiary had committed no wrong against those who suffered harm, for example, where the subsidiary enjoyed some immunity against suit which the parent lacked or the risk in question was foreseeable only by the parent company. However, too much should not be made of this point. As we shall see below, the question of whether the parent owes a duty to those suffering harm turns in large part on the closeness of the control exercised by the parent over the subsidiary's activities. The correct analysis appears to be that the duty is owed in law by the parent to the claimant, but it arises out of an analysis of the degree of factual control exercised by the parent over the subsidiary in relation to the hazardous activities carried on within the subsidiary.

Because the 'parent tort' theory is a theory of direct liability of the parent towards the claimants, not a theory of vicarious liability of the parent for the torts of the subsidiary, the central question becomes one of determining the situations in which the courts will recognise that the direct duty has arisen. Unlike with vicarious liability, where the liability of the principal/employer is automatic provided the relevant relationship exists, the direct liability of the parent does not flow automatically from the parent–subsidiary relationship.

(ii) 'Ordinary' Tort Law or Not?

In *Chandler*, apparently the first case in which liability was established on the basis of a duty of care owed by the parent to those who suffered harm as a result of the subsidiary's actions, the trial judge regarded himself as presented with a novel situation for the application of a tortious duty of care. He therefore directed himself according to the tripartite tests laid down in *Caparo Industries plc v Dickman*[11] for the recognition of a duty of care in situations not previously considered by the court. The same approach was followed by the Court of Appeal in that case. Of course, Lord Bridge had commented in *Caparo* that 'the concepts of proximity and fairness embodied in these additional ingredients [additional to foreseeability] are not susceptible to any such precise definition as would be necessary to give them utility as practical tests' and are really conclusionary rather than analytical statements. Nevertheless, the fact that the courts in *Chandler* took them as the framework for analysis indicates that they regarded themselves as treading new ground, even though the harm at issue in *Chandler* was personal injury caused by physical means, a fact pattern hardly new to the law of tort, rather than economic loss caused by negligent misstatement, as in *Caparo*.

By the end of the last decade, however, the Supreme Court had decided that the courts no longer needed the *Caparo* check on their inventiveness. In *Vedanta Resources plc v Lungowe*,[12] Lord Briggs said of the *Caparo* test that 'it did not lead to the identification of a wider basis in law for the recognition of the relevant parental duty of care than that which in my view, the law actually provides, by reference to

[11] *Caparo Industries plc v Dickman* [1990] 2 AC 605 (HL).
[12] *Vedanta Resources plc v Lungowe* [2019] UKSC 20, [2020] AC 1045.

basic principle'.[13] He approved the approach of Sales LJ (as he then was) in *AAA v Unilever plc*,[14] who said:

> There is no special doctrine in the law of tort of legal responsibility on the part of a parent company in relation to the activities of its subsidiary, vis-à-vis persons affected by those activities. … The legal principles are the same as would apply to in relation to the question whether any third party (such as a consultant giving advice to the subsidiary) was subject to a duty of care in tort owed to a claimant dealing with the subsidiary.[15]

To similar effect was the decision in *Okpabi v Royal Dutch Shell*: it was 'not the correct approach' to focus on the threefold test for a duty of care set out in *Caparo*.[16]

At one level, this development was to be expected. Once it was decided, on *Caparo* principles, that a duty of care could be owed by a parent company towards those harmed by the activities of a subsidiary, it was not helpful to revert constantly to those very imprecise criteria to establish the circumstances in which that duty would arise. To perform that second-stage task, the courts needed to move beyond the generalities of *Caparo* and focus directly on the characteristics of the parent–subsidiary relationships which would lead the courts to regard the imposition of a duty of care on the parent towards third parties as appropriate.

However, there appears to have been a second incentive for the courts to move in this direction. *Chandler* involved a UK subsidiary of the UK parent company. This was a classic case of the wrongdoing subsidiary not being worth suing, because its insurance policy for some reason failed to cover the risk of harm in question (pneumoconiosis caused by the inhalation of asbestos dust) or the particular class of claimant (who had not been employed directly in the part of the business that handled asbestos).[17] The subsequent cases, *Vedanta, AAA* and *Okpabi*, all involved foreign subsidiaries of an English parent company, which carried on substantial continuing businesses in their respective jurisdictions.[18] Although some doubts were expressed on this score, it was certainly never shown that the subsidiary would be incapable of meeting any judgment that might be made against it or that the parent would not support the subsidiary. The driving force behind the claimants' desire to sue in the English courts seems to have been what were referred to in the cases as 'access to justice' arguments. In particular, the availability of funding and legal expertise to support large-scale litigation against a multinational company was, the claimants argued, substantially greater in the United Kingdom than in the subsidiaries'

[13] ibid [56].

[14] *AAA v Unilever plc* [2018] EWCA Civ 1532, [2018] BCC 959.

[15] ibid [36]. For an extension of this argument to the controlling shareholders of at least state-owned entities, see E Lim, *Sustainability and Corporate Mechanisms in Asia* (Cambridge University Press, 2020) 267–73.

[16] *Okpabi v Royal Dutch Shell* [2021] UKSC 3 [24]–[25], [2021] 1 WLR 1294.

[17] The subsidiary in fact had been dissolved, but presumably it could have been restored to the register, had its insurance policy been of any value.

[18] Zambia, Kenya and Nigeria, respectively.

jurisdictions.[19] Although too polite to mention it, the claimants may have felt also that they would be likely to obtain a more open hearing in an English court, since in both the *Vedanta* and *Okpabi* cases the government in whose territory the operations were conducted had a substantial economic interest in the subsidiary, either directly or indirectly.[20]

In addition to the duty of care issue, there was therefore a jurisdictional issue. Since the harm had occurred outside the United Kingdom, were the English courts the appropriate forum to hear the claims? As the law then stood, this was not a serious issue in relation to the parent company, since the Brussels Regulation[21] had been interpreted by the Court of Justice of the European Union as permitting only very narrow exceptions to the rule that companies domiciled in the European Union may be sued in the jurisdiction of their domicile in respect of breaches of duty by them, no matter that the harm was inflicted elsewhere.[22] However, in addition to the parent (the 'anchor defendant'), the claimants also sought to sue in the English courts the subsidiaries directly responsible for the alleged harm. This was in all likelihood for the same reasons as motivated the litigation against the parent in the English courts, coupled with the desire to avoid the risk of inconsistent judgments if the subsidiary were sued in its operating jurisdiction and found not liable.

This put the claimants in the position of having to obtain the court's permission to serve legal process on the subsidiary out of the jurisdiction. In turn, this brought back centre-stage the question of whether there was a triable issue against the parent, this being one of the tests to determine whether the subsidiary was a 'necessary and proper party' to the litigation against the parent.[23] However, the courts were concerned to avoid extensive hearings at this preliminary stage. In both *Vedanta* and *Okpabi* the Supreme Court was clear that the parties had overstepped the line: the litigation over the preliminary jurisdiction issues had been 'disproportionate' and had approached the 'self-defeating' position that it was necessary to have a trial to determine whether a trial was necessary. In *Okpabi*, where the Supreme Court viewed the lower courts as having conducted a mini-trial, it was said that at the jurisdictional stage the focus should be on the particulars of claim and a decision made on the arguability point on the basis of the facts so alleged, without the defendant seeking to dispute the factual allegations with its own evidence, except in rare cases. Moving to the view that the parent's liability was a matter of

[19] These issues did not relate only to the claimants' motivations to sue in the English courts but also the legal question of whether the English courts should take jurisdiction over the tort claim against the foreign subsidiary. See *Vedanta* (n 12) [66]–[87].

[20] See further below the discussion of host state involvement in human rights abuses.

[21] Article 4 of the Recast Brussels Regulation on Jurisdiction etc in Civil and Commercial Matters, Regulation (EU) 1215/2012.

[22] The court in *Vedanta* (n 12) discussed the CJEU jurisprudence at [23]–[41]. It rejected the defendants' argument that it was an abuse of EU law to use Art 4 to establish jurisdiction against the parent for the sole purpose of establishing jurisdiction against foreign defendants who were the real objects of the claim. This argument failed largely on the facts, since the parent as well as the foreign subsidiary was a real object of the claims. For the possible resurgence of *forum non conveniens* issues in relation to parent companies post-Brexit, see E Aristova, 'The Future of Tort Litigation against Transnational Corporations in the English Courts: Is Forum [Non] Conveniens Back?' (2021) 6 *Business and Human Rights Journal* 399.

[23] CPR, Pt 6, Practice Direction 6B, para 3.1.

ordinary tort law might be seen as further discouraging defendants from making elaborate arguments at a preliminary stage in the litigation that jurisdiction should be rejected.[24]

(iii) What Does 'Ordinary' Tort Law Require?

Although the most recent and authoritative decisions on the tort liability of parent companies concerned preliminary issues, it is now tolerably clear where the courts will focus their attention when determining whether the parent owed a duty of care to the claimants.[25] They will focus on the extent of the control of the parent over the subsidiary. It is equally clear that control here is not what a corporate lawyer understands by that term in the context of parent–subsidiary relationships. Under the Companies Act 2006, control is defined, principally, in terms of holding a majority of the voting rights of another company or having the right to appoint or remove the majority of its board of directors.[26] On the company law approach, therefore, a company would always have control of another majority-owned or wholly owned company.

For the purposes of the duty of care in tort, by contrast, the capacity to control the actions of the subsidiary is not enough. The focus is on what might be termed 'managerial' control. To what extent has the parent involved itself in the management of those aspects of the subsidiary's activities which are alleged to have generated the harm of which the claimants complain – or, possibly, has held itself out as being so involved? A company with control of another on the company law tests is not necessarily one with control on the tort tests. It may have the authority to exercise the tort level of control, but have decided not (or simply failed) to do so, presumably for commercial reasons related to its view of the benefits of leaving a high level of discretion to the subsidiary as to how it might best conduct its activities.

Although not to be treated as exhaustive, the Supreme Court in *Okpabi* regarded the decision in *Vedanta* as having identified at least four routes to managerial control of the subsidiary:

(1) The parent taking over the management or joint management of the relevant aspects of the subsidiary's activities.
(2) The parent providing defective advice or defective group-wide policies which the subsidiary implemented without further analysis.
(3) The parent promulgating group-wide policies and taking active steps to secure their implementation by subsidiaries.

[24] In *Vedanta* (n 12) the defendants sought to argue that the court should not take jurisdiction over the subsidiary, inter alia, because 'this was by no means a *Chandler* type of case' ([49]), ie the very approach which was rejected by the Supreme Court in *Okpabi* (see text at n 16 above).

[25] But it follows that the appeal courts have not yet addressed in any detail the questions of whether the duty of care was broken, whether it caused harm to the claimants and how compensation should be assessed.

[26] Companies Act 2006, ss 1159 and 1162. For reasons related to EU law there are slightly different definitions for 'holding' companies and 'parent' companies, but the core of both definitions is as stated in the text.

(4) The parent holding out that it exercises a particular level of control over the subsidiary.[27]

In *Okpabi*,[28] the Court's view was that there was an arguable case under both headings (1) and (3). In *Vedanta*,[29] the focus was primarily on (3).

At first sight, managerial control is a more difficult thing for claimants to demonstrate than corporate control. For share ownership, the data are publicly available, both for legal ownership (in all cases) and for beneficial ownership (in publicly traded companies at the 3 percent level and above and at the 25 percent level in nearly all cases).[30] Managerial control, by contrast, requires information about the internal arrangements of the group, a matter that has traditionally been regarded as of private business concern and so not subject to mandatory disclosure. However, there are at least two ways in which claimants may seek to address this difficulty. First, effective group-wide policies and their implementation are likely to require both internal administrative arrangements for the production of those policies and their dissemination to the relevant levels of parent and subsidiary management. The policies cannot be locked away in the CEO's safe if they are to have an impact, and nor can the source of their authority be obscured; on the contrary, they will become available to a significant number of employees of the parent or subsidiary. In *Okpabi*, the claimants relied on information provided by former employees of Shell as to both the administrative arrangements and the content of the policies.[31]

Second, over the course of this century, publicly traded companies have come under obligations to publish documents relating to matters that might previously have been regarded as of only internal concern. Thus, under the Companies Act 2006, companies are required to produce as part of their annual accounts a 'strategic' report, which in the case of 'quoted'[32] UK companies includes "non-financial" information on:

- environmental matters (including the impact of the company's activities on the environment);[33]
- the company's employees;
- social matters;

[27] This list omits a possible further basis of liability identified in *Chandler*, ie superior knowledge. This arises where '(1) the businesses of the parent and subsidiary are in a relevant respect the same; (2) the parent has, or ought to have, superior knowledge on some relevant aspect of health and safety in the particular industry; (3) the subsidiary's system of work is unsafe as the parent company knew, or ought to have known; and (4) the parent knew or ought to have foreseen that the subsidiary or its employees would rely on its using that superior knowledge for the employees' protection' ([80]).

[28] *Okpabi* (n16) [153].

[29] *Vedanta* (n 12) [61].

[30] P Davies, S Worthington and C Hare (eds), *Gower's Principles of Modern Company Law*, 11th edn (London, Sweet & Maxwell, 2021) paras 27-011ff, 13-022ff and 28-024 (this last dealing with the disclosure of 'control arrangements').

[31] *Okpabi* (n 16) [133]–[140].

[32] ie officially listed in the United Kingdom or an EEA state or traded on the NYSE or Nasdaq.

[33] In the case of climate change disclosures the Companies Act's requirements are enhanced by the Listing Rules (LR 9.8.6(8)).

- respect for human rights;
- anti-corruption and bribery matters.

This information must include descriptions of the corporate policies or due-diligence policies pursued in relation to these matters (or an explanation of why the company does not have policies on a particular matter), of the outcomes of these policies, of the risks the company faces in these areas which are likely to have an adverse impact, and of how it manages these risks.[34] Reputational incentives are likely to encourage large publicly traded companies to adopt policies rather than report that they have no such policies.[35]

Consequently, there will be in the public domain a significant amount of material relating to the level of control exercised by parent companies over subsidiaries. So, in *Vedanta*, Lord Briggs, whilst discounting the significance of a management services agreement between parent and subsidiary, concluded that the parent exercised the requisite degree of control over the subsidiary:

> But I regard the published materials in which Vedanta may fairly be said to have asserted its own assumption of responsibility for the maintenance of proper standards of environmental control over the activities of its subsidiaries … and not merely to have laid down but also implemented those standards by training, monitoring and enforcement, as sufficient on their own to show that it is well arguable.[36]

In *Okpabi*, the Court of Appeal, although, unlike the Supreme Court, finding in favour of Shell, held that the first-instance judge had been wrong to place no reliance on 'publicly available Shell corporate documentation which had been produced in the context of fulfilment of listing obligations'.[37]

When the strategic report was proposed by the Company Law Review (under the title of an 'Operating and Financial Review'), the Steering Committee for the Review attached importance to putting 'the onus on the directors to give their own account, based on their own judgement, of the matters which are important in assessing the performance and prospects of the business. This is calculated to ensure that boilerplate formulae will be treated by the market with the distrust they deserve.'[38] To this end, two amendments were made to the standard regime applying to the annual accounts. First, the strategic review is not subject to a full audit (which might make the review the auditors' review rather than the directors') but is checked by auditors only for consistency with the corporate documents which are subject to full audit.[39] Second, to encourage directors to be forthcoming in the strategic review, statements it contains will trigger director liability to the company only if they are at least recklessly made (and so not on the otherwise applicable negligence standard).[40]

[34] Companies Act 2006, s 414CB (operative from December 2016).
[35] See further text to n 60.
[36] *Vedanta* (n 12) [61].
[37] *Okpabi* (n 16) [111].
[38] Company Law Steering Group, *Modern Company Law for a Competitive Economy: Final Report* (2001) vol 1, para 3.40.
[39] Companies Act 2006, s 496.
[40] ibid s 463. Directors' liability to persons other than the company is excluded entirely.

There is a risk that the developments in tort liability for parent companies have undermined this policy. Directors now have an incentive to reveal the minimum necessary to comply with the statutory and regulatory requirements. If they do more, they may be increasing the liability risk of the company. One can imagine that, after these Supreme Court decisions, the parent company's lawyers will have a greater input into the documents posted on the company's website, and the company's communications departments a lesser one. It will be interesting to see how this tension is resolved. On the one hand, there is growing regulatory and investor pressure on companies to reveal increasing amounts of and increasingly detailed non-financial information; on the other hand, the company's lawyers will be well aware of the litigation risks. My guess is that the former will win out.[41]

It is inherent in the courts' approach to the direct duty of care that the control tests developed above will not necessarily lead to the conclusion that a duty of care on the part of the parent has been triggered in relation to the activities of the subsidiary. In *AAA v Unilever plc*,[42] where Sales LJ articulated the 'ordinary tort' approach which was subsequently endorsed by the Supreme Court, the court refused to categorise the parent as an anchor defendant, because the evidence did not disclose an arguable case that the parent owed a duty of care to the claimant employees of the subsidiary. Those employees had been victims of intertribal violence following presidential elections in Kenya, when the tea plantation in which they worked and the associated housing in which they lived had been attacked by 'marauding mobs' as part of a national breakdown in law and order. The Court of Appeal upheld the first-instance judge's conclusion (Elisabeth Laing J, as she then was) that the parent owed the employees of the subsidiary no duty to protect them from such an event. The evidence showed that the subsidiary carried out its own crisis management training, drafted its own policies and received no specific advice from the parent. Although the parent was seeking to run the Unilever group as a single operating unit and had developed group-wide policies, in particular, a crisis management policy, that policy made it clear that responsibility for producing crisis management procedures lay below the parent company level.[43]

B. The Dangerous Situation Theory

In *Begum v Maran (UK) Ltd*,[44] the Court of Appeal refused to strike out a claim that A is liable to C where A is responsible for or has created a danger which B has then exploited and, in so doing, has caused harm to C. The defendant was a ship-broker which had undertaken to dispose of ships owned by other group companies when

[41] See further the discussion below.

[42] *AAA v Unilever plc* [2018] EWCA Civ 1532, [2018] BCC 959.

[43] See also *Thompson v The Renwick Group plc*, [2014] EWCA Civ 635, [2015] BCC 855, holding that a company with purely coordinating functions owed no duty of care to an employee of a subsidiary. This was so even though the parent had appointed a director to the subsidiary to be responsible for health and safety at the subsidiary (asbestos risk again).

[44] *Begum v Maran (UK) Ltd* [2021] EWCA Civ 326, [2022] 1 All ER (Comm) 940.

they reached the end of their useful lives. The defendant disposed of the tanker in question for cash to Hsejar Maritime Inc, a company incorporated in Nevis, on the basis that Hsejar would arrange for the ship to be broken up. Hsejar arranged this with the Zumar Enterprise Yard in Bangladesh. The 'yard' consisted essentially of tidal mud flats on which the tanker was beached and was then broken up without significant dockside support structure and in extremely unsafe working conditions. The claimant's husband fell and died in the breaking-up process.

The Court held that, on the assumed facts, it could not be said that there was no reasonable prospect of success for the argument that the claim fell within an exception to the *novus actus interveniens* doctrine. Although most of the previous cases dealing with this exception had arisen in the public sector, it was arguable that the defendant played an active role by sending the vessel to Bangladesh, knowingly exposing workers to the significant dangers which working on this large vessel in Bangladesh entailed.[45] The knowledge arose from two main facts of which the defendant was aware. First, the structure of the industry was that, for ships of this size, the only safe break-up yards were in China, while it was known that Bangladesh (and some other countries) operated extremely unsafe 'beaching' operations. Second, the price paid to the defendant by Hsejar was one which was appropriate only on the basis that the ship was not to be broken up in China, where costs were higher, but in Bangladesh. Finally, the defendant could have protected itself by including and enforcing a safe break-up clause in the contract with Hsejar.[46]

What are the implications of this decision for the subject-matter of this chapter? It is clear that the 'dangerous situation' theory is narrower than the managerial control theory. Managerial control on the part of the parent over at least some elements of subsidiaries' activities is likely to arise routinely out of the centralisation of the group's businesses. Whilst groups vary in the extent to which they centralise decision-making, a completely decentralised approach, akin to a portfolio of passive investments, is a rarity. A dangerous situation, by contrast, is not likely to arise routinely from group centralisation but only episodically in the context of particular business activities. Even then, 'it will only be in a relatively extreme case that the "creation of danger" exception will operate'.[47]

On the other hand, the 'dangerous situation' theory is not linked necessarily to the activities of parent companies and their capacity to exert managerial control over subsidiaries and contractors. The defendant in the case was not the group parent but rather a subsidiary providing ship-broking services to the group as a whole. More important, the implication of the case for companies is that they need to supervise the activities of all those in the value chain, both contractors (Hsejar) and subcontractors (Zumar). That supervision need not involve day-to-day monitoring of contractors and might not need to go beyond the inclusion and supervision of appropriate contractual provisions. But complete inattention once a dangerous

[45] ibid [64].

[46] In fact, the contract contained such a clause but the court concluded that neither the defendant nor Hsejar expected it to be enforced (ibid [69]).

[47] ibid [63].

situation has been created clearly will generate a liability risk. In the light of the extension of due-diligence requirements under the regulatory law discussed below to the whole of the company's 'value chain', *Marin* is a potentially important development in tort liability.

IV. THE ISSUE IN REGULATORY LAW

A. The Approach Stated

Courts using duty-of-care concepts to fashion direct parent company liability for wrongs committed within subsidiaries need to take as given the managerial arrangements between the parent and the subsidiary that the parent has chosen to put in place or has purported to do so. Most human rights and environmental lawyers will have none of this. For them, the *capacity* of the parent to exercise control over the subsidiaries should be the basis for imposing on the parent a duty to prevent or minimise wrongdoing occurring in subsidiaries and for imposing liability on them if they do not. Indeed, the capacity argument is extended so as to include wrongdoing by contractors, both direct and indirect, to the company and its subsidiaries. In the jargon, the company should be required to exercise control over its entire value chain, ie all the established business relationships that exist between it and its suppliers and customers.

Traditionally, those taking this view have been in favour of the 'single economic entity' theory of parental liability, which was rejected in *Adams*. Today, however, they tend to support a turbocharged version of the tort theory as the best way forward. Under this theory, a parent should be subject to legal incentives to exercise a proactive control over subsidiaries and contractors to reduce the risk that human rights (and other) violations will be committed within these other entities. While it is true that the risk of direct tort liability may induce parent companies ex ante to exercise control over the subsidiary's activities, the regular tort theory leaves the parent with more freedom than the turbocharged version to craft intra-group functions as it wishes. First, under the ordinary tort theory the company is free to decide to what extent it will run the risk of tort liability ex post even if it does involve itself in the subsidiary's decisions ex ante. In other words, there is no scrutiny ex ante of how good a job the parent does in reducing risks within the subsidiary and, if no harm in fact occurs, it will be subject to no liability ex post. Second, and more important, the parent is free to steer clear of involvement in the subsidiary's decision-making in the areas most likely to generate tort litigation (subject to the reputational factors discussed below).

So the more demanding duty imposed on the company involves a shift from standards developed by courts using private law to regulation crafted by the legislature. Nevertheless, the regulation is still reliant on the corporate structure: essentially, it co-opts the board and senior management of the company to implement an enhanced oversight and monitoring duty in relation to the company's observance of human rights standards. A 'due-diligence' obligation is imposed that requires parent company involvement in reviewing and controlling the risks arising in subsidiaries (and contractors), at least in the areas of human rights infringements and environmental damage. The company no longer has the freedom to leave to individual subsidiaries the task of developing and implementing policies in relation to these risks. Failure to discharge this duty may lead significant administrative penalties for the company, even if no harm to third parties occurs, as well as to civil liability if it does. Thus, while at one time the decision in *Chandler v Cape* was seen revealing domestic tort law as a promising way to bring human rights abuses before the courts,[48] the majority view today among human rights lawyers is probably that *Chandler* represented only an interim step in the necessary legal development towards a more intrusive legal structure.

It is true that the regulatory strategy has been advanced to date only in relation to breaches of core human rights and environmental protections located in international treaties and conventions. This is in contrast to the tort theory which in principle applies to all interests protected by the law of tort. However, the situations where the parent company is most likely to be found to owe a direct legal duty to third parties under the tort theory are precisely those where significant numbers of third parties are at risk of harms inflicted in breach of the international standards, because it is precisely in such cases that the company has the strongest incentives to involve itself in the controlling the subsidiaries' activities. Thus, in all the post-*Chandler* cases discussed above, the argument was that the company owed a duty of care to prevent the occurrence of events which were both tortious and in breach of international human rights or environmental standards.

B. The Role of the United Nations

This regulatory approach to parent company liability can be traced back to a 2008 report by Professor John Ruggie (Kennedy School of Government, Harvard), acting as the Special Representative of the Secretary General of the United Nations on the issue of human rights and transnational corporations. His report to the General Assembly's Human Rights Council advanced the propositions that transnational companies should 'respect' human rights and that effective remedies for breaches should be provided in the case of non-respect.[49] The report led initially to the UN's *Guiding Principles on Business and Human Rights* (2011),[50] to which multinational companies were invited to subscribe on a voluntary basis, as many did. However, in 2014 the Human Rights Council established an 'open-ended intergovernmental working group' on transnational businesses and human rights. Its brief was to develop an instrument that would make human rights standards embodied in international

[48] D Palombo, '*Chandler v Cape*: An Alternative to Piercing the Corporate Veil beyond *Kiobel v Royal Dutch Shell*' (2015) 4 *British Journal of American Legal Studies* 453.

[49] J Ruggie, *Protect, Respect and Remedy: a Framework for Business and Human Rights: report of the Special Representative of the Secretary-General on the Issue of Human Rights and Transnational Corporations and Other Business Enterprises* (2008), available at https://digitallibrary.un.org/record/625292?ln=en (accessed 15 October 2023).

[50] United Nations, Office of the High Commissioner on Human Rights, 2011 (HR/PUB/11/04).

treaties and conventions directly and legally binding on companies. These international instruments had previously operated, by and large, only between and among states. The establishment of the working group was thus an acknowledgement that the traditional system of inter-state international law had operated with only partial success in the human rights field. The aim now was to develop an instrument that would be binding on companies irrespective of whether their state of incorporation or the state of operation had ratified and implemented effectively the international agreements[51]

C. The Proposed EU Directive on Corporate Sustainability Due Diligence

(i) An Overview of the Proposed Directive

Of course, the proposed treaty, making human rights standards binding on companies, suffers from the same core defect as the treaties containing the substantive human rights standards, ie that it will be binding only on companies operating in states which have ratified and implemented the proposed treaty. It is in this context that a proposal from the European Commission for a Directive on Corporate Sustainability Due Diligence[52] is important. The Commission's draft was heavily influenced by that of the working group, perhaps not surprisingly in view of the Commission's membership of the group.[53] At the time of writing, the proposal has achieved a common position in the Council, which took a somewhat more cautious approach than the Commission but left the basic structure of the proposal intact.[54,55] What can be said is that the proposal, when adopted, will pre-empt the decisions of the Member States whether to sign any document which may emerge from the UN working group, by making its underlying ideas mandatory

[51] For the working group's latest draft of 2021, see OEIGWG Chairmanship, *Legally Binding Instrument to Regulate, in International Human Rights Law, the Activities of Transnational Corporations and Other Business Entities* (Third Revised Draft, 17.08.2021), available at www.ohchr.org/sites/default/files/Documents/HRBodies/HRCouncil/WGTransCorp/Session6/LBI3rdDRAFT.pdf (accessed 27 September 2023).

[52] COM(2022) 71 final, 23.2.2022, available at https://eur-lex.europa.eu/resource.html?uri=cellar:bc4dcea4-9584-11ec-b4e4-01aa75ed71a1.0001.02/DOC_1&format=PDF (accessed 27 September 2023). The Commission's draft applies to all companies which meet the relevant size standards, based on the number of employees and turnover (art 2), but it seems clear that its main impact in practice will be on parent companies.

[53] Also influential were the French reforms of 2017 (law no 2017-399 of 27 March 2017), which also reflected the UN initiatives. See A Pietrancosta, 'Codification in Company Law of General CSR Requirements: Pioneering Recent French Reforms and EU Perspectives' (ECGI Law Working Paper 639/2022), available at www.ssrn.com/abstract=4083398 (accessed 27 September 2023).

[54] Note from Personal Representatives Committee (Part 1) to Council, 'Proposal for a Directive of the European Parliament and of the Council on Corporate Sustainability Due Diligence and amending Directive (EU) 2019/1937 – General Approach', 30 November 2022, available at https://data.consilium.europa.eu/doc/document/ST-15024-2022-REV-1/en/pdf (accessed 27 September 2023). There will now be tripartite negotiations among the Commission, the Council and the Parliament before a final version emerges.

[55] Unless otherwise indicated, the references are to the common position of the Council.

on EU Member States and, thus, the international standards binding on covered companies via the 'due-diligence' obligation.

The Commission's proposal sought to make those standards binding throughout the 'value chain' of the companies it applies to, even, in fact especially, those parts of the value chain located outside Europe. In short, the backsliding of non-European states in relation to human rights and environmental standards is to be made good, at least in part, by establishing in the laws of EU Member States a requirement that companies incorporated (or in some cases, simply operating) in the European Union abide by those standards when operating outside the Union. This point is recognised, albeit in more diplomatic language, in the *travaux préparatoires* of the Directive:

> By including European companies' global supply chains into their scope, and by recognising that the most salient adverse impacts on human rights and on the environment occur mainly outside the EU, the policy options have a strong external dimension through their impacts on supply chain actors and stakeholders in third and developing countries.[56]

The definition of the value chain, as adopted in the Commission's proposal, has turned out to be a hotly debated issue. As proposed, the term covered not just subsidiaries and affiliates of the company, but also their contractors and subcontractors, across the whole of the company's 'value chain'. However, the Council's common position is more cautious about going beyond the company's supply chain and including the 'downstream' activities of customers. In fact, it eschews the term 'value chain' and prefers the more open term 'chain of activities'. How this question will be resolved is unclear at the time of writing.

(ii) A Little Detail on the Proposed Directive

It is probably very difficult for governments these days to put forward corporate proposals that do not contain the word 'sustainability' in the title or the rationale. Sustainability is, of course, a word of many possible meanings, but in the context of the Commission's proposal it has a rather limited meaning, which reveals its links with the work of the United Nations. It creates 'obligations for companies regarding actual and potential human rights adverse impacts and environmental adverse impacts' (Article 1) and those adverse impacts are defined as those resulting from breaches of a list of international conventions laid down in an Annex to the proposed Directive (Article 3(b) and (c)). Although the source of human rights and environmental obligations to be made binding on companies is confined to the international sphere, the Commission has drunk heavily from it. The Annex in the Commission's

[56] Commission Staff Working Document, *Impact Assessment Report accompanying the document Proposal for a Directive of the European Parliament and of the Council on Corporate Sustainability Due Diligence and amending Directive (EU) 2019/1937*, SWD(2022) 42 final, 23.2.2022 para 6.1.5, available at https://eur-lex.europa.eu/legal-content/EN/TXT/PDF/?uri=CELEX:52022SC0042 (accessed 15 October 2023). The authors did not investigate the further question whether host countries will always welcome the corporate intervention. See, for example, the reaction in China to H&M, the Swedish retailer, when it announced it did not use products from a Chinese province where slave labour was said to be deployed. The retailer was excluded from online sales engines for a while and Chinese consumers switched away from its products ('H&M and Nike Face China Backlash over Xinjiang Stance' *Financial Times*, 31 March 2021).

proposal identified twenty human rights provisions (reduced to fourteen in the Council's version) and twelve environmental ones in relation to which the company must perform due diligence. It should be noted that the obligation to carry out due diligence is not dependent upon these international standards being binding (apart from the proposed Directive) on the company or any of its business partners, whether in their country of incorporation or the country of operation.

Due Diligence

The central element in the proposal is the duty on the companies falling within its scope to carry out an assessment of the human rights and environmental risks contained in its business relationships and to take steps to prevent those risks eventuating or to minimise their likely impact. The duty thus goes beyond the idea that you should identify risks before you decide whether to enter into a transaction or a new line of business. Having identified those risks (as required by Article 6), the company must take steps to prevent the occurrence of potential adverse impacts or to reduce the probability of their happening (Article 7, including risks that should have been identified under Article 6 but were not). The company must also take steps to bring actual occurrences to an end or to minimise their impact, including the payment of financial compensation (Article 8). Under both Articles 7 and 8 companies may be required as a final step to end the business relationship in which the breaches are occurring, either temporarily or permanently. How to deal with the risk of human rights abuses in subsidiaries' operations is, thus, no longer to be a matter for the parent company – subject to the risk of tort liability ex post – but is specified in a regulatory instrument.

Monitoring and Enforcement

The regulatory credentials of the proposal are demonstrated very clearly in its provisions on enforcement and monitoring. As to monitoring, the company itself must review at least every two years its implementation of its due-diligence obligations (Article 10). Those likely to be harmed by the adverse impacts, employee representatives and non-governmental organisations (NGOs) active in the human rights field, may monitor the company through a 'complaints procedure' which the company must establish where they have 'legitimate concerns regarding actual or potential adverse impacts' (Article 9). Governments and the wider society may monitor the company by reacting to the annual report on the discharge of its due-diligence obligations which the company is required to make (Article 11). Finally, governmental supervisors (to be established in each Member State, not at EU level) may demand information from the company and initiate investigations into the company's discharge of its obligations, either on their own motion or on a complaint from a third party (Article 18).

As to enforcement, the supervisors are to have the usual wide range of administrative sanctions, including the imposition of financial penalties related to the size of the company's turnover. But private enforcement is provided for as well. Those actually harmed through the failure of the company to discharge its due-diligence responsibilities under Articles 7 and 8 are to have a right of action against the company in the courts of the Member State in which the company is incorporated, provided the company's breach was intentional or negligent (Article 22).[57] This provision does not extend to making the company liable for the harm caused by its business partners alone, even if, apparently, the company was in breach of its obligations under those articles. Since the Directive imposes due-diligence obligations only on the 'top' company, Article 22 presumably does not operate so as to make entities lower down the chain liable for the harm cause by breaches of Articles 7 and 8 at the top of the chain. However, national law, if any, which makes subsidiaries and business partners liable for the harm caused by them, is preserved.

Non EU-incorporated Companies

The proposal applies only to large companies defined by reference to turnover and number of employees, with a lower threshold for companies operating in businesses where there is thought to be a high risk of human rights and environmental abuses. The criteria will trigger the application of the Directive only if they are met over two consecutive years (Article 2).

Figure 5.1 Criteria triggering the Directive

	Incorporated in EU	**Incorporated in third country**
General rule	500 employees + €150m turnover world-wide	€150m EU
'High-risk sectors'	250 employees + €40m world-wide (€20m high risk)	€40m EU (€20m high risk)
Estimated coverage	13,000 companies	4,000 companies

As Figure 5.1 makes clear, the proposal applies not only to companies incorporated in an EU Member State, but also to companies incorporated in third countries which do substantial amounts of business in the EU. (The specification of the appropriate regulator for third-country companies is to be found in Article 17.3.) The extension may raise hackles in some quarters, but it is not a new approach. Thus, the Modern Slavery Act 2015 (UK), Part 6 (Transparency in Supply Chains etc) requires an annual statement of the steps the company has taken, if any, to eliminate slavery and human

[57] This liability will be shaped by national law (eg on causation and remoteness).

trafficking in its supply chain. This obligation applies, subject to thresholds, to 'a body corporate (wherever incorporated) which carries on a business, or part of a business, in any part of the United Kingdom'.[58]

While the principle of applying human rights law to companies incorporated outside the jurisdiction but carrying on business has become uncontroversial, there is likely to be some debate about whether the criteria for the inclusion of outside companies are equivalent to those for inside companies. However, one may wonder how important the issue is in fact. It seems likely that most companies, incorporated in third countries but carrying on significant business within the European Union, do so via EU-incorporated subsidiaries, which will be subject to the same rules as any other EU-incorporated company. If this is so, the third-country provisions can be seen mainly as a prophylactic against decisions by companies incorporated in third countries to move their EU business from a subsidiary to a branch.

V. TWO FUNDAMENTAL QUESTIONS ABOUT TORT LIABILITY AND DUE-DILIGENCE OBLIGATIONS

A. Why Do Companies Breach Human Rights and Environmental Standards?

We noted above the economists' take on externalities. In the economists' model, the company shifts costs onto third parties without compensation or, if they naturally fall on third parties, the company leaves them there, because this reduces the company's costs of production and thus increases its profits. In a competitive market, companies are no doubt incentivised to reduce their production costs, and thereby take advantage of externalities, in order to maintain or strengthen their competitive position. Incentive payment structures for managers may operate in the same direction. However, the outcome is not socially efficient because the company's production costs are artificially lowered. It follows from this analysis that efficiency from a societal point of view requires some mechanism whereby externalised costs are required to be taken into account by the company when calculating its production costs.[59]

However, the economists' discussion does not investigate the existence of any counter-incentives to managers robotically taking advantage of any externalisation opportunities that arise. In this they are followed by many human rights and environmental activists. In the area under discussion, there may in fact be constraints on the willingness of senior management of large companies simply to trample on the human rights of others or to degrade the environment in the name of operational efficiency. The weight of these countervailing incentives needs to be assessed if the optimal legal rules in this area are to be designed.

[58] Section 54(12).

[59] As Coase famously pointed out, in a world of zero transaction costs that mechanism could simply be the law of contract: those harmed and those inflicting the harm would simply bargain about how the costs of the harm should be allocated amongst them (R Coase, 'The Problem of Social Cost' (1960) III *Journal of Law and Economics* 1).

Recent research from the United States shows that large US companies have introduced policies and procedures designed to secure the company's compliance with international conventions the United States has never signed or, during Mr Trump's presidency, was in the business of resiling from.[60] While this research does not establish the effectiveness of the policies introduced, the research suggests that large companies are not indifferent to their impact on human rights and the environment. The research further suggests that the two main explanations for the adoption by large US companies of non-binding international standards lie in the areas of reputation and risk management. As to risk management, as indicated above, breaches of the international standards are likely to count as independent torts in the jurisdictions where the company operates, so that compliance with the standards reduces the risks of such litigation. Second, and more interesting, are the reputational reasons for the steps taken. Directors and senior managers of large public companies are not likely to want to view themselves or to be viewed by others as trampling on human rights or degrading the environment; talented employees may be less willing to work for companies with a bad reputation in these areas; increasingly investors are interested in the performance of their company along non-financial dimensions as well as along financial ones, as witnessed by the rise in 'ESG' funds;[61] and customer-facing companies may suffer a backlash from consumers if their record in these areas is poor. Moreover, provided competing companies comply with the international standards, the market position of any one company is not necessarily undermined by adherence to them.

The EU's Regulatory Scrutiny Board, when delivering a (second) negative opinion on the Commission's proposal, criticised the Commission for not exploring this line of argument. The Board stated that:

> The problem description remains vague. … It does not provide convincing evidence that EU businesses … do not already reflect sustainability aspects or do not have sufficient incentives to do so.[62]

If supported, this argument does not remove the case for the use of law to promote compliance with international standards in these areas, but it does point in the direction of providing incentives for companies to comply voluntarily with the international standards ('nudging'), perhaps via mandatory disclosure of corporate policies, whilst reserving liability for cases where the company has not in fact implemented

[60] O Hathaway, C Ewell and E Nohle, 'Has the Alien Tort Statute Made a Difference?' (2022) 107 *Cornell Law Review* 1205; K Parella, 'International Law in the Boardroom' (2023) 108 *Cornell Law Review* 839.

[61] See W-G Ringe, 'Investor Led Sustainability in Corporate Governance', ECGI Law Working Paper 615/2021 (also available in (2022) 7 *Annals of Corporate Governance* 93) for a review of the data on ESG investing and the argument that bottom-up investor pressure is a better mechanism for fostering corporate sustainability than top-down legislation.

[62] *Regulatory Scrutiny Board Opinion, Proposal for a Directive … on Sustainable Corporate Due Diligence and amending Directive (EU) 2019/1937*, SEC(2022) 95, 26.11.2021, 1; available at https://eur-lex.europa.eu/legal-content/EN/TXT/PDF/?uri=PI_COM:SEC(2022)95 (accessed 16 October 2023).

adequately its adopted policies. Authoritative guidance on what compliance entails in the human rights area already exists in the shape of the UN's *Guiding Principles on Business and Human Rights*,[63] and the OECD's *Due Diligence Guidance for Responsible Business Conduct* (2018),[64] which are linked to the OECD's *Guidelines for Responsible Business Conduct* (2011),[65] while liability for non-compliance with adopted policies is a task that, as we have seen, national tort law is already undertaking. Nevertheless, civil society groups generally regard this approach as too lax and they succeeded in persuading both the Human Rights Council of the UN and the EU Commission not to adopt it.[66]

B. How to Cope with State Complicity in Human Rights Abuses?

In the previous section it has not been argued that there have never occurred significant breaches of human rights and environmental standards in which companies are involved nor that such breaches will never occur in the future. However, it is not often noticed or remarked upon that many of the most highly distressing, widespread and difficult-to-fix human rights cases have a common feature. This common feature is that the host state where the wrongdoing has occurred is complicit in the abuses, and perhaps even initiated them. Although putting the emphasis the other way around, the Ruggie Report for the UN Human Rights Council made this same factual point. Having surveyed the worst allegations of corporate-related human rights harm, it reported that 'a significant fraction of the allegations involved companies being complicit in the acts of government or armed factions'.[67]

The reported cases from around the world give support to this statement. In *Kiobel v Royal Dutch Petroleum Co*,[68] the allegation was that the Nigerian government engaged in violent suppression of Nigerian communities protesting against pollution resulting from a pipeline operated by Shell. (The US Supreme Court held the claim did not fall within the Alien Torts Statute.) In *Nevsun Resources Ltd v Araya*,[69] the Supreme Court of Canada refused to strike out (but did not substantively decide) a claim that Nevsun had breached the human rights of Eritrean citizens who had been subject to a system of forced labour in the construction and operation

[63] United Nations, Office of the High Commissioner on Human Rights, 2011 (HR/PUB/11/04). This was the UN's first formal response to the Ruggie Report (n 49) and is not to be confused with the binding Treaty which the Working Group of the Human Rights Council has been developing (n 51).

[64] See mneguidelines.oecd.org/mneguidelines/ (accessed 27 September 2023).

[65] These can be found at: https://doi.org/10.1787/9789264115415-en (accessed 27 September 2023).

[66] Given the origin of the proposed Directive in the UN Human Rights Committee's working group, this is perhaps not a surprising stance. The non-state members of that working group, of which there are many, are overwhelmingly human rights NGOs, with whom the reputational and risk avoidance arguments mentioned above probably carry little weight. For the list of members see the Annex to the minutes of the 49th Session of the Human Rights Council, 2022 (A/HRC/49/65).

[67] Above (n 49) para 16.

[68] *Kiobel v Royal Dutch Petroleum Co* 569 US 108 (2013), US Supreme Court.

[69] *Nevsun Resources Ltd v Araya* 2020 SCC 5, [2021] 1 SCR 166.

of a mine operated by the defendant, and that this breach of customary international law was justiciable in the Canadian courts. The forced labour system took the form of a mandatory national service programme operated by the government, under which workers were supplied to those constructing and operating the mine. The construction companies were owned and operated by persons who were part of the political and social elites of Eritrea. It seems likely that the governments in both these cases were prepared to commit these abuses against their own citizens because they regarded the multinational investment as essential to the development of their economy and to the government's revenues. In addition, the government and individuals closely associated with it had a significant economic interest in the business, through an equity stake in the group's local operations held by a host state-owned company (which is common) or through lucrative contracts linked to the multinational's business.

In other cases, the harm was not initiated by the host state; but that state failed in its duty to maintain law and order. In *Okpabi v Royal Dutch Shell*[70] (UK Supreme Court), the claim by the local communities was that their drinking water had been contaminated by spills from a pipeline operated by a Nigerian subsidiary. The spills were apparently the result of sabotage and other criminal acts by third parties, which the state had not prevented and perhaps even in some part condoned. In *AAA v Unilever*[71] (English Court of Appeal), the claim arose out of a national breakdown of law and order and widespread inter-tribal violence, during which employees of the defendant, living and working on tea plantations, suffered violent personal attacks.

The difficult question these stark cases raise is: what is it appropriate to require the company to do in response? On the one hand, it is not appropriate to permit the company to turn a blind eye to the abuses simply because they result from the action or inaction of the host state. On the other hand, bringing them to an end on a permanent basis or even significantly moderating them is likely to require the resetting of embedded political and social structures in the host state, something it is unlikely the company has either capacity or the legitimacy to bring about by itself. In a few rare cases, the company's threat of exit will give it the necessary leverage to bring about a change in the host state's behaviour. Generally, however, there will be a competitor, either local or based in a home state with a different view of human rights, which is willing, indeed anxious, to replace the incumbent, acquiring its assets at a discounted price.

In the absence of such leverage, the incumbent will be faced with the choice between actual exit, and remaining and exercising voice, which, given the limitations on the company's leverage, will probably produce a less than complete remediation of the abuses. If one runs the facts of the above cases through Article 8 of the proposed Directive, it is far from clear what analysis the supervisory bodies or courts of the Member States would apply. There is some general language in Article 8 upon which the company could seek to rely to justify the (limited) extent of its reaction, such that

[70] Above n 16.
[71] Above n 14.

the company is required to take only 'appropriate measures' to bring actual adverse impacts to an end or to minimise them; or to take mitigating measures only to the extent that they are 'proportionate' to the 'contribution of the company's conduct to the adverse impact'. However, it will be very difficult for the company to judge ex ante how supervisors or courts will make the judgements inherent in these tests, whilst the mere fact of litigation, even if the company is successful, may entail a reputational harm that the board assesses as too severe for the company.

Thus, companies are likely to favour exit in this class of case. It is true that Articles 7 and 8 require exit only as a 'last resort' and do not require it at all when 'there is a reasonable expectation that the termination would result in an adverse impact that is more severe than' the actual or potential adverse impact that would exist if the company remained (Articles 7(7) and 8(8)). But, as a commercial matter, exit is always available to companies, even when not required by the proposed Directive. The reactions of some of the companies involved in the above litigation suggests that exit will often be the most attractive of the available options. Thus, Unilever, although winning the case against it in the English Court of Appeal, shortly afterwards decided to dispose of its tea plantations and associated brands to a private equity company. According to an analysis in the *Financial Times*[72] this was because Unilever feared the reputational harm it would suffer if it held onto them and, in particular, a downgrading of its ESG ratings, risks to which the private equity purchaser was thought to be less exposed. Equally, the decision by Shell, which has faced litigation in both the UK and the Netherlands, to exit its onshore oil production activities in Nigeria (but to retain the offshore ones) was apparently driven in part by a desire to reduce the reputational harm it was suffering from repeated litigation.[73] There is nothing in either company's actions which suggests that, in the first case, the risk of harm to the employees from intercommunal conflict or, in the second, of environmental degradation from the pipeline will be reduced by the exit.

An alternative, albeit probably less likely, form of exit, would be for the (parent) company to exit from the state in which it faces liability. In the wake of the judgment on jurisdiction, Vedanta Resources plc delisted from the London Stock Exchange in October 2018 when its Indian controlling shareholder and founder bought out the minority shareholders.[74] The company remains incorporated and so domiciled in England (though now as a private company) and so is still open to tort suits brought against it by foreign claimants. However, it is no longer subject to the disclosure requirements of the Companies Act, because it is no longer 'quoted', or of the Listing Rules, so that such litigation will be more difficult to mount. (The company itself explained the decisions as part of a plan to simplify the

[72] 'How Unilever's Tea Business Became a Test of Private Equity's Conscience', *Financial Times* 16 February 2022. However, the private equity buyer was reported shortly afterwards as seeking to dispose of the plantation: 'CVC explores sale of troubled Kenyan tea plantation', *Financial Times* 10 August 2023.

[73] The CEO of Shell is reported to have said: 'We cannot solve community problems in the Niger Delta – that's for the Nigerian government perhaps to solve. … We can do our best, but at some point in time, we also have to conclude that this is an exposure that doesn't fit with our risk appetite any more.' 'Nigerians Blame Shell for "Community Problems" in Niger Delta', *Financial Times*, 1 April 2022.

[74] 'Vedanta's London Exit Fails to Stem Scrutiny of Indian Miner', *Financial Times*, 17 October 2018.

group structure.) This was a relatively low-cost step for the company to take. The overwhelming bulk of its operations are located outside the United Kingdom and so its presence in London was mainly for financing purposes. However, the parent holds a majority stake in a Mumbai-listed company which, with the development of Indian capital markets, can be used as a possibly better-informed conduit for the company's financing needs.[75]

In my view, litigation and straight-down-the-line supervisory action are unlikely to bring about a satisfactory forward-looking resolution to these deep-seated problems. Indeed, in some cases litigation may impede more promising efforts aimed at addressing the underlying problems. In *Nestlé USA Inc v Doe*,[76] the US Supreme Court was presented with an Alien Tort Statute claim against the US subsidiary of Nestlé, arising out of the use of child labour on cacao farms in the Ivory Coast. Nestlé neither owned nor operated the farms, but had an exclusive supply contract with the farm operators. It was accused of aiding and abetting the use of child labour. The US Supreme Court turned down the claim on the grounds that the harm had occurred outside the United States and the supply contract was not enough to implicate the US company in the wrongdoing. Assume, however, the same facts but involving an EU subsidiary of Nestlé after the enactment of the proposed Directive. The EU subsidiary would fall within the Directive and so be required to discharge its obligations under Articles 6–8 of the Directive. It would be at significant risk of administrative fines and civil damages because of its involvement with the produce of the cacao farms. Yet, this would be a counterproductive outcome. A significant background fact in this case – which was legally irrelevant to the litigation, except that it caused the US government to support Nestlé – is that there was in place a partnership agreement between the US Department of Labor, the government of the Ivory Coast and the company, aimed at resetting the economics of cacao production in the country. As part of its partnership, Nestlé supplied various resources and training to the farmers. As some of the Justices commented, these were 'the same kinds of activity that respondents contend make petitioners liable for violations of international law. Companies or individuals may be less likely to engage in intergovernmental efforts if they fear those activities will subject them to private suits.'

If exit is to be a true last resort for companies covered by the proposal, what is needed is an inducement for companies to exercise voice rather than exit, when voice is likely to be more effective than exit in addressing human rights violations. But however hard one looks, no such safe-harbour provisions are to be found in the Commission's proposal. In fact, Article 18(4) specifically rules out protection against supervisory sanctions and private litigation when the company engages in remedial

[75] The Zambian mine at the heart of the litigation was later expropriated by the Zambian government. 'Investors Rattled by Takeover of Zambian Mining Operation', *Financial Times*, 18 February 2022). But Vedanta appears recently to have reacquired control of the mine after it struggled operationally under state control and under the threat of litigation.' Vedanta to take back ownership of Zambian copper mine', *Financial Times*, 5 September 2023.

[76] *Nestlé USA Inc v Doe* 141 S Ct 1931 (2021).

action after being found in breach. It is not as if the Commission's attention was not drawn to the point by the Regulatory Scrutiny Board (again). As the Board put it, the Commission

> should better assess the risk of 'sustainability leakage'. If EU companies will ultimately have to withdraw from certain suppliers due to sustainability issues, third-country companies (if out of the personal scope) could take over these suppliers and thereby gain a competitive advantage and supply chain control, while leaving no improvement in overall human rights and environmental performance.[77]

There is thus scope for a Morton's fork argument here. In the standard case, the reputational pressures on management and companies make the adoption of rules on due diligence as strong as those contained in the proposed Directive a form of overkill, whereas, when the host state lies at the origin of the abuses, corporate liability rules generate exit by the company without improving the lot of those suffering from them.

VI. CONCLUSION

This chapter has argued that UK law has moved away from the position where the parent was not liable for the subsidiary's torts because the tort victims of the subsidiary could not pierce the corporate veil of the subsidiary so as to make the shareholder (the parent company) liable. Now, under domestic tort law, depending on the degree of control exercised by the parent over the risky activities of the subsidiary, the parent may owe a direct duty of care to those harmed by the subsidiary's activities. The EU proposal would make the parent liable to those harmed if the parent has not exercised the level of control over risky activities the court or a regulator thinks it should have exercised, so that the parent's freedom of action in this regard is narrowed.

Consequently, in this area, through both tort and regulatory developments, the rule against veil piercing and, *pro tanto*, asset partitioning between the parent and the subsidiary has been sidestepped. Arden LJ (as she then was), as a leading judicial voice in the company law area, was alive to the company law implications of the Court of Appeal's decision in *Chandler*, which set the UK courts off on this new tack. She said, 'I would emphatically reject any suggestion that this court is in any way concerned with what is usually referred to as piercing the corporate veil. A subsidiary and its company [*sic*] are separate entities.' Although this statement is doctrinally clearly correct, it does not meet the functional point. The decision did restrict the scope of the limited liability of the parent for the subsidiary's wrongdoing, and thus the partitioning of the assets as between parent and subsidiary. In the specified circumstances, the company is now directly liable for the harm caused by the wrongdoing of the subsidiary by virtue of a control failure on the part of the parent. The separate legal personalities of the parent and

[77] Above n 62, 4.

subsidiary are maintained, but the victims of the subsidiary's wrongdoing now have access to the assets of the parent to satisfy their claims. In other words, asset partitioning requires more than the maintenance of the separate legal personalities of the parent and the subsidiary. After all, if the subsidiary were routinely treated as an agent of the parent – this was one of the arguments unsuccessfully advanced in *Adams v Cape* – the separate legal personalities of the parent and subsidiary would be maintained (indeed, agency doctrine demands this) but functionally the parent would routinely be liable for the obligations of its subsidiary.

Does the above mean that, under either the domestic developments or the EU proposals, we have moved, almost without realising it, to accepting the qualifications to asset partitioning which law and economic scholars have advocated for some time? The answer is clearly in the negative. Hansmann and Kraakman's argument[78] for unlimited, pro-rata shareholder liability for corporate torts was advanced mainly on the basis of an analysis of free-standing companies, whereas the domestic and EU developments have their core application in relation to groups of companies, though both to a limited extent have an application outside groups. Despite these extensions, the crucial point from the perspective of unlimited liability for corporate torts is that, if a parent company falls foul of either the domestic rules or the EU proposals, there is nothing in them which removes the limited liability protection of the shareholders of *that* company.[79] The rules are about expanding corporate liability for torts and breaches of international standards committed by other entities over which the company has exercised, or could have exercised, some relevant level of control, not about the implementation of a general policy of shareholder liability for corporate torts.

This might suggest that the rules considered in this chapter score more highly as an implementation of the proposal by Hansmann and Squires[80] for qualifying limited liability, ie a more open approach on the part of the courts to piercing the corporate veil within groups. Quite apart from the fact that the rules considered in this chapter do not make use of the doctrine of piercing the veil, the more important point is that Hansmann and Squires were proposing a qualification in relation to all the debts of the subsidiary, not only those arise out of tortious liability. So the rules under consideration are in part only a partial implementation of the Hansmann and Squires proposal as well – although in another part the EU proposal goes beyond what these two authors envisaged because its reach extends all the way down the company's supply chain.

In short, the rules considered in this chapter require, at least in the overwhelming majority of case, the presence of both the factors which, it has been suggested, should qualify limited liability, ie both (serious) tort liability and a group (or a network) context. Although more limited in scope than either of the academic papers would indicate, the proposals (it can be argued) nevertheless achieve an important social

[78] Above n 3.
[79] Unless tort liability is developed in the way envisaged by Lim (n 15).
[80] Above n 4.

function. They discourage the allocation of hazardous activities to undercapitalised or litigation-proof entities in a supply chain, and encourage the parent to reflect on what it can do to avoid or mitigate the harms resulting from the allocation.

Judged as techniques for discouraging externalities, the EU proposals on their face do a better job than the domestic tort law developments, even though the EU proposals relate, formally, to a somewhat smaller set of wrongs than do the domestic rules. Two elements in the EU proposals are important here:

(1) The domestic tort rules leave the parent company in a position where it can avoid liability by not exercising – or purporting to exercise – control over the hazardous aspects of the subsidiary's activities. The EU proposals require top companies to exercise control over subsidiaries which are part of the top company's chain of business relations. However, in practice, this distinction may be less important than it seems at first sight, because the reputational and regulatory pressures on top companies to exercise control over subsidiaries, or to assert that they do so, may generate tort liability, even in the absence of a formal due-diligence duty.

(2) On the face of it, the EU rules take a broader view of the scope of the top company's duty to exercise control because it expressly includes within the due-diligence duty the hazardous activities of contractors, direct and indirect, as well as those of subsidiaries. This extension is somewhat diluted by provisions which exempt the company from liability for damage caused by contractors.[81] Nevertheless, the principle of extension of the due-diligence duty so as to embrace contractors is important because there is some evidence that, without it, companies are incentivised to engage in further level of delegation, beyond subsidiaries, to contractors.[82] Again, it is possible that this contrast with the tort rules is less important than it seems. The *Maran* decision explicitly embraces contractors within its limited scope. Additionally, reputational and disclosure rules may put pressure on companies to control the hazardous activities of contractors and, if they do or hold themselves out as so doing, the theory underlying parental tort liability in relation to subsidiaries may apply to contractors as well. The parent would then fall, in relation to the contractor, into the same category as the consultant identified by Sales LJ.[83]

The choice between the direct tort and due-diligence duties is likely to turn on two factors. The first is the strength of the incentives on group management to comply with human rights and environmental standards, even where they are not directly binding on the company. We have suggested that these incentives are stronger than is commonly acknowledged. The second is the capacity of regulators and courts to apply the due-diligence obligation appropriately in the common and very distressing cases where the host state is a prime mover in the abuses that have taken place.

[81] Text at n 57 above.

[82] See A Pacces, 'Supply Chain Liability in the Corporate Sustainability Due Diligence Directive Proposal', Oxford Business Law Blog, 20 April 2022, www.law.ox.ac.uk/business-law-blog/blog/2022/04/supply-chain-liability-corporate-sustainability-due-diligence (accessed 27 September 2023).

[83] Text at n 15 above.

The risk here of blunt application of the due-diligence law is that it will result in exit from host states by companies whose parents are subject to the due-diligence obligation rather than any significant alleviation of the position of those abused. Of course, this risk attaches, as we have seen, to tort liability, but at least tort law develops incrementally, through a form of judicial conversation, which provides greater scope for backtracking if a misstep seems to have occurred. Courts are experienced at shaping the content of a reasonableness obligation so as to take account of the complexities of the situation in which the tortfeasor finds itself. Even judicially developed standards, however, do not entirely negate the reputational pressures on companies to exit, rather than to remedy, difficult situations, even when they win the litigation, as the *AAA* case demonstrates. To some extent, however, those reputational pressures exist independently of the company's exposure to liability and, for better or for worse, are part of the environment for the conduct of modern business, at least in Western countries.

6

Networks as a Legal Concept: Mythical Beast No More?

HUGH COLLINS*

I. THE LEGAL IDEA OF A NETWORK

IN ABOUT 1990, several scholarly papers were published about business networks. Two famous examples had the titles 'Neither Market nor Hierarchy: Network Forms of Organisation' and 'Neither Friends nor Strangers: Informal Networks of Subcontracting in French Industry'.[1] The papers were published within the disciplines of sociology, economics and business studies. It is striking that both of those influential papers began their titles with the word 'Neither'. The scholars were clear that they were describing a new (or perhaps revived) form of business organisation. Both advanced a similar claim: the laws and practices used for coordinating productive activities not only include markets (ie contracts) and firms (ie corporations, partnerships and other kinds of business associations), but also include a new kind of business undertaking that they called a network. Unfortunately, these theorists of business structures were unable to provide a precise definition of the core features of a network and the business practices they described seemed rather diverse.[2] Adding to the confusion, the terminology of networks shortly afterwards became fashionable in many disciplines, from anthropology to neurology, as we entered what Castells called the 'Network Society'.[3]

* I am grateful for comments on an earlier draft from many members of the private law discussion group at LSE, and to participants at the workshop 'Law at the Cutting Edge', especially Lord Burrows, Lord Leggatt, Sir Marcus Smith and Rob Stevens.

[1] W W Powell, 'Neither Market nor Hierarchy: Network Forms of Organisation' (1990) 12 *Research in Organisational Behaviour* 295; E H Lorenz, 'Neither Friends nor Strangers: Informal Networks of Subcontracting in French Industry' in D Gambetta (ed), *Trust: Making and Breaking of Cooperative Relations* (Oxford, Blackwell, 1989) 194.

[2] The term 'network' has been applied, for instance, to industrial districts and science parks, but although networks in the more precise sense may flourish in such contexts, those locations are not in themselves networks for the purpose of legal analysis.

[3] M Castells, *The Rise of the Network Society* (Oxford, Blackwell, 2000).

In the context of studies of the organisation of businesses, the term 'network' gradually assumed a relatively precise meaning.[4] Network forms of business organisation were not contained in a single company or a group of companies with common ownership and control. A network comprises independently owned businesses that contract with each other at arm's length. There might be direct contracts between all the parties to a network, but often some business relationships within the network would rely on custom, practice and mutual dependence rather than any formal agreement. Yet these independent businesses within the network typically work together so closely that their relationship is very similar to an integrated business organisation or firm. All parties expect to cooperate closely and be loyal to the business relationships within the network and to the commercial purpose of the network.[5] The contracts within a network are closely connected in the sense that together they function interdependently to produce a business outcome such as a product or a service. The coordination between the performance of each contract is close, so that the functioning of these contracts resembles in some ways the types of command and control exercised by managers within a single integrated corporate entity, but the businesses and participants in the network remain separate legal entities that are free to act independently in their own interests by performing or breaking their contracts, as they decide. Two common instances of networks occur in supply chains and retail and distribution.[6]

In a supply chain or production network, the core business, perhaps a manufacturer or a major retailer, acquires raw materials, component products and items for retail sales through a supply chain of independent businesses. This chain might be global with many links. Superficially, the supply chain appears to be a collection of completely independent contracts between separate businesses dealing at arm's length. However, the core business cannot function efficiently without managing the supply chain from one end to the other in considerable detail. Each component part or item for the supermarket shelves must arrive just in time, be perfect and conform exactly to the specification fixed by the core business. That demand requires effective control over the whole chain. Managerial control is often achieved through computer links: as soon as a product is taken off the shelf or removed from the factory inventory, computerised ordering systems send detailed instructions for prompt fulfilment

[4] G Teubner, *Networks as Connected Contracts* (ed with an introduction by H Collins) (Oxford, Hart Publishing, 2011).

[5] This feature sometimes leads to a confusion between networks and relational contracts, where close cooperation and loyalty to the purpose of the contract is also present, but there is no necessary connection between bilateral relational contracts and multilateral networks of connected contracts.

[6] Legal theorists of business networks are unsure whether these different types of business organisation are really the same kind of thing at all, except of course, that they are all neither exactly market nor hierarchy. Compare the informal structure of networks in P Krebs and S Jung, 'Introductory Remarks on the Phenomenon of Business Networks and on this Volume' in S Jung, P Krebs and G Teubner (eds), *Business Networks Reloaded* (Baden Baden and Farnham, Nomos/Ashgate, 2015) 11, 15, with the organised hierarchical structures emphasised in S Grundmann, F Cafaggi and G Venturi (eds), *The Organisational Contract* (London, Routledge, 2020). A similar tripartite division is found in EM Weitzenboek, *A New Legal Framework for Emerging Business Models: Dynamic Networks as Collaborative Contracts* (Cheltenham, Edward Elgar, 2012) 5–9.

all along the supply chain.[7] Businesses along the supply chain may also try to control their own suppliers in similar ways.

A retail or distribution network typically assumes the form of a hub-and-spokes organisation. A business format franchise such as the burger restaurant Macdonald's is a typical example. Here, the core business enters into contracts with many independent businesses to retail goods and services in accordance with the successful retail formula. The control exercised by the core business or franchisor over its satellite contractors or franchisees is usually intense, including setting the prices they can charge to customers and specifying the presentation of the goods and services. That is why every Macdonald's restaurant run by a franchisee looks identical, sells the same products and offers much the same prices. A slightly looser framework for networks has been deployed in the gig economy in businesses such as Uber, where the core business operates through a large number of purportedly independent contractors, the drivers.

It is an interesting question why networks appear to have proliferated as a form of business organisation in recent decades. This development may be linked to such factors as the globalisation of the economy and the expansion of the service sector in postindustrial economies. Communications technology has clearly facilitated the rise of networks by reducing the transaction costs of coordination and by offering instantaneous messages. Many connect the rise of networks to their alleged superior potential to develop innovative products and services through their distinctive mixture of multilateral cooperation and competition.[8] It is argued that the independent businesses have greater freedom to experiment than if they were merely part of a large, vertically integrated business. At the same time, the need to cooperate with other businesses to further the project may create opportunities for mutual learning, dissemination of knowledge and fertile collaborations. The independent businesses may become highly specialised, but then use interfirm collaboration to develop new and more complex products and services. No doubt, there are many other explanations for the proliferation of networks as a form of business organisation.

Interesting as those theories may be, my question here is different: should networks be recognised as a legal concept that refers to a particular kind of business organisation? Like the idea of 'relational contracts', discussed in scholarly articles for many years,[9] the concept of a network has been mooted in law books and journals,

[7] H Collins, 'The Weakest Link: Legal Implications of the Network Architecture of Supply Chains' in M Amstutz and G Teubner, *Networks: Legal Issues of Multilateral Co-operation* (Oxford, Hart Publishing, 2009) 187.

[8] Li-Wen Lin and Josh Whitford, 'Conflict and Collaboration in Business Organisation: A Preliminary Study' in J Braucher, J Kidwell and W C Whitford (eds), *Revisiting the Contracts Scholarship of Stewart Macaulay* (Oxford, Hart Publishing, 2013) 191; R Gilson, C Sabel and R Scott, 'Braiding: The Interaction of Formal and Informal Contracting in Theory, Practice, and Doctrine' (2010) 110 *Columbia Law Review* 1377; P M Baquero, *Networks of Collaborative Contracts for Innovation* (Oxford, Hart Publishing, 2020).

[9] I Macneil, 'Contracts: Adjstment of Longterm Economic Relations Under Classical, Neoclassical and Relational Contract Law' (1978) 72 *Northwestern University Law Review* 854, and other works collected in I Macneil, *The Relational Theory of Contract: Selected Works of Ian MacNeil* (ed D Campbell) (London, Sweet & Maxwell, 2001); C Goetz and R Scott, 'Principles of Relational Contracts' (1981) 67 *Virginia Law Review* 1089; H Collins, 'Is a Relational Contract a Legal Concept?' in S Degeling, J Edelman and J Goudkamp (eds), *Contract and Commercial Law* (London, Thomson Reuters, 2016) 37.

but it has remained a theoretical entity, a non-existent mythical beast.[10] Now that the legal concept of a relational contract has been recognised in the common law of England,[11] the question arises whether the time has come for networks also to be mythical beasts no more. The main consequence of the legal recognition of the category of relational contracts has been the acceptance that relational contracts as a class contain a term implied by law that requires good faith in the performance of the contract.[12] My question here is: what might be the legal consequences of the recognition of networks in law?

Although there have been some judicial references to a network in an appropriate context,[13] the idea is not been imbued with any legal significance.[14] Since network is not yet a legal concept, it is not possible to illustrate the legal consequences that flow from its application. Instead, what I shall try to demonstrate is how legal reasoning becomes confused and contorted because it fails to acknowledge the presence and legal significance of a network. The legal reasoning goes wrong either in the sense that the result appears deeply unsatisfactory from a commercial point of view, or that the reasoning employs artificial and convoluted techniques, often involving fictions, to reach a commercially sensible result. My argument is that the network, though invisible to the legal mind, is like a goblin that disrupts the conventional rules of the common law and leads it into error and confusion.[15]

If the presence and significance of the network were acknowledged by the law, however, these errors and confusions might be avoided. Sometimes, the recognition of the presence of a network explains the need to make minor adjustments to the normal rules of contract law or to interpret the commercial arrangements in the light of the context of a network. In other cases, the legal consequence that flow from the recognition of a network may require the implication of a contract in order to regulate the commercial relationships in the way that was intended and makes sense within the relations of interdependent businesses. Finally, networks may provide a way of handling claims both for and against members of a network by treating it as a collective actor that makes it members jointly and severally liable.

This chapter proceeds by examining four situations where arguably the goblin has been present and tempted courts into paradoxical reasoning that seems to flout basic tenets of the common law. The argument in each case is that once the network becomes visible to legal reasoning, the solution that the law should supply becomes much clearer and the paradoxes can be resolved by reference to the concept of a

[10] R Buxbaum, 'Is "Network" a Legal Concept?' (1993) 149 *Journal of Institutional and Theoretical Economics* 698, 704.

[11] *Yam Seng Pte Ltd v International Trade Corporation Ltd* [2013] EWHC 111, [2013] 1 All ER (Comm) 1321; *Braganza v BP Shipping Ltd* [2015] UKSC 17, [2015] ICR 449.

[12] *Bates v Post Office (No 3)* [2019] EWHC 606; H Collins, 'Employment as a Relational Contract' (2021) *LQR* 426.

[13] eg the legal arrangements for the consumer's use of credit cards was described as a 'network' by Lord Mance in *Office of Fair Trading v Lloyds TSB Bank plc and others* [2007] UKHL 48, [2008] 1 AC 316 [23].

[14] The economic concept of 'network effects' is used in competition law, but the meaning of network is different in that context.

[15] A goblin is defined as a wandering sprite that is usually mischievous but often malicious: *Encyclopedia Britannica* (www.britannica.com/art/goblin (accessed 29 September 2023)). The word 'goblin' derives from the Greek *kobalos* ('rogue').

network. Often the courts reach the commercially sensible result, but their reasoning is hard to explain and justify without resort to fictions and inconsistences. It is contended that if the concept of a network were acknowledged by the law, it could provide a principled and coherent basis for achieving those appropriate results.

II. BATTLE OF FORMS AND THE INTERPRETATION OF CONTRACTS

Under the normal rules of contract law, the interpretation and legal enforcement of one contract is not affected by the existence of other separate contracts. Each contract is regarded as an autonomous entity. It is interpreted and enforced according to its terms. But in the context of a network such as a supply chain, the parties to a contract may have the expectation that the existence of the chain of contracts should have a bearing on how each contract should be interpreted. Since the contracts function interdependently, a reasonable expectation is that the interpretation of each contract in the network should bear in mind the content of relevant terms in the connected contracts. The contracts need to function harmoniously rather than interfere with the successful production scheme of the network. That need may guide the interpretation of a contract or require the implication of suitable terms that reflect the interdependence of contracts inside the network.

An example arises in the law of offer and acceptance in connection with the 'battle of forms'. In these cases, both parties claim that their own standard terms of business apply to a transaction. The general rule that emerges from the application of the classical analysis of offer and acceptance is that the 'last shot' wins. In other words, the party who last communicates that the contract will be on their terms will succeed in having their own terms govern the contract. That rule derives from an application of the classical rules of offer and acceptance, because the final offer or counteroffer is accepted by conduct. An exception will arise where it is clear on the evidence that the parties both intended a different outcome, although proof of such a common intent is difficult.

The question of whether an exception to the 'last shot' rule should be recognised arose in *Tekdata Interconnections Ltd v Amphenol Ltd*.[16] The context of the case was a lengthy supply chain comprising at least five independent businesses. Rolls Royce was the ultimate purchaser. It bought engine control systems from a company called Goodrich, which itself bought cable harnesses for internal wiring from Tekdata. In order to manufacture the harnesses, Tekdata purchased connectors from Amphenol. Amphenol in turn acquired electronic filters from further suppliers. Quality control and just-in-time delivery were essential aspects of all these business relations. A dispute arose between Tekdata and Amphenol about late delivery and defective quality. Tekdata claimed that the terms of the contract were fixed by its purchase order. However, in its response to the purchase order, Amphenol had put on its confirmation a statement that it accepted the order on its own standard terms of business, which excluded or limited liability. The Court of Appeal applied the 'last shot' rule to confirm that Amphenol's terms applied to the dispute.

[16] *Tekdata Interconnections Ltd v Amphenol Ltd* [2009] EWCA Civ 1209, [2010] 1 Lloyd's LR 357.

Unlike the judge at first instance, the Court of Appeal declined to attach any weight to the context of the transaction in a highly coordinated supply chain. For instance, Goodrich had instructed Tekdata that it must acquire all its supplies of connectors from Amphenol to a specification required by Goodrich and at a price determined by Goodrich. Furthermore, Goodrich had a direct contract with Amphenol pursuant to which Amphenol agreed to supply connectors to Tekdata for the price determined by Goodrich. Furthermore, the terms on which Goodrich contracted with Tekdata were almost identical to those issued by Tekdata to Amphenol. These business relations had persisted for more than twenty years. The judge at first instance was also impressed by the point that, of course, in this high-tech environment, where safety was paramount, every participant in the supply chain would expect to deliver on time in absolute conformity to the specifications, so that the exclusions contained in the standard terms of business relied upon by Amphenol were wholly inappropriate. The judge concluded that the parties could not have intended those exclusion clauses to apply, with the consequence that the case represented an exception to the 'last shot' rule based upon the common intention of the parties.

Instead of looking at the context of the supply chain, the Court of Appeal examined the contract in isolation. Network theory argues that this approach is a mistake. It gives almost no attention to the purpose of the network, the interdependence of the parties and their contracts, and how each should be loyal to the interests of the whole network. The most important party in this case was really Goodrich, which was not a party to the contract in dispute, but which in effect forced the parties to contract with each other on terms and specifications largely fixed by Goodrich. It was the arrangements that Goodrich were seeking to make, themselves no doubt dictated by Rolls Royce, which were the crucial context of the case. It was therefore the terms of the Goodrich and Tekdata contracts which were the most significant ones for an interpretation of the contractual relation between Tekdata and Amphenol. The terms issued by Tekdata replicated those imposed by Goodrich. Tekdata was therefore right to assume that those terms governed its contract with Amphenol. What the Court of Appeal should have done is to recognise that in the context of a network like a supply chain, the battle of forms needs to be resolved in a different way because the terms of the contracts will almost certainly be driven by the requirements of the quasi-integrated system of production. As Catherine Mitchell has correctly observed about this case:

> [T]he stark error displayed in a case like Tekdata is to impose the discrete contract model on the network and regard an isolated instance of transacting as the prime focus of the legal analysis, ignoring the other aspects of the relationship and its 20-year history and the expectations amongst participants to which this would give rise.[17]

But the error of the Court of Appeal was not merely one of interpreting the contract out of context. The error was to apply the 'last shot' rule in a closely integrated

[17] Catherine Mitchell, *Contract Law and Contract Practice: Bridging the Gap between Legal Reasoning and Commercial Expectation* (Oxford, Hart Publishing, 2013) 59.

network. The 'last shot' rule must be ignored in the context of supply chains, because the terms of the purchase order are the commercially significant rules for the transaction. A different rule should be applied to the battle of forms in a supply chain network: the buyer's terms should govern the transaction whatever may have been the history of the exchange of the boilerplate. If that rule is ignored for the sake of the theoretical purity of conformity to the search for consensus during the battle of forms, the result will be disruption to integrated supply chains that will lead to inefficiency and commercially undesirable results.

III. IMPLIED TERM OF EQUITABLE TREATMENT BETWEEN MEMBERS OF THE NETWORK

In a second example of network theory, we should consider implied terms that may arise in contracts within the network. A particular term may not satisfy the orthodox test of business necessity if one focuses solely on the isolated contract in question. Yet if the context is expanded to include the operations of the whole network and its business model, it may be appropriate to imply terms that conform to the business logic of the network form of organisation. For example, there may be a need for an implied term that requires equal treatment or the absence of discrimination between different members of a network. This implied term is likely to arise in business format franchises and distribution networks.

For instance, in a distribution network of petrol stations, the oil company usually owns some petrol stations, but most are run by independent businesses according to a business format franchise or 'solus agreement'. These businesses take a lease of the premises and manage the operation according to strict instructions from the oil company concerning appearance, services, sources of oil products and prices at the pump. Each franchise is technically a separate contract between the franchisor and the franchisee. According to the classical law of contract, the content of the obligations and the performance of each franchise contract are strictly separate, with no bearing on the others. Network theory suggests, however, that because all the different franchisees depend on each other, as well as on the franchisor, for the successful functioning of the business model, it would be an error not to give weight to the connected contracts that surround each franchise agreement.

For example, in *Shell UK Ltd v Lostock Garages*[18] the context was a glut of petrol resulting from a major price increase imposed by the OPEC cartel. Lostock, a small garage, was compelled to charge 75p a gallon to customers because it was tied by a 'solus agreement' to Shell for supplies, whereas other independent garages could obtain cheaper supplies and remain profitable at a pump price of 70p a gallon. Two other Shell garages operated nearby and both of those were also able to sell at 70p a gallon because Shell provided them with rebates. One of those garages was directly owned by Shell. Lostock Garage sought to break the solus agreement that tied it to Shell. It claimed that Shell's conduct in discriminating against Lostock in its prices

[18] *Shell UK Ltd v Lostock Garage Ltd* [1977] 1 All ER 481, [1976] 1 WLR 1187.

and rebates was either contrary to the restraint-of-trade doctrine or a breach of an implied term. Lord Denning MR held that the restraint-of-trade doctrine invalidated the contract even though it seemed that when the agreement was formed it was reasonable and compatible with public policy. Here is the goblin at work: refashioning the doctrine of restraint of trade to function as a technique for ensuring fairness in contracts. In contrast, Bridge LJ held that there was an implied term in the contract that Shell would not discriminate against Lostock in the rebates it offered for the purpose of permitting them to compete with independent petrol stations. Price discrimination was a repudiatory breach of the implied term if it rendered it commercially impracticable to continue the franchise arrangement according to its express terms. Here the goblin finds a way to make conduct permitted by the express terms of the contract – the discretionary setting of rebates – a repudiatory breach of contract. On either view (both rejected by Ormrod LJ as contrary to the law), Lostock was entitled obtain cheaper supplies elsewhere, because it was no longer bound by the solus agreement.

Today, we might say that the franchisor was in breach of an implied term of good faith in performance that arose in this kind of relational contract when it discriminated against a particular franchisee in a way that was bound to put it out of business, thereby defeating the purpose of the franchise.[19] From the point of view of network theory, what Bridge LJ correctly appreciated is that the franchisor's treatment of other franchisees is relevant to the question of whether it is in breach of a good-faith requirement in a particular franchise contract. Unless the franchisor treats each franchisee fairly and does not discriminate in favour of its directly owned retail outlets, it will undermine the purpose and structure of the franchise operation as a network of connected contracts. In this example, legal recognition of the concept of a network would have explained why the conduct of the franchisor was a breach of the implied term of good faith even though the franchisor acted within its express rights under the contract. In networks, an implied obligation of good faith requires a hub business to treat its retail outlets equitably.

IV. IMPLIED CONTRACTS IN NETWORKS

Earlier it was noted that networks are comprised of functionally interdependent contracts, but it was also observed that not all of its members are joined by express contracts. In a supply chain, as we observed in the Rolls Royce case, although each link in the chain is formed by a contract, there may or may not be direct contracts between different participants in the chain. Similarly, in the hub-and-spokes model of retail distribution, there may not be direct contractual links between the different spokes. The absence of direct contracts between some parties to the network can be accounted for by the cost of formalising those relationships combined with an assumption that no such contracts are necessary when the network is functioning well. When something goes wrong, however, the absence of a direct contractual relationship to govern the risks requires a legal intervention.

[19] eg *Yam Seng* (n 11); *Bhasin v Hrynew* [2014] SCC 71, [2014] 3 SCR 494.

Carriage of goods by sea has sometimes provoked this issue. In a typical transaction, an owner of goods enters a bill of lading with a carrier to transport goods by sea to the destination required by the buyer or consignee. The carrier enters into a contract with a stevedore company to unload the goods at their destination port. The contract between the owner of the goods and the carrier includes a limitation-of-damages clause. A similar limitation-of-damages clause is contained in the contract between carrier and stevedore. If the goods are damaged by the stevedores, the owner may claim damages for the loss of the goods in the tort of negligence. There is no direct contract between the stevedores and the owner of the goods. As illustrated by *Scruttons Ltd v Midland Silicones Ltd*,[20] the doctrine of privity of contract holds that as a third party the stevedores cannot take the benefit of the limitation-of-damages clause in the contract between owner and carrier; nor can the stevedores rely on the limitation-of-damages clause in their contract with the carrier, because the owner of the goods cannot be subject to a burden in a contract to which it is not a party. The result that the owner of the goods can claim full compensation from the stevedores is commercially unsatisfactory, for it subverts the intended scheme of risk allocation for the loss of the goods as evidenced in the bill of lading, which is no doubt backed up with insurance arrangements.

Network theory suggests instead that where functionally interdependent contracts are connected in a production chain, as in the example of carriage of goods by sea, contracts should be implied, where appropriate, to complete the intended allocation of risks. On that view, there is a contract between the stevedores and owners of the goods that limits their liability when unloading the goods. The implied contract serves the functional purpose of the network, although it may not be strictly necessary for the network to operate. In the absence of such a legal concept of a network and a willingness to imply contracts to serve its purpose, the goblins quickly got to work to try to reconcile legal doctrine with the commercially sensible result.

Picking up on a suggestion by Lord Reid, the drafters of contracts for the carriage of goods by sea constructed an artificial framework for conferring a benefit on the stevedores by means of a slightly fanciful agency relation. Using a so-called *Himalaya* clause,[21] the revised contract of carriage stated that the carrier, when entering the bill of lading as principal, also entered the contract as an agent for subcontractors such as the stevedores for the purpose of creating a collateral contract containing the limitation of liability clause. By a majority, the Privy Council accepted this device in *New Zealand Shipping Co Ltd v Satterthwaite & Co Ltd (The Eurymedon)*.[22] This result was achieved despite the points that the stevedores did not know about this arrangement and nor was it certain that they would be used by the carriers, so it was unclear how there could be the necessary authority conferred on the carriers by an unascertained principal.[23] Similarly, since the stevedores were ignorant of the collateral contract, it was hard to fit the facts into the requirements for an offer, acceptance and consideration. The acceptance and consideration for the collateral contract could

[20] *Scruttons Ltd v Midland Silicones Ltd* [1962] AC 446 (HL).

[21] Following the name of the ship involved in *Adler v Dickson* [1955] 1 QB 158 (CA).

[22] *New Zealand Shipping Co Ltd v Satterthwaite & Co Ltd (The Eurymedon)* [1975] AC 154 (PC).

[23] See *Southern Water Authority v Carey* [1985] 2 All ER 1077 (QB).

only be the act of unloading the goods which provided the acceptance and consideration for the stevedores' contract with the carrier. This rickety scaffolding of an artificial agency relationship creating a collateral contract was challenged in subsequent cases by seeking factual distinctions that undermined the plausibility of the fiction of agency. Lord Wilberforce discouraged this practice, because it was abundantly clear that there was a commercial need to confer the benefit of exemptions on stevedores and other subcontractors, even though they were not parties to the original bill of lading.[24] Finally, in *The Mahkutai*,[25] Lord Goff asked when the perhaps inevitable step should be taken of recognising in these cases 'a fully-fledged exception to the doctrine of privity contract', thus escaping from all the technicalities.[26] In other words, the goblin tempted the judges to create a bypass of privity of contract of uncertain dimensions and dubious legal reasoning.

This mischief-maker tempted other courts to take a different approach to the problem caused by the absence of direct contracts between parties to networks. When constructing a building, it is typically the case that a main contractor will subcontract out much of the work to specialist subcontractors, which in turn may allocate work to sub-subcontractors. Within this network of contracts, it is unlikely that there will be direct contracts between all the different parties. Nevertheless, there is an integrated scheme of production, with the main contractor at its core. The presence of the network should permit the implication of contracts in order to confer benefits on network participants in support of the functioning and commercial purpose of the network. In this context, however, the goblin tempted the courts to solve the commercial problem by rewriting the law of tort.

In *Norwich City Council v Harvey*,[27] a building contractor agreed with the owner to make major renovations to an existing building. The work of rewiring the building was subcontracted. Since the owner of the building already possessed comprehensive fire insurance, the terms of the main contract with the builder excluded liability for fire damage to the building during the construction work. When the building was damaged by a fire caused by the negligence of the electrical subcontractor, the doctrine of privity prevented the electrical subcontractor from taking advantage of the benefit of the exclusion clause in a defence to a claim in tort because it was not a party to the main contract. In order to avoid that result and uphold the commercially sensible solution of protecting the subcontractor from liability, the Court of Appeal resorted to drastic action. It claimed that it was dealing with a novel situation in the law of negligence, so it had to decide whether the imposition of a duty of care was just and reasonable. It held that an exclusion of liability for fire in the main contract made it inappropriate to impose a duty of care to prevent damage by fire owed by the subcontractor in the tort of negligence.[28] Although the result makes

[24] *Port Jackson Stevedoring Pty Ltd v Salmond & Spraggon (Australia) Pty Ltd (The New York Star)* [1981] 1 WLR 138 (PC) 144.

[25] *The Mahkutai* [1996] AC 650 (PC).

[26] A step taken in Canada in *London Drugs Ltd v Kuehne & Nagel International Ltd* (1992) 97 DLR 4th 261.

[27] *Norwich City Council v Harvey* [1989] 1 All ER 1180 (CA).

[28] If the further question arose of whether the exclusion clause was invalid under the Unfair Contract Terms Act 1977, the reasonableness test should consider the presence of the network as highly relevant

commercial sense, the legal reasoning seems unsound. Was this situation of burning down a building with blowtorch really a novel one where the existence of a duty of care was uncertain?[29] Was it appropriate to use the rules designed to control the extent of recovery for pure economic loss to prevent a duty of care arising for damage to property? Perhaps the legal reasoning would have been more orthodox if the subcontractors had relied on a defence of *volenti non fit injuria*, by using the exclusion clause in the main contract as the necessary expression of consent. The problems with that argument were both that it had been rejected implicitly in *Midland Silicones v Scruttons*,[30] and that on its face the contract term only conferred the immunity on the main contractor.

As well as distorting the normal rules governing the duty of care in negligence, it is possible that the goblin was at work at the Law Commission. The Contracts (Rights of Third Parties) Act 1999 tries to sort out some of the problems of networks, without, of course, ever mentioning that mythical beast. The Law Commission justified the need for reform primarily on the ground that the doctrine of privity sometimes thwarts the intentions of the parties to the contract.[31] Section 1(1)(a) permits a third party to enforce a contractual term where the contract expressly provides that he may. That reversal of *Tweddle v Atkinson*[32] is clearly justified as merely an enforcement of the express intentions of the parties. But the reform could not stop there, because it would not address the commercial problems arising in networks described above.[33] Section 1(1)(b) also permits a third party to enforce a contractual term where the contract merely 'purports to confer a benefit on him'. To tie down this exception to privity, the statute also requires the third party to be identified by name, as a member of a class, or as answering a particular description.[34] As has been observed by critics of the legislation, the reform may tackle some aspects of problems for third-party beneficiaries of contracts, but at the expense of uncertainty regarding what counts as a 'purported' benefit. To grant the third party a right may also flout the intentions of the parties to the contract, who might not have wanted to give any enforceable right to the third party.[35]

in the circumstances. An exclusion clause that might look unreasonable when examined from a bilateral contract point of view, might appear an efficient and fair allocation of risk when viewed within the context of the network as a whole: R Brownsword, 'Network Contracts Revisited' in Amstutz and Teubner (n 7) 31.

[29] Compare *Marc Rich & Co AG v Bishop Rock Marine Co Ltd* [1996] AC 211 (HL) in the context of carriage of goods by sea where the duty of care owed by a classification society was truly a novel situation and the duty of care was negatived by the context of the bill of lading and its inclusion of the elaborate code to govern the network provided by the Hague–Visby Rules scheduled to the Carriage of Goods by Sea Act 1971.

[30] As pointed out by Lord Simon, dissenting, in *New Zealand Shipping v Satterthwaite* (n 22).

[31] Law Commission, *Privity of Contract: Contracts for the Benefit of Third Parties* (Law Com No 242, Cm 3329, 1996).

[32] *Tweddle v Atkinson* (1861) 1 B&S 393, 121 ER 762.

[33] A Burrows, 'The Contracts (Rights of Third Parties) Act 1999 and its Implications for Commercial Contracts' [2000] *LMCLQ* 540, 542–46.

[34] Section 1(3).

[35] See M Chen-Wishart, *Contract Law*, 7th edn (Oxford, Oxford University Press, 2022) 176–77; R Stevens, 'The Contracts (Rights of Third Parties) Act 1999' (2004) 120 *LQR* 292. The weakness of the justification based on the intention of the parties is revealed by the reversal of the burden of proof in s 1(2): the promisor has to show that the parties did not intend the term to be enforceable by the third party.

These problems of uncertainty and unwanted third-party rights are arguably illustrated in *Chudley v Clydesdale Bank plc*.[36] The bank accepted a letter of instruction from a property investment company to put the money of investors into a segregated client account, where the funds could only be removed under specific conditions. The property investment company collapsed, its owners were imprisoned for fraud, and the bank manager (who had failed to set up the segregated client account) was dismissed for gross misconduct. As a third party to the letter-of-instruction contract, one client successfully sued the bank for having failed to segregate his investment, thereby causing loss of his capital. The Court of Appeal held that the letter of instruction purported to confer a benefit on the class of investors in the property company. It was unnecessary for the investors to have knowledge of the benefit at the time of the letter of instruction. Although this result probably fits an analysis based on networks, arguably it goes further than the claimed justification of the reform to prevent the frustration of the intentions of the parties to a contract. In its interpretation of the statute, the Court was perhaps tempted by the goblin to stretch its provisions to address the commercial problem presented by a network.

In each of these examples, it has been claimed that judges have been tempted to distort the application of the traditional rules of law to address the commercial needs of networks. One device was an artificial construction of a collateral contract created by a tenuous agency arrangement. Another device was the denial of a duty of care in tort for damage to property in a standard situation normally covered by the law of negligence. A third device was to find a purported benefit under the statute when arguably the bank was not trying to benefit third parties at all and certainly not intending to give these unknown persons rights. Although the legal reasoning is questionable, the outcomes of the judgments make commercial sense. Where business is being conducted through connected and interdependent contracts between several parties, as in networks, the absence of a direct contract between the parties may have to be remedied to fulfil the purpose of the network.

In contrast to those complex devices, a more straightforward solution is to imply a contract between the parties in order to fulfil the purpose of the network. That is the solution proposed by network theory. It is true that the implication of contracts runs up against the important principle of freedom of contract: no one should have a contract imposed on them without their consent. For this reason, the courts have insisted that they will only imply a contract where it is necessary to give business efficacy to the arrangements.[37] In practice, that test of necessity has proven to be a high hurdle that prevents the implication of a contract in a network, because it is evident that the network can function normally without the implication of such a contract.

[36] *Chudley v Clydesdale Bank plc* [2019] EWCA Civ 344, [2020] QB 284.

[37] Bingham LJ in *The Aramis* [1989] 1 Lloyds LR 213 (CA) 224: 'necessary … in order to give business reality to a transaction and to create enforceable obligations between parties who are dealing with one another in circumstances in which one would expect that business reality and those enforceable obligations to exist'.

In the case of temporary agency workers, for instance, an employment agency supplies a worker who has a contract with the agency under which the agency finds the worker jobs and agrees to pay wages when work has been performed. The agency also has a contract with its client or end-user to supply workers in return for a fee. Under the contract between agency and worker, the latter agrees to perform the job according to the instructions of the client/employer as if he or she were an employee of the client. There is no express contract between the client employer and the worker. Nor can such a contract be implied according to the Court of Appeal because it is not necessary to give business efficacy to the arrangements.[38] As a consequence, the worker normally cannot claim any employment law or discrimination law rights against the client employer. Accordingly, if a manager of the client employer uses racial abuse against the worker, the client employer cannot be liable for discrimination; in the absence of a contract between worker and employer, there is no legal responsibility under the law of discrimination.[39] Nor can the agency be vicariously liable for the actions of the manager, who is an employee of a different legal entity. There is no inkling in these decisions about agency workers that the theory of networks might justify the implication of a contract between agency workers and the end-user, so that the workers can avoid exclusion from basic employment law rights.

In the Supreme Court in *Uber BV v Aslam*,[40] however, a glimmer of network theory can perhaps be detected. In that case, the responsibility of the defendant Uber for the drivers' statutory rights such as the right to a minimum wage depended on a finding that the drivers had a contract of employment or a contract to perform services personally on behalf of the defendant. A major obstacle in the way of the claim was that Uber argued that it did not have contracts of this type with the drivers. There was a written contractual arrangement between the drivers and Uber BV, the Dutch holding company, which owned the app through which taxi rides were booked, but that contract purported only to be an agreement for the drivers' use of electronic services through the app, including payment services. There was another business, Uber London, a subsidiary of Uber BV, which held the legally necessary licence for private car hire services in London. That licence covered the drivers. To comply with the licensing regime, Uber London had to carry out various checks on the drivers. However, there was no written contract between Uber London and the drivers. There was a written contract, however, between passengers and Uber BV which was formed when they downloaded the app onto their phones. That contract explained that the only transportation contract which the passengers formed by using the app was with the driver, not Uber BV or Uber London. At most, it was claimed, Uber London acted as an intermediary or booking agent between driver and passenger. In the UK Supreme Court, the idea that Uber London acted as a booking agent for the drivers was rejected on the ground that the drivers had never actually or ostensibly conferred authority on Uber London to act as their agent. Instead, the court inferred from the

[38] *James v Greenwich London Borough Council* [2008] EWCA Civ 35, [2008] ICR 545.
[39] *Muschett v HM Prison Service* [2010] EWCA Civ 25, [2010] IRLR 451.
[40] *Uber BV and others v Aslam* [2021] UKSC 5, [2021] ICR 657.

evidence that there was an implied contract each time a driver accepted a booking that amounted to a contract to provide a service personally for Uber London.

One feature of this reasoning is that the Supreme Court implies a contract in order to hold Uber London responsible for infringements of statutory employment rights in circumstances where the only express contractual agreement was between the driver and Uber BV. Uber London claimed that such an implication was unnecessary for the business efficacy of the arrangements. The Court implied the contract by insisting that 'the nature of the relationship has to be inferred from the parties' conduct, considered in its relevant factual and legal context'.[41] The Court applied a kind of network analysis (without using the terminology of networks) when Lord Leggatt said:

> In these circumstances Uber London would have no means of performing its contractual obligations to passengers, nor of securing compliance with its regulatory obligations as a licensed operator, without either employees or subcontractors to perform driving services for it. Considered against this background, it is difficult to see how Uber's business could operate without Uber London entering into contracts with drivers (even if only on a per trip basis) under which the drivers undertake to provide services to carry out the private hire booking accepted by Uber London.[42]

In other words, for the network operation to provide the taxi service to customers, it was necessary to imply a contract between Uber London and the drivers for the personal performance of services. The implication was necessary because, without the implied contract, Uber could not comply with the relevant regulations, nor could it perform the contracts to provide a taxi that it entered into with customers through the app.

Network theory suggests that such implied contracts will be common in the context of networks where direct contracts between all the members are missing. The drivers' contracts for work were implied by the Supreme Court to fulfil the purpose of the network and to secure compliance with the licensing regime. Similarly, a collateral contract was implied in *New Zealand Shipping v Satterthwaite* to complete the network allocation of risk with respect to the cargo, although the reasoning used the fiction of agency to do so. Similarly, Lord Denning's brilliant dissenting judgment in the earlier case of *Scruttons v Midland Silicones*,[43] following the earlier reasoning of Scrutton LJ,[44] described the stevedores as 'agents' in a non-technical sense, in order to convey the point that the stevedores were functioning within an integrated scheme of contracts for the carriage of goods in which third parties were impliedly bound by the allocation of risks in the bill of lading.

To imply contracts within networks, the test should not be the current strict test of necessity. Instead, the test for the implication of contracts should be concerned

[41] ibid [45].
[42] ibid [56].
[43] *Scruttons Ltd v Midland Silicones Ltd* [1962] AC 446 (HL).
[44] *Mersey Shipping and Transport Co Ltd v Rea Ltd* (1925) 21 LlLR 375 (KB) 378. See also *Elder, Dempster & Co Ltd v Paterson, Zochonis & Co. Ltd* [1923] 1 KB 420 (CA), where Scrutton LJ, dissenting, applied the same principle to protect an 'agent', in that case the shipowner.

to achieve the purpose of the network as an efficient system of production according to its intended allocation of risks. In the carriage of goods by sea, the bill of lading serves as a framework agreement that regulates the risks and liabilities of all the parties involved in the network even if they do not have express contracts with the parties to the bill of lading. Those arrangements for the allocation of risks are best fulfilled by the implication of a direct contract between third parties and parties to the bill of lading. The carriage of goods could take place without such an implied contract, but the purpose of the network and its allocation of risks would be undermined. Similarly, the business model as a kind of booking agency envisaged by Uber has been successful the world over without the need to imply a contract with the driver. Yet the purpose of the network of providing taxi rides efficiently to customers under the protections afforded by a licensing system could only be achieved through the implication of a contract between drivers and Uber London, for the provision of their services personally. Contrary to the reasonable expectations of the allocation of risks in the network, without the direct contract for work, customers would not have any rights against Uber for failure to comply with the contract of hire and they would not be fully protected by the licensing regime. The scope of the production network and those participating in it would determine which third parties could take the benefit of implied contracts in their favour. The range of protection would extend to all those participating in the carriage of goods by sea or in the provision of taxi services. That scope of protection for third parties might also justify the protection of third-party investors for the failure of the bank to segregate their investments even though they were not direct clients of the bank.

V. THE PRINCIPLE OF TRANSFERRED LOSS AND THE NETWORK AS A COLLECTIVE ACTOR

In my last example of the goblin at work, the presence of a network of connected contracts may help to explain the otherwise mysterious principle of 'transferred loss'. The problem arises from a basic principle that a claimant can only be awarded damages for breach of contract for its own loss and not those of third parties. Thus, if all the loss has been suffered by a third party, the claimant or promisee should not be able to recover more than nominal damages. The idea of a claim for 'transferred loss' is one that permits the promisee to claim damages against the promisor for the third party's loss, a clear breach of the normal compensatory principle of damages. Lord Denning MR introduced the idea of transferred loss in *Jackson v Horizon Holidays*,[45] where he permitted the father of a family to claim damages for a disastrous holiday not only for himself but also for the bad experience of the members of his family. That decision was subsequently doubted or confined to its special facts, perhaps revealing a suspicion that the goblin had been at work again. Yet the idea of recovery for a third party's loss has been extended occasionally to commercial contexts.

[45] *Jackson v Horizon Holidays Ltd* [1975] 1 WLR 1468 (CA).

In the case of goods being transported by sea by a carrier, it is usually anticipated that the owner of the goods (the consignor) will transfer ownership to a consignee or buyer prior to the arrival of the goods at their destination. If the goods are damaged after transfer of ownership to the consignee on route, the consignee may have no direct contractual right of redress against the carrier. In *The Albazero*, Lord Diplock held that:

> [W]here it is in the contemplation of the parties that the proprietary interests in the goods may be transferred from one owner to another after the contract has been entered into and before the breach which causes loss or damage to the goods, an original party to the contract, if such be the intention of them both, is to be treated in law as having entered into the contract for the benefit of all persons who have or may acquire an interest in the goods before they are lost or damaged, and is entitled to recover by way of damages for breach of contract the actual loss sustained by those for whose benefit the contract is entered into.[46]

Subsequently, the question has arisen whether that decision represents a broader principle of uncertain scope, in which a promisee may claim damages for breach of contract when the losses fall on a third party even where the promisee is under no obligation to carry out the repairs or compensate the third party.[47] For the present, although the position is uncertain, the furthest that the Supreme Court has been prepared to go is to acknowledge obiter a principle that permits the promisee to recover damages for the third party's loss if the known objective of a transaction is to benefit a third party or a class of persons to which a third party belongs, and the anticipated effect of a breach will be to cause loss to that third party, and the third party suffers loss as the intended transferee of property affect by the breach.[48]

The theory of networks holds that where the contracts in this triangular relation are interconnected to such an extent that they are a quasi-integrated organisation, the normal rule that limits the promisee's damages to its own loss should be displaced. Since the network functions to a considerable extent as a single entity for its productive purpose, it should be permitted to defend its interest in the performance of contracts by its members or by external parties by permitting the promisee to claim damages on behalf of the network as a collective actor. The presence of a network should ensure that in some way the claimant is accountable to other members of the network for the allocation amongst them of any successful claim for damages.

To view a network as a collective actor approximates to treating it in some respects as having a legal personality. The promisee can claim damages on behalf of all members of the network because they owe each other express and implicit obligations to further the purpose of the network. The principle of transferred loss in *The Albazero* functions in accordance with this interpretation of network theory. The consignor can sue for the losses to the consignee caused by damage to the goods sold because the purpose of the network was to transfer property under a regime that

[46] *The Albazero* [1977] AC 774 (HL) 847 (Lord Diplock).

[47] *Darlington Borough Council v Wiltshier Northern Ltd* [1995] 1 WLR 68 (CA); *Alfred McAlpine Construction Ltd v Panatown Ltd* [2001] 1 AC 518 (HL).

[48] *Linden Gardens Trust Ltd v Lenesta Sludge Disposals Ltd* [1994] 1 AC 85 (HL); *Swynson Ltd v Lowick Rose LLP* [2017] UKSC 32, [2018] AC 313 [14] (Lord Sumption).

allocated risks and liabilities to all members of the network. In effect, the consignor claims substantial compensation on behalf of the network when the goods are damaged, and then compensation is allocated where the loss happens to lie.

This view of the network as a collective actor would reject the limitation on the principle of transferred loss approved in *Alfred McAlpine Construction Ltd v Panatown Ltd*.[49] The judicial committee of the House of Lords agreed that the problem addressed by the principle of transferred loss was a 'black hole' created by the doctrine of privity of contract, in which the promisee who had suffered no loss could not claim substantial damages against a defendant even though a third party had suffered substantial loss from the promisor's breach. Having defined the problem in that way, once the third party turned out to have a direct contract with the defendant, the privity issue disappeared and there was no need to adopt the principle of transferred loss. According to the theory of networks as connected contracts, however, the real black hole in that case was not the doctrine of privity of contract but the absence of a legal concept of a network. If the courts had appreciated the legal significance of the network in that case (where all the companies concerned were cooperating to employ the contractor to construct a building), the presence of a direct contract between the third party and the defendant contractor would only have been of marginal relevance to the dispute. The more important question would have been whether, when viewed in the context of the network of contracts, the promisee should be entitled to sue for substantial damages on behalf of the network viewed as a collective actor. From that point of view, the presence of a direct contract between third party and the defendant contractor merely strengthened the argument that the contracts were interconnected and mutually dependent, as in a network, and that therefore it was possible to treat the network as a collective actor whose members could sue on behalf of the network as a whole.

To regard a network as a kind of legal person is hard to contemplate, however, because the common law is reluctant to recognise new types of legal person. In the law of property, the idea that there are only a limited and closed number of proprietary interests that are legally recognised in the law is a well-known, if controversial, proposition, sometimes called the *numerus clausus* principle.[50] I think that a similar statement could be made about the law of persons: there are only a limited number of persons or entities with legal personality through which they can obtain legal rights and fall under legal obligations. The main categories are adult persons and corporations, but there are also trusts, partnerships, agents, unincorporated associations, statutory bodies, and some special statutory kinds of legal entities such as trade unions. The theory of networks hints at the claim that there is a need to recognise another kind of legal entity: the business network. Recall that a network is more than a contract or collection of contracts, but it is less than a business organisation such as a corporation or partnership. To recognise networks as a new kind of legal person

[49] *Alfred McAlpine Construction Ltd v Panatown Ltd* (n 47).

[50] Sarah Worthington appears to believe, however, that *numerus clausus* does not apply to proprietary interests in the common law: S Worthington, 'Revolutions in Personal Property: Redrawing the Common Law's Conceptual Map' in S Worthington, A Robertson and G Virgo (eds), *Revolution and Evolution in Private Law* (Oxford, Hart Publishing, 2018) 227.

would therefore breach the principle of *numerus clausus* in the law of persons. The idea of networks possessing legal personality is dismissed by even those who recognise the existence and economic importance of networks as far too 'visionary'.[51]

The proposition advanced here differs, however, from a fully fledged legal personality for networks. The argument is rather that a member of the network should be able to sue and be sued on behalf of all the members of the network. If any one member of the network were liable in contract and tort, they would all be liable jointly and severally. The rules and allocations of risks within the network would then be used to distribute any costs and benefits. On this model, a claimant who is external to the network does not need to identify its responsible member. The legal claim could be brought against any member of the network. The members of the network would have to decide among themselves which members would actually pay the damages. It would also be possible for a member of the network to bring a claim against an external third party on behalf of the network, with any compensation paid by the third party to be distributed appropriately among members of the network. That representative action on behalf of the network and the subsequent distribution obligation within the network appears to lie at the core of the apparently anomalous principle of transferred loss.

The view of networks as a collective actor might have an interesting application to supply chains in business, particularly those involved in fashion.[52] In order to stock their high-street retail stores in the United Kingdom, businesses such as Primark and Next acquire clothing from suppliers, who themselves acquire goods from subcontractors and sub-subcontractors. The supply chain spans the globe. To minimise costs and to ensure just-in-time delivery of stock, the retailers insist that all its contractors use a computer monitoring and ordering system. The working conditions in the sweatshops of south-east Asia are often appalling, although this work may still be the most attractive option for earning a living for the workers involved. Imagine that in one sweatshop in Thailand, the local authorities find that the workers have not been paid the local statutory minimum wage. Their direct employer is liable to pay all the compensation, which may bankrupt it and throw the workers out of a job. Can anyone else be held responsible for the arrears of wages? There have been many attempts to hold the core business, in this case the UK retailers, to account, in part because they have deep pockets and in part because they are within a jurisdiction where the legal system functions effectively. The main obstacle to holding such hub businesses legally responsible is (apart from the fact that they are not the employer of the complainant workers) that they may have made reasonable efforts to stop the underpayments, and that most of the fault for lack of monitoring of compliance with local laws may be the responsibility of an intermediary in the supply chain.

[51] S Grundmann, 'Contractual Networks in German Private Law' in F Cafaggi (ed), *Contractual Networks, Inter-firm Cooperation and Economic Growth*, 1st edn (Cheltenham, Edward Elgar, 2011) 116, 124–25. Cf Teubner, *Networks as Connected Contracts* (n 4), 1–3, 72, 145ff.

[52] The Circle, *Fashion Focus: The Fundamental Right to a Living Wage* (London, 2017) www.thecircle.ngo/wp-content/uploads/Fashion-Focus-The-Fundamental-Right-to-a-Living-Wage-Compressed.pdf (accessed 29 September 2023).

The idea of regarding the network as being a collective actor supports the suggestion that the whole supply chain or production network should be held responsible for violations of labour rights by businesses within the network. Liability for the compensation would be shared jointly and severally among all members of the network. The members could then argue about their respective shares of liability depending on their levels of responsibility and their ability to afford the cost. In particular, the underpaid workers in Thailand could recover their wages from other members of the network without bankrupting their employer and putting themselves out of work. In this way, the concept of a network may help us address better one of the most troubling questions of globalisation, which is how we might hold to account the powerful Western corporations of the vanguard Western economies in their control, regulation and exploitation of supply chains or production networks in the rear-guard economies, which lack the economic and technological capabilities to compete in the knowledge economy.[53]

A similar argument for a collective actor might be applied to the triangular relations of temporary agency workers. Instead of inventing a contract between the agency worker and the end-user, it could be said instead that both the agency and the end-user are party to a network that is jointly responsible for compliance with employment and discrimination law. Again, the agency workers would be able to claim their legal rights against any or all parties to the network, leaving it to those businesses to sort out their respective liabilities to pay the compensation awarded by a tribunal. This development of a status of joint employers has not been accepted in England but has been recognised in some US states.[54]

In all these examples, the argument for extending the whole liability to the network as a collective actor for this purpose is that it functions economically very much like a firm or an integrated business organisation, even though it remains in law a collection of functionally connected contracts between independent businesses. The presence of formal legal boundaries between organisations belies the substance of an economically integrated system of production. The main practical reason for treating the network as a collective entity and responsible for the breach of contract or regulations that harms a third party is to prevent networks from evading responsibility for their actions by claiming to be unconnected businesses that cannot be responsible for the wrongs of other businesses. The network's liability could be strict, even if ultimately the costs were distributed according to culpability or ability to pay.

VI. CONCLUSION

The traditional contrast between the choice of a business either to make goods and services within the organisation or to buy them externally from other independent businesses breaks down in the context of networks. The production network uses

[53] R Unger, *The Knowledge Economy* (London, Verso, 2019); H Collins, 'Fat Cats, Production Networks, and the Right to Fair Pay' (2022) 85 *MLR* 1.

[54] G Davidov, 'Joint Employer Status in Triangular Employment Relationships' (2004) 42 *British Journal of Industrial Relations* 727. Joint employer liability may be possible through vicarious liability in tort.

contracts and understandings about a shared business purpose between independent businesses to bind them together to such an extent that it makes sense to conceive of networks as a new kind of business organisation. Networks are neither markets nor firms: neither contracts within the organisation nor contracts between strangers. They are invisible to legal reasoning, yet accommodating them forces legal reasoning into uncharted waters.

Like goblins, business networks frequently cause mischief in commercial law, because they disrupt the binary legal framework of firms or markets and tempt courts into inexplicable doctrinal paradoxes such as an agency without authority, the implication of unnecessary contracts and recovery for another's loss. Once the nature of networks is properly understood, these paradoxes become easier to understand. The courts appreciate that they should try to uphold the purpose of the network as an innovative commercial structure, but they lack the legal concept of a network that would enable them to carve out these instances as requiring a rational and closely confined qualifications of fundamental principles such as freedom of contract, privity of contract and the compensatory rule for awards of damages.

7

*The Importance of Classes in Insolvency and Restructuring**

SIR ANTONY ZACAROLI

I. INTRODUCTION

THE TECHNIQUE OF dividing creditors into classes for the purposes of considering a proposal by a debtor, for example to restructure its debt arrangements, has been around since the introduction of the scheme of arrangement for companies in the mid-nineteenth century (now governed by Part 26 of the Companies Act 2006).

Broader recourse to the idea of a class – the interests of which must be considered when considering the entitlement of those within it to vote on a proposed action or arrangement concerning an individual or company – has been around for considerably longer. In addition to schemes of arrangements for companies, the concept of class in this sense has arisen in the following contexts: compositions and arrangements in bankruptcy; meetings of shareholders of companies; meetings of holders of debt governed by multilateral contracts, such as deeds of indenture or debentures; voluntary arrangements between a company (or individual debtor) and its creditors (under Parts I or VII of the Insolvency Act 1986); and restructuring plans under Part 26A of the Companies Act 2006.

The common feature in all such cases is that the decision of the class is reflected in the decision of the majority within it. In other words, the decision of the majority is imposed on the minority. Whenever a court is required to consider the validity of a decision reached in these circumstances, it is alive to the risk that the decision, purportedly reached by the class, is not a fair and true reflection of the class as a whole. That has led to the development of principles designed to protect a minority within a class from the wrongful exercise of a power by the majority. These principles are of ancient origin, traceable back (according to Page-Wood V-C in *Blisset v Daniel*[1]) to Justinian's Institutes.

* A copy of this chapter first appeared as an article in the South Square Digest, www.southsquare.com.

[1] *Blisset v Daniel* (1853) 10 Hare 493, 68 ER 1022. See also *Assenagon Asset Management SA v Irish Bank Resolution Corp Ltd* [2013] EWHC 2090 (Ch), [2014] 2 BCLC 116 [41].

The type of questions that arise in each of the circumstances in which a statutory or contractual framework expressly empowers a majority of the relevant class to bind the whole class, include: when may a court override the wishes of the majority? What principles should a court apply in considering when to do so? To what extent should differences in the rights and interests of different stakeholders, or different groups of stakeholders, enable the court to interfere with the wishes of the majority? To what extent should connections between one or more of the members of the class and the company or individual to whom the decision relates be taken into account? Is it open to the court to ignore the wishes of the majority by reference to its own perception of the fairness or otherwise of the decision?

This chapter draws together, and traces the development of, the tests formulated by courts in considering the power of a majority within a class to bind the minority, in each of the different contexts referred to above. It will consider the difficulties that arise when creditors with different rights or interests are considered to be part of the same class, and the benefits of subdividing them into separate classes.

II. COMPOSITIONS AND ARRANGEMENTS IN NINETEENTH-CENTURY BANKRUPTCY LAW

In bankruptcy, the relevant 'class' has generally comprised the whole body of unsecured creditors. The power of a majority of creditors of a bankrupt debtor to approve an arrangement so as to be binding on the whole class of unsecured creditors has a long pedigree. From the earliest days, the courts have been astute to prevent abuse, developing principles of good faith and equality among members of the class.

Many of the cases arose in the context of secret inducements to one or other of the creditors in order to achieve the necessary majority in favour of the arrangement. For example, in one of the earliest cases, *Cockshott v Bennett*,[2] where creditors subscribed to a deed accepting 11s in the pound in satisfaction of their debts, one creditor was induced to agree by being provided by the debtor with a promissory note for the remainder of his debt. The rationale for preventing that creditor from recovering on the note was that all creditors mutually contracted with each other that the defendants should be discharged from their debts, and it was a fraud on the other creditors for one of them to obtain a benefit from the debtor not available to others.[3] The same rationale applied where the additional inducement came not from the debtor, but from a third party, as in *Knight v Hunt*.[4]

The deceit on other creditors in most of these cases consisted of a *secret* inducement to one, or a few only, of the debtor's creditors. The courts' refusal to permit such behaviour was underpinned by principles of good faith,[5] and secret inducements to one or more creditors were clearly contrary to 'the ordinary principles of

[2] *Cockshott v Bennett* (1788) 2 Term Rep 763, 100 ER 411.
[3] ibid 765; 100 ER 411, 412–13 (Lord Kenyon).
[4] *Knight v Hunt* (1829) 5 Bing 432, 130 ER 1127.
[5] ibid 433–34; 130 ER 1128.

morality recognised by all mankind'.[6] The courts recognised that creditors may not be capable of deciding for themselves whether to accept an arrangement, but 'would rather trust to the judgment of a body of creditors than to his own'.[7]

The principle was extended to cases where the court inferred that one or other creditor had an ulterior motive for voting in favour of an arrangement, even without a secret side deal. In *Re Cowen*[8] (a case decided under section 192 of the Bankruptcy Act 1861), for example, an arrangement provided for a payment of 2s 6d in the pound, whereas the evidence indicated that the assets were sufficient to pay a dividend of 10s in the pound. The Court of Appeal rejected an argument that wherever a court finds a deed to be unreasonable, for example because of the amount of composition is not in fair proportion to what the debtor can afford to pay, it may strike it down. Nevertheless, such a state of affairs is obvious cause for enquiry as to the bona fides of the majority. The arrangement was in fact struck down because a majority of the creditors was connected to the debtor, either through family connection or friendship, and in that capacity expected to be paid in full, although there was no agreement to that effect. Turner LJ identified the underlying principle as being that the arrangement must be free from all taint of fraud, and must be made and entered into bona fide with a view to the benefit of all the creditors.[9] Lord Cairns LJ agreed:

> [E]ven without any ingredient of fraud, if the creditors, from motives of charity and benevolence, which might be highly honourable to them, were willing to give the debtor a discharge on payment of a composition wholly disproportioned to his assets, that would not be such a bargain as the Act requires, and would not bind the non-assenting minority.[10]

In another case, *Re Page*,[11] it appears from the short report that the inference that the creditors had voted for an improper (albeit benevolent) reason was inferred simply from the miserable amount offered by way of composition, compared with what the debtor could actually afford.

Other cases stressed the importance of equal treatment – for example, *Mare v Sandford*,[12] *McKewan v Sanderson*[13] and *Re Milner*.[14] In the last case, the agreement of certain creditors to a composition, which was not made under the applicable

[6] *Mare v Sandford* (1859) 1 Giff 288, 294–95; 65 ER 923, 926 (Stuart-VC). This was another case concerned with a private agreement between the debtor and a creditor, inducing the creditor to support an arrangement with all creditors.

[7] *Dauglish v Tennent* (1866–67) LR 2 QB 49 (QB) 53–54 (Cockburn CJ).

[8] *Re Cowan* (1867) LR 2 Ch App 563 (CA).

[9] ibid 567–68.

[10] ibid 570.

[11] *Re Page* (1876) 2 Ch D 323 (CA).

[12] ibid 294–95: 'the object of the bankrupt laws is to secure an equal distribution of property among the creditors, so that none shall have any advantage over another'.

[13] *McKewan v Sanderson* (1875) LR 20 Eq 65, 72-73 (Malins V-C): 'Now I take it to be thoroughly settled, both in Court of Law and Equity, that where there is a bankruptcy, or an arrangement with creditors by composition or insolvency, when insolvency exists as contradistinguished from bankruptcy, it is the duty of all creditors who have once taken part in the proceedings of bankruptcy or composition to stand and share and share alike.'

[14] *Re Milner* (1885) 15 QBD 605 (CA).

provisions of the Bankruptcy Acts, was procured by an inducement from a third party. Brett MR held that the very essence of such a composition was that all creditors were obliged to participate on a 'footing of equality', implied by law from the very nature of the transaction.[15]

In most of the cases, the problem stemmed either from attempts to garner support by secret deals, or from the ulterior motives of certain of the creditors. It seems to have been uncommon for an arrangement to provide, openly and transparently, for differential treatment of different creditors *within* an arrangement. Where that did occur, however, as in *Thompson v Knight*,[16] the court was strongly opposed to it. In that case, relying on the basic proposition that bankruptcy required all creditors to be treated equally, an arrangement that did provide – even only potentially – for such differential treatment was struck down altogether. The arrangement (entered into under section 192 of the Bankruptcy Act 1861) provided that creditors' debts would be compromised by a payment of 10s in the pound, payable in instalments, but where the trustee administering the arrangement was given a discretion to pay any creditor whose debt was less than £20 the full amount of its composition at such time as he thought fit. In finding that the arrangement was invalid, Kelly CB said it was 'only when the provisions of the deed are just and equal that the deed ought to be held binding upon all'.[17]

III. VOTING UNDER MULTILATERAL CONTRACTS; COMPANY GENERAL MEETINGS

The starting point in considering the exercise of a power given to a majority by contract is the contract itself. In one case,[18] this was also seen as the end point: any limitation on the contractual power could only exist as a matter of construction or implication of terms, and a term could only be implied if it was required for business efficacy purposes, or was a matter of obvious inference, or was necessary to give effect to the reasonable expectations of the parties.[19] In *Assenagon*, however, Briggs J preferred the view that 'an additional basis for the implication of this principle into provisions conferring powers on majorities to bind minorities' was that such a term is generally implied by the law in contracts or arrangements of particular types,[20] albeit that it would still be regulated by any contrary intention demonstrated by the parties' agreement.[21] This reflects the approach taken in, for example, *British America Nickel Corpn Ltd v O'Brien Ltd*,[22] a case concerned with the power of a majority of

[15] ibid 612.

[16] *Thompson v Knight* (1866-67) LR 2 Ex 42 (Ex).

[17] ibid 44.

[18] *Redwood Master Fund Ltd v TD Bank Europe Ltd* [2002] EWHC 2073 (Ch) [2006] 1 BCLC 149.

[19] ibid [92] (Rimer J).

[20] See *Liverpool City Council v Irwin* [1977] AC 239 (HL) 253–55 (Lord Wilberforce).

[21] *Assenagon* (n 1) [46] (Briggs J). It may also be possible to read down an apparently wide power through a process of purpose construction, as in *Mercantile Investment and General Trust Co v International Company of Mexico* [1893] 1 Ch 484 (Note) (CA), where a power to modify the rights of debenture holders against the company was construed as not extending to a power to relinquish all their rights.

[22] *British America Nickel Corpn Ltd v O'Brien Ltd* [1927] AC 369 (PC) 371 (Viscount Haldane).

debenture holders to modify the terms of the debenture so as to bind the minority: such a power 'must be exercised subject to a general principle, which is applicable to all authorities conferred on majorities of classes enabling them to bind minorities, namely that the power given must be exercised for the purpose of benefitting the class as a whole, and not merely individual members only'.

As to the content of the principle, Briggs J in *Assenagon* considered that it was best reflected in the judgment of Lord Evershed MR in *Greenhalgh v Arderne Cinemas Ltd*,[23] a case concerned with the power of shareholders by special resolution to amend the articles of association of the company. He held that 'bona fide for the benefit of the company as a whole' meant two things: the shareholder must proceed upon what, in his honest opinion, is for the benefit of the company as a whole; and 'the company as a whole' meant the corporators as a general body. He paraphrased the test as follows: 'a special resolution of this kind would be liable to be impeached if the effect of it were to discriminate between the majority shareholders and the minority shareholders, so as to give to the former an advantage of which the latter were deprived'.

On the facts in *Assenagon* the court found[24] that the majority had acted unlawfully in voting for a resolution to approve the bank's offer to exchange €0.20 new notes for each €1 of existing subordinated notes, but on terms that the noteholders were required to commit themselves at a noteholders' meeting to vote for a resolution introducing an amendment allowing the bank to redeem all outstanding notes for a nominal price of €0.01 per €1,000 face value. Briggs J concluded that the only function of the resolution was the intimidation of a potential minority, based upon the fear of any individual member of the class that, by rejecting the exchange and voting against the resolution, it would left out in the cold. That form of coercion was 'entirely at variance' with the purposes for which power was given to majorities to bind minorities.[25]

The restriction on the power of a majority of shareholders to bind the minority is itself derived from the limitation on the power of a majority of partners to expel a partner: see *British America Nickel Corp Ltd v O'Brien Ltd*,[26] *Re Westbourne Galleries Ltd*[27] and *O'Neill v Phillips*.[28] In *Blisset v Daniel*,[29] the principle was applied to a power given to a majority of partners to expel one of their number. Page-Wood V-C said, of this power, that it was inserted 'not for the benefit of any particular parties holding two-thirds of the shares, but for the benefit of the whole society and partnership'.[30]

[23] *Greenhalgh v Arderne Cinemas Ltd* [1951] Ch 286 (CA) 291.

[24] This conclusion was obiter because the court had concluded that the notes held by the majority were, by the time of the meeting, held for the benefit of the bank, and thus were to be excluded by contract from voting at the meeting.

[25] *Assenagon* (n 1) [84]–[86].

[26] *British America Nickel Corp* (n 22) 371 (Viscount Haldane).

[27] *In re Westbourne Galleries* [1973] AC 360 (HL) 381 (Lord Wilberforce).

[28] *O'Neill v Phillips* [1999] 1 WLR 1092 (HL) 1098–1101 (Lord Hoffmann).

[29] *Blisset v Daniel* (1853) 10 Hare 493, 68 ER 1022.

[30] ibid 523–24; 68 ER 1035.

IV. COMPANY SCHEMES OF ARRANGEMENT

The earliest provisions permitting arrangements between creditors and a company to be made binding on all, if approved by a majority, were in the Companies Act 1862, sections 136, 159 and 160. These provisions were, however, restrictively interpreted.[31] Once enlarged (by section 2 of the Joint Stock Companies Arrangement Act 1870) extended to arrangements with members (by section 24 of the Companies Act 1900), and applied to companies not in the course of being wound up (by section 38 of the Companies Act 1907), the statutory provision became that which in materially the same form exists today in Part 26 of the Companies Act 2006. This provides that an arrangement or compromise between a company and its creditors, or members, or a class of creditors or members, is binding on all creditors, or members, if approved by a majority in number representing three-fourths in value of the creditors, or members, or any class of them, and if sanctioned by the court.

The most important innovation introduced by these provisions was the possibility of subdividing the creditors into separate classes, so enabling an arrangement to be made with a class, or two or more classes, of them. As Chadwick LJ put it a century later in *Re Hawk Insurance*,[32] it enabled a company to enter into a series of linked arrangements with different classes of creditors.

Before getting to that, however, in the earliest cases under these new provisions the courts followed the earlier bankruptcy authorities in protecting minorities against majorities influenced by special interests. In *Re Wedgwood Coal and Iron Company*,[33] for example, a reconstruction scheme was resolved upon, by the requisite majority, at a meeting of debenture holders. The vote was carried by debenture holders who were also shareholders with substantial liabilities to the company, of which they were relieved by virtue of the scheme. Although the case was decided on the narrow ground that the holders of debentures passing by delivery were not eligible to vote, Malins V-C also rejected the resolutions on the basis of the principle derived from *Re Cowen* and *Re Page* (above): wherever there is a power in a majority to bind a minority, that power must be exercised bona fide 'by persons who really have regard to the interests of the company'. That did not include those who voted merely for the purposes of getting out of a liability.

That was an extreme case, but in *Re Alabama, New Orleans, Texas and Pacific Junction Railway Co*[34] the circumstances were more familiar to those involved in modern schemes of arrangement. There were three classes of debt (first and second debenture holders and unsecured creditors). The restructuring involved an exchange of existing debt for new debentures, with a view to returning the company to solvency. There was no question that the majority was acting in good

[31] Section 136, which applied only to a company about to be, or in the course of being, wound up, was held not to apply to an arrangement that was intended to return the company to solvency, and was rarely used: In *Re Contal Radio Ltd* [1932] 2 Ch 66 (Ch) (see the judgment of Maugham J); ss 159 and 160 were held to include limited, if any, power to bind minorities: In *Re Alabama, New Orleans, Texas and Pacific Junction Railway Co* [1891] 1 Ch 213 (CA) 235 (Lindley LJ).

[32] *Re Hawk Insurance* [2001] EWCA Civ 241, [2001] 2 BCLC 480.

[33] *Re Wedgwood Coal and Iron Company* [1877] 6 Ch D 627 (CA).

[34] *Re Alabama, New Orleans, Texas and Pacific Junction Railway Co* [1891] 1 Ch 213 (CA).

faith, but – with four class meetings – it raised the question of how to assess votes of creditors in one class who held debt or shares in another class (eg debenture holders who also held shares). Lindley LJ formulated the following test, which has largely been applied ever since:[35] is the majority acting bona fide? Is the minority being overridden by a majority 'having interests of its own clashing with those of the minority whom they seek to coerce'? Is the scheme one that persons acting honestly, and viewing the scheme in the interests of those whom they represent, take a view that can reasonably be taken by business men?[36] Bowen LJ also addressed[37] the issue of cross-class holdings. He concluded that, while it was open to each member of a class 'to do that which is best for himself', it was for the court to see what was just and reasonable for the whole class, and it would no doubt be influenced if it turned out that the majority 'was composed of persons who had not really the interests of the class at stake'.

The following year, in *Sovereign Life Assurance Company v Dodd*,[38] the Court of Appeal turned its mind to the question of what was meant by 'class' in the statutory provisions. The statute did not define the term. Bowen LJ, describing it as 'vague', said that to find out what it meant it was necessary to look at the scope of the section, concluding:

> [I]t seems plain that we must give such a meaning to the term 'class' as will prevent the section being so worked as to result in confiscation and injustice, and that it must be confined to those persons whose rights are not so dissimilar as to make it impossible for them to consult together with a view to their common interest.[39]

This is the test that has been applied ever since, reiterated in more recent times by the Court of Appeal in *Re Hawk Insurance*.[40] As applied recently, the test has been interpreted as going to jurisdiction: if creditors are wrongly placed into the same class, then that deprives the court of the ability to sanction the scheme. Case law has developed subtle distinctions between, on the one hand, the rights of creditors and, on the other hand, interests held by creditors falling short of rights.

The rights in question are either existing rights against the company, or the rights to be conferred under the scheme.[41] The former are the rights the creditors would have against the company in the event that the scheme was not sanctioned, ie the relevant 'comparator'. Where, for example, creditors' claims carry different interest rates, those differences will not be relevant if the comparator is an insolvent liquidation, because unless and until there is a surplus in such liquidation, no interest is payable on proved debts – see, for example, *Re ED&F Man Treasury Management plc*.[42]

[35] ibid 239 (Lindley LJ).

[36] At 247 Fry LJ expressed this last question in oft-quoted language: '[The court] must be satisfied that the proposal was at least so far fair and reasonable, as that an intelligent and honest man, who is a member of that class, and acting alone in respect of his interests as such a member, might approve it.'

[37] ibid 244.

[38] *Sovereign Life Assurance Company v Dodd* [1892] 2 QB 573 (CA) 583 (Bowen LJ).

[39] ibid.

[40] ibid [26] (Chadwick LJ).

[41] See eg *Re UDL Holdings Ltd* [2001] HKCFA 19, [2002] 1 HKC 172 [27] (Lord Millett).

[42] *Re ED&F Man Treasury Management plc* [2020] EWHC 2290 (Ch) [11]; *Re Obrascon Huarte Lain SA* [2021] EWHC 859 (Ch).

The strictness of this rule, and the trap for the unwary that it creates, is mitigated to some extent by the inherent flexibility in the test. A class is not split merely because it contains creditors with different rights; it is split only if the differences in rights are such that the creditors cannot consult together with a view to their common interest. As Hildyard J put it in *Re Apcoa Parking Holdings GMBH*,[43] if there are differences in rights, then the court is required to go on to 'postulate, by reference to the alternative if the scheme were to fail, whether objectively there would be more to unite than divide the creditors in the proposed class, ignoring for that purpose any personal or extraneous interest or subjective motivation operating in the case of any particular creditor(s)'.

Where there is a minority of creditors who either do not support, or actively oppose, a scheme, therefore, there are two important layers of protection: the division of creditors into classes at the stage of convening meetings of creditors, which ensures that creditors with similar rights are not outvoted by others with materially different rights; and the broad discretion applied at the stage of sanctioning the scheme, including the principles borrowed from the bankruptcy arrangements in the nineteenth century, and applied in multilateral contracts, of good faith and equal treatment.

The precise content of the broad discretion exercised at the sanction stage is harder to define, but is often encapsulated (picking up the threads identified in *Re Alabama, New Orleans, Texas and Pacific Junction Railway Co* (above)) in the following points: was the class fairly represented at the meeting or meetings? Was there any coercion of the minority by the majority in order to promote an interest adverse to those of the class which they represent? Was the scheme one that an intelligent and honest person, a member of the class concerned, acting in respect of their own interest could reasonably approve? Is there any 'blot' or defect in the scheme that would make it unlawful or inoperative?[44]

It is in fact a rare event that an English court has exercised its discretion by declining to sanction a scheme of arrangement. The fact that groups of creditors have special interests not shared with the class (eg by reason of cross-holdings of different classes of debt, or of shares) has rarely been considered a reason to refuse to sanction the scheme. A recent example is *Re ALL Scheme Limited*,[45] but the reason for refusing to sanction the scheme was that the court was not satisfied that the vote at the single meeting of creditors was representative of the class, in circumstances where the turnout was extremely low (9 percent of the creditors by number) and there had been insufficient explanation of the proposal and its consequences to enable creditors to make an informed decision.[46]

It is less common to find a subgroup of creditors within a voting class with a special interest that is not shared by the other members of the class (but which does not amount to a difference in rights so as to fracture the class), where that subgroup

[43] *Re Apcoa Parking Holdings GmbH* [2014] EWHC 3849 (Ch), [2015] 4 All ER 572 [52].

[44] *Re Telewest Communications* [2004] EWHC 1466 (Ch), [2005] BCC 36 [20]–[22] (David Richards J); *Re TDG plc* [2008] EWHC 2334 (Ch), [2009] 1 BCLC 445 [29] (Morgan J).

[45] *Re ALL Scheme Limited* [2021] EWHC 1401 (Ch).

[46] ibid [138]–[139] (Miles J).

are motivated to approve the scheme by reason of that special interest and their vote is material in obtaining the requisite majority in the class.

The problems to which that can give rise were grappled with by Hildyard J in *Re Lehman Brothers International (Europe) (No 10)*.[47] The possible approaches were either (i) to discount the weight to be given to the majority vote, and consider the fairness of the scheme without adopting any presumption in favour of the majority, or (ii) to disregard altogether the votes of the 'special interest' creditors, so that they did not count at all towards the statutory majority. The latter approach – if applied strictly – would seem to cut across the rules for class composition. Creditors are only placed in the same class if their rights are not so dissimilar as to make it impossible for them to consult together. The corollary is that if they are in the same class they should be permitted to vote. Hildyard J concluded that the question was one of discretion,[48] to be exercised according to all the circumstances of the case. An important factor, in his view, was that the court has always been especially disposed to guard against coercion of a minority by a self-interested majority. In light of that, the most important circumstances would often be the level of support from creditors who did not share the special interest and the court's own views on the balance of the benefit offered by the scheme. As will be seen, this notion of 'balancing the benefit' offered by the scheme echoes the approach taken in the remaining two contexts: voluntary arrangements and Part 26A restructuring plans.

V. VOLUNTARY ARRANGEMENTS

Voluntary arrangements owe far more to the nineteenth-century arrangements and compositions in bankruptcy than they do to schemes of arrangement. The legislation provides for a single arrangement between the debtor and all of its creditors. In both the corporate and individual versions, 'voluntary arrangement' is defined as the proposal made by the debtor to 'its creditors' for a composition in satisfaction of its debts or a scheme of arrangement of its affairs. Notice of the 'qualifying decision procedure' (which may, but need not be, a meeting) must be given to *all* of the debtor's creditors of whom the nominee is aware,[49] and all creditors who are given notice are entitled to vote in respect of the arrangement.[50] There is no provision, therefore, for an arrangement with a class of creditors, or for linked arrangements with multiple classes.

The report of the Cork committee, which preceded the 1986 Insolvency Act, focused mostly on voluntary arrangements for individuals: the extension to companies

[47] *Re Lehman Brothers International (Europe) (No 10)* [2018] EWHC 1980 (Ch), [2019] Bus LR 1012 [107]–[111].

[48] The same judge had noted, in *Apcoa Parking* (n 43) [54], that the approach advocated by Bowen LJ in *Re Alabama*, 'chimes … with the inclination of judges to prefer the more flexible tool of discretion and an overall appreciation of fairness tested by reference to real alternatives rather than the straight-jacket [*sic*] of jurisdiction, especially where rigidity may result in fragmentation of classes to avoid jurisdictional issues, but at the cost of enabling a small group to hold out unfairly against a majority'.

[49] Insolvency Act 1986, ss 3(4), 257(2B).

[50] Insolvency (England and Wales) Rules 2016, SI 2016/1024, r 15.28(5).

was dealt with in just a few paragraphs. It was the expectation of the Cork committee that company voluntary arrangements would be used only in relatively simple cases, for example where the company's debt profile resembled that of a sole trader, and where there were not substantially different rights and interests among creditor groups.[51]

There are, however, two significant developments compared to the nineteenth-century bankruptcy arrangements. First, the problem of creditors being motivated to approve an arrangement by reason of family or other close connections with the debtor is addressed head-on in the rules. While the overall majority required to approve a voluntary arrangement is 75 percent by value, a decision otherwise approving an arrangement is deemed not to be made if more than half of the total value of unconnected creditors vote against it.[52]

Second, court involvement in the approval of an arrangement is removed: an arrangement is brought into effect solely as a consequence of its approval by the requisite majority of creditors. The court is involved only if there is an appeal relating to voting rights, or an objecting creditor applies to revoke the approval of the arrangement on one of two grounds: material irregularity or unfair prejudice.[53]

In recognition of the fact that the rights of secured creditors to enforce their security are retained in the case of their debtor's bankruptcy or winding-up, the legislation provides special treatment for them. Although they are included within 'all creditors' entitled to be given notice of, and to vote in respect of, a proposal, the proposal cannot modify their security rights without their consent,[54] and they are only entitled to vote in respect of the unsecured portion (if any) of their debt.[55]

In interpreting and developing the first ground of challenge (material irregularity) the courts have continued to apply the principles of good faith and equality from the nineteenth-century cases referred to above.[56]

For example, in *Somji v Cadbury Schweppes plc*[57] the Court of Appeal concluded that a secret inducement to a creditor to vote in favour of the arrangement constituted a material irregularity. Robert Walker LJ[58] considered that the intellectual freight of the pre-1986 insolvency law that was least likely to have been jettisoned by the Insolvency Act 1986 were the basic doctrines – such as proportionate treatment of unsecured creditors – which were features of bankruptcy law from its earliest days.

A further example is *National Westminster Bank plc v Kapoor*,[59] where an assignment from a connected creditor to one who was unconnected with the debtor (so as to avoid the arrangement failing under Rule 15.34(4)) was held to be a material

[51] See Department of Trade and Industry, *Report of the Review Committee on Insolvency Law and Practice* (Cmnd 8558, 1982) (Cork Report) para 430.

[52] Insolvency Rules 2016 (n 51), r 15.34(4).

[53] Insolvency Act 1986, ss 6, 262.

[54] ibid s 4(3) and s 258(4).

[55] Insolvency Rules 2016 (n 51), r 15.31(4) and (5).

[56] See, for a fuller treatment of the case law, *Lazari Properties 2 Ltd v New Look Retailers and others* [2021] EWHC 1209 (Ch), [2021] Bus LR 915 (*New Look*) [86]–[105].

[57] *Cadbury Schweppes plc v Somji* [2001] 1 WLR 615 (CA).

[58] ibid [24].

[59] *National Westminster Bank plc v Kapoor* [2011] EWCA Civ 1083, [2012] 1 All ER 1201.

irregularity, on the basis that 'material irregularity' was coloured by the principles of good faith and equal treatment laid down in, for example, *Dauglish v Tennent* and *Mare v Sandford*.[60] In *Gertner v CFL Finance Ltd*,[61] the Court of Appeal applied the same principles in the context of a separate deal with one creditor, notwithstanding that it was not kept secret from others. In that case, an arrangement under which creditors would receive 0.07p in the pound was approved by a meeting of creditors at which the largest creditor, Kaupthing Bank hf, voted in favour. Kaupthing, however, had the benefit of a settlement agreement with the debtor under which it received considerable benefits that were not made available to other creditors. This was held to constitute a material irregularity, as it breached the good-faith principle. Importantly, although there was a complaint of inadequate disclosure, Patten LJ's reasoning did not depend upon non-disclosure of the settlement agreement. Thus, it was not merely a lack of good faith by reason of a secret inducement (as in most of the nineteenth-century bankruptcy cases) that caused the arrangement to fail. It was the fact that the side-deal offered to Kaupthing alone meant that the creditors were not on an equal footing in considering the merits of the proposal, and put Kaupthing in a position of conflict with other creditors.[62]

Each of these cases involved something more than merely differential treatment of creditors: either a secret side deal, an arrangement (the assignment in *Kapoor*) whose purpose was found to be to subvert the statutory policy relating to connected creditors, or – while falling short of 'vote-buying' – an arrangement intended to provide a significant inducement to a creditor to vote in favour. Moreover, these cases all involved a transaction outside the terms of the arrangement.

More difficult is where the arrangement transparently provides for differential treatment. This is made more complicated by the fact that, contrary to the expectation of the Cork committee, company voluntary arrangements have in recent years been used for companies with ever-more complex debt profiles and in order to effect materially different outcomes for different groups of creditors. Cases, that is, in which the creditors would be placed into different classes if the restructuring were effected via a scheme of arrangement. Without the concept of class to fall back on, this places particular stress on the concept of 'unfair prejudice'.

Soon after the introduction of voluntary arrangements, it was established that unfair prejudice meant that which stemmed from the terms of the arrangement itself:[63] it referred to a degree of prejudice to one creditor or class of creditors as compared with other creditors, or classes of creditors.[64]

Latterly, the courts have developed two 'useful heuristics'[65] for assessing whether an arrangement is unfairly prejudicial. The first (the vertical comparator) compares the outcome for each creditor in the arrangement with the outcome that they would

[60] See above, nn 6, 7.

[61] *Gertner v CFL Finance Ltd* [2018] EWCA Civ 1781, [2018] BPIR 1605.

[62] ibid [63] and [80] (Patten LJ).

[63] *Re a Debtor (No 259 of 1990)* [1992] 1 WLR 226 (Ch) 228 (Hoffmann J).

[64] *Doorbar v Alltime Securities Ltd (No 2)* [1995] 2 BCLC 513 (Ch) 518 (Knox J). See also *Re a Debtor (No 222 of 1990), ex p the Bank of Ireland* [1992] BCLC 137 (Ch) 145D-E (Harman J).

[65] *Discovery (Northampton) Limited v Debenhams Retail Limited* [2019] EWHC 2441 (Ch), [2020] BCC 9 [12] (Norris J).

have achieved in the event that the arrangement had not been approved, typically a liquidation. The return that a creditor would have received in a liquidation or bankruptcy has been described as 'the irreducible minimum' below which an arrangement cannot go.[66] It is difficult to envisage a court not interfering with an arrangement that was 'likely to result in creditors, or some of them, receiving less than they would in a winding up of the company, assuming that the return in a winding up would in reality be achieved and within an acceptable time-scale'.[67]

The second (the horizontal comparator) compares the outcome as between different creditors or groups of creditors. The mere fact that differences exist between creditors – either in their existing rights or in the rights conferred by the arrangement – does not in itself constitute unfair prejudice. It will give cause for inquiry, but may turn out to be justified.[68] In some cases, differential treatment is essential to *ensure* fairness. For example, if in the absence of the arrangement the debtor company would go into liquidation where a group of creditors would be entitled to special treatment, then fairness requires that treatment to be replicated in the arrangement.[69]

The most oft-cited justification for giving preferential treatment to some creditors is that it is necessary to ensure the continuation of the debtor's business *and* that the continuation of the business is essential to the success of the arrangement.[70] Beyond that, however, there is little guidance as to the principles to apply in determining when differential treatment may be justified. The cases where arrangements have been struck down as being unfairly prejudicial are often ones where the treatment of the objecting creditor was such that it was worse off than in the event of the company's liquidation. In *Prudential Assurance Co Ltd v PRG Powerhouse Ltd*,[71] for example, the arrangement purported to deprive landlords of their valuable rights of guarantee against third parties (which would have survived the company's liquidation) in return for a relatively small dividend in the arrangement. Similarly, in *Mourant & Co Trustees Ltd v Sixty UK Ltd*[72] the treatment of landlords was held to be worse than they would have received in a winding-up of the debtor company.

It is for those proposing a voluntary arrangement to justify the differential treatment of 'critical' creditors. Failure to provide a robust explanation for why they should be paid in full, or at a higher rate of dividend than others, may well lead to the failure of the arrangement. That was one of the reasons advanced for revoking the

[66] *Mourant & Co Trustees Ltd v Sixty UK Ltd* [2010] EWHC 1890, [2011] 1 BCLC 383 (Ch) [67] (Henderson J).

[67] *Re T&N Ltd* [2004] EWHC 2361 (Ch), [2005] 2 BCLC 488 [82] (David Richards J).

[68] *Re a Debtor (No 101 of 1999)* [2001] 1 BCLC 54 [63] (Ferris J,).

[69] *Sea Voyage Maritime Inc v Bielecki* [1999] 1 All ER 628 (Ch), where certain creditors would have had the right, in the winding-up of the debtor, to be indemnified by the debtor's insurer under the Third Party (Rights Against Insurers) Act 1930. This approach mirrors that taken in schemes of arrangement (see above), where the differences in the rights of creditors are measured against the rights that they would have in the relevant alternative.

[70] *Prudential Assurance Co Ltd v PRG Powerhouse Ltd* [2007] EWHC 1002, [2007] BCC 500 [90] (*Powerhouse*) (Etherton J) and the cases there cited.

[71] ibid.

[72] *Mourant & Co Trustees Ltd v Sixty UK Ltd* (n 66).

arrangement in *Mourant & Co v Sixty*,[73] and was critical to the court's conclusion in *Carraway Guildford (Nominee A) Limited v Regis UK Limited* ('*Regis*').[74] In that case, a debt of nearly £600,000 owed to the immediate parent company of the debtor was left unimpaired by the arrangement. The arrangement was expected to generate, from trading, approximately the same sum, to be made available to all impaired creditors so that, over time, they would receive 7p in the pound. Although that was likely to be higher than they would recover in the event of the company's liquidation, the absence of a proper explanation for leaving the shareholder's debt wholly unimpaired led the court to conclude that this was unfair prejudice.

The real difficulty with differential treatment of creditors within a voluntary arrangement is the fact that, irrespective of their treatment, all creditors are entitled to vote in the qualifying decision procedure. In the simpler cases, and in the case of the most often cited reason for preferential treatment – ie that payment of certain creditors is critical to the continuation of the debtor's trading – the number of creditors and volume of debt involved are unlikely to be significant. They are unlikely, in other words, to have a material impact on the outcome of the vote.

In recent years, however, with the use of company voluntary arrangements in evermore complex cases, there has been a tendency to treat large numbers of creditors as critical, and thus unimpaired by the arrangement (or at least afforded substantially better treatment), where the combined voting power of such creditors is sufficient to swing the vote in favour of the arrangement. Given that there is no provision for placing creditors into different classes for voting purposes, this has created a clear tension with the principles established in the nineteenth-century cases on compositions and arrangements. According to these principles, a majority of creditors should only bind the minority where they are treated equally (or at least sufficiently similarly) with the minority.[75]

The problem arises most acutely where the differential treatment can be justified on the basis that payment of the relevant creditor is critical to ensure the success of the arrangement, and where the arrangement enables all of the unimpaired creditors to obtain a better return than if the company went into liquidation, but where unimpaired creditors as a group do not approve the arrangement by the requisite majority. That issue potentially arose in *Regis*, but as a result of the court's refusal on case management grounds to permit amendments to the pleadings, this was not a point that it was open to the objecting landlords to take.

Such a restructuring could not be achieved via a scheme of arrangement, because the impaired creditors would clearly be entitled to form a separate class, and their negative vote would deprive the court of jurisdiction to sanction the scheme.

One possible answer to this problem is that a voluntary arrangement cannot, as a matter of jurisdiction, be used to implement separate deals with different creditor

[73] ibid.

[74] *Carraway Guildford (Nominee A) Limited v Regis UK Limited* [2021] EWHC 1294 (Ch), [2022] 1 BCLC 709.

[75] As noted above in section II, the nineteenth-century cases were mostly concerned with precluding secret side-deals, but where there was differential treatment under the arrangement (as in *Thompson v Knight* (n16), the lack of equal treatment was in itself sufficient to invalidate the arrangement.

groups. That argument was, however, rejected in *New Look*, as was the contention that this would necessarily amount to unfair prejudice.[76]

The fact that a voluntary arrangement could *not* be achieved via a scheme of arrangement is nevertheless a powerful factor in considering whether unfair prejudice exists.[77] In *Powerhouse*,[78] Etherton J noted that not only would the impaired landlords have formed a separate class in a scheme, but a scheme would not have needed to include, and would not have included, the unimpaired creditors. An arrangement whereby the vote of the impaired landlords was 'swamped' by the vote of those who were to receive payment in full was one that it was 'obvious' was outside the contemplation of the Cork committee. The facts were extreme, as noted above, because the impaired landlords stood to lose least (if anything) upon liquidation of the debtor, but stood to lose the most of all creditors in the company voluntary arrangement.

It is, however, not in itself determinative: see *SISU Capital Fund Ltd v Tucker*.[79] In *Re Portsmouth City Football* Club,[80] the arrangement was voted through by virtue of the votes of a group of creditors who had no real interest in its outcome, because they would be paid in full. These were 'football creditors' who under Football League rules would be paid in full by the Football League (by way of deduction from amounts that would otherwise be paid by the League to the club). The proposal offered ordinary unsecured creditors 20p in the pound. Mann J rejected the argument that the ordinary unsecured creditors (predominantly HMRC) were unfairly prejudiced. The differential treatment of the football creditors (assuming that the arrangement provided for them to be paid in full, rather than merely acknowledging they would be paid in full elsewhere) was objectively justifiable because they were to be paid out of assets that would not otherwise have been available to the company in the voluntary arrangement. They were not being paid, therefore, at the expense of other creditors of the company. Two points were made in answer to the objection that the compromise was being forced on creditors by the vote of those who were unaffected by the arrangement: first, the unsecured creditors were better off under the arrangement than in the company's liquidation (ie the vertical comparator test was satisfied); and, second, the football creditors were sufficiently *interested* in the arrangement by virtue of the fact that their contracts would be honoured if the arrangement was approved, whereas in a liquidation their employment would cease.

In *New Look*, the company contended that it was sufficient to answer a charge of unfair prejudice that any differential treatment could be objectively justified, and that the impaired creditors would achieve a better outcome than in the relevant alternative.

[76] *New Look* (n 56) paras 156–86.

[77] As David Richards J pointed out in *Re T&N Ltd* (n 67) [81], the crucial difference between a scheme and a voluntary arrangement is that in a voluntary arrangement there is just one meeting, so that necessarily means that there may be subgroups who would constitute a separate class for a scheme: 'in considering unfair prejudice, the court will have regard to the different position of different groups of creditors'.

[78] *Powerhouse* (n 70) [108].

[79] *SISU Capital Fund Ltd v Tucker* [2005] EWHC 2170 (Ch), [2006] BCC 463 [133]–[134] (Warren J).

[80] *Re Portsmouth City Football* [2010] EWHC 2013, [2011] BCC 149.

The court rejected that argument, which failed to pay sufficient regard to the horizontal comparator. In that case, one group of creditors consisted of compromised landlords of numerous retail premises occupied by the company. Their claims were substantially impaired by the arrangement. There were two other groups of creditors who received materially different treatment, but whose votes counted towards the statutory majority in approving the arrangement: secured noteholders were unaffected by the arrangement, but were compromised by a separate scheme of arrangement; and the ordinary unsecured creditors and landlords of premises deemed necessary for the success of the business were unimpaired by the arrangement.

It was accepted by the objecting landlords that the preferential treatment of the second group of creditors was justified on the grounds that they were critical creditors. As their combined vote was insufficient to have made a material difference to the outcome of the meeting, the fact that they had preferential treatment was held not to be unfairly prejudicial.

As to the first group, the Court reasoned as follows: their right to enforce their security could not be impaired by the arrangement without their consent; consent of all noteholders could not in practice be obtained, so the scheme of arrangement was best analysed as a mechanism for achieving the consent of all noteholders to the impairment of their security (by exchanging their existing rights for new security rights); it was a statutory requirement that the unsecured portion of their claim be admitted to vote; in relation to that unsecured portion they in fact received nothing, so their treatment was significantly *worse* than that of the impaired landlords; and the fact that they may nevertheless have been incentivised to vote in favour of the arrangement because their treatment under the scheme may have ensured a better outcome than in the relevant alternative was not sufficient to constitute unfair prejudice.

The court identified the following as factors relevant in considering whether it was unfairly prejudicial that the vote of unimpaired, or lesser impaired, creditors influenced the vote to approve a voluntary arrangement. First, has there been a fair allocation of the assets available within the arrangement between the compromised creditors and other groups? That might involve considering the source of the assets from which the treatment of the different subgroups derives, and whether they would or could have been made available to all creditors in the relevant alternative. This necessarily contemplates the court considering whether a different allocation to that proposed by those who formulated the arrangement would have been possible.[81] Second, what is the nature and extent of the different treatment, the justification for that treatment, and its impact on the outcome of the qualifying decision procedure? Unfair prejudice might more readily be found where an arrangement that compromised the claims of a subgroup of creditors was achieved only because of the votes of a large swathe of creditors who are unaffected by it, even if there was an objective justification for those creditors being unaffected by the company voluntary

[81] Contrast the position in relation to schemes of arrangement under Part 26 of the Companies Act 2006, where the court is not concerned to see whether another arrangement might be fairer for one or other group of creditors: see for example *In re Co-operative Bank plc* [2017] EWHC 2269 (Ch) [37] (Snowden J).

arrangement.[82] Third, was there a significant body of creditors, in the same position as those objecting to the arrangement, who approved it?[83]

VI. RESTRUCTURING PLANS

By reference to the restructuring toolkit in English law, the restructuring plan under Part 26A of the Companies Act 2006 is clearly the offspring of the scheme of arrangement.[84] Like the scheme, it divides creditors into classes for the purposes of voting and requires court involvement both at the stage of defining the classes and at the stage of sanction. Its major innovation, however – the cross-class cram-down power[85] – makes it particularly suited as a replacement for the voluntary arrangement in those complex cases where substantively different deals are sought to be imposed on different groups of creditors.

As noted above, the question of particular difficulty that arises in relation to voluntary arrangements is how to determine whether an arrangement that gives preferential treatment to one or more subgroups of creditors is unfairly prejudicial, where the disadvantaged subgroups will obtain under the arrangement at least as good an outcome as they would achieve in the relevant alternative.

Under Part 26A, it appears that the mere fact that creditors in the dissenting classes will be no worse off under the plan than in the relevant alternative is not sufficient to justify the sanction of the plan. That is because the requirement of 'no worse-off treatment' is a condition for the cross-class cram-down power to be exercised, not a reason – in itself – for exercising it. Two early cases on the new regime provided preliminary guidance on the operation of the cross-class cram-down: *Re DeepOcean 1 UK Ltd*[86] and *Re Virgin Active Holdings Ltd*.[87]

In *DeepOcean*, Trower J identified the following as relevant to the exercise of the cram-down power.[88] First, no plan creditor objected that the plan was unfair. Second, creditors in the dissenting class would not merely be no worse off than in the relevant alternative (which was held to be a formal insolvency process of some kind): they would have received nothing in the relevant alternative, but stood to receive a dividend

[82] See for example *Powerhouse* (n 70).

[83] Compare *Lehman Brothers* (n 47) [129–30], in the case of a scheme of arrangement; and *Re DeepOcean 1 UK Ltd* [2021] EWHC 138 (Ch), [2021] BCC 483 [59], in the case of a Part 26A restructuring plan.

[84] Although the cross-class cram-down is derived from the plan of reorganisation under Chapter 11 of the US Bankruptcy Code.

[85] The court may sanction a restructuring plan, under Companies Act 2006, s 901G, even if the requisite majority is not obtained at one or more of the class meetings (of creditors or shareholders), provided that: (1) none of the members of the dissenting class or classes would be any worse off under the plan than they would be in the event of the relevant alternative; and (2) the plan has been agreed by the requisite majority of at least one class of creditors who would receive a payment, or have a genuine economic interest in the company, in the relevant alternative.

[86] *DeepOcean* (n 83).

[87] *Re Virgin Active Holdings Ltd* [2021] EWHC 1246 (Ch), [2022] 1 All ER (Comm) 1023. It is interesting to compare and contrast this case with *New Look*. Both cases involved a restructuring of a retail business conducted over numerous premises, the creditors of which therefore included a large number of landlords. One was restructured via a company voluntary arrangement, the other via the new Part 26A procedure.

[88] *DeepOcean* (n 83) [34]–[66].

of approximately 4 percent on their claims under the plan. Third, the approach adopted by the court in deciding whether to sanction a scheme of arrangement was an appropriate starting point, but with the important difference that the court's reluctance to differ from the meeting (in a scheme context) did not have the same place in the court's approach to sanctioning a plan to which section 910G applies. That is because by its very nature the power under that section contemplates the court overriding the wishes of a class meeting. Fourth, where the evidence is that members of the dissenting class are out of the money in the relevant alternative, such that they could have been excluded from a Part 26 scheme by virtue of the principle in *Re Tea Corp*,[89] their receipt of any benefits under the plan means that they are unlikely to have been treated in a manner that was not just and equitable.[90] Fifth, the fact that the benefits under the plan were to be provided by a group company other than DSC, combined with the fact that the creditors in the dissenting class were out of the money in the relevant alternative, was a powerful pointer towards exercising the cross-class cram-down power. Sixth, it was also relevant to take into account the overall support for the three companies' proposals taken as a whole and the extent to which the plan creditors were fairly represented at their respective meetings.

Finally, it was appropriate to have regard to the 'horizontal comparison' test usually carried out when considering a challenge to a voluntary arrangement on the basis of unfair prejudice (as in the *Debenhams* case). The court would be particularly concerned to ascertain whether there had been a fair distribution of the benefits of the restructuring[91] between those classes who had agreed the restructuring plan and those that had not. As to this, (i) the difference between the treatment of the secured creditors and those in the dissenting class was readily explained because of the secured nature of the former's claims; (ii) the horizontal comparison test was less significant where the benefits under the plan are derived from sources other than the plan company and the dissenting class would be out of the money in the relevant comparator; and (iii) so far as some creditors had been excluded altogether from the plan, that was justified on commercial grounds.

In *Virgin Active*, one of the issues was that the shareholders of a company which, in the relevant alternative, was insolvent were nevertheless provided with benefits under the restructuring plan. Snowden J considered this to be a fair allocation of the benefits arising in the plan in circumstances where the shareholders had committed under the plan to introduce new monies into the group.

Since this chapter was first presented, there has been a run of cases in which the discretion to exercise the cram-down power has been examined, and the limits of the exercise of that power have begun to emerge. A consideration of these is beyond

[89] *Re Tea Corp* [1904] 1 Ch 12 (CA).

[90] In this regard it was relevant to note that under s 901C(4) it may not have been necessary for such creditors to be summoned to a meeting at all.

[91] Referred to by some commentators as the 'restructuring surplus': see, for an illuminating discussion of this concept, two articles by Professor Riz Mokal: 'The Two Conditions for the Pt 26A Cram Down' (2020) 35(11) *Butterworths Journal of International Banking and Financial Law* 730; and 'The Court's Discretion in Relation to the Pt 26A Cram Down' (2021) 36(1) *Butterworths Journal of International Banking and Financial Law* 12.

the scope of this chapter, but a helpful analysis of some of the issues arising can be found in Sarah Paterson and Adrian Walters's article, 'Selective Corporate Restructuring Strategy'.[92]

VII. CONCLUSION

In most of the contexts, historically, in which creditors have been called on to vote as a class, or in classes, to consider a compromise or arrangement involving their debtor, the court's role has been – at least ostensibly – relatively limited. It has been concerned to ensure that the arrangement complies with principles of good faith and equality; in particular, to ensure that no one is induced to vote in favour by special treatment. Even with the greater complexity of restructuring deals under the scheme-of-arrangement regime, the court's role was generally limited to ensuring that creditors were placed into the appropriate classes, and that those within the classes were voting in the interests of the class and not motivated by some special interest. When it came to considering the 'fairness' of the arrangement in a broader manner, the limit of the court's role was generally to ensure that a reasonable and honest person, being a member of the relevant class, could reasonably approve it. It was not for the court to consider whether some other arrangement might have been fairer to one or other group of creditors.

In recent years, however, the ingenuity of those promoting restructuring schemes has begun to push the envelope, in two ways in particular: by exploring the limits of what amounts to a sufficient similarity in rights, as opposed to interests, so as not to give power to minorities in the context of schemes; and by moulding considerably more complex arrangements within the framework of company voluntary arrangements. One result of this is that it subtly changes the nature of the question the court is required to ask. In the schemes context, as Hildyard J put it in *Lehman Brothers*,[93] the court may be required to consider, among other things, the balance of the benefit offered by the scheme to creditors within a class. In the voluntary arrangement context, as well as ensuring that no creditor is worse off than in the relevant alternative (the vertical comparator) the court is required to consider the fairness of the arrangement as between different subgroups of creditors (the horizontal comparator).

This is essentially the same question facing the court in a Part 26A restructuring plan. While the Part 26A procedure has to some extent reduced the significance of the class test, as compared to schemes of arrangements, it is a confirmation of the relevance and importance of dividing creditors into classes for the purposes of considering arrangements that impact on creditors' rights.

There are important advantages, both to those promoting a scheme and to the court, in using the Part 26A structure (where creditors are divided into classes) as opposed to a voluntary arrangement (where they are not) or a scheme (where they

[92] S Paterson and A Walters, 'Selective Corporate Restructuring Strategy' (2023) 86(2) *MLR* 436.
[93] *Lehman Brothers* (n 47).

are, but there is an incentive to ensure that as many creditors as possible are included within a class so as avoid giving a power of veto to a minority).

First, by ensuring that creditors with the same or substantially similar rights against the debtor are divided into groups at the outset of the process, there is much better scope for creditors to consult with each other than there is in a voluntary arrangement. That will facilitate coordination of responses from creditor groups, improving their negotiating position and potentially leading to improved outcomes.

Second, when the court is called upon to consider the fairness of the arrangement (at the sanction of a scheme, or upon a challenge to a voluntary arrangement), it is better informed in the scheme context, because it can see the voting pattern among each group of creditors. That will assist in determining to what extent it can be said that a person within a dissenting class could reasonably approve the scheme.

Third, with the benefit of that information, the court (and the parties) can focus directly on the extent to which the scheme provides a fair distribution of value, including such value as is generated by reason of the restructuring. While that is essentially similar to the exercise when considering the horizontal comparator test in voluntary arrangements, it is better carried out with a clear picture of the groups into which creditors are to be divided, and voting patterns among those groups.

Fourth, when these issues are considered in relation to a voluntary arrangement, it is often against the backdrop that a successful objection to the arrangement will result in the loss of any chance to restructure the company and save the business. The arrangement is a fait accompli, and it is often too late to go back to the drawing board. If these issues are faced, with full transparency for creditors, before the scheme becomes effective, then (while it has to be acknowledged that the company's dire financial position in reality may often provide only a short window in which to achieve a restructuring) there is at least more prospect of the proposed scheme being remodelled – before it is too late – to take account of the court's conclusions on the objections raised.

Fifth, the court has much greater control over the information the debtor should provide to creditors in the context of a restructuring plan. As noted above, there is no court involvement in the preparation of a voluntary arrangement. Moreover, the time periods for the provision of information to creditors are significantly shorter in a voluntary arrangement. One of the common complaints, therefore, is that creditors were given insufficient information, and given insufficient time to consider it. Under the scheme procedure, the court can tailor the quantity, quality and timing of dissemination of information to suit the case.

8

Proprietary Restitution: The Primary Remedy for Unjust Enrichment?

MICHAEL BRYAN*

I. INTRODUCTION

SARAH WORTHINGTON HAS been writing on proprietary restitution for over a quarter of a century.[1] That an academic writer's arguments have not altered much over the course of that twenty-five years or so would not ordinarily be a matter for commendation; on the contrary, it might be taken as evidence of intellectual rigidity. That the arguments have not required alteration is, however, a genuine achievement. Professor Worthington has had little cause to modify her first thoughts; later iterations have altered some of the terminology but little, if any, of the substance of her arguments.[2]

Her publications on proprietary restitution for unjust enrichment attempt, as do the writings of every other writer on this much-fought-over battleground in the law of restitution, to make sense of what looks like a dunghill of isolated precedents. But her analysis rests on a disarmingly simple premise, namely that the function of the law of unjust enrichment is to restore the economic benefit of an asset to the party entitled to that benefit. The aim of this chapter is to examine the implications of

* The chapter is an inadequate return for the intellectual stimulation gained from co-teaching with Sarah at Melbourne University in LLB Trusts 1989, 1991 and LLM Commercial Law 2010–18. Elise Bant provided invaluable assistance, but the author is solely responsible for any errors.

[1] The publications on which this chapter principally focuses are *Equity*, 2nd edn (Oxford, Clarendon Press, 2006) 290–317 (*Equity*); 'The Commercial Triple Helix: Contract, Property and Unjust Enrichment' in P Devonshire and R Havelock (eds), *The Impact of Equity and Restitution in Commerce* (Oxford, Hart Publishing, 2019) 33–64 ('The Commercial Triple Helix'); and, with W Day, 'Proprietary Restitution' in W Day and S Worthington (eds), *Challenging Private Law: Lord Sumption in the High Court* (Oxford, Hart Publishing, 2020) 193–216 ('Proprietary Restitution').

[2] Lord Browne-Wilkinson's 'fundamental propositions' of trusts law, set out in *Westdeutsche Landesbank Girozentrale v Islington London Borough Council* [1996] AC 669 (HL) 705–06 (*Westdeutsche*), appeared shortly after Worthington's *Proprietary Interests in Commercial Transactions* (Oxford, Clarendon Press, 1996) had been edited, and were discussed in an addendum to that book. Her disagreement with some of the propositions is a consistent theme of her writings in this area.

this functional understanding of unjust enrichment. Not all are obvious. But first Sarah Worthington's scheme of unjust enrichment will be summarised. At the risk of serious oversimplification, its essential propositions are as follows:

(1) Proprietary restitution for unjust enrichment is not subordinate to personal restitution. A successful claimant in unjust enrichment ought to recover her property, or its traceable substitute, by application of trust machinery, unless a defence or equitable bar precludes proprietary restitution. If the property no longer exists, she will be remitted to personal restitution.
(2) The truth of proposition (1) has been concealed by a failure to recognise that proprietary restitution is already established as the primary response to unjust enrichment in many cases. The cases include: (a) rescission of a contract where a party's consent to contracting has been vitiated; and (b) the enforcement of a resulting trust, whether 'automatic' or by application of a presumption.[3]
(3) Although there is (in crude terms) 'more' proprietary restitution for unjust enrichment than is generally acknowledged, some disjunctions, historically explicable but not justifiable, have prevented the development of coherent principles governing the availability of proprietary remedies. That 'usual suspect', the pre-Judicature Act separation of the administration of common law and equity, is not solely to blame. Distinctions between void and voidable transfers, and between different types of property (land, chattels, shares, money), have also contributed to the blurred image of proprietary restitution. The principles applicable to specific restitution of property transferred pursuant to a void contract, for example, vary widely depending on the identity of the property.[4]
(4) The availability of restitution for unjust enrichment turns on a critical distinction between unintended transfers, on the one hand, involving no allocation of commercial risk, and losing commercial deals, on the other hand, where risk has been expressly or implicitly allocated. Restitution is justified only in the former case. The unjust factors of 'mistake' and 'failure of consideration (or basis)' are overbroad and do not accurately reflect this distinction. Commercial certainty will be promoted by applying contract law's objective approach to determining whether a claimant intended to transfer property. Restitution for unjust enrichment should be awarded only if the transferor did not objectively consent to the transfer, or if the consent was objectively conditional and the condition has totally failed.[5]

Worthington acknowledges that these propositions run against the grain of both the law and of legal writing at several points. The textbooks discuss proprietary

[3] 'Proprietary Restitution' (n 1) 200–01.
[4] *Equity* (n 1) 297–98.
[5] The terminology varies across successive accounts of unjust enrichment, but no change of substance is intended: *Equity* (n 1) 294–309 (proprietary restitution available for unintended transfers and unintended gifts); 'The Commercial Triple *Helix*' (n 1) 64 (vitiated consent and cases where transfer was objectively conditional and the condition failed); 'Proprietary Restitution' (n 1) 198–204 (defective intention and cases of conditional intention where there was no obligation to provide counterperformance).

restitution, if at all, as a secondary and somewhat problematic measure of relief.[6] Moreover, the unjust factors recognised by the English law of unjust enrichment, particularly mistake, are not premised on the contractual grounds of invalidation, as Worthington favours, and are defined less restrictively.[7]

In place of the isolated precedents usually discussed under the rubric of proprietary restitution Worthington draws upon established lines of authority to show how the law of unjust enrichment restores the full economic benefit of an asset to its owner. In fulfilling this function, unjust enrichment resembles trust law in being a law relating to assets, in contrast to contract and tort law, where the primary objective is to restore individuals, not assets, to the position in which they would have been if the contract had been performed or the tort not committed.[8] The model of proprietary restitution is, on this reading, part of the 'big picture' of an internally consistent private law.

The principal focus of this chapter is on trusts simply because Worthington views court-imposed trusts as equitable machinery for restoring the full economic value of assets to claimants entitled to that value. But the policy objective of distinguishing unintended transfers of property from risk-taking is not one that can, or should, be limited to establishing the criteria for awards of resulting or constructive trusts. Risk-takers ought to be no more entitled to personal restitution than to the award of a proprietary remedy. As will become clear when we examine Worthington's critique of the unjust factors of mistake and failure of consideration, the model she proposes encompasses both personal and proprietary restitution. A critical issue for the law of unjust enrichment is to identify, with greater precision than is currently the case, the risk-takers who should be denied restitution of their assets or their value.

Worthington has a general interest in the law of unjust enrichment, but she places special emphasis on the restitution of assets.[9] The asset may consist of an interest under a trust, a leasehold or security interest, or a right of possession.[10] Since the function of the trust is to restore economic value to a successful claimant, her analysis is understandably confined to those rights that can validly be held on trust. Awards of restitution for services are implicitly excluded from her model of unjust enrichment. This is in spite of the fact that the policy of not remunerating risk-takers is applied with arguably greater rigour to the provision of services than to the transfer of assets.[11] The cases on restitution for services raise many of the same issues as those dealing with restitution of assets. There are, however, discrete questions relating to an individual's freedom to reject a service that have no counterpart

[6] A Burrows, *The Law of Restitution*, 3rd edn (Oxford, Oxford University Press, 2011) 168; G Virgo, *The Principles of the Law of Restitution*, 3rd edn (Oxford, Oxford University Press, 2015) 12–17; J Edelman and E Bant, *Unjust Enrichment*, 2nd edn (Oxford, Hart Publishing, 2016) 33–46; W Swadling, 'Unjust Enrichment: Value, Rights and Trusts' (2021) 137 *LQR* 56, 76.

[7] *Barclays Bank Ltd v Simms* [1980] QB 677 (QB); *Chase Manhattan Bank NA v Israel-British Bank (London) Ltd* [1981] Ch 105 (Ch).

[8] 'The Commercial Triple Helix' (n 1) 63.

[9] ibid 36, 38–39.

[10] ibid 41, discussing a thief's possessory title.

[11] *Chief Constable of the Greater Manchester Police v Wigan Athletic AFC Ltd* [2008] EWCA Civ 1449, [2009] 1 WLR 1580.

in asset transfer cases. Importantly, liability to pay for the full economic value of a service cannot be imposed on someone who has not accepted responsibility to pay for the service.[12]

Space precludes an evaluation of all aspects of Worthington's model. This chapter singles out three issues for discussion. All three are critical to her model gaining intellectual support and perhaps, ultimately, judicial acceptance. First, and most striking, is the proposition that proprietary restitution should be recognised as the primary response to unjust enrichment, always assuming the existence of traceable property which can be restored. Secondly, the proposed grounds of unjust enrichment are reviewed. The third issue is whether a trust – resulting or constructive – is necessary or sufficient to restore the economic benefit of an unjust enrichment.

II. PROPRIETARY RESTITUTION AS THE PRIMARY RESPONSE

Arguments for an award of proprietary restitution as the primary response to an unjust enrichment claim can be constructed from more than one theoretical premise. Ordering *in specie* restitution of an asset that has been unintentionally transferred can be defended on the ground that it achieves complete corrective justice since 'the enrichment itself represents something that is the plaintiff's'.[13] More speculatively, perhaps, an Aquinian natural law perspective might be adopted, based on the moral supposition that no one should be allowed to benefit from an unintended transfer of wealth.[14] Worthington's starting point is economic: the wealth of a society is maximised if property is securely protected:

> Strong proprietary protection is warranted in the interests of preserving property to ensure greater productivity for all.[15]

The incidents of ownership recognised by a capitalist society include the right to the income derived from an asset, and to capital appreciation.[16] The function of the law of unjust enrichment is to restore the value of these incidents to an owner who has been deprived of the right to enjoy them by an unintended or misconceived transfer of title. The function of the trust is to effectuate restoration of the full value of the asset.[17]

[12] *Benedetti v Sawiris* [2013] UKSC 50; [2014] AC 938; *Mann v Paterson Constructions Pty Ltd* [2019] HCA 32, [2019] 267 CLR 560.

[13] EJ Weinrib, *The Idea of Private Law* (Cambridge, MA, Harvard University Press, 1995) 141; EJ Weinrib, 'The Corrective Justice of Liability for Unjust Enrichment' in E Bant, K Barker and S Degeling (eds), *Research Handbook on Unjust Enrichment and Restitution* (Cheltenham, Edward Elgar, 2020). Weinrib does not, however, promote a principle of 'proprietary primacy'. See also L Smith, 'Philosophical Foundations of Proprietary Remedies' in R Chambers, C Mitchell and J Penner (eds), *Philosophical Foundations of the Law of Unjust Enrichment* (Oxford, Oxford University Press, 2009) 281; C Webb, *Reason and Restitution: A Theory of Unjust Enrichment* (Oxford, Oxford University Press, 2016,) 178–81.

[14] cf Smith, 'Philosophical Foundations' (n 13) 286–89.

[15] *Equity* (n 1) 293.

[16] AM Honoré, 'Ownership' in AG Guest (ed), *Oxford Essays in Jurisprudence* (Oxford, Oxford University Press, 1961) 107.

[17] 'The Commercial Triple Helix' (n 1) 37.

It is important to keep this economic rationale of unjust enrichment clearly in mind when assessing Worthington's model. Her aim is not just to organise private law concepts and categories on a coherent basis, although that is certainly one of her objectives. Her basal concern is to establish how private law can most effectively protect property rights in a capitalist society. The trust plays a necessary role, on this account, in promoting economic stability by ensuring that the investment value of property is restored to the party entitled to exploit that value.

Some examples of proprietary restitution are easy to explain in terms of safeguarding a stable economic order. They include proprietary restitution of the proceeds of theft, although, in this instance, corrective justice and natural justice justifications for primary proprietary protection are also available.[18] Similarly, proprietary restitution as the primary response to undue influence or unconscionability can be explained in terms of safeguarding the exercise of rational choice in taking decisions affecting economic entitlements.[19] It is controversial whether individuals do in fact make rational, utility-maximising decisions, but it is elementary that an owner transferring title under undue influence is disabled from exercising genuine choice to obtain the full economic benefit from her property. As far as proprietary restitution from third parties is concerned, a combination of the doctrine of notice and the acquisition of title by registration establish, between them, clear economic boundaries to the availability of proprietary restitution. The burden of increased transaction costs, including the cost of time, associated with making inquiries has been judicially recognised as a reason for rejecting the application of the doctrine of constructive notice to determine whether a third party will be bound by notice of an equitable interest in personal property.[20]

None of these examples explicitly relate to the rationale of proprietary restitution, but all are consistent with Worthington's aim of promoting wealth maximisation by enabling claimants to recover the full economic value of their property rights.

Even if this rationale were to be accepted, objection can be taken on pragmatic grounds to awarding trusts as the primary response to unjust enrichment. Opponents of proprietary overreach often point to the creation of a new class of creditors who, by virtue of their status as trust beneficiaries, stand outside the pool of unsecured creditors.[21] Insolvency law's principle of 'creditor collectivism' assumes that

[18] *Black v Freedman & Co* [1910] HCA 58, (1910) 12 CLR 105. For a natural law rationale, see Aquinas, *Summa Theologica* Art 6, discussed by Smith, 'Philosophical Foundations' (n 13) 281, 287–89. In Australia the question whether a constructive trust imposed over the proceeds of stolen property reverses unjust enrichment, protects pre-existing property rights or is a restitutionary remedy for wrongdoing is contested: see K Handley, 'The *Black v Freedman* trust: Vindicating Proprietary Rights or Remedying Wrongs?' in E Bant and M Bryan (eds), *Principles of Proprietary Remedies* (Sydney, Lawbook, 2013) 117; R Chambers, 'Trust and Theft' in E Bant and M Harding (eds), *Exploring Private Law* (Cambridge, Cambridge University Press, 2010) 223.

[19] A Sen, 'Rational Behaviour' in *The New Palgrave Dictionary of Economics*, ed SN Durlauf and LE Blume, 2nd edn (Basingstoke, Palgrave Macmillan, 2008) R 1–12.

[20] *Manchester Trust v Furness, Withy & Co Ltd* [1895] 2 QB 539 (CA) 545 (Lindley LJ).

[21] Court-imposed trusts also confer priority over later equitable mortgagees, applying the 'first in time' principle. In *Muschinski v Dodds* (1985) 160 CLR 583 the imposition of the constructive trust was declared to take effect from the date of judgment so as not to prejudice potential third-party claims: 623 (Deane J).

the post-insolvency distribution of assets should mirror as closely as possible pre-insolvency entitlements, subject to statutory policy-based exceptions.[22] There are limits to the principle of 'creditor collectivism', one of which concerns property held by an insolvent on trust for a third party. Insolvency orthodoxy holds that property beneficially owned by a third party has no part to play in 'creditor collectivism'.[23] This is not because the law has carved out an exception to collective asset distribution but because property beneficially owned by a third party never belonged to the creditor pool in the first place. Liquidators, and even more unsecured creditors caught up in the insolvency, can nonetheless be excused for regarding this reasoning as casuistical when applied, not to a pre-existing property interest (as will be the case, for example, with an interest held an express trust), but to a new equitable interest arising from the receipt of the enrichment.[24] The suspicion that the interest was judicially created precisely in order to establish priority status on bankruptcy may be hard to dispel.

Judicial perceptions of the unfairness to creditors of restitutionary trusts inform two recent developments in Australian equity. Although well intentioned, they have the potential to complicate the ascertainment of a claimant's right to proprietary restitution. The first involves the application of one of the 'fundamental' tenets of trusts law identified by Lord Browne-Wilkinson in *Westdeutsche Landesbank Girozentrale v Islington London Borough Council*.[25] This is the principle that, since equity operates on the conscience of the owner of the legal interest, that owner cannot be a trustee if he is unaware of the matters that are alleged to affect his conscience. Lord Browne-Wilkinson's 'fundamental principle' received a practical application in the New South Wales decision of *Wambo Coal Pty Ltd v Ariff*.[26] A mistake of identity caused two payments to be made to the wrong payee company. The first defendant, Ariff, who was the administrator of the payee company when the mistaken payments were made, and who subsequently became the company's liquidator, caused the payments to be transferred into the account of the second defendant, a company he controlled. It was found that the payee company did

[22] TH Jackson, *The Logic and Limits of Bankruptcy Law* (Cambridge, MA, Harvard University Press, 1986). This rationale for the *pari passu* principle is controversial: E Warren, 'Bankruptcy Policy' [1984] *University of Chicago Law Review* 97; R Mokal, 'Priority as Pathology: The *Pari Passu* Myth' (2001) 60 *CLJ* 581. For a review of the debate and an argument for a natural law justification of the *pari passu* principle, see J Purcell, 'A Corrective and Distributive Justice Analysis of Creditor Entitlements in Bankruptcy' (PhD thesis, Melbourne University 2014).

[23] cf the doctrine of reputed ownership, which had brought some of these cases within the *pari passu* principle, now abolished by the omission of the words 'goods in the reputed ownership of the bankrupt' from the definition of the bankrupt's estate in Insolvency Act 1986 (UK) s 283(1).

[24] *Equity* (n 1) 290–92; Burrows, *Law of Restitution* (n 6) 168–69. Contrast Virgo, *Principles of the Law of Restitution* (n 6) 11–17.

[25] *Westdeutsche* (n 2) 705. Cp *Bailey v Angove's Pty Ltd* [2016] UKSC 47, [2016] 1 WLR 3179 (*Angove's*) [29]–[30] (Lord Sumption), discussed in 'Proprietary Restitution' (n 1) 213–16.

[26] *Wambo Coal Pty Ltd v Ariff* [2007] NSWSC 589, (2007) 63 ACSR 429. See also *AE Brighton Holdings Pty Ltd v UDP Holdings Pty Ltd* [2020] VSCA 235 [30]–[32]; B Macfarlane, 'Trusts and Knowledge: Lessons from Australia' in J Glister and P Ridge (eds), *Fault Lines in Equity* (Oxford, Hart Publishing, 2012) 169, 180–82.

not have knowledge of the mistake when the first payment was made but should have known that the second payment was mistaken.[27] A direct application of Lord Browne-Wilkinson's 'conscience' principle meant that a constructive trust was imposed over the second payment, but not the first.

The 'conscience' approach adds a new layer of uncertainty to the process of ascertaining the pool of assets available for distribution to creditors. A payment conferring beneficial title on the payee, and therefore prospectively available for distribution to the payee's creditors in the event of insolvency, subsequently becomes trust property and is then taken out of the creditors' asset pool once knowledge of the mistake is sheeted home to the payee. Determining precisely when it is removed from the asset pool depends on the court's determination of the date on which the payee is found to have known, or ought to have known, the facts entitling the payer to restitution. The payee's knowledge is relevant even though he may well not be an interested party in the dispute between the unjust enrichment claimant and the unsecured creditors. The size of the insolvency pool available to the unsecured creditors will depend on the answer to this knowledge inquiry.[28]

The second proposed limitation on the enforcement of trust interests against creditors is that the beneficiary's right to the full economic benefit of her interest ought to be enforceable outside, but not inside, insolvency. This suggestion was floated as an obiter dictum in *Grimaldi v Chameleon Mining NL (No 2)*.[29] The case concerned fiduciary liability for an undisclosed personal interest and is therefore a decision on restitution for equitable wrongdoing, not on unjust enrichment. The dictum of the Full Federal Court on constructive trust relief is nonetheless relevant to the analysis of the impact of insolvency on beneficial title. Applying binding High Court of Australia authority, the court stated that a constructive trust should not be imposed if other orders are capable of achieving full justice.[30] The court proceeded to give an example of withholding the award of a trust:

> Such could be the case, for example, where a bribed fiduciary, having profitably invested the bribe, is then bankrupted and, apart from the investment, is hopelessly insolvent. In such a case a lien on that property may well be sufficient to achieve 'practical justice' in the circumstances. This said, a constructive trust is likely to be awarded as of course where the bribe still exists in its original, or in a traceable, form, and no third party issue arises.[31]

[27] *Wambo* (n 26) [48]–[55] Since Ariff was controlling the company at the relevant times, his knowledge was attributed to the company. 'Knowledge' was defined, oddly in this context, as knowledge required to establish liability under the second (assistance) limb of *Barnes v Addy*: *Wambo* [44]. Assistance liability in Australia is posited on proof of 'knowing', not 'dishonest', assistance: *Farah Constructions Pty Ltd v Say-Dee Pty Ltd* [2007] HCA 22, (2007) 230 CLR 89 [174]–[178].

[28] cf *Ali v Dinc* [2020] EWHC 3055 (Ch) [225] (Sarah Worthington QC (Hon) sitting as a Deputy High Court Judge): 'The constructive trust analysis advocated in *Westdeutsche* leaves the messy problem of needing to determine when a defendant should be considered to know that particular receipts were not his to treat as his own.'

[29] *Grimaldi v Chameleon Mining NL (No 2)* [2012] FCAFC 6, (2012) 200 FCR 296.

[30] *Bathurst City Council v PWC Properties Pty Ltd* [1998] HCA 59, (1998) 195 CLR 566 [42].

[31] *Grimaldi* (n 29) [583].

This dictum is consistent with the recognition in Australia of the remedial constructive trust.[32] It is important, however, to confine its scope to restitution for wrongs (and specifically to breaches of fiduciary duty) and not to extend it to unjust enrichment claims. If applied to a trust claim to the proceeds of a mistaken payment, it departs from the principle of 'creditor collectivism'. Assuming that the claimant is entitled to the benefit of a constructive trust at the time of the defendant's receipt of the payment, the entitlement will possibly be lost in the event of the defendant's insolvency. The qualification 'possibly lost' reflects the reality that the availability of trust relief depends on the exercise of equitable discretion. Viewed from an insolvency perspective, the payer's post-insolvency rights will not mirror her pre-insolvency entitlement. Pre-insolvency, the invested or appreciated value of the payment will be recoverable. Post-insolvency and applying this dictum, the claimant may lose her entitlement to the full economic benefit of her property. Proprietary relief will be limited to the amount of the payment received.

The methods employed in these cases to reconceptualise the criteria for the award of a trust are unconvincing, even though the *Grimaldi* approach evokes sympathy as a valiant attempt to improve the position on insolvency of that perennial loser, the unsecured creditor. They either ignore the principle of 'creditor collectivism', or else artificially manipulate the size of the pool of assets available to unsecured creditors, or they do both.

Worthington's model is designed to promote doctrinal coherence. In doing so, it avoids the uncertainties attending either the application of Lord Browne-Wilkinson's 'conscience' approach or judicial attempts to manipulate the size of the creditor pool. But the model's coherence with the rest of private law is not the only consideration. The analysis of a trust reversing unjust enrichment as one based on the creation of a new equitable interest, and not on the enforcement of pre-existing title, may well encounter resistance in an insolvency setting. Legal logic is not the only factor determining the acceptability of a scheme of proprietary restitution. Considerations of legal method and policy must also come into play. Some of these considerations will be examined at the end of this chapter.

III. THE GROUNDS OF RESTITUTION

Possible criticism of Worthington's scheme on the ground of its potential proprietary overreach, and reduction of the asset pool available to unsecured creditors, is countered by the adoption of a strict approach to the definition of the two unjust factors, mistake and failure of consideration, that are most often in play in insolvency cases. The purpose of re-examining the grounds of restitution is to differentiate cases of genuinely unintended transfers of assets from commercial risk-taking. Only the former ought to attract a restitutionary response.

It is trite law that an unjust enrichment claim requires proof of an unjust factor. Unjust factors are identified by simple conceptual labels – mistake, duress, total

[32] *Muschinski v Dodds* (n21); *Baumgartner v Baumgartner* [1987] HCA 59, (1987) 164 CLR 137.

failure of consideration, and so forth. Labelling is dangerous because it encourages the misconception that the dictionary definition of a concept, such as mistake, is correlated to what must be proved to establish a legal ground of restitution. The legal meaning of mistake does not coincide with the dictionary meaning: not all mistakes entitle a mistaken payer to restitution.[33] Arguments about the recognition of some unjust factors have been bedevilled by misunderstandings of the purpose of labelling.[34] What matters is not the label, which is simply a convenient shorthand for the unjust factor, but the criteria for restitution that are concealed by the label.

Worthington's concern is that, under cover of the labels of 'mistake' and 'failure of consideration', courts award proprietary restitution to claimants who should not be allowed to recover the full economic value of a payment made or of property transferred. Specifically, proprietary relief ought not to be granted to a risk-taker whose only claim against a non-performing counterparty should lie (if anywhere) in contract law, even though that claim may have been rendered worthless by the counterparty's insolvency.[35] How is risk-taking to be removed from the ambit of the law of unjust enrichment? Worthington's answer to this question is to redefine the unjust factors so that they are more closely aligned with the bargaining flaws or failed conditions that justify the invalidation of a contract.[36] The defective intention entitling a payer to restitution from a payee should be the same as the defective intention that invalidates a contract with that payee. Conversely, no restitution should be allowed to the payer who objectively intended to make the payment, even if she is subjectively mistaken.

The 'defective intention' category of unjust factors includes grounds that may also prevent the formation of a valid contract, such as mistake, duress and undue influence. Mistake is the most problematic in this group. The causative mistake test for establishing this ground of restitution ('did the mistake cause the payment to be made?') has a strong pro-restitutionary bias, thereby undermining the countervailing policy of 'security of receipts' which favours the recipient. The concept of 'mistake' has considerable restitutionary reach, even allowing for the irrecoverability of payments based on mispredictions. The late Peter Birks's vision of unjust enrichment, based on broadly defined unjust factors but subject to vigorous defences, does not, on Worthington's analysis, achieve the right balance between restoring the economic value of property to the claimant and safeguarding the security of completed transactions.[37]

[33] Edelman and Bant, *Unjust Enrichment* (n 6) 172–79, including the discussion of risk-taking at 178–79. See also F Wilmot-Smith, 'Replacing Risk-Taking Reasoning' (2011) 127 *LQR* 610; Virgo, *Principles of the Law of Restitution* (n 6) 36–37.

[34] See, for example, the argument that 'ignorance' should not be recognised as an unjust factor because on the ground of lack of authority for the label: *Farah Constructions* (n 27) [156]. The relevant question should be whether the principles encapsulated by the label 'ignorance' have been recognised as justifying restitution for unjust enrichment.

[35] Lord Sumption's dicta in *Angove's* (n 25) [29] disapproving Bingham J's reasoning justifying the constructive award in *Neste Oy v Lloyd's Bank plc* [1983] 2 Lloyds Rep 658 (QB) is endorsed from this perspective in 'Proprietary Restitution' (n 1) 214.

[36] 'Proprietary Restitution' (n 1) 198.

[37] P Birks, *An Introduction to the Law of Restitution* (Oxford, Clarendon Press, 1985). Contrast 'The Commercial Triple Helix' (n 1) 58.

In response, she identifies two distinct types of asset transfer. The first, 'unintended transfers', adopts the definition of mistake applied in contract law. Contract law usually applies an objective standard to determine whether a contract is void or voidable, although a subjective test applies if the mistake was induced by the defendant, for example, by a misrepresentation or by 'snapping up' an offer.[38] The second category, 'unintended gifts', picks up some cases of failure of consideration, as well as others conventionally analysed under the rubric of 'mistake'. The customer who pays her gas bill twice will be entitled to a trust (if her payment is traceable) not because she made a mistake but because she made an unintended gift of the second payment to the gas company. In *Chase Manhattan Bank v Israel-British Bank*,[39] on which that double-paying customer will rely, the plaintiff bank made an unintended gift of US$2 million, justifying the award of a trust (again assuming traceability of the payment) – arising on receipt, and liberated from the knowledge requirement on proprietary restitution imposed by Lord Browne-Wilkinson in *Westdeutsche*.[40] The facts of *Westdeutsche* itself will, on this analysis, also justify a trust award.[41]

Granted that 'causative mistake' is too blunt an instrument to distinguish between genuinely unintended enrichments and risk-taking property transfers, one might nonetheless doubt whether Worthington's model contributes much to enhancing commercial certainty in this branch of the law. Most successful claims based on 'causative mistake' will also entitle the mistaken payer to restitution under her scheme, not because the payment was mistaken but because an unintended gift has been made.[42] Her model does, however, make a difference in one type of case. Restitution, under current law, will be granted to a mistaken payer who has a donative intent if that intent rests on a misapprehension of the facts motivating the payment.[43] For Worthington, this is not an unintended transfer that ought to entitle the payer to restitution.

Many early 'mistaken motive' cases involved family property settlements, and posed no special threat to commercial certainty, even though the impact of the law of unjust enrichment on the administration of these settlements would have been considerable. But the *Pitt v Holt*[44] litigation, when read together with the post-*Pitt v Holt* authorities, carried the right to restitution based on 'mistaken motive for payment' far beyond family arrangements, and has the potential to unsettle the security of commercial transactions.

Worthington is right to argue that the payer whose motive is mistaken should have no right to restitution. Motivation is a weak reason for recovering an asset if

[38] *Hartog v Colin & Shields* [1939] 3 All ER 566 (KB); *Taylor v Johnson* [1983] HCA 5, (1983) 151 CLR 422.

[39] *Chase Manhattan Bank v Israel-British Bank* [1981] Ch 105 (Ch).

[40] *Westdeutsche* (n 2) 714–15 (Lord Browne-Wilkinson).

[41] 'The Commercial Triple Helix' (n 1) 59, n 118 (both parties made unintended gifts to each other since the contract supposedly governing the swaps arrangement was void).

[42] Other 'unintended gift' cases include *Barclays Bank Ltd v WJ Simms Ltd* [1980] QB 677 (QB) and *David Securities Pty Ltd v Commonwealth Bank of Australia* [1992] HCA 353, (1992) 175 CLR 353.

[43] *Lady Hood of Avalon v Mackinnon* [1909] 1 Ch 476 (Ch). cf *Ogilvie v Littleboy* (1897) 13 TLR 399 (CA), upheld sub nom *Ogilvie v Allen* (1899) 15 TLR 294 (HL).

[44] *Pitt v Holt; Futter v Futter* [2013] UKSC 26, [2013] AC 108 [104]–[135].

the intention to transfer is in all other respects unimpaired. The comparison with contract law on this point is convincing. It is hard to see why an erroneous motive justifies restitution of an asset when it does not justify rescission of a contract. The difference between the two situations cannot be rationalised by arguing that considerations of sanctity of contract explain the disallowance of rescission in the latter case. The real question in both cases ought to be whether there is a sound reason for unsettling the recipient's security of title to property received under the relevant transaction.

The problem here is not with Worthington's model but with the direction English law has taken. In *Pitt v Holt*, Lord Walker reasserted the equitable jurisdiction to set aside voluntary dispositions on the ground of causative mistake where the mistake is so grave that it would be unconscionable to leave it uncorrected.[45] The revived jurisdiction is inconsistent with Worthington's approach: the mistakes in these 'unconscionability' cases relate to assumptions made by the donor, usually as to the fiscal implications of the disposition, and not to whether the disposition itself was intended. A steady flow of post-*Pitt v Holt* authority on 'unconscionable mistake' has been sensitive to commercial considerations, including whether the claimant has taken the risk of being mistaken.[46] But the suspicion remains that the litigation costs involved in evaluating factors relevant to applying the discretionary 'in the round' approach favoured by Lord Walker to mistakes of motive are high. Moreover, 'unconscionable mistake' perpetuates a distinction between mistake at common law and mistake in equity that English courts have been concerned, elsewhere in the law, to eliminate.[47]

The other unjust factor examined by Worthington is the failure of the consideration (or basis) for transferring an asset.[48] This factor is also open to criticism. Like mistake, the cases sometimes fail to distinguish between a genuinely unintended transfer and a transfer consequential on a misjudged commercial risk.[49] Worthington's model permits proprietary restitution if the recipient of an asset was under no contractual obligation to provide counterperformance.[50] This includes cases where property rights have been transferred pursuant to a void or voidable contract objectively assumed to be valid. Failure of the contractual basis for making the transfer in these cases will mean that the transferor has made an unintended gift. 'Unintended

[45] E Bant, 'Constructive Trusts, Unconscionability and the Necessity for Working Criteria' (2014) 8 *Journal of Equity* 259, 273–82 ('Constructive Trusts'), discussing practical application of the unconscionability test. *Bhaur v Equity First Trustees (Nevis) Ltd* [2021] EWHC 2581 (Ch), [2021] BTC 31 [107]–[126] identifies some of these considerations including the causation requirement, tax implications of the mistake, the mistake/misprediction distinction, and risk acceptance.

[46] *Co-operative Bank plc v Hayes Freehold Ltd* [2017] EWHC (Ch) 1820; *Bhaur v Equity First Trustees (Nevis) Ltd*, ibid [124]–[126].

[47] *Great Peace Shipping Ltd v Tsavliris Salvage (International) Ltd* [2002] EWCA Civ 1407, [2003] QB 679. Cp Bant, 'Constructive Trusts' (n 45) 275, observing that that the differences between mistakes at law and in equity 'are more apparent than real' when regard is had to the factors relevant to determining whether a mistake justifies relief.

[48] The analysis assumes that restitutionary claims based on failure of consideration are not confined to money: see Virgo, *Principles of the Law of Restitution* (n 6) 311–12; Burrows, *Law of Restitution* (n 6) 346–47; Edelman and Bant, *Unjust Enrichment* (n 6) 256–57.

[49] *Neste Oy v Lloyd's Bank plc* (n 35), disapproved in *Angove's* (n 25) [29] (Lord Sumption).

[50] 'Proprietary Restitution' (n 1) 203.

gifts' also captures dispositions made under illegal contracts, provided that public policy permits restitution,[51] and under frustrated contracts where the transferor of an asset has not received counterperformance.[52] Worthington also recognises the availability of proprietary restitution, on the ground of 'failure of an objective condition', where the contract provides for payment to be applied on *Quistclose* terms which have not been carried out.[53]

Bringing *Quistclose* arrangements into the scheme of proprietary restitution for unjust enrichment raises some awkward questions. The creation of a *Quistclose* trust is an exercise of autonomy by informed legal actors. Should commercial parties be allowed to stipulate the circumstances in which proprietary restitution for unjust enrichment will be available?[54] Then there is the question of the *Quistclose* trust's function. Although formally a trust, the arrangement substantively secures, not the repayment of an obligation, but the application of a loan for its stipulated purpose. Does the lender's resulting trust enforce the economic benefit of ownership, or does it operate functionally as a species of equitable charge? Arguments have been adduced on both sides of these questions.[55] A *Quistclose* arrangement is a doubtful candidate for inclusion in a scheme of proprietary restitution designed to restore the right to an asset to its owner. It is better analysed as an example of contractual restitution *in specie*, the trust operating as a 'default trust' in the absence of express provision governing the destination of such part of a loan as has not been applied for its specified purpose. To judge by dicta in recent decisions, the law is heading in this direction.[56]

IV. TRUSTS THAT REVERSE UNJUST ENRICHMENT

The question here is whether the trust conclusion logically follows from the unjust enrichment premise. If, as Worthington argues, the goal of unjust enrichment law is to restore the economic benefit of an asset to its dis-enriched owner, is the award of a court-imposed trust the most effective means of achieving that goal?[57] The answer

[51] *Patel v Mirza* [2016] UKSC 42, [2017] AC 467.

[52] Law Reform (Frustrated Contracts) Act 1943. See also the category of failure of consideration described by Burrows, *Law of Restitution* (n 6) 398–99, as instances of a 'failure of an unpromised future event', citing *Chillingworth v Esche* [1924] 1 Ch 97 (CA); *Roxborough v Rothmans of Pall Mall of Australia Ltd* [2001] HCA 68, (2001) 208 CLR 516. The contracts in these cases were not frustrated but did not allocate the risk that materialised.

[53] *Barclays Bank Ltd v Quistclose Investments Ltd* [1970] AC 567 (HL); 'The Commercial Triple Helix' (n 1) 59. cf *Ali v Dinc* (n 28) [321]–[323] on overreaching interests under *Quistclose* trusts.

[54] Courts are astute about preventing simple debts from being recharacterised as *Quistclose* trusts: *Prickly Bay Waterside Ltd v British American Insurance Company (Grenada) Ltd* [2022] UKPC 8, [2022] 1 WLR 2087.

[55] R Stevens, 'Insolvency' in W Swadling (ed), *The Quistclose Trust: Critical Essays* (Oxford, Hart Publishing, 2004) 153, 165–66. In Australia s 8(1)(h) of the Personal Property Securities Act 2009 (Cth) excludes the *Quistclose* trust from the statutory definition of a security interest.

[56] cf *Twinsectra v Yardley* [2002] UKHL 12, [2002] 2 AC 164 (HL), [100] (Lord Millett); *Prickly Bay* (n 54) [22] (Lady Arden), emphasising the default role performed by *Quistclose* trusts in commercial lending.

[57] 'The Commercial Triple Helix' (n 1) 36–37. Space precludes consideration of the taxonomic question whether the trust should be classified as resulting or constructive.

to the question given in this chapter is a qualified affirmative. Court-imposed trusts capture, more completely than their alternatives,[58] the full economic value of ownership for the successful claimant. In this sense they accomplish 'perfect restitution'. But there are well-known doctrinal and practical limitations on trust enforcement. They include the loss or destruction of the asset, or its acquisition by a good faith purchaser. The limitations can only be overcome by developing 'partial trust' alternatives. This means in practice that personal and proprietary remedies for unjust enrichment must be better integrated than they are at present. A more radical step would be to pursue further the idea of proprietary restitution without trusts. Why should 'perfect restitution' be limited to the existing menu of equitable remedies? There is a respectable case to be argued for the law to develop an order of specific restitution, instead of relying on court-imposed trusts with their imperfect analogies to the express trust.[59]

Trusts that reverse unjust enrichment must comply with many, though not all, of the requirements of any other trust. One requirement is the necessity for identifiable trust property. No trust can be imposed if the property has been destroyed, or for some other reason cannot be specifically restored (eg, if it is not situated within the court's jurisdiction). Moreover, the trust cannot be enforced against a good faith purchaser of the legal interest in the property for value without notice of the claimant's interest. But the good faith purchase defence is not necessarily the end of the story. The claimant can assert a trust over the consideration paid by the good faith purchaser to the unjustly enriched recipient if the consideration can be traced. If the 'consideration trail' runs out, the claimant will be remitted to a personal award of restitution. Loss or destruction of the trust property are of course fatal to any proprietary claim. Additionally, a claimant will often be content with a money award obtained against a solvent recipient for the value of the property received, plus interest, even if a trust remedy is available. Just as it is not always necessary to claim the benefit of a constructive trust over property if an account of profits will achieve full disgorgement, so also personal restitution for unjust enrichment may well be rationally preferred to the constructive trust where both remedies are available.

Leaving aside bankruptcy concerns, considered in part II above, a scheme such as Worthington's for imposing trusts as the primary remedies for unintended transfers is unlikely to result in more proprietary restitution than occurs at present. For a host of doctrinal and pragmatic reasons, personal remedies for unjust enrichment will remain more common than proprietary alternatives. The theory of Worthington's scheme is therefore more radical than, if implemented, its likely practice. The scheme raises, however, a little-discussed question about the relationship between personal and proprietary remedies.

[58] Alternatives which are often overlooked include: (i) a continuing, secured account of profits order, not confined to profits accrued at the date of judgment, and typically made in cases where delinquent trustees have profited from developing a mine: *Primeau v Granfield* 184 F 480 (SDNY 1911) (Learned Hand J); *Grimaldi* (n 29) [541]–[546]; (ii) a mandatory restorative injunction, discussed in *Smethurst v Commissioner of Police* [2020] HCA 14, [2020] 376 ALR 575 [248]–[260] (Edelman J).

[59] L Smith, 'Unravelling Proprietary Restitution' (2004) 40 *Canadian Business Law Journal* 317; K Mason, 'Deconstructing Constructive Trusts in Australia' (2010) 4 *Journal of Equity* 98; E Bant and M Bryan, 'Specific Restitution without Trusts' (2012) 6 *Journal of Equity* 181.

Arguments for the primacy of either personal or proprietary restitution minimise the frequent situations where they are combined. Complete restitution often means *both* imposing a trust *and* making a personal restitution award. The case law on equitable rescission, arguably the most fully evolved species of proprietary restitution, provides many examples of the interplay of proprietary and personal measures of relief. If a contract for the sale of a business is rescinded for misrepresentation, the terms of relief may include the imposition of a trust over physical and intangible assets transferred by the vendor, as well as over the traceable proceeds of the price paid by the purchaser for the assets. The terms of rescission will sometimes also include personal adjustment orders to reflect depreciation, deterioration or disposal of business assets.[60]

Even the sophisticated version of proprietary-cum-personal relief awarded in the equitable rescission cases sometimes falls short of achieving full restitution. An example that has attracted some academic attention is that of the claimant who transfers an asset under a voidable contract that is later sub-sold to a good faith purchaser, the consideration for the sub-sale being spent by the sub-seller on a holiday. The suggestion has been made that the claimant should be entitled to what has been described as 'pecuniary rescission' against her contractual counterparty (the sub-seller), assessed as the value of the asset received by the counterparty, unless the latter can show that he changed his position in good faith.[61] Although Worthington does not discuss this question in the publications with which this chapter is concerned,[62] application of her scheme ought to result in the claimant receiving an award of personal restitution for the unintended transfer of her property, provided that she has elected to rescind the contract. If the aim of the law of unjust enrichment is to restore to the claimant the full economic value of the asset of which she has been deprived, the quantum of the money award will be the value of the property in the hands of the third party, assessed at the date of trial. But the price paid by the good faith purchaser to the sub-seller may be a convenient proxy for the value if it proves difficult to obtain access to the asset, for valuation purposes, from the good faith purchaser.

A second problem, which Worthington's scheme solves neatly, concerns the application of the resulting trust to reverse unjust enrichment. The extensive modern literature on the resulting trust's rationale and practical application can, for the most part, be put aside.[63] That it functionally reverses unjust enrichment has been recognised.[64] But incorporating resulting trusts doctrinally within the law of

[60] *Adam v Newbigging* (1888) 13 App Cas 308 (HL); *Alati v Kruger* (1955) 94 CLR 216. The line between restitution and compensation can be hard to draw in this area: D O'Sullivan, S Elliott and R Zakrzewski, *The Law of Rescission* (Oxford, Oxford University Press, 2008) paras 17.53–17.58.

[61] P Birks, *Unjust Enrichment*, 2nd edn (Oxford, Oxford University Press, 2005) 226–28. There are isolated but ambiguous precedents for an award of pecuniary rescission: *Mahoney v Purnell* [1996] 3 All ER 61 (QB); *Hartigan v International Society for Krishna Consciousness* [2002] NSWSC 810.

[62] But see S Worthington, 'The Proprietary Consequences of Rescission' [2002] *Restitution Law Review* 28.

[63] The literature is briefly reviewed in 'The Commercial Triple Helix' (n 1) 49–52.

[64] *El Ajou v Dollar Land Holdings plc* [1993] 3 All ER 717 (Ch), 734; *Evans of Robb Evans & Associates v European Bank Ltd* [2004] NSWCA 82 [112]–[114] (Spigelman CJ).

unjust enrichment is challenging. The second part of Robert Chambers's scholarly monograph on resulting trusts tried to fit the case law on resulting trusts within the framework of the unjust factors recognised by the law of unjust enrichment.[65] It was, he later admitted, 'not an easy fit'.[66] The historical divide between common law and equity is one of the problems. The classification of resulting trusts that emerged in fifteenth-century equity from volunteer feoffees holding title of land for the benefit of feoffors, or from the failure of an express trust (or use), differs from the categories into which the authorities on the common law action for money and received are organised, even though there are underlying factual similarities between the two types of case.

Worthington's answer is not to force the resulting trust authorities into the strait-jacket of unjust factors. Instead, the unjust factors and the presumption of resulting trust are aligned with each other. The mistakes and failures of consideration that, as we saw in the previous section, can be analysed as unintended gifts of assets also provide the factual foundation for applying the presumption of resulting trust. She argues that the fact presumed to give rise to a resulting trust is not that the provider of property intended the recipient to hold the property on trust for the provider (as Lord Browne-Wilkinson, adopting the analysis of Swadling, held[67]), nor that the provider did not intend to benefit the recipient (as Chambers argued[68]). The presumption is that the provider did not intend to benefit the recipient *by gift*. We saw earlier that the customer who double-pays her gas bill is entitled to restitution of the second payment on the ground that it was an unintended gift to the gas company. Applying the resulting trust path, we arrive at the same conclusion: the gas company presumptively holds the payment on resulting trust for the customer because she did not intend to benefit the company by way of gift. If the gas company's impenetrable accounts system is an obstacle to imposing a resulting trust over the proceeds of the payment, personal restitution of the value of the unintended gift will still be ordered. Although she does not explain it quite in these terms, Worthington is advocating a unitary scheme of restitution for unintended gifts combining both common law unjust enrichment and equitable resulting trust principles, and resting on identical grounds for awarding personal and proprietary remedies.

In an Australian decision concerning restitution of the proceeds of fraud, it was argued that personal restitution was available if the criteria for recognising a resulting trust were satisfied but the trust property no longer existed.[69] The argument failed for want of authority. Under Worthington's scheme, absence of subject matter will also, inevitably, defeat the claim to proprietary restitution. But the claimant will be entitled to personal restitution, for precisely the same reason that, had trust property existed,

[65] R Chambers, *Resulting Trusts* (Oxford, Clarendon Press, 1997).

[66] R Chambers, 'Constructive and Resulting Trusts' in C Mitchell (ed), *Constructive and Resulting Trusts* (Oxford, Hart Publishing, 2010) 267, 287.

[67] *Westdeutsche* (n 2) 708; W Swadling, 'A New Role for Resulting Trusts?' (1996) 16 *LS* 110.

[68] Chambers, *Resulting Trusts* (n 65) 33.

[69] *Port of Brisbane Corp v ANZ Securities Ltd (No2)* [2002] QCA 158, [2003] 2 Qd 661 [28]–[37] (McPherson JA). The defences of change of position and ministerial receipt defeated a common law unjust enrichment claim based on *Lipkin Gorman v Karpnale Ltd* [1991] 2 AC 548 (HL).

the resulting trust would have been awarded: the victim of the fraud had made an unintended gift of her property to the fraudster.

Achieving doctrinal coherence in the law of unjust enrichment is still work in progress. This becomes clear if we do not reason, as in the previous paragraph, from the availability of a trust to an award of personal restitution, but in the opposite direction, arguing for the availability of proprietary restitution from the starting point that personal restitution can certainly be awarded on the facts. A deficiency, sometimes attributed to the common law/equity jurisdictional chasm, is that the factors entitling the claimant to personal restitution do not, if traceable property exists, necessarily entitle the claimant to proprietary restitution. Restitution for failure of consideration is the best example of the misfit between personal and proprietary restitution. Writers have drawn an arcane and awkward distinction between initial and subsequent failure of consideration in order to distinguish cases where the removal of the basis of the defendant's enrichment entitles the claimant to a proprietary remedy from others where only a personal award of restitution can be made.[70] The distinction disappears in Worthington's vision of the law. This is not because she favours proprietary restitution whenever the basis for passing title to property has failed and the claimant's property can be traced. It is simpler than that: her redefined grounds of restitution limit both personal and proprietary recovery to unintended gifts. An intended transfer of an asset will never, under her scheme, entitle the transferor to either personal or proprietary restitution.

The nirvana of a law of unjust enrichment, at which Worthington is aiming, that awards personal and proprietary restitution based on identical unjust factors (such as 'unintended transfer') is very far from being realised in English law. But it is certainly an ideal worthy of realisation. An even more idealistic proposal would be to abandon, at least for the purposes of the law of unjust enrichment, the sometimes random division of trust orders between resulting and constructive trusts, and to replace both by orders of 'specific restitution'.[71] One advantage of the proposal is that a specific restitution order would be unambiguously remedial, so that there would be no room for arguments about whether constructive trustees are fiduciaries and are subject to some or all of the duties of an express trustee. But does this proposal exceed the limits of what can be achieved by the recognised processes of developing the law by judicial decision? Judges, even in the highest appellate courts, can only travel a limited distance in the pursuit of establishing coherence in private law, applying the established principles of legal reasoning. How 'to get from here to there' is a recurring question in the law of unjust enrichment.

V. ACADEMIC AND JUDICIAL METHODS

Sarah Worthington has focused her analytical torch on the role of the trust in reversing unjust enrichment because the trust provides the necessary equitable machinery

[70] Birks, *Unjust Enrichment* (n 61) 185–98.

[71] E Bant and M Bryan, 'A Model of Proprietary Remedies' in Bant and Bryan (eds), *Principles of Proprietary Remedies* (n 18) 213–14. See also the articles listed in n 59.

for restoring the full economic value of an asset to the claimant who has been deprived of that value. But we have seen that her model is not confined to identifying the circumstances in which proprietary restitution will be available. Her justification for redefining the unjust factors of mistake and failure of consideration apply equally to both personal and proprietary restitution. What she has proposed is a coherent model of the law of unjust enrichment, applicable to any common law system recognising legal and equitable rights, albeit one that remains highly aspirational.

Her analytical reach in fact extends even further. In her most ambitious publication in this area, Worthington situates unjust enrichment in the overall design of private law, or at least that part of private law concerned with commerce.[72] According to her functional division of private law, unjust enrichment, like trusts law, is concerned with the allocation of assets. Conversely, the focus of tort and contract law is on the rights and liabilities of individuals.[73]

This binary division may be accepted, subject to qualifications. First, 'asset allocation' does not necessarily presuppose the existence of an asset. The dissipation of trust property or the expenditure of a mistaken payment on a holiday do not preclude the application of trusts law or the law of unjust enrichment. Personal remedies can still come into play. Paradoxical as it may seem, allocation rules are often applied even though there may be no asset to allocate. Secondly, although the emphasis of contract and tort is primarily on individual rights and liabilities, aspects of those areas of law have an allocative function. Negotiating damages have been held to be compensatory, but they arguably allocate the right to control the use of an asset.[74] Similarly, an account of profits awarded for breach of contract is not so much concerned with individuals as with allocating the productive output of a breach of contract.[75]

These qualifications are just quibbles on the margins of Worthington's functional analysis of private law. In general terms, it is correct to say that unjust enrichment restores the value of *unintended* transfer of assets, whereas the law of express trusts enforces the value of *intended* transfers of assets. In both cases, the aim is to ensure that the claimant or beneficiary receives the full economic value of the asset, although that aim may be qualified by the application of defences (such as change of position to the unjust enrichment claim), equitable bars such as delay (to either claim) or by the loss of destruction of the asset, which remits the claimant to a personal remedy. In the case of an express trust, the terms of the trust may specify that the beneficiary is not entitled to the full economic value of the trust property, for example where the trust stipulates that the beneficiary shall only be entitled to a right of occupation of trust property.

In summary, what Worthington offers us is therefore a functional account of private law that explains the functions of each of the basic categories of private

[72] Significant areas of private law are concerned are not concerned with the allocation of commercial risk. See the discussion of family law in H Dagan, 'The Limited Autonomy of Private Law' in *Reconstructing American Legal Realism and Rethinking Private Law Theory* (Oxford, Oxford University Press, 2013) ch 5, especially the discussion of marital property at 115–19.

[73] 'The Commercial Triple Helix' (n 1) 63–64.

[74] *Morris-Garner v One Step (Support) Ltd* [2018] UKSC20, [2019] AC 649 [30] (Lord Reed).

[75] *A-G v Blake* [2000] UKHL 45, [2001] 1 AC 268.

law, including the law of unjust enrichment which performs the necessary role of correcting unintended transfers of assets.

What is the utility of this kind of functional analysis? One obvious disadvantage is that 'big thinking' of this order is unlikely to win wholesale judicial acceptance, even by the apex court of a legal system. There are a host of practical reasons why a case law system is an unsatisfactory vehicle for making anything more than piecemeal improvements to the overall coherence of a body of private law. One is the random operation of civil litigation, which sometimes brings a cluster of cases on the same question to judicial attention within a short space of time, while leaving other areas of law untouched for decades.[76] Another is the doctrine of precedent which preserves even irrational rules until either the legislature or an ultimate appellate court loses patience and intervenes.[77] Finally, even if development of the law proceeds in the general direction indicated by the model, divergences from that path cannot be ruled out – as is shown in English law by the revival of the jurisdiction for setting aside mistaken voluntary dispositions post-*Pitt v Holt*, discussed above.

From the perspective of common law judicial method, Worthington's model does not come within Lord Goff's definition of an 'interstitial development', being more than a 'very modest development, of existing principle'.[78] Even though the model could be considered a logical extension of the existing principles governing unintended transfers, the reformulation of the criteria of mistake and failure of consideration, together with the assertion of the trust as the primary mode of restitution, amounts to what Lord Goff termed a 'judicial development … of a more radical nature', as a 'a departure … from what has previously been considered to be established principle, and leading to a realignment of subsidiary principles within that branch of the law'.[79] All schemes for reorganising areas of private law will be 'radical' in this sense, although unjust enrichment lends itself more readily to academic schematisation by reason of both its late recognition in English law and its uncertain boundaries.[80]

It would be obtuse, however, to dismiss Worthington's model of unjust enrichment solely because it is unlikely to be judicially adopted in its entirety. There are at least two reasons why her model is analytically significant. First, she has successfully demonstrated that every developed legal system requires recognition of the unjust enrichment principle in order to correct unintended transfers. This reason is important in jurisdictions, such as Australia, characterised by unjust-enrichment scepticism, and where disputes about unintended transfers are adjudicated under a variety of doctrinal labels.[81] Secondly, the adjustments to the definition of 'mistake' and 'failure

[76] Within the law of unjust enrichment, the swaps decisions and authorities on the award of compound interest arising out of European Court of Justice decisions are an example of the former, while the paucity of cases on necessitous intervention is arguably an example of the latter.

[77] cf the 'mistake of law' bar to restitution of a mistaken payment, eliminated in *Kleinwort Benson Ltd v Lincoln City Council* [1999] 2 AC 349 (HL).

[78] ibid 378 (Lord Goff).

[79] ibid.

[80] cp Birks's vision of an English law version of unjust enrichment based on the civilian 'sine causa' approach, rejected in *Deutsche Morgan Grenfell Group plc v Inland Revenue Commissioners* [2006] UKHL 49, [2007] 1 AC 558 [28] (Lord Hoffmann), [152]–[158] (Lord Walker).

[81] *Farah Constructions* (n 27) [150]–[153].

of consideration' that she recommends would, if adopted, more effectively prevent risk-takers from obtaining restitution than is currently the case.

Practical, as well as doctrinal, considerations will prevent the trust from being the primary response to unjust enrichment. But the reasons Worthington gives for limiting the grounds of restitution to objectively unintended asset transfers are compelling, even if English law has so far failed to recognise them. It will be fascinating to see whether the law will follow the path to reinvigorating the law of unjust enrichment that she has richly illuminated in her writings.

9

Exporting Fiduciary Obligations: The Case of Advisors

SIMONE DEGELING AND LIONEL SMITH*

SARAH WORTHINGTON HAS made extraordinary contributions to our understanding in many fields: commercial law, insolvency, property, security and equity. In relation to equity, her scholarship on fiduciary relationships is well known for its thoroughness and its clear and careful analysis. This chapter – in the form of a dialogue – is our tribute to Sarah and to her extraordinary academic career.

I. INTRODUCING OUR CONVERSATION

LDS: We have been asked to address the topic of 'To what extent do or should equitable notions of loyalty and stewardship inform other areas of law?' One area that is interesting in this respect is the application of the law of fiduciary relationships to advisors. Most fiduciaries – we can take agents, company directors, trustees, personal representatives – have been entrusted in one way or another with legal powers that they must use for and on behalf of others. They do not hold those powers as personal wealth; they acquired them for the benefit of others. The result is that we can conclude that 'the very *function* or *purpose* or *reason* for one party's role in the relationship demands that the party operate on the basis of self-denial'.[1] The case of advisors is different inasmuch as any power they hold over the beneficiary is purely factual. Financial advisors have been held, by the Supreme Court of Canada and the High Court of Australia, to be fiduciaries, even if they are not agents who can buy and

* This chapter is a dialogue between the coauthors. Simone Degeling (SD) specialises in equity and trusts, remedies, the law of restitution and unjust enrichment, and the intersection of civil procedure and private law doctrine. Lionel Smith (LDS) also specialises in equity and trusts and restitution, as well as comparative private law. They agree about many things, but not about everything. The authors thank the conference organisers for the invitation to participate. They also thank Sir Guy Newey who made perceptive comments in relation to the chapter, and conference participants who shared insights and observations.

[1] S Worthington, 'Fiduciaries: When Is Self-denial Obligatory?' (1999) 58 *CLJ* 500, 506 (emphasis in original).

sell in the name of the client.[2] Such a financial advisor does not have legal powers to bind the client. The advisor says, 'I suggest this investment', but the client makes the decision.

II. WHEN AND WHY ARE ADVISORS FIDUCIARIES?

LDS (cont): My own view is that the factual power of an advisor may, in some circumstances, justify characterising the advisor as a fiduciary.[3] In the case of legal powers, the mere presence of the power is not enough; lots of people have legal powers that may seriously affect other persons. Every employer can dismiss their employee. What is also needed is that the legal power is held by its holder in order to allow them to pursue some other-regarding mission, such as the trustee's role of managing the trust. In the case of advice, it seems to me that advice, properly so called, can *only* be given in the interest of the advisee. Giving advice means telling the advisee what you think is *their* best course of action in the circumstances. But not every case of giving advice rises to the level of being comparable to the holding of a legal power. This is because in the case of a legal power, the power holder is capable of unilaterally affecting the other person; in the case of an advisor, the advisee makes their own decision, and may reject the advice. This is why the cases seem to suggest that what we are looking for is an advisory relationship in which the advice is very likely to be followed. Then we are close to the situation in which the advisor actually makes the decision, at least in a practical sense; that is, to the case in which a fiduciary holds a legal power.

Do you think that the law of 'legal power fiduciaries' can rightly be applied to advisors?

SD: I am attracted to the idea of the advisor holding sufficient factual power such that equity treats them 'as if' they hold a legal power and the consequent practical ability to alter the legal status of the client. It potentially explains cases such as *Daly v Sydney Stock Exchange*[4] in which, despite the lack of agency or other entrustment of legal power, inherent in the giving of financial advice, a stockbroker was held to owe fiduciary duties to the client. The explanation also has relevance to the so-called status category of solicitor–client where there may similarly be an absence of legal power in the solicitor.[5] A solicitor who is retained to advise their client may not be a trustee, for example if no client funds are held on trust, and similarly will not necessarily be an agent.[6] The same could also be said in relation to doctors who give

[2] *Daly v Sydney Stock Exchange Ltd* [1986] HCA 25, (1986) 160 CLR 371; *Hodgkinson v Simms* [1994] 3 SCR 377; AB Laby, 'Advisors as Fiduciaries' (2020) 72 *Florida Law Review* 953.

[3] L Smith, 'Fiduciary Relationships: Ensuring the Loyal Exercise of Judgement on Behalf of Another' (2014) 130 *LQR* 608, 618–19; see now L Smith, *The Law of Loyalty* (Oxford, Oxford University Press, 2023) 264–72.

[4] *Daly* (n 2).

[5] *Hospital Products Ltd v USSC* [1984] HCA 64, (1984) 156 CLR 41, 96 (Mason J).

[6] *Nocton v Lord Ashburton* [1914] AC 932 (HL) is an example where the solicitor Nocton gave advice which was bound by an obligation of loyalty. However, Lord Ashburton had also conferred an agency on Nocton, encompassing, for example, applying for a loan on Lord Ashburton's behalf. Len Sealy argued

advice,[7] leaving to one side, for example any statutory power a doctor has to prescribe medication. Lionel's model of factual power also enriches our understanding of other well-accepted judicial accounts of fiduciary responsibility. For example, in *Hospital Products v USSC*,[8] Mason J listed the following 'accepted fiduciary relationships' as the 'illustrations' from which he 'distill[ed] the essence or the characteristics' of the fiduciary relationship: trustee and beneficiary, agent and principal, solicitor and client, employee and employer, director and company and partners. Mason J's list is not a complete list of per se fiduciary relationships, omitting, for example, guardian and ward, and tenant for life and remainderman. However, solicitor–client is unique in this list by the absence of legal power held by the solicitor. Yet Mason J's 'critical features' include the 'exercise of a power or discretion' by the fiduciary. So what is this power? Taking Lionel's approach, in the absence of agency or trust, it includes factual power which is assimilated to a legal power.

In fully understanding 'as if', it would be useful to explore some of the assumptions that underpin, and consequences of, this approach.

LDS: I think the solicitor–client relationship is a crucial example, because this relationship is treated as a per se fiduciary relationship throughout the common law world, but as you say, only sometimes does it involve legal powers. It seems clear as a matter of positive law that no legal powers are needed for this relationship to be a fiduciary one.[9]

Of course, even where someone holds legal powers that can affect another person, the relationship is not necessarily fiduciary. Lots of ordinary contractual relationships involve powers which may greatly affect the interests of the other contracting party. The crucial question is how powers are held: for oneself, as a kind of asset, or to equip one to carry out an other-regarding mission. Only in the latter case is the power a fiduciary one.[10] It is the interpretation of the grant or the source of the power that tells us whether the holder of the power holds it for their own benefit.

that Nocton was liable for breach of trust in the strict sense: LS Sealy, 'Some Principles of Fiduciary Obligations' (1963) 21 *CLJ* 119, 138–39. The argument is difficult to follow and seems to be (138) that non-disclosure converted Nocton into a trustee; but he also says that Ashburton's money 'passed through [Nocton's] hands' (139). See also LS Sealy, 'Fiduciary Obligations, Forty Years On' (1995) 1 *Journal of Contract Law* 37, text at footnote 101. In *London Loan & Savings Co v Brickenden* [1934] 3 DLR 465 (PC), it was taken to be self-evident that every solicitor is in a fiduciary relationship with their client.

[7] *Breen v Williams* [1996] HCA 57, (1995) 186 CLR 171, 134 (Gummow J) relying on the reasoning of Gibbs CJ in *Daly* (n 2) 377, 584–85.

[8] *Hospital Products Ltd v USSC* (n 5).

[9] In *Sheikh Tahnoon Bin Saeed Bin Shakhboot Al Nehayan v Kent* [2018] EWHC 333 (Comm), [2018] 1 CLC 216 [159], Leggatt LJ noted that the purely advisory solicitor–client relationship is fiduciary; and it is taken for granted in innumerable statements, in decided cases and in solicitors' codes of ethics, that the relationship is a fiduciary one.

[10] It seems to me that Sarah Worthington misreads Paul Miller and others on this point, in saying that his theory would work 'a radical redefinition of the fiduciary terrain' by greatly expanding the range of fiduciary relationships to include any situation where legal powers are held: S Worthington, 'Fiduciaries Then and Now' (2021) 80 *CLJ* S154, S169. Miller certainly does not think that all legal powers are held in a fiduciary capacity. He insists (eg PB Miller, 'The Fiduciary Relationship' in AS Gold and PB Miller (eds), *Philosophical Foundations of Fiduciary Law* (Oxford, Oxford University Press, 2014) 63, 70–71) that fiduciary power is power held for the benefit of the beneficiary, excluding, for example, merely contractual powers. In fact, on this point Miller's theory does not seem to be that different from Sarah's own, because she agrees with Len Sealy that fiduciary duties apply where 'the [fiduciary] *has control of another's property or has undertaken to act on another's behalf and for that other's benefit and not the fiduciary's*

Paul Miller has suggested that only legal (as opposed to factual) powers can be constitutive of the fiduciary relationship.[11] Miller's position is certainly cleaner analytically, because it dispenses with the need to say that some advisors are treated 'as if' they have legal powers. It does not, however, fit the positive law well; and there is reason to think that his view is ahistorical. The modern idea of a fiduciary relationship is one that attracts the well-known rules that fiduciary powers can only be used for proper purposes, that they cannot be used unimpeachably in a conflict, that the fiduciary cannot extract unauthorised profits, and that the fiduciary must disclose to the beneficiary all information in the possession of the fiduciary that is relevant to the beneficiary's decision-making process. (SD: I am well aware that Australians may not see fiduciary relationships in quite this way![12]) Historically, however, these rules evolved from principles governing relationships involving significant power imbalances.[13] In this historical sense, therefore, it seems inaccurate to suppose that legal powers, as opposed to factual influence, are essential for a fiduciary relationship.

A good illustration is the case of *Tate v Williamson*, decided in 1866 by Lord Chancellor Chelmsford before the fusion of the administration of common law and equity.[14] A young man, William Tate, had contracted bad habits and debts of about £1,000 while at Oxford University, and his 'father's doors were closed against him'.[15] He applied to his great-uncle by marriage, HH Williamson, for assistance and advice, and the great-uncle, being in poor health, deputed his nephew, the defendant, Robert Williamson, to meet with Tate. The defendant thought that the creditors' charges were excessive and could be settled for half of what was claimed; Tate refused any suggestion of negotiating with his creditors to reduce the claims, as he thought it would reflect badly on his character. Tate's only asset was a 50% interest in an estate in land. Robert Williamson had a valuation of Tate's interest at about £14,000, and he purchased Tate's interest for £7,000. Tate died intestate and his heir succeeded in having the contract set aside for non-disclosure by Robert Williamson.

This was a purely advisory relationship, and outside of any of the per se fiduciary categories known to the modern law. Chelmsford LC said:

> Wherever two persons stand in such a relation that, while it continues, confidence is necessarily reposed by one, and the influence which naturally grows out of that confidence is possessed by the other, and this confidence is abused, or the influence is exerted to obtain an advantage at the expense of the confiding party, the person so availing himself of his

own benefit' [emphasis in original]; see also S168. Even being in control of another's property is not enough; mortgagees are not fiduciaries when they enforce their security (as Sarah notes at S169). The power must always be one that was conferred for the pursuit of other-regarding objectives.

[11] Miller (n 10) 83–84. He also argues that only *discretionary* legal powers can constitute fiduciary relationships. Here, I agree with Sarah Worthington's critique (Worthington (n 10) S169)), where she points out that trustees are always fiduciaries even if their powers are not discretionary. See also the detailed discussion of whether discretion is essential in Laby (n 2) 980–89.

[12] L Smith, 'Prescriptive Fiduciary Duties' (2018) 37 *University of Queensland Law Journal* 261.

[13] See generally J Grower, *From Disability to Duty: From Constructive Fraud to Equitable Wrongs* (PhD thesis, University College London, 2021).

[14] *Tate v Williamson* (1866) 2 Ch App 55 (LC).

[15] ibid 61.

> position will not be permitted to retain the advantage, although the transaction could not have been impeached if no such confidential relationship had existed.[16]

This sounds in modern terms somewhat like a relationship of undue influence, but the decision proceeds on the basis that Robert Williamson was under a genuine duty of disclosure, as exists in a fiduciary relationship, and which would not have arisen in relation to any other purchaser, and which does not arise out of a relationship of undue influence.[17] He also owed a fiduciary's duty of care in relation to the giving of advice:

> It seems to me that the Defendant had placed himself in a position which rendered it incumbent upon him to give the best advice to the intestate how to relieve himself from his debts, and no one can doubt that if [the Defendant's] judgment had been unbiased that he would have recommended a mortgage and not a sale [because Tate's interest was worth far more than the debts he owed]. ... This being so, the Defendant, pending the agreement, was bound to communicate all the information he acquired, which it was material for the intestate [Tate] to know in order to enable him to judge of the value of his property.[18]

In short, it is only with modern eyes that we may think that an advisory relationship is an 'extension' of the fiduciary relationship.

III. WHAT IS ADVICE?

SD: To what extent is it necessary to identify advice, or advice-giving, as a discrete integer? Treating some advisory relationships as fiduciary because of the factual power of the advisor in part rests on the conclusion that they have given 'advice'. But what is 'advice'? As a concept, does it do any work here? This is a question which arises in relation to the 'as if' account, but also more broadly in those cases which consider the fiduciary responsibility of advisors. The *OED* defines 'advice' as an 'opinion given or offered as to action' and 'counsel' but it also includes 'information giving'. Part of the difficulty is that cases which consider the fiduciary responsibility of advisors generally assert or assume the giving of advice and focus instead on the course of dealing surrounding the advice. For example, as Brennan J said in *Daly*: 'Dr Daly sought advice from Patrick Partners on the investment of his money and they advised him.'[19]

A rare exception in which advice was found *not* to have been given is *Pilmer v Duke Group Ltd (in liq)*.[20] Kia Ora (ultimately Duke Group) successfully took over Western United Ltd. Both companies were listed on the Australian Stock Exchange. In compliance with the Stock Exchange listing rules, an accountant's opinion was

[16] ibid.

[17] We discuss undue influence below, Section V.

[18] ibid 64, 65.

[19] *Daly* (n 2) 384 (Brennan J).

[20] *Pilmer v Duke Group Ltd (in liq)* [2001] HCA 31, (2001) 207 CLR 165 [73] (McHugh, Gummow, Hayne and Callinan JJ). See also *Townsend v Collova* [2005] WASC 4 [171]–[172] (Le Miere J) upheld on this point *Townsend v Roussety & Co (WA) Pty Ltd* [2007] WASCA 40, 33 WAR 321 [130] (Buss JA) with whom Wheeler JA and McLure JA agreed, where an accountant who prepared cashflow projections about their client's business in response to a request from a lender was held not to be providing advice.

solicited stating that the price to be offered by Kia Ora to Western United shareholders was 'fair and reasonable'. The report was incompetently prepared, the price offered was too high and Kia Ora was later wound up. The liquidators of Kia Ora sued the accountant, including for breach of fiduciary duty as advisor. The foundation for this plea lay in the allegation that that the accountant had had a 'past and continuing "alignment"'[21] with the Kia Ora directors and therefore that the accountant acted with an undisclosed conflict of interest in accepting the retainer and writing the report. A majority of the High Court held that the opinion did not constitute 'advice in the relevant sense for the purposes of liabilities as a fiduciary'[22] since it was merely an opinion as required by a retainer entered into in conformity with the listing rules and not a statement intended to be guiding or influencing Kia Ora as to the wisdom of the takeover.[23] Even in this case it is therefore difficult to separate out the consideration of whether the conduct amounted to advice from other elements engaging fiduciary responsibility. The majority approved the reasoning in *Daly*.[24] Implicitly at least, in emphasising that the accountant was merely expressing an opinion pursuant to its retainer as required by the listing rules, and thus addressed to shareholders of Kia Ora, their Honours appear also to have held against satisfaction of the integers in *Daly* of an undertaking to advise and reliance by Kia Ora.

Whilst the decision of the Court in *Pilmer* was undoubtedly correct in holding that the certification did not constitute advice, in the sense that it was not a *recommendation* directed to Kia Ora shareholders, it does lead to a further question, which is whether a parallel category of 'opinion giving' ought to be recognised for an obligation of loyalty? The accountant was fulfilling a duty to the public, or at least a section of it, in certifying (albeit negligently) that the price offered to Western United shareholders was fair and reasonable. The certification relied on expertise, knowledge and skill, and was institutionally privileged; it was sought by and given the imprimatur of the Stock Exchange and only a person holding the necessary professional qualifications was authorised to give it. Unless the facts exceptionally support the characterisation of the work of accountants as advice givers, accountants will not owe fiduciary duties to their clients.[25] However, it is important to distinguish between the case where an accountant may or may not give advice and one where, as in *Pilmer*, an accountant gives a professional opinion or in some way performs a public duty. Depending on the circumstances, such 'opinion' giving may well hold the same potential for factual power as 'advice'. This is shown by the dissenting judgment of Kirby J in *Pilmer*. ASX rule 3J(3) provided that the necessary notice of any meeting of shareholders of Kia Ora required to approve the takeover be 'accompanied by copies of [reports and valuations] from independent qualified persons sufficient to establish that the … [price] … [was] a fair price'.[26] Relying on the terms of the listing rule and

[21] *Pilmer v Duke Group* (n 20) [81].
[22] ibid [72].
[23] ibid [73], citing at [74] the findings of the trial judge with approval.
[24] ibid [72].
[25] *Re Porter* [2021] VSC 572; *Pavan v Ratnam* (1996) 23 ACSR 214 (NSWCA); *Townsend v Collova* (n 20).
[26] *Duke Group v Pilmer* (1999) 73 SASR 64, [35] (The Court).

the surrounding circumstances, Kirby J held that by providing the valuation on these terms, the chartered accountant owed a fiduciary duty to Kia Ora shareholders.[27]

The other distinction is between advising and 'informing'. As Lionel points out, merely providing information is not generally considered to be providing advice.[28] However, we must not be too quick to label conduct as mere information giving if it involves, for example, filtering, selection or ordering. Depending on the circumstances, this may instead be giving advice. Take, for example, a mortgage broker who, after interviewing the client, is asked by the client to select, compile and provide a list of ten loan products and issuers to meet the client's needs in financing the purchase of their home. Despite not being accompanied by any specific recommendation as to suitability, does provision of this list constitute advice? Arguably yes, as the mortgage broker has filtered the loan products and issuers against a set of criteria, which the client may infer were generated by the earlier interview. Recent decisions of the Court of Appeal for England and Wales hold that such a relationship may indeed be fiduciary.[29] There may of course be subsequent interactions between the parties, in which the advisor will give further counsel as to the suitability of a particular product, but this should not obscure the earlier advice.

LDS: I agree that the dictionary distinctions between, for example, advice and information can be very difficult to apply in practice. 'My view is that this course of action is better than that one' may formally be a provision of information about my personal state of mind, but substantively it is a piece of advice, which I would say generically takes a form such as 'I counsel you to do the following …' or 'if I were you, I would do the following …'. Scholars have also tried to pull these functions apart in the law of duress. If I say 'should you insist on your contractual rights against me, I will surely go bankrupt', am I making a threat, or simply providing information?[30] In working out whether advice has been given, substance must prevail over form. In the context of the public law regulation of advice relating to investments, the Court of Appeal for England and Wales has indicated that information that is combined with a value judgment may amount to advice.[31]

If factual powers can be assimilated to legal ones for the purposes of fiduciary analysis, then it will be just as crucial in the case of factual powers as it is in the case of legal powers to ask whether the power-holder holds the power for their own benefit, to do with as they wish, or rather for the benefit of the other. My thought is that advice, properly so called, is inherently given for the benefit of the advisee. It is not given to *persuade* the advisee, but to help them. In this kind of potentially fiduciary relationship (although I do not think it applies in all of them), an undertaking on the

[27] *Pilmer v Duke Group* (n 20) [141]–[144] (Kirby J).

[28] Smith (n 3) 618.

[29] *McWilliam v Norton Finance (UK) Ltd (t/a Norton Finance (In Liquidation))* [2015] EWCA Civ 186, [2016] 1 All ER (Comm) 1026 [35]–[48] and *Adams v Options Sipp UK LLP* [2021] EWCA Civ 474, [2021] Bus LR 1568 [75]; cf DA DeMott, 'Breach of Fiduciary Duty: On Justifiable Expectations of Loyalty and Their Consequences' (2006) 48 *Arizona Law Review* 925, 941; S Degeling and J Hudson, 'Credit Advisers, Consumer Credit and Equitable Fiduciary Obligations' (2019) 47 *Federal Law Review* 64, 69–73.

[30] SA Smith, 'Contracting under Pressure: A Theory of Duress' (1997) 56 *CLJ* 343, 346–47. Similarly, advice *as such* is not procurement (such as inducement to breach a contract): *Lewis v Yeeles* [2010] EWCA Civ 326 [22]–[24]. We thank Janet O'Sullivan for this reference.

[31] *Adams* (n 29) [73]–[75].

part of the advisor may be crucial: the advisor must accept that their advice is being given on the basis that it is intended to advance the advisee's interests; the advisor is not simply trying to persuade the advisee.[32] Once we think that an advisor can only rightly use their advice-giving function for the benefit of the advisee, a crucial question is whether there is enough commonality between that advisory function and the holding of legal powers that we can rightly attach similar legal consequences to the two situations. This is why I think that the *form* of the communication is less important than the substantive inquiry into whether the communication is an exertion of other-regarding power.

IV. WHAT IS FACTUAL POWER AND HOW IS IT MEASURED?

SD: How does equity determine whether the advisor holds factual power and whether this is sufficient to justify fiduciary responsibility? The 'as if' account argues that where the client trusts the advisor and relies on the advice to the extent that it is usually likely to be followed, practically speaking it is the advisor who is making the decisions, not the client. If we are going to explain cases of mere advisors as sufficiently similar to agency, in which the advisor does hold legal power, the question arises as to how we evaluate the nature and extent of the advisor's factual power. What are the criteria for admission to the set? Relating to this question, are these essentially relationships of undue influence? Is this a potentially competing explanation? At one level, there is no difficulty in conceding that these 'as if' advisory relationships may also attract the doctrine of undue influence.[33] But in identifying relationships of sufficient 'factual power' are we being duplicative? Is this a distinction without difference? Further, our discussion here might be labelled 'back to the future' or 're-exporting fiduciary concepts'. As we know, historically the relational or presumed undue influence category arose in relationships of fiduciary responsibility.[34] These are described by Rick Bigwood as a being a contextual application of fiduciary accountability, concerned with the 'narrow mischief of disloyal opportunism by those … required to act for, on behalf of or in the interests of another'.[35] We return to undue influence further below.[36]

[32] We return to this in the next section, in the discussion of *Hodkginson* (n 2).

[33] To be clear, the facts may of course support an argument of both an advisor fiduciary relationship and also an independent relationship of influence. See eg *Calvo v Sweeney* [2009] NSWSC 719. However, this discussion is exploring a categorical problem, which is whether in identifying a fiduciary relationship inherent in the giving of advice, we are thereby *necessarily* identifying a relationship of undue influence.

[34] Category 2A relationships (presumed undue influence): solicitor and client, medical advisor and patient, parent and child, guardian and ward, trustee and beneficiary, spiritual leader and follower. However, the categories are not completely coextensive. For example, per *Leeder v Stevens* [2005] EWCA Civ 50, there may be a relationship of presumed undue influence between a fiancé and fiancée. However, this is not an accepted per se fiduciary category.

[35] R Bigwood, 'From Morgan to Etridge' in J Neyers et al (eds), *Exploring Contract Law* (Oxford, Hart Publishing, 2009) 381. Paul Finn, in his seminal monograph on fiduciary obligations, covered undue influence: PD Finn, *Fiduciary Obligations* (Sydney, Law Book, 1977) ch 16. Even at that time, it was arguable that fiduciary relationships and undue influence were analytically distinct, as noted by a reviewer: WM Gummow, 'Review: *Fiduciary Obligations*' (1978) 2 *University of New South Wales Law Journal* 408, 410.

[36] Section V.

On the question of identifying factual power, could *Daly* assist? In that case, the High Court of Australia identified that an advisor will owe fiduciary obligations, inherent in the giving of advice, where there is an undertaking to advise, holding out of relevant expertise and reliance by the client.[37] Could these be understood more generally as indicators of the existence of the necessary factual power? Dr Daly, a medical practitioner, approached a stockbroking firm after he inherited a large sum of money. Apart from a small parcel of shares purchased some time earlier, Daly had not previously invested in the share market, although he had read a book entitled *Investment for Everyone*.[38] Daly made an appointment and ultimately met with Tolz who was employed by the firm as a 'client advisor' or 'sales advisor'.[39] Tolz gave Daly a tour of the firm's offices and shared with him some material 'Statistics and Earnings Projections',[40] selecting a number of companies in the shares of which Daly might 'safely, or profitably, invest'.[41] Unfortunately, according to Tolz, the news was not good. The market and yields were falling and had yet to 'bottom out'. Accordingly, instead of purchasing shares, Tolz 'suggested to, or advised, Dr Daly that he should "put (his) money on deposit with (the firm)" until "the time was ripe to buy"'.[42] After confirming that the firm would offer 14 percent in interest, Tolz further reassured Daly that although the investment would be unsecured, '[the firm is] as safe as a bank'.[43] Daly and his wife (for whom he was agent) proceeded to lend the firm $29,000. However, the firm was later declared insolvent and these funds were lost. Daly and his wife claimed under a statutory fidelity fund which required them to demonstrate that the firm had received the funds as constructive trustee. It was for this reason that the court heard arguments on the question whether a fiduciary relationship existed between Daly and the firm.

In holding that the firm owed a fiduciary duty to Daly as advisor, the High Court of Australia identified as diagnostic the elements of an undertaking to advise, holding out of relevant expertise and the client's reliance.[44] Given that no shares were purchased or sold by the firm for or on behalf of the Daly's, it is difficult to see how this was an agency. Rather, the course of dealing shows that the firm gave advice leading to a debt. The case is undoubtedly a contender for 'as if' factual power. Arguably, therefore, the High Court has given us criteria for identifying when factual power is present.[45]

[37] *Daly* (n 2) 377 (Gibbs CJ) and 385 (Brennan J).
[38] *Daly v Sydney Stock Exchange* [1981] 2 NSWLR 179, 183 (Powell J).
[39] ibid.
[40] ibid.
[41] ibid.
[42] ibid.
[43] ibid 184 (Powell J).
[44] *Daly* (n 2) 377 (Gibbs CJ) and 385 (Brennan J).
[45] It must be conceded that there are advisor cases in which a fiduciary relationship is found inherent in the giving of advice which do not rely on *Daly*, or do not rely exclusively on *Daly*-type reasoning. *Daly* is not the exclusively competent method by which such advisor relationships may be identified. For example, *Wingecarribbee Shire Council v Lehman Brothers Australia Ltd (in liq)* [2012] FCA 1028, (2012) 301 ALR 1 [737]–[743] (Rares J), which also purports to apply *Hospital Products* in support of the advisor's fiduciary obligations. Notwithstanding these deviations, *Daly* was approved in *Pilmer v Duke Group)* (n 20) [74] (McHugh, Gummow, Hayne and Callinan JJ) and followed in key cases such as *Aequitas v AEFC* [2001] NSWSC 14, [307] (Austin J) and *ASIC v Citigroup* [2007] FCA 965 [283]–[284] (Jacobson J).

LDS: To my mind, *Daly*, like *Tate v Williamson*, is an example of a fiduciary duty to disclose. Non-fiduciaries do not generally have to disclose information that they hold to their contractual counterparty. As both cases show, a fiduciary who does not disclose all material information will find that the beneficiary can set the contract aside; the breach of a duty of disclosure has, in this context, the same legal result as a misrepresentation. And this is not just information about the conflict of interest; when you are contracting with someone, it is obvious that your interests conflict with theirs. An advisory fiduciary, unlike a non-fiduciary, must disclose everything relevant (such as, in *Daly*, the firm's precarious financial condition). The advisory fiduciary, as such, must give advice in the interests of the advisee. This cannot sensibly be done without revealing all relevant information.

Another good case study is *Hodgkinson v Simms*.[46] The claimant Hodgkinson was himself a stockbroker and so hardly an unsophisticated investor. The defendant Simms was an accountant who specialised in helping clients to find tax shelters. Hodgkinson went to Simms for the latter's unbiased and expert opinions on tax-sheltered investments, particularly relating to 'MURBs', that is, multiple-unit residential buildings, which provided tax advantages in Canada at the time. Simms held himself out as providing independent advice, and Hodgkinson usually (though not always) took Simms's advice. Simms advised Hodgkinson to invest in certain MURB developments, and this advice was taken. It was found as a fact that this was good advice, in the sense that at the time it was given it was suitable to Hodgkinson's needs in terms of tax savings and of the relationship between risk and expected return. However, Simms was also acting for the developers and received commissions from them when he found investors. The real estate market fell in 1981 and Hodgkinson, having found about Simms's double dealing, sought to recover his losses. It is important to note that, as in many such cases (eg *Nocton*), the most obvious cause of the claimant's loss was a movement in market values. The true complaint of the claimant in such cases rests on the breach of a prescriptive fiduciary duty of disclosure: the claimant says, 'If you had informed me, as you were bound to do, of all relevant information in your possession, I would never have made this investment, and so your unlawful non-disclosure was a but-for cause of my loss.'[47]

The case divided the Supreme Court of Canada, four–three, on the question whether there was a fiduciary relationship. The judges all agreed that an advisory relationship *could be* a fiduciary relationship but was not necessarily so. The minority held that there would not be a fiduciary relationship unless there was a 'ceding by one party of effective power to the other'.[48] The majority's legal test was a little less clear. They said that 'what is required is evidence of a mutual understanding that one party has relinquished its own self-interest and agreed to act solely on behalf

[46] *Hodgkinson* (n 2).

[47] For a full argument: L Smith, 'Prescriptive Fiduciary Duties' (n 12). As in *Nocton* (n 6) and many other cases, the conflict of self-interest and duty, as such, is not a but-for cause of the loss: if the advisor had given the same advice but had not been conflicted, the same loss would have befallen the claimant. It is the non-disclosure that is the but-for cause of the claimant's loss.

[48] *Hodgkinson* (n 2) 466.

of the other party'.[49] The judgments are not always easy to follow, but it is at least arguable that there is some convergence between them in relation to the presence of factual power on one side of the relationship, and trust and reliance (and therefore vulnerability to factual power) on the other. In my contemporaneous note on the case, I suggested that both groups of judges were of the view that in an advisory relationship, some kind of undertaking by the advisor to advise solely in the interests of the advisee may be a crucial factor.[50] It confirms that the power is held in an other-regarding way, which is just as necessary in advisory relationships as it is in cases of relationships involving legal powers.

As we have discussed above, some sufficient *level* of power is still needed in order to assimilate advice to legal power. In a recent and thorough analysis of whether an advisory relationship can be fiduciary, Arthur Laby concludes that it can.[51] Subjective trust on the part of the beneficiary is not an essential element of all fiduciary relationships: for example, an infant of six months may be a trust beneficiary. But actual subjective trust on the part of an advisee/beneficiary is one way in which actual power on the part of an advisor/fiduciary can be created. A relationship of this kind brings us close to a situation in which the advisor actually makes the decision, at least in a practical sense.[52] It is not surprising that such relationships may also, in the common law, attract a presumption of undue influence.[53]

Sir Guy Newey, who commented on the draft of this text when it was presented, made a powerful observation on this issue. In my own words, his insight was this: an advisor can well be held to be a fiduciary *whether or not* their advisory 'power' rises to the level that approximates a legal power in which the fiduciary can decide unilaterally what will happen. In Sir Guy's words, 'A solicitor whose client sometimes rejects his advice is still a fiduciary.' This is clearly correct. Perhaps a better way to frame the law's response here must make reference to the nature of human decision-making, which of course is closely tied to advice. There are many aspects of the law (including, for example, the law of duress[54]) which have concluded that human decision-making is rather inscrutable so that if we know that some input was a *factor* in the making of a decision, we may treat that factor as legally significant even if we cannot say

[49] *Hodgkinson* (n 2) 409–10.

[50] L Smith, 'Fiduciary Relationships – Arising in Commercial Contexts – Investment Advisor: *Hodgkinson v Simms*' (1995) 74 *Canadian Bar Review* 714.

[51] Laby (n 2).

[52] On the role of trust in these advisory fiduciary relationships, see also AS Gold, 'Trust and Advice' in P Miller and M Harding (eds), *Fiduciaries and Trust: Ethics, Politics, Economics and Law* (Cambridge, Cambridge University Press, 2020) 35. Laby (n 2) argues (997) that '[t]rust leads to clients' reliance on the advisor and to vulnerability with respect to matters related to the advice'. This is a description of a factual (not a legal) power held by the advisor.

[53] This presumption arises in all fiduciary relationships, but also in some other relationships such as husband–wife. In the common law, the law on fiduciary relationships and on undue influence grew out of common roots: Grower (n 13). They were not treated as fully separate until quite recently (eg *Geffen v Goodman Estate* [1991] 2 SCR 353, 81 DLR (4th) 211; cf *Lloyds Bank Ltd v Bundy* [1975] QB 326 (CA), in which the majority do not clearly distinguish undue influence from the fiduciary relationship and its duties of disclosure); see also Worthington, 'Fiduciaries: When Is Self-denial Obligatory?' (n 1) 503, footnote 18. The interrelationship between fiduciary relationships and undue influence is discussed immediately below in Section V, where there is further discussion of *Bundy*.

[54] *Barton v Armstrong* [1976] AC 104 (PC).

with certainty that the input was *decisive*. There are two clear examples of this in fiduciary law itself. First, the exercise of a fiduciary power while the holder of the power is in a conflict is always voidable: this is simply because no one can know whether the holder's judgment was affected by an improper purpose.[55] This is seen particularly in the context of the 'self-dealing' rule, but the principle applies more widely.[56] It is never necessary to show that the conflict *actually* influenced the power-holder. The second example is seen in the context of the 'fair-dealing' rule, when a fiduciary deals with his own beneficiary.[57] The fiduciary – whether an advisory fiduciary or one holding a legal power – is obliged to disclose any information that he holds and that is potentially relevant to the beneficiary's decision-making process.[58] A breach of this duty allows the beneficiary to set aside the contract,[59] or to recover loss of which the non-disclosure was a but-for cause, even where the loss was also caused by a business failure or fall in the market.[60] And in *Brickenden*,[61] the Privy Council has held that once unlawful non-disclosure is established, it should be presumed unless proven otherwise that the claimant's loss was caused by the wrongful non-disclosure. This is also a recognition of the impossibility of unpacking the details of human decision-making. The Singapore Court of Appeal recently recognised the importance of the *Brickenden* principle, after a thorough discussion of case law and commentary from all over the common law world.[62]

In this perspective, the long tradition of protecting the advisee in advisory relationships may rest on this insight about decision-making: the advice, as an influencing factor, is treated as if it were decisive, without the need to prove that it was. That would mean that it is treated as if it were equipollent to a legal power.

The Court of Appeal of England and Wales has recently proposed another solution to this difficult question. In *Wood v Commercial First Business Ltd*,[63] it was held that an advisor could be subject to the rule against unauthorised profits

[55] The improper purpose being the advancement of his own self-interest, in the case of a conflict of self-interest and fiduciary duty, or the advancement of the interest of another, in the case of a conflict of between one fiduciary duty and another.

[56] *Re Lamb* [1894] 2 QB 805 (CA) 820 (AL Smith LJ): 'It is obvious – everybody knows it who has any knowledge of life – that when a man has a pecuniary interest, his mind is naturally warped in favour of his own interest. It is human nature, and no one can doubt it.'

[57] In these cases, the fiduciary is *not* exercising a fiduciary power but only their own contractual capacity.

[58] He is obliged, in other words, to prioritise the other-regarding fiduciary relationship over the pursuit of his own interests, an obligation that would not apply to one who was not a fiduciary. For a clear statement of long standing, see *Gibson v Jeyes* (1801) 6 Ves Jun 266, 31 ER 1044 (LC).

[59] As in *Tate* (n 14); *McKenzie v McDonald* [1927] VLR 134; *Maguire v Makaronis* [1997] HCA 23, (1997) 188 CLR 449; *Daly* (n 2).

[60] As in *Nocton* (n 6), *Brickenden* (n 6) and *Hodgkinson* (n 2). In *Swindle v Harrison* [1997] 4 All ER 705 (CA), each judge explicitly stated that the wrong in question was non-disclosure (718 (Evans LJ), 720 (Hobhouse LJ), 735 (Mummery LJ)). The claim failed because the claimant failed to prove a causal link between the wrong and the loss, which was also the only reason that a claim for non-disclosure failed in *Canson Enterprises Ltd v Boughton & Co* [1991] 3 SCR 534. In *Swindle*, Mummery LJ (at 732) interpreted *Nocton* (n 6) as a claim based on the breach of a fiduciary duty of disclosure, as did Kirby J in *Maguire* (n 59) 495, the majority in *Canson* (ibid) 570–71, and the majority in *Hodgkinson* (n 2) 415.

[61] *Brickenden* (n 6) 469.

[62] *Sim Poh Ping v Winsta Holding Pte Ltd* [2020] SGCA 35 accepting ([240]) that the burden of proof should be reversed. See also *Southwind v Canada* 2021 SCC 28 [82].

[63] *Wood v Commercial First Business Ltd* [2021] EWCA Civ 471, [2022] Ch 123.

without needing to be classified as being in a fiduciary relationship. The reasoning is interesting, because the Court's conclusion was that a person who owes a duty 'to be impartial and to give disinterested advice, information or recommendations'[64] is liable to give up any unauthorised profit, and this, without the need to engage in 'complex analyses of the nature of a fiduciary relationship or the duties which may be associated with a fiduciary relationship'.[65] Personally, I don't think that analysis is especially complex, even though it is contested. More importantly, if the rule against unauthorised profits, typically considered to be a characteristic feature of a fiduciary relationship, operates against non-fiduciaries, then surely some equally complex analysis must be required to explain why and when. The case of solicitors makes it clear that advisory fiduciary relationships exist. The idea that we have advisory relationships that are not fiduciary relationships but that attract the essential characteristics of fiduciary relationships is not, in my personal view, necessarily a step in the direction of simplifying this complex area of the law.

V. RELATIONSHIP TO UNDUE INFLUENCE

SD: In relation to a potential overlap with undue influence, as I understand Lionel's argument, factual power is present when the advisor has 'influence over the choices of the advisee' and not simply 'influence over the fortunes of the advisee'[66] such that the advisor's influence is so powerful that it is 'as if' the advisor held legal powers to affect the legal position of the client. Alternatively, returning to *Daly*, are the elements of the presence of an undertaking, holding out of expertise and reliance a way of detecting the presence of undue influence, at least in a subset of cases?[67] Undue influence occurs where the claimant lacks the self-awareness or capacity to be alive to her own interest in her dealings with the defendant and where the influence of the defendant is *undue*, never mind that the influence may be 'benign, welcome or otherwise'.[68] Whilst jurisdictions may vary as to the precise models employed,[69] undue influence is concerned to determine whether the claimant's assent is a 'free act'[70] or instead whether assent is produced by 'undue influence of such effect as to overbear the [claimant's] independence and voluntariness of free will'.[71] This inquiry encompasses not only the particular legal act, but a 'consideration of the extent to

[64] ibid [102].

[65] ibid.

[66] L Smith, 'Parenthood Is a Fiduciary Relationship' (2020) 70 *University of Toronto Law Journal* 395, 425, footnote 129.

[67] The further question of whether, for example, the claimant will be able to demonstrate emancipation must also be determined.

[68] J Edelman and E Bant, *Unjust Enrichment*, 2nd edn (Oxford, Hart Publishing, 2016) 231. See also *Thorne v Kennedy* (2017) 263 CLR 85 [30] (Kiefel CJ, Bell, Gageler, Keane and Edelman JJ): 'since pressure is only one of the many sources for the influence that one person can have over another, it is not necessary that the pressure which contributes to a conclusion of undue influence be characterised as illegitimate or improper'.

[69] *Royal Bank of Scotland plc v Etridge (No 2)* [2002] 2 AC 773 (HL); *Thorne* (n 68).

[70] *Johnson v Buttress* (1936) 56 CLR 113, 134 (Dixon CJ).

[71] *Hsiao v Fazarri* [2020] HCA 35, (2020) 270 CLR 588 [70] (Nettle and Gordon JJ).

which the [claimant] was constrained in assessing alternatives and deciding between them'.[72]

Lloyd's Bank v Bundy[73] is arguably a case where the facts were held to establish undue influence and also to demonstrate the presence of factual power. More importantly, the criteria applied by the Court of Appeal in raising a presumption of undue influence in substance appear to map the fiduciary elements of advice, an undertaking, a holding out of expertise and reliance. Mr Bundy gave further guarantees to secure his son's business debts to Lloyd's Bank. These further guarantees were secured by a charge on Bundy's farm. The value of the debts ultimately secured exceeded the value of the farm. The son defaulted and the bank foreclosed, seeking to exercise its power of sale over the farm. Bundy successfully resisted, avoiding the guarantees on the ground of undue influence.[74] Bundy had signed the relevant guarantee and charge at his farm in a meeting at which the bank's employee, Mr Head, brought the relevant documents for execution. Bundy received no independent advice prior to signing the documents but instead sought and received advice from Head. As described by Sir Eric Sachs: 'the bank gave him advice, … he relied on that advice, and the bank knew of the reliance'.[75]

That the relationship was between banker and customer is no barrier to finding a fiduciary relationship as advisor.[76] In determining that a presumption of undue influence existed, and that the bank had not discharged the onus of demonstrating emancipation via the presence of independent advice, Sir Eric Sachs (with whose reasons Cairns LJ agreed) focused on the circumstances of Head's advice. Although as a formal matter his Lordship's reasons are not expressed in the language of the fiduciary responsibility of advisors,[77] the substance of Sir Eric Sach's analysis arguably rests on the presence of 'advice' and whether there was an undertaking, expertise and reliance. On the question of whether Head had actually 'advised' Bundy, the answer was in the affirmative. It was similarly clear that Bundy had relied on this advice. In relation to expertise, Sir Eric Sachs pointed to the fact that in a rural community, 'senior [bank] officials may become trusted councillors of customers of those whose affairs they have an intimate knowledge. Confidential trust is placed in them because of a combination of status, goodwill and knowledge'[78] and that Head had stood in this position and was 'familiar with the finance and business of the Bundy's and the relevant company'.[79] The question of whether or not Head had undertaken to advise Bundy is more difficult. Head stated in evidence that 'I would think … [Bundy] relied on me implicitly to advise him about the transaction as bank

[72] ibid [32].

[73] *Lloyd's Bank v Bundy* (n 53).

[74] ibid 340 (Cairns LJ) and 346 (Sir Erich Sachs). Lord Denning MR based his conclusion on a broader range of considerations which he labelled (339) 'inequality of bargaining power'. However, he also held (340) that the facts supported a finding for Bundy based on 'the second class' of undue influence.

[75] ibid 344 (Sir Erich Sachs). See also para (2), 339 (Lord Denning MR).

[76] See eg *Commonwealth of Australia v Smith* (1991) 42 FCR 390.

[77] Sir Erich Sachs's judgment in *Lloyd's Bank v Bundy* (n 53) was also framed (340) about whether or not Head, in obtaining Bundy's signature, had breached a duty of 'fiduciary care'. As observed in *Hsiao* (n 71) [53] (Nettle and Gordon JJ) '[the judge's] reasons reflect … the arguments that were put to him.'

[78] *Lloyd's Bank v Bundy* (n 53) 344 (Sir Eric Sachs).

[79] ibid.

manager.'[80] Therefore, it might be argued that, given their relationship, and his role as bank manager, Head had impliedly given the necessary undertaking in proffering the advice.

Returning to the criteria articulated in *Daly*, assuming that we accept these as indicative of the presence of 'as if' factual power, will satisfying these criteria inevitably reveal a presumption of undue influence? Similarly, does Sir Eric Sachs's reasoning in *Bundy*, which arguably raised a presumption of undue influence by reference to the presence of advice, an undertaking, expertise and reliance, suggest that the satisfaction of these integers will necessarily indicate a presumption of undue influence? If the key features of factual power for the purposes of advice are that the client is not likely to be able to exercise his own judgment, and will usually follow the advisor's recommendation, this seems virtually indistinguishable from undue influence's inquiry as to whether the claimant's assent is a 'free act', including whether the claimant is able to weigh and evaluate alternatives.

LDS: I have certainly been conscious of the difficulty of the question of overlap, or perhaps of superfluity or error, in trying to work out the relationship between fiduciary duties and undue influence in the advisory context. The reasons for the overlap are not hard to find: both are aspects of equity's regulation of relationships involving imbalances of power.[81] It was not that long ago that 'fiduciary relationships' were understood to include not only relationships of undue influence[82] but also duties relating to confidential information.[83] As recently as 1998, Peter Millett described them as three different kinds of fiduciary relationship.[84] But the law was already changing, and it has certainly changed now. Obligations relating to confidential information can arise outside of a fiduciary relationship;[85] and while a fiduciary relationship may import a presumption of undue influence, the reverse is not true. A relationship of actual or presumed undue influence does not require us to look for any of the characteristics of a fiduciary relationship.[86]

And yet to say that an advisory relationship can rightly be fiduciary because the advisor has the same kind of other-regarding power as an agent or a trustee seems to focus precisely on the advisor's high (undue?) level of influence on the advisee. So what does it add, and is that addition analytically justified? To take the first question first, it adds a great deal. Undue influence may allow the influencee to resile from a transaction; even a transaction with a third party, if that person ought to have known of the influence. As a legal argument, it will *not* allow the influencee to resile from the transaction on the basis of a breach of a duty of disclosure, as a fiduciary relationship may do.[87] It will not allow the influencee to recover compensation for a loss suffered

[80] ibid 343 (Sir Eric Sachs).
[81] Grower (n 13).
[82] See n 35.
[83] Paul Finn discussed both confidential information and undue influence in his 1977 monograph, and again a contemporary reviewer wondered whether this was overinclusive on both counts (n 35).
[84] P Millett, 'Equity's Place in the Law of Commerce' (1998) 114 *LQR* 214, 219–21.
[85] *LAC Minerals Ltd v International Corona Resources Ltd* [1989] 2 SCR 574; *Attorney-General v Guardian Newspapers (No 2)* [1990] 1 AC 109 (HL); *Cadbury Schweppes Inc v FBI Foods Ltd* [1999] 1 SCR 142, 167 DLR (4th) 577.
[86] eg *Geffen* (n 53).
[87] See the cases in n 59.

due to a fall in the market, on the basis that the loss would not have been suffered if the advisor had fully disclosed their conflict of interest; a fiduciary advisory relationship does allow such a claim.[88] Undue influence will also not allow the advisee to recover from the advisor unauthorised profits that the advisor may have extracted from the relationship; a fiduciary relationship, of course, allows this.[89] As for the second question: are these recourses justified in a purely advisory relationship? The only way to answer that, of course, is to have a theory of what makes a relationship fiduciary; in my view, arguments based on such considerations as 'legitimate expectations' do not assist in this respect, as they do not relate closely enough to the facts to help us to decide difficult questions.

A fiduciary relationship is one in which one person is empowered to act for and on behalf of another (or others, or a purpose): presumptively, for the sole benefit of that other (although as we know, the fiduciary can be a member of a 'beneficiary class'). I think the law has been correct to say that an advisory relationship of the right kind can certainly fit that bill. It has long been the case for solicitors, and I agree with you, Simone, that it promises explanatory assistance also in relation to the advisory part of a physician–patient relationship. This would explain our natural instinct, that advising physicians should disclose financial conflicts of interest.[90]

All fiduciaries are accountable in the broad sense that they must account for how they have conducted themselves in their other-regarding role. This may require them to 'account' for unauthorised profits in the technical sense that those profits will be brought into an account to surcharge it. Their accountability in a wider sense, to account for their conduct in the role, also requires them to disclose past wrongdoing.[91] Only in this way can a beneficiary know what are their rights and where they stand. This could also apply to physicians.[92] We have seen above that an advisory fiduciary has an obligation to disclose to the advisee all information in the possession of the fiduciary that is relevant to the advisee's decision-making. There is no other way to give advice that is truly other-regarding. The failure to disclose will make any contract between the fiduciary and the beneficiary voidable;[93] but it will also give rise to a claim

[88] See the cases in n 60.

[89] cf *Strother v 3464920 Canada Inc* 2007 SCC 24, [2007] 2 SCR 177, noted R Valsan and L Smith, 'The Loyalty of Lawyers: A Comment on *3464920 Canada Inc v Strother*' (2008) 87 *Canadian Bar Review* 247.

[90] SR Latham, 'Conflict of Interest in Medical Practice' in M Davis and A Stark (eds), *Conflict of Interest in the Professions* (New York, Oxford University Press, 2001) 279; B Lo and MJ Field (eds), *Conflict of Interest in Medical Research, Education, and Practice* (Washington, DC, National Academies Press, 2009). For discussion of some effects of undisclosed conflicts in medical practice, see Atul Gawande, 'The Cost Conundrum', *The New Yorker*, 25 May 2009. In *Breen v Williams* (1995) 186 CLR 71, 93–94, Dawson and Toohey JJ said that an undisclosed financial conflict of interest on the part of a physician could 'give rise to fiduciary obligations'. This seems to be the wrong way around; we have to decide first whether the relationship is fiduciary in order to see whether norms about conflicts apply, in this case in relation to the giving of advice.

[91] *Item Software (UK) Ltd v Fassihi* [2004] EWCA Civ 1244, [2005] 2 BCLC 91. The decision followed earlier first-instance holdings to the same effect which are cited in the judgment. For similar holdings in US law, see 'Neel' in 6 Cal3d 176, 491 P2d 421 (Magana, Olney, Levy, Cathcart and Gelfand: SC, 1971). and 'Merrill Lynch, Pierce, Fenner & Smith, Inc' in 901 F2d 1124 (Cheng: DC Cir, 1990), 1128–29, discussed in DeMott (n 29) 941.

[92] GB Robertson, 'When Things Go Wrong: The Duty to Disclose Medical Error' (2002) 28 *Queen's Law Journal* 353.

[93] See the cases in n 87.

for compensation for loss caused by the non-disclosure.[94] Applying this to physicians, we have a convincing explanation for the physician's obligation to disclose the risks of a procedure or treatment that is being advised.[95] Again, it relates to information in the possession of the advising physician that is relevant for the patient in making their own decision.

VI. WHEN AND HOW DOES A FIDUCIARY RELATIONSHIP BASED ON FACTUAL POWER END? TO WHAT EXTENT DO THE FIDUCIARY OBLIGATIONS ALSO END?

SD: When do fiduciary responsibilities come to an end? We know that those who hold offices such as trustees, company directors and executors of estates may be removed by the court or, potentially, by the principal or beneficiary. More controversially, the fiduciary may themselves resign. But in a relationship where the power held by the fiduciary is purely factual power, such as that held by an advisor or some solicitors, when and how does this fiduciary relationship end? How can we tell? As a general matter, understanding this question has two parts. First, identifying that the underlying relationship giving rise to fiduciary responsibility may itself end or change. Secondly, asking whether, even though the underlying relationship has ended or changed, the fiduciary may or may not continue to owe fiduciary obligations to their principal. For example, a company director after resignation may not ' use … for his own benefit property of the company or information which he has acquired while a director'.[96] But in a relationship where the power held by the fiduciary is purely factual power, such as an advisor or some solicitors, when and how does this fiduciary relationship end? And what obligations, if any, may continue to be owed by the 'as if' fiduciary?

LDS: Not all fiduciary relationships involve an 'office'. A core case that does not is that of principal and agent. Either side can end the relationship (unless perhaps it is 'agency coupled with an interest' of the 'agent', which is not a fiduciary relationship and arguably not an agency relationship). Where the advisee is fully capacitated, my thought is that an advisory fiduciary relationship is of that kind. The court does not have a supervisory role, as it does where there is a legally recognised office. But I agree: this does not mean that the advisor is completely unfettered in relation, for example, to information acquired while acting in the fiduciary role. The rule against unauthorised profits should apply, just as it does to fiduciaries with legal powers.

SD: Turning to the first question above, has the underlying relationship between the parties ended or altered? As with the initial inquiry determining that a fiduciary

[94] See the cases in n 88.

[95] In the common law, this duty of the physician is fully recognised but courts and commentators have struggled to explain it; A Beever, *A Theory of Tort Liability* (Oxford, Hart Publishing, 2016) ch 15. Some courts, however, have tied it to the fiduciary nature of the advisory physician–patient relationship (eg 'Moore' in 51 Cal3d 120, 793 P2d 479 (Regents of University of California: SC, 1990)). In *Kenny v Lockwood* [1932] OR 141, [1932] 1 DLR 507 (CA), the Ontario Court of Appeal applied the fiduciary duty of disclosure recognised in *Nocton* (n 6) to an advising physician.

[96] *Ultraframe (UL) Ltd v Fielding & Ors* [2005] EWHC 1638 (Ch) [1391] (Lewison J).

relationship exists, it is necessary to confirm the extent to which the facts now engage the elements of fiduciary responsibility.

There may well be a contract between the parties, for example, a contract to provide advice or a solicitor's retainer. The client or the fiduciary might terminate the contract, which may or may not have contractual remedial consequences. However, the determination of whether the advisor or solicitor remains a fiduciary is a discrete inquiry. The termination of the contract may, as a matter of evidence, remove the necessary elements of advice giving and/or undertaking, but is not of itself conclusive. What is relevant is whether the underlying elements giving rise to the fiduciary relationship in the first instance still subsist. This is shown by the position of parties prior to contract, where equity takes the view that 'a fiduciary relationship can arise and fiduciary duties can exist between parties who have not reached, and who may never reach, agreement'.[97] In *UDC v Brian*, Mason, Brennan and Deane JJ held that 'a fiduciary relationship with attendant fiduciary obligations may, and ordinarily will, exist between prospective partners who have embarked upon the conduct of the partnership business or venture before the precise terms of any partnership agreement have been settled'.[98] There are parallel examples confirming that a solicitor may owe fiduciary obligations to their client prior to any retainer or costs agreement.[99] If fiduciary obligations potentially accrue prior to a retainer, depending on the facts, surely they may continue after its termination? This appears to fly in the face of *Prince Jefri Bolkiah v KPMG*,[100] in which Lord Millett, with whom the other members of the House agreed, held that 'the fiduciary relationship which subsists between solicitor and client comes to an end with the termination of the retainer'. However, Lord Millett was not directly addressing the situation where the course of dealing extended beyond any termination of the retainer. The point is always, as identified in *Demerara Bauxite Co v Hubbard*,[101] 'whether in any particular transaction any duty exists which makes the relationship between the parties that of solicitor and client, will depend on all the circumstances of the particular case'[102] and that 'even if a solicitor is no longer retained or acting, his duty, in the contemplation in a Court of equity [may still be such as to place fiduciary obligations on him]'.[103]

[97] *United Dominions Corporation Ltd v Brian Pty Ltd* [1985] HCA 49; (1985) 157 CLR 1, 12 (Mason, Brennan and Deane JJ). There may be a question of differing scopes.

[98] ibid. Gibbs CJ (5) was in 'general agreement' with the reasons of Mason, Brennan and Deane JJ and held on the facts that a fiduciary relationship between the parties existed (8) 'as if a formal partnership deed had been executed' but also held (6) that it was 'unnecessary to decide whether persons negotiation for a partnership always stand in a fiduciary relationship' [but did not doubt that it could]. Dawson J (14) similarly agreed with the reasons of Mason, Brennan and Deane JJ and held that a fiduciary relationship existed. His Honour also confirmed (16) that 'a fiduciary relationship may arise during negotiations for a partnership or … joint venture, before any … agreement has been finally concluded'.

[99] See eg *Demerara Bauxite Co v Hubbard* [1923] AC 673 (PC) 675–76 (Lord Parmoor); *Rahme v Benjamin & Khoury* (2019) 100 NSWLR 550 (NSWCA) [86]–[98] (Macfarlan JA), [1] (Bathurst CJ) and [142] (McCallum JA) agreeing; *Law Society of New South Wales v Foreman* (1994) 34 NSWLR 408 (NSWCA), 435–36 (Mahoney JA).

[100] *Prince Jefri Bolkiah v KPMG* [1999] 2 AC 222 (HL) 235 (Lord Millett).

[101] *Demerara Bauxite Co v Hubbard* (n 99).

[102] ibid 676 (Lord Parmoor).

[103] ibid 675 (Lord Parmoor).

Arguably, therefore, the answer still comes down to the course of dealing. We examine the whole of the course of dealing, including the retainer (if any) and its terms, determining whether the elements equity determines as relevant to raising a fiduciary relationship continue to exist.[104] In the advisor context, this may be one important reason to delineate what we mean by 'advice', and to insist on the need for an undertaking or holding out, because one who holds factual power may cease to give advice even though the other elements of trust and reliance remain. Practically speaking, it is only the advice and undertaking elements which are in the control of the factual power holder, including one who wishes no longer to stand in a fiduciary relationship.

LDS: In *Strother*,[105] the defendant Strother was a lawyer who had advised the claimant on tax-shelter-driven opportunities for about four years; Strother's contract with the client forbade him from acting for other clients in this kind of business. The law changed and the opportunities came to an end. Strother continued to do routine corporate work for the client, now under an oral retainer that was not carefully delineated. Only about two years after telling the claimant that the tax-shelter-driven business was finished, Strother realised that the tax-shelter opportunities could indeed again be made into profitable investments. He went into business with a former employee of the claimant and they made tens of millions of dollars in profit. Was Strother accountable for his profits to the claimant? This divided the Supreme Court of Canada by a margin of five–four. The dissenting judges thought that the relationship between the parties had come to an end and Strother had no positive obligations towards the claimant to tell them about what he had learned or was doing. The bare majority, however, said that Strother was accountable. According to them, even the informal oral contract obligated Strother to tell the claimant that Strother's previous negative advice was subject to reconsideration. They were not willing to interpret the contract against the client's interest. Moreover, Strother was liable to account for profits; not all of them, but those earned up to the point that that he resigned from the law firm through which the claimant had engaged him. To me, this is not so much a question of being accountable for information acquired from acting in the fiduciary role. It is more like *Industrial Development Consultants Ltd v Cooley*:[106] the defendant acquired the opportunity independently, but the ongoing contract obliged him to render that benefit, or at least to offer it, to the claimant.

SD: The second question is about the substance of the obligations owed. If the above analysis is correct, the fiduciary relationship may potentially continue even after the termination of the retainer. In this case, within the scope of that relationship, including, for example, whether it has altered, the advisor or solicitor is obligated not to act when they are in a conflict of interest and they must account to their client for any benefit obtained by reason or use of so acting.

[104] These will include an undertaking, irrespective of whether or not it is packaged in a retainer: *Beach Petroleum NL v Kennedy* (1999) 48 NSWLR 1 (NSWCA) [188] (the Court); *Birchnell v Equity Trustees, Executors and Agency Co Ltd* (1929) 42 CLR 384, 408 (Dixon J); *Bristol and West Building Society v Mothew* [1998] Ch 1 (CA) 18 (Millett LJ); *Demerara Bauxite* (n 99).

[105] *Strother* (n 89).

[106] *Industrial Development Consultants Ltd v Cooley* [1972] 1 WLR 443 (F).

LDS: I am not sure we need to say that the 'fiduciary relationship may continue'. Take this case: I agree to sell you goods but fail deliver by the due date. You accept this repudiation and the obligations on both sides come to an end. However, I am liable to you in damages. In one way, the contract is at an end, but this liability (which may turn into a duty) continues. It is a creature of the contract, and so in another way, the contract continues. Or another one: I am your employee and I agree that after ceasing to be your employee, I will not compete with you for two years. I quit the job. I am no longer employed by you. In one way, our contract is over, but in another way, it is not: this obligation, born of the contract, remains in force.

So if I extract information from a fiduciary role and then resign, the rule against unauthorised profits will apply to any profit I extract from that information. When the leading Canadian case on this point was decided, much discussion was in terms of fiduciary relationships continuing after the contractual relationship that gave rise to the fiduciary relationship.[107] My answer is: yes and no. The former fiduciary is no longer in a fiduciary relationship in the strict sense that they hold powers for the sole benefit of another. That relationship is over, and the power to resign is not a fiduciary power.[108] But there may be liabilities that continue; in this restricted sense, the fiduciary relationship continues.

SD: This still leaves the case where, after construing the course of dealing, we are satisfied that there is no longer a fiduciary relationship between the parties. What fiduciary obligations may still be owed? In relation to solicitors, Lord Millett in *Prince Jefri*[109] held that, following the termination of the retainer and therefore the fiduciary relationship, '[t]hereafter the solicitor has no obligation to defend and advance the interests of his former client. The only duty which survives the termination of the client relationship is a continuing duty to preserve the confidentiality of information imparted during its subsistence.'[110] However, courts do not speak with one voice on this issue. Brooking JA in the Victorian Court of Appeal in *Spincode Pty Ltd v Look Software Pty Ltd*[111] held obiter that a duty of 'loyalty', which survived the termination of a retainer, was an independent ground for a former client to restrain a solicitor from acting for a client with an interest adverse to that of the former client.

LDS: The Supreme Court of Canada has released a whole series of cases on these issues in recent years. As law firms get bigger, it gets easier and easier for a concerned party to argue that a firm should not be allowed to act for the other side, because

[107] *Canadian Aero Services Ltd v O'Malley* [1974] SCR 592.

[108] *Foster Bryant Surveying Ltd v Bryant* [2007] EWCA Civ 200, [2007] BCC 804 [8], quoting with approval an earlier decision.

[109] *Prince Jefri Bolkiah* (n 100) 235 (Lord Millett). *Prince Jefri* concerned the ability of a former client to restrain an accountant providing litigation support services from undertaking work for another client with an interest adverse to the former client. It was accepted that, in this context, accountants should be treated in the same way as solicitors.

[110] ibid.

[111] *Spincode Pty Ltd v Look Software Pty Ltd* (2001) 4 VR 501 [53] (Brooking JA); cf [61] (Ormiston JA) and [63] (Chernov JA), who did not unequivocally support Brooking JA's view. However, in *Schmidt v AHRKalimpa Pty Ltd* [2020] VSCA 193 [142] (the Court) the Victorian Court of Appeal confirmed that 'depending on the circumstances of a particular case, fiduciary duties may survive the termination of the relationship that first called those duties into being'.

there was some prior dealing (however unrelated) between the concerned party and the firm, or between the concerned party and a lawyer who has since joined the firm in question.[112] The problems arising here are often generically described as relating to 'conflicts'; they are not usually, however, conflicts of self-interest and duty, which is the commonest kind of 'conflict' in fiduciary discourse. They may be conflicts of duty and duty: that is, conflicts between fiduciary duties owed to different clients. That serious problem, however, classically arises where the same lawyer or firm acts for multiple clients with opposing interests. It *may* be a threat in these cases, and the Supreme Court of Canada rightly expresses the overriding concern as to whether a lawyer's judgement may be affected by the conflict.[113] In this context, that means judgement in giving advice. In fiduciary conflict rules more generally, the concern is with how conflicts of both kinds can have unknowable effects on the fiduciary's judgement in relation to discretionary powers that they hold in a fiduciary capacity.

But I agree with you that if the lawyer or law firm is no longer in a fiduciary relationship with the former client, it is not obvious how they can be in a conflict of duty and duty. My own view is that in these cases, the wider and more enduring concern relates to confidential information. Clients have to be free to be completely candid with their lawyers; this underlies legal professional privilege. That concern, in my view, should rightly be a controlling factor that may prevent a lawyer, or other advisory fiduciary or professional, from acting against a former client.

VII. CONCLUSION

LDS: In some ways, it is obvious that there are advisory fiduciary relationships, since the solicitor–client relationship is clearly fiduciary. This means that a good account of fiduciary relationships has to make room for advisory relationships, and cannot restrict itself to situations in which the fiduciary holds legal powers.

In my view, the solicitor–client relationship also pushes the fiduciary envelope in a different direction. Some argue that fiduciary relationships are confined to ones in which the fiduciary's powers are over the financial or pecuniary interests of the beneficiary.[114] This argument may be made to exclude the physician–patient advisory relationship from fiduciary regulation, since the patient's relevant interests are physical and mental rather than pecuniary. So too, some people have legal powers, but not over pecuniary interests. For example, one person may have the legal authority to make medical decisions for and on behalf of another person who lacks full capacity. If fiduciary relationships only arose in relation to pecuniary interests, there would be grounds for saying that such a relationship could not be fiduciary. But: imagine a case in which a parent is seeking custody or visiting access to children, while the other parent is resisting. Assume that the parties are in litigation, but there is no pecuniary claim being made on either side. Surely the relationship between each client and their

[112] See *Canadian National Railway Co v McKercher LLP* [2013] 2 SCR 649, [2013] SCC 39 and the earlier cases discussed therein.

[113] ibid [38].

[114] eg *Paramasivam v Flynn* [1998] FCA 1711, 90 FCR 489, 160 ALR 203 (FCFCA) [65]–[79].

solicitor would be a fiduciary relationship?[115] If so, the solicitor–client relationship not only shows us that advisory relationships can be fiduciary, but also that powers over non-financial interests can also be held in a fiduciary capacity.

SD: I agree. What this discussion hopefully also highlights is that properly to understand the law requires detailed excavation and attention below established categories and labels. Sarah's work stands as an exemplar of this type of scholarship, seeking to cut through established categories and language to provide clarity of principle, policy and doctrine. I suspect that Sarah may not wholly agree with the conclusions reached above.[116] However, that scholars sometimes disagree is not unexpected. What is important is that her scholarship stands as a shining example of lucidity and precision.

[115] The test proposed by Sarah Worthington (set out in n 10) could incorporate fiduciary relationships in relation to power over non-financial interests. This is because it is based on two alternatives; in the absence of control over property, a fiduciary relationship can alternatively arise where there has been an undertaking to act on behalf of another. Personally, I believe that an undertaking may be sufficient but that it is not necessary (Smith (n 66) 402–04).

[116] In addition to Worthington, 'Fiduciaries and Self-denial' (n 1) and Worthington, 'Fiduciaries Then and Now' (n 10), see, among many other contributions: S Worthington, 'Fiduciary Duties and Proprietary Remedies: Addressing the Failure of Equitable Formulae' (2013) 72 *CLJ* 720; S Worthington, 'Four Questions on Fiduciaries' (2016) 2(2) *Canadian Journal of Comparative and Contemporary Law* 723, 735–36; S Worthington, 'Fiduciaries: Following Finn' in T Bonyhady (ed), *Finn's Law: An Australian Justice* (Alexandria, NSW, Federation Press, 2016) 64.

10

Achieving Coherence in Equity's Responses to 'Breach of Trust'

JESSICA HUDSON AND PAULINE RIDGE

I. INTRODUCTION

A COMPLEX MATRIX of claims and remedies respond to breach of trust. They include claims against the trustee and/or third parties, and personal and proprietary remedies. Adding to the complexity, some of the rules extend beyond the express trust context to different fiduciary and non-fiduciary custodial relationships. Moreover, there are doctrinal uncertainties as to the availability, assessment and priority of various forms of personal and proprietary claims and remedies, and deeper theoretical questions about when and why liability to equitable relief arises. These complexities and uncertainties make it challenging to determine whether the rules are coherent, in the sense of being normatively intelligible.

Concerns about the coherence of the claims and remedies responding to breach of trust have previously been expressed in doctrinal critiques of the relationship between the common law and equity. However, our aim in this chapter is to highlight the importance of a more localised inquiry that elucidates the predominantly equitable rules and their supporting norms (variously described as organising principles, rationales, pragmatic purposes and general values) that respond specifically to breaches of trust. Understanding a given rule and how it serves its supporting norm(s) is a prerequisite to making sense of that individual rule, as well as its relationship to the body of rules providing for remedies in response to a breach of trust.

The arguments in the chapter proceed as follows. Part II explains our understanding of 'coherence' and why it matters, and sets out the analytical processes we think are involved in achieving it. We argue that achieving coherence depends on iterative processes of assessment of the operation of a rule and elucidation of its supporting norms. As we will see in Part III, the outcome of these processes when applied to the rule providing for the trust beneficiary's proprietary claim requires a re-examination of the accepted or orthodox justification of equitable title. In this instance, achieving coherence requires us to rethink our reliance on equitable title to justify why an innocent recipient should give up her title in response to a beneficiary's proprietary claim. The chapter goes on in Part IV to show how achieving coherence is particularly complex when both the operation of a rule and its supporting norms are contested, as is the case with the knowing receipt rule. Achieving coherence here may involve consideration of, and have repercussions for, the coherence of other rules.

We have chosen to illustrate our arguments concerning coherence with examples taken from the rules providing for equitable remedies against third parties in response to breach of trust. We agree on the importance of coherence, and the means by which coherence is achieved, however, we do not fully agree as to the implications in relation to this law, in large part owing to different views we take about the rules themselves and their supporting norms. Accordingly, we illustrate our joint arguments about coherence in Part II through our separately authored Parts III and IV.

We consider the law in Australia (our home jurisdiction) and England and Wales,[1] with some reference to Privy Council decisions.

II. COHERENCE

A. What is Coherence and Why Does it Matter?

'Coherence' is understood in different ways in different legal contexts. The term has a technical and contested meaning in legal philosophy,[2] for example, that may differ from popular meanings,[3] and from its usage in case law. It is not always obvious which meaning is intended in any given context. The High Court of Australia, for instance, has been criticised for a failure to articulate what it means when requiring that the interaction of common law, including equity, and statute be 'coherent'.[4] Hence, it is important to be clear about the sense of 'coherence' we think should inform doctrinal analysis and any critique of equity's responses to a breach of trust.

Dame Sarah Worthington equates coherence with rational consistency and the rule of law aphorism that 'like cases must be treated alike' in her influential critique in *Equity* of the dualism of the common law.[5] This sense of coherence demands that rules that deal with the same issue or situation should do so in the same way and to the same extent, regardless of jurisdictional origin.[6] She, and others,[7] argue that there are inconsistencies in how the common law and equity deal with similar or

[1] This is referred to as the 'English law' in the chapter.

[2] The coherence literature is extensive. For an overview of three influential theories, see A Amaya, *The Tapestry of Reason* (Oxford, Hart Publishing, 2015) ch 1. See also N MacCormick, *Legal Reasoning and Legal Theory* (Oxford, Clarendon Press, 1978); B Baum Levenbook, 'The Role of Coherence in Legal Reasoning' (1984) 3 *Law and Philosophy* 355.

[3] J Raz, 'The Relevance of Coherence' (1992) 72 *Boston University Law Review* 273, 276.

[4] See eg *Miller v Miller* [2011] HCA 9, (2011) 242 CLR 446 [15]. A Fell, 'The Concept of Coherence in Australian Public Law' (2018) 41 *Melbourne University Law Review* 1160.

[5] S Worthington, *Equity* (Oxford, Oxford University Press, 2003) 4.

[6] There is a different view according to which equity and common law can and do coherently fulfil the same ends albeit via different means. See eg H Smith, 'Equity as Meta-Law' (2021) 130 *Yale Law Journal* 1050, 1054. See also B McFarlane, 'Form and Substance in Equity' in A Robertson and J Goudkamp (eds), *Form and Substance in the Law of Obligations* (Oxford, Hart Publishing, 2019) ch 9; J Hudson, 'Equity's Gloss on Authority' in S Elliott and B McFarlane, *Equity Today: 150 Years After the Judicature Reforms* (Oxford, Hart Publishing, 2023), ch 2.

[7] See eg A Burrows, 'We Do This at Common Law But That in Equity' (2002) 22 *OJLS* 1.

identical scenarios; and they call for principled reform of the substantive law. Dame Sarah describes the evolution of rules made up by children playing a ball game and the problems that arise if two sets of rules are applied to regulate the same game in different ways.[8] Her argument is that the common law, like the evolving rules of the children's ball game,

> must remain coherent and rational. Like situations must be treated alike; different situations must be treated differently, and, crucially, in rationally different ways. … Experience may throw up instances of lack of coherence, and the rules will then need to adapt to reassert coherence.[9]

This idea of coherence is critical. Different games may have different rules, but each set of rules must be designed to be internally coherent.

Just as children cannot adopt contradictory rules for the one ball game, it would be undesirable for the one legal system to have rules that treat the same situation in contradictory ways and arrive at contradictory outcomes. How are we to know which rule applies and on what basis can differences in outcome be justified? Incoherence undermines the normative force of law and risks its abuse.

Coherence is more than consistency or likeness in treatment alone. The criteria of 'likeness' need to be identified before we can know whether claims and remedies are indeed alike in non-superficial ways, such that they should be treated alike.[10] Keith Mason describes coherence in this sense as a 'fundamental legal norm that assumes and works towards integration of legal principles'.[11] Coherence understood as 'making sense'[12] of the law assumes that any given legal rule and/or body of rules is informed and supported by one or more norms that provide justificatory and explanatory foundations. As discussed further in Part II.B below, these norms can be expressed at different levels of practice, policy and theory and derived from a range of legal, political and moral values. Either way, coherence stands for the proposition that law must be normatively intelligible. To make sense of the law overall, or one or more legal rules, requires that those rules embody their supporting norms.

A *coherent* legal system is thus one in which the operation and outcomes of specific legal rules can be explained and interpreted in line with the general norms they express. And, conversely, judges have a predictable and stable set of norms which can be derived from the cases when faced with facts that do not fit within one or more of a set of established legal rules. The value of coherence is explained by Gummow J in *Esanda Finance Corporation Limited v Peat Marwick Hungerfords*[13] in the following way:

> [T]he very essence of accepted judicial method … is the combined purposes of developing the law, maintaining its continuity and preserving its coherence. Accepted means of

[8] Worthington, *Equity* (n 5) ch 1.

[9] Worthington, *Equity* (n 5) 4.

[10] MacCormick, (n 2) 266.

[11] K Mason, 'Fusion: Fallacy, Future or Finished?' in S Degeling and J Edelman (eds), *Equity in Commercial Law* (Sydney, Lawbook, 2005) 41, 62.

[12] MacCormick (n 2) ch VII.

[13] *Esanda Finance Corporation Limited v Peat Marwick Hungerfords* [1997] HCA 8, (1997) 188 CLR 241 [159].

> effecting those purposes include (i) extending the application of accepted principles to new cases; (ii) reasoning from the more fundamental of settled legal principles to new conclusions; and (iii) subsuming unforeseen instances under a category which, in reason, is not closed against them.

Coherence – that is, the normative intelligibility of one or more legal rules – is thus essential to a legal system's commitment to the rule of law. It supports judges in being able to give transparent and persuasive reasons and it helps ensure that law is capable of being understood and adopted as a reason for individual action.

B. Achieving Coherence

Our understanding of coherence is consistent with that of Dame Sarah when asking whether equity and common law can be rationalised. However, we think that coherence is not simply concerned with comparing and rationalising the common law and equity: there is also the matter of internal coherence within each set of rules. Coherence demands that a legal system overall makes sense, which in turn depends on the constituent subsystems themselves being coherent.

Therefore, before we can ask whether two or more rules, or sets of rules, are coherent as a whole, these rules need to be normatively intelligible on an individual basis. We need to know what issue, interest, or situation a rule(s) deals with and the norms it serves before we can sensibly ask whether it is purporting to deal with the same situation or serve the same norm as another rule. No matter the scale of inquiry, it will ultimately depend on localised coherence between any given rule and its underlying norm(s). Expressed in terms of the rule of law aphorism of treating like cases alike, before we treat one case like another, we first need to know whether one case is, indeed, like another such that it should be treated the same.

We thus consider that there are some important prerequisites to achieving coherence, whether this be to make sense of one rule or a set of rules. One is a localised or internal coherence inquiry as to the underlying norm(s) supporting a legal rule. The second is a stable and accurate understanding of the relevant rule itself. We do not think that either prerequisite must be met before the other; rather, there can be a co-dependency between them, making these analytical inquiries part of the one iterative and complex process towards achieving coherence, as will now be explained.

The first prerequisite to achieving coherence across any set of rules (a localised inquiry into an individual rule's supporting norms) does not entail that such law constitute 'the outworking of a single principle', that is, this chapter does not assume that legal coherence requires monist normativity.[14] Instead, it seems to us that a local[15] coherence account of (predominantly) case law is likely to reveal alignment with more than one legal norm and that these norms might not necessarily be consistent, such

[14] R Grantham and D Jensen, 'Coherence in the Age of Statutes' (2016) 42 *Monash Law Review* 360, 361.
[15] See Levenbook (n 2).

that some holistic balancing of norms may be required.[16] The content of a rule may well represent a compromise between conflicting norms. Relatedly, it seems to us that a coherent version of *judge*-made law must accommodate overlapping claims with different normative foundations; the common law can be both 'disorderly' (within reason) and normatively intelligible.[17] It also may be the case that some of the norms underpinning trusts law are unique to that law; hence, in relation to some equitable claims and remedies there may not be 'like' cases at common law at all.[18] Nonetheless, where the same norms occur in other areas of law (eg in contract or tort), one would expect to find that the claims and remedies operate in a similar fashion or at least are directed towards the same ends; that is, that like cases are treated alike.

The second prerequisite to any coherence inquiry is a stable and accurate understanding of the relevant rule itself: the persuasiveness of an inquiry's outcomes depends on the accuracy of its understanding of the relevant law(s) and how they relate to one another.

Coherence means that individual legal rules and their interactions with other rules will be understood and interpreted in light of the supporting norms. Sometimes those norms will have an existence independent of the rules they support, and be derived from some ex ante moral or political values accepted by a legal system. For those public and private laws that instantiate basic individual rights and liberties, the supporting norms will be ascertainable independently of the rules themselves.

Sometimes, however, the supporting norms may themselves be derived from how certain legal rules have been applied over a body of cases. Trust law, for example, does not instantiate some basic individual right or liberty; it does not express some fundamental moral or political imperative necessary to the function and legitimacy of state authority.[19] This is not to say that trust law exists outside of or in conflict with these basic imperatives. Indeed, we can track alignment between many rules of trust law and basic individual rights and liberties. Nonetheless, we do not think it is possible to justify the existence of trust law, and the remedies that enforce it, as being prescribed or necessitated by some ex ante norm, as might be possible for other areas of law, such as those securing an individual's freedom from physical interference, for example.

Instead, making sense of trust law and the remedies in response to a breach of trust requires a different analytical starting point. It is necessary to adopt what McLachlin J in *R v Van der Peet*[20] described as the 'the time-honoured methodology of the common law' of evaluation and reasoning from the experience of decided cases. This methodology, sometimes referred to as inductive or bottom-up reasoning, ascertains the

[16] R Bigwood and J Dietrich, 'Uncertainty in Private Law: Rhetorical Device or Substantive Legal Argument?' (2021) 45 *Melbourne University Law Review* 60, 95.

[17] *Fistar v Riverwood Legion and Community Club Ltd* [2016] NSWCA 81, (2016) 91 NSWLR 732 [53]. See also MacCormick (n 2) 266.

[18] See L Smith, 'Fusion and Tradition' in Degeling and Edelman (eds), *Equity in Commercial Law* (n 11) 32.

[19] J Penner, 'An Untheory of the Law of Trusts, or Some Notes Toward Understanding the Structure of Trusts Law Doctrine' (2010) 63 *Current Legal Problems* 653; J Hudson and C Mitchell, 'Justificanda' in I Samet et al, *The Philosophical Foundations of the Law of Express Trusts* (Oxford, Oxford University Press, 2023, forthcoming).

[20] *R v Van der Peet* [1997] 2 SCR 507; (1996) 137 DLR (4th) 289, 377.

organising principle(s) or norms(s) underpinning one or more of a body of rules from their application in the cases and is in contrast with reasoning from first principles (sometimes referred to as deductive or top-down legal reasoning).[21] Leaving aside for now the debates[22] as to the roles and interconnections between each type of reasoning, what matters for present purposes is that the 'time-honoured methodology' can itself be fraught when the rules themselves are not well understood or consistently applied in the cases. While instability at the level of the doctrine may be resolved by turning to the supporting norm(s), this assumes that that norm(s) is stable in the first place. The analytical processes of ascertaining the operation and content of a rule or set of rules, and its supporting norm(s) may thus occur as dynamic and iterative processes rather than perfectly sequential.

All this can make achieving coherence a complicated analytical process but nonetheless does not make it any less of a worthwhile aim. Our objective in the remainder of this chapter is to illustrate how these processes of analysis and argument might be used to achieve greater coherence in relation to the rules dealing with a third party's liability for unauthorised receipt of trust property. Jessica considers the trust beneficiary's proprietary claim (Part III) and Pauline considers the claim for knowing receipt of trust property (Part IV).

III. THE TRUST BENEFICIARY'S PROPRIETARY CLAIM

A. The Trust Beneficiary's Proprietary Claim

This part considers how coherence might be achieved in relation to a rule that has previously been identified, including by Dame Sarah,[23] as raising the spectre of incoherence: that which is sometimes referred to as the express trust beneficiary's proprietary claim or the assertion of equitable title. According to this rule, a beneficiary can assert or 'vindicate' her 'equitable proprietary interest' (variously labelled as 'equitable ownership', 'beneficial ownership' or 'equitable title', for example) via a claim for orders requiring the recipient of the trust property or its traceable substitute to transfer her title to the (possibly a replacement) trustee.[24] To make out this claim for proprietary restitution, the beneficiary is *not* required to plead or prove the recipient's knowledge of the facts giving rise to the claim,[25] albeit the

[21] *Roxborough v Rothmans of Pall Mall Australia Ltd* [2001] HCA 68, (2001) 208 CLR 516, 544 (Gummow J).

[22] See generally: *McGinty v Western Australia* [1996] HCA 48, (1996) 186 CLR 140, 232 (McHugh J); R Posner, 'Legal Reasoning from the Top Down and from the Bottom Up: The Question of Unenumerated Constitutional Rights' (1992) 59 *University of Chicago Law Review* 433, 433; K Mason, 'Do Top-Down and Bottom-Up Reasoning Ever Meet?' in E Bant and M Harding (eds), *Exploring Private Law* (Cambridge, Cambridge University Press 2010).

[23] Worthington, *Equity* (n 5) 15, ch 4.

[24] See eg *Yorkshire Miners' Association v Howden* [1905] AC 256 (HL) 281–83; *Strang v Owens* (1925) 42 WN (NSW) 183, 184–85; *Foskett v McKeown* [2001] 1 AC 102 (HL); *Independent Trustee Services Ltd v GP Noble Trustees Ltd* [2012] EWCA Civ 195, [2013] Ch 91.

[25] *Re Montagu's Settlement Trusts* [1987] 1 Ch 264 (Ch) 271–72; *Krnjulac v Lincu* [2015] NSWCA 367 [2]–[6]. Bathurst CJ expressly observed on appeal that B did not plead or prove X's knowledge of B's claim and upheld relief in response to the beneficiary's proprietary claim [24].

recipient will probably have some knowledge at least via the processes for initiation of litigation and pleading. The claim and the recipient's liability will be limited to the property that they have.[26] The recipient is not liable to the extent she no longer has the subject property, leaving the beneficiary to make out a claim based on the recipient's knowledge; this is discussed in Part IV below.

The existence and parameters of this rule are considered 'orthodox',[27] however, there is uncertainty as to the scope of the rule, with some confining it to property held on express trust,[28] while other cases extend the concept of 'trust property' to property held subject to other trusts or other custodial fiduciary relationships.[29] Further, the rule and claim it defines lack consistent labels, and are referred to variously as, for example, the 'equitable tracing claim',[30] 'tracing remedy',[31] 'proprietary claim'[32] or 'equitable proprietary claim'.[33] For ease of exposition, this essay will refer to the rule by reference to the claim it recognises under the label of the 'beneficiary's proprietary claim' or, 'the claim', but as we will see below, this is inapt given the availability of the claim to a non-beneficiary, such as a trustee.

If the elements to the claim are made out, the recipient will be required to transfer the subject property to the (repentant or replacement) trustee,[34] or potentially the beneficiary in the event the beneficiary is absolutely entitled to the property,[35] and unless the recipient can make out a defence, such as the plea of bona fide purchaser of legal title.[36] The recipient's insolvency or death will make no difference and her successors in title, such as a trustee in bankruptcy, and personal representative, are all bound.[37]

The beneficiary's proprietary claim thus effects a significant disruption to the ex ante body of legal rules that generate the recipient's title, such as property law or contract law. According to the ex ante rules, the recipient, as the titleholder, has the authority to decide what to do with her title, and how she will or will not exercise the legal entitlements held as an incident of that title. When subject to a beneficiary's proprietary claim, however, that authority is curtailed and redefined by orders requiring the recipient to exercise her powers as titleholder to transfer that title to the trustee. Once made, the recipient is subject to a court-imposed duty, enforceable

[26] As in *Re Montague* (n 25); *Krnjulac* (n 25).

[27] *Farah Constructions Pty Ltd v Say-Dee Pty Ltd* [2007] HCA 22, (2007) 230 CLR 89 [140] (the Court).

[28] See eg *Grimaldi v Chameleon Mining NL (No 2)* [2012] FCAFC 6, (2012) 200 FCR 296 [254].

[29] See eg *United States Surgical Corps v Hospital Products Int'l Pty Ltd* (1983) 2 NSWLR 157, 233–38; *Clegg v Pache (Deceased)* [2017] EWCA Civ 256 [87] (Lord Briggs, with whom Thirlwall and McCombe LJJ agreed). The differing conception of 'trust property' is an issue raised again in relation to knowing receipt in Part IV.

[30] *Boscawen v Bajwa* [1996] 1 WLR 328 (CA) 334 (Millett LJ).

[31] *McNally v Harris* [2008] NSWSC 659 [155] ('tracing claim'), [89] ('tracing remedies').

[32] *Bank of Cyprus UK Ltd v Menelaou* [2015] UKSC 66, [2016] AC 176 [59], [100] (Lord Neuberger P).

[33] *Great Investments Ltd v Warner* [2016] FCAFC 85, (2016) 243 FCR 516 [55] (the Court); *Fistar* (n 17) [46].

[34] See further: *Akers v Samba Financial Group* [2017] UKSC 6, [2017] AC 424 [46], [82].

[35] As in *Foskett* (n 24) 103.

[36] *Pilcher v Rawlins* (1872) LR 7 Ch App 259 (CA); *Independent Trustee Services* (n 24).

[37] *Space Investments Ltd v CIBC Trust Co (Bahamas) Ltd* [1986] 1 WLR 1072 (PC) 1074; *Foskett* (n 24) 127; Bankruptcy Act 1966 (Cth), s 116(2)(a); Succession Act 2006 (NSW), s 4(5); Probate and Administration Act 1898 (NSW), s 45.

by contempt of court, to exercise her powers in the required manner. Coherence as between trusts law and other areas of law depends on a secure justification as to why the, *sometimes innocent and unknowing*, recipient should give up her title.

Further, the beneficiary's proprietary claim is impacting upon the property available for distribution in the event of the trustee's bankruptcy or insolvency, or divorce, for example. The availability of assets for distribution in insolvency/bankruptcy is largely[38] the purview of various statutory regimes,[39] which carve out of the assets for distribution those subject to the beneficiary's proprietary claim.[40] The claim is thus impacting upon a range of bodies of law dealing with significant personal, social and economic interests, and the coherence of the law overall demands, as a start, a sure basis upon which the existence and parameters of this claim may be justified.

B. The Proprietary Rationale for the Claim

A proprietary rationale, sometimes expressed in terms of 'equitable title' or 'equitable ownership', is a justification for the beneficiary's proprietary claim, and remedies in response.[41] The Full Federal Court of Australia in *Grimaldi v Chameleon Mining NL (No 2)*, for example, rationalised the claim as 'proprietary, *in rem*, proceedings to make specific restitution to the "true owner"' which 'in essence [is] a claim to priority'.[42] English examples of the reliance on a beneficiary's proprietary title as justifying the claim include Lord Browne-Wilkinson's judgment in *Westdeutsche*[43] and the House of Lords' decision in *Foskett v McKeown*.[44]

These and other cases show that the claim is understood as the beneficiary's assertion of 'hey, that's mine, give it back!' and her (equitable) ownership justifies the orders in response. This proprietary rationale has strong support in the academic literature as well.[45] Peter Birks, for example, referred to the beneficiary's proprietary

[38] Bankruptcy Act 1966 (Cth), s 116(2)(a). Note that there is not a parallel provision for insolvency in the Corporations Act 2001 (Cth); nonetheless, it is 'elementary and fundamental' that property held on trust by a company is not available for distribution on insolvency: *Carter Holt Harvey Woodproducts v Commonwealth of Australia* [2019] HCA 20, (2019) 268 CLR 524 [25]–[27] (Kiefel CJ, Keane and Edelman JJ).

[39] See further *Carter Holt* (n 38) [27].

[40] Subject, of course to the trust terms permitting the trustee to benefit from the trust property, such as if she as an unsatisfied indemnity for properly incurred expenses, see *Carter Holt* (n 38) [28].

[41] A sample includes: *Shropshire Union v R* (1865) LR 7 (HL) 496, 511 (Lord Hatherley), see also 506 (Lord Cairns LC); *Re Diplock* [1948] Ch 465 (CA) 522 (the Court); *Strang* (n 34); *Boscawen* (n 30) 334; *Grimaldi* (n 28) [251].

[42] *Grimaldi* (n 28) [251].

[43] *Westdeutsche Landesbank Girozentrale v Islington LBC* [1996] AC 669 (HL) 705. See also *Akers* (n 34) [46]–[52] (Lord Mance), [82]–[83] (Lord Sumption).

[44] *Foskett* (n 24) 12–29 (Lord Millett); see also 108–09 (Lord Browne-Wilkinson).

[45] Lord Millett, 'Proprietary Restitution' in Degeling and Edelman (eds), *Equity in Commercial Law* (n 11) 313–14; G Virgo, *The Principles of the Law of Restitution*, 3rd edn, (Oxford, Oxford University Press, 2015) 1–18, 559–65.

claim as the 'equitable vindication',[46] drawing an analogy with the Roman law *vindicatio*.[47]

This reliance on the proprietary rationale matters for coherence. Equitable title is not just being used as convenient shorthand to assert the existence of the rule and the claim it creates. It is being used as a general justificatory norm according to which the rule is made sense of, and it is with this norm that the rule, and the interconnections with other rules, are made to conform.

For example, equitable title dictates how the scope of the rule is defined, and in particular the extension to recipients of traceable substitutes, as in *Foskett* itself. While there are different views taken as to whether equitable title does[48] or does not[49] justify the claim to traceable substitutes, the point for now is that both sides assume that the answer is derived from the proprietary nature of the right asserted, and the extension to traceable substitutes is a matter of property law. Another example is that the range of permissible defences, and in particular the inapplicability of change of position, and equitable discretion, have been excluded owing to the 'proprietary' nature of the rights asserted by the claim.[50]

Equitable title also dictates how the beneficiary's proprietary claim is understood in relation to other rules providing for remedies for breach of trust against third-party recipients (discussed further below in Part IV). For example, Leeming JA in *Fistar v Riverwood Legion & Community Club Ltd* distinguished the proprietary claim from claims in knowing receipt on the basis the latter 'turn upon conscience, rather than property'.[51]

The reliance on equitable title is part of a broader phenomenon by which equitable title and the proprietary rationale are driving how courts make sense of what is a trust, and how trust law interacts with other areas of law.[52] Further, the proprietary rationale impacts on coherence between the equitable remedies in response to the beneficiary's equitable title and the different remedies afforded at law for legal title,[53] as is highlighted by Dame Sarah in her book.[54] As Dame Sarah points out,

[46] A label used in P Birks, 'Receipt' in P Birks and A Pretto (eds), *Breach of Trust* (Oxford, Hart Publishing, 2002) 213, 215–17; A Burrows, *The Law of Restitution*, 3rd edn (Oxford, Oxford University Press, 2011) 13, 169.

[47] B Nicholas, *An Introduction to Roman Law* (Oxford, Clarendon Press 1962) 100–01.

[48] See eg *Foskett* (n 24) 110 (Lord Browne-Wilkinson), 115 (Lord Hoffmann), 127–29 (Lord Millett); Lord Millett, 'Proprietary Restitution' (n 45) 315–16.

[49] P Birks, 'Tracing, Property, and Unjust Enrichment' (2002) 54 *Common Legal Problems* 231, 244–45; R Chambers, 'Tracing and Unjust Enrichment' in JW Neyers et al (eds), *Understanding Unjust Enrichment* (Oxford, Hart Publishing, 2004) 273–74. See too A Burrows, 'Proprietary Restitution: Unmasking Unjust Enrichment' (2001) 117 *LQR* 412.

[50] See eg *Foskett* (n 24) 127, 129.

[51] *Fistar* (n 17) [44], see also [45]–[46]. See also *Re Montague* (n 25) 276. Compare with the view that the *proprietary claim* depends on the recipient's conscience being affected by knowledge in S Agnew and B McFarlane, 'The Paradox of the Equitable Proprietary Claim' in S Agnew and B McFarlane (eds), *Modern Studies in Property Law*, vol 10 (Oxford, Hart Publishing, 2019) ch 17.

[52] See eg *Shell UK Ltd v Total UK Ltd* [2010] EWCA Civ 180, [2011] QB 186. A phenomenon that has been criticised, see eg B McFarlane and R Stevens, 'The Nature of Equitable Property' (2010) 4 *Journal of Equity* 1; J Edelman, 'Two Fundamental Questions for the Law of Trusts' (2013) 129 *LQR* 66.

[53] Worthington, *Equity* (n 5) 15.

[54] Worthington, *Equity* (n 5) 184.

the proprietary rationale generates at least a spectre of incoherence between the equitable rules affording remedies to protect equitable property that differ from their common law counterparts. I do not aim to reconcile or justify these differences. This is because the beneficiary's proprietary claim and remedies in response are not responding to property and thus should not be compared to those common law remedies that do. Achieving coherence (and avoiding incoherence) depends first on making sense of the beneficiary's proprietary claim and its rationale. Coherence requires us to rethink our reliance on equitable title even in the face of the weight of case authority otherwise. This is because equitable title does not help us to make sense of the cases, and it is logically impossible as a justification for the rule and remedies that enforce it. Each problem is discussed in turn.

C. Equitable Title Does Not Make Sense of the Cases

As discussed in Part II, the law of express trusts does not instantiate some basic individual right or liberty, and it does not express some fundamental moral or political imperative necessary to the function and legitimacy of state authority. This means that we cannot ground a beneficiary's proprietary claim in her basic rights and interests as an individual. However, this is exactly what reliance on the proprietary rationale does by grounding the claim in the norms underpinning property law. Leaving aside the broader question of whether property is a basic individual right or interest to which the law must give effect,[55] property cannot be the justification for the beneficiary's proprietary claim.

The beneficiary is *not* the owner or titleholder, the trustee is. Adding the equitable epithet to the beneficiary's 'equitable ownership/title/proprietary right' does not change this and only obscures the justification for the rule behind a misunderstanding of an express trust as affecting a split between legal and equitable title. Properly understood, however, the express trust is a legal relationship that is impressed or engrafted onto, not carved out of, or effects a split to, the trustee's title.[56] The trustee's title, the 'trust property', may not even be property in the sense of a right to a tangible thing, and may be some other legal entitlement defined by laws other than property law, such as a personal chose in action recognised in contract.[57] The essence of the express trust relationship is that the trustee must hold and use

[55] About which may be controversial itself and about which there is a vast literature justifying or not property law, see eg H Dagan, *A Liberal Theory of Property* (Cambridge, Cambridge University Press, 2021).

[56] *DKLR Holding Co (No 2) Pty Ltd v Commissioner of Stamp Duties* [1980] 1 NSWLR 510, 518–20 (Hope JA); *First City Monument Bank Plc v Zumax Nigeria Ltd* [2019] EWCA Civ 294, [2019] WTLR 511 [16] (Newey LJ); *Commissioner of State Revenue v Rojoda Pty Ltd* [2020] HCA 7, (2020) 268 CLR 281 [44] (the Court); F Maitland, *Lectures on Equity* (Cambridge, Cambridge University Press, 1929) 19–20; Hudson and Mitchell, 'Justificanda' (n 19).

[57] See eg *Lord Strathcona Steamship Co Ltd v Dominion Coal Co Ltd* [1926] AC 108 (PC) 124. What counts as 'trust property' may not count as 'property' for other purposes, see eg S Douglas and B McFarlane, 'Defining Property Rights' in J Penner and H Smith (eds), *Philosophical Foundations of Property Law* (Oxford, Oxford University Press, 2013) ch 10.

her title in accordance with the trust terms.[58] Those terms may sometimes generate a complex of legal entitlements that have been analogised with ownership or other proprietary rights,[59] but this is not necessarily the case for all private express trusts,[60] and is not the case for charitable trusts.

All this should raise concerns about the transplantation of the norms inherent in property law to trust law. These concerns are further substantiated when the proprietary rationale is tested according to the 'time-honoured tradition of the common law'[61] by looking backwards to the body of relevant cases and asking whether the equitable title is a norm according to which we can make sense of the cases. While the proprietary rationale has a weight of express case support, it nonetheless fails to make sense of the rule and the operation of the claim across a range of cases, for the following four reasons.

First, the beneficiary's proprietary claim is not an assertion of ownership and is not a claim of 'that's mine, give it back'. The claim is for orders requiring the recipient to transfer the subject property to the (possibly a replacement) trustee so that it can be held administered according to the trust terms.[62] When those terms confer upon a beneficiary a present and absolute entitlement to the benefit of trust property, and if other conditions[63] are met as per the so-called rule in *Saunders v Vautier*,[64] then she may be able to seek relief that 'short circuits'[65] the step of return to the trustee, and require a direct transfer. The nature of relief as facilitating return back into trust is harder to see when the beneficiary also exercises her power to call for the trust property, however, it has not changed and makes the *vindicatio* rationale harder to accept.

Second, the proprietary labels may describe certain features of the content and operation of the rule, but they do not change the in personam nature of all equitable relief. This can be seen from the reasons of Lord Sumption in *Akers*,[66] where, after stating that the beneficiary 'had a true proprietary right', Lord Sumption goes onto explain this is because the beneficiary's interest 'possess[es] the essential hallmark of any right in rem, namely that it is good against third parties into whose hands the property or its traceable proceeds may have come'.[67] 'In rem' and 'proprietary' are labels describing the availability of orders for specific relief against an innocent and

[58] *DKLR* (n 56) 520.

[59] A characterisation that itself has been subject to criticism, see eg FW Maitland, *Lectures on Equity* (1929) chs 9–11; H Stone, 'The Nature of the Rights of the "Cestui Que Trust"' (1917) 17 *Columbia Law Review* 467, esp 477–80; McFarlane and Stevens, 'Equitable Property' (n 52); B McFarlane, 'The Persistence of Equity: Lessons from the Trust' (Inaugural Lecture, Oxford 2022): recording available at: www.youtube.com/watch?v=TNUQ96ik2tQ (accessed 10 January 2023).

[60] Cases have rejected the as false the 'dogma' that an essential attribute of a trust is that it confers a complex of legal relations which may be called ownership, see eg *CPT Custodian Pty Ltd v Comr State Revenue* [2005] HCA 53, (2005) 224 CLR 98 [25]; *Glenn v Federal Comr Land Tax* (1915) 20 CLR 490, 497.

[61] *R v Van der Peet* (1996) 137 DLR (4th) 289, 377.

[62] *Akers* (n 34) [46], [82].

[63] See further: *CPT Custodian* (n 60) [42]–[44], [47]; J Harris, 'Trust, Power and Duty' (1971) 87 *LQR* 31, 63.

[64] *Saunders v Vautier* (1841) 4 Beav 115, 49 ER 282, affd on appeal (1841) Cr & Ph 240, 41 ER 482.

[65] J Hudson, 'Equitable Ownership and Restitution of Misapplied Trust Property' (2017) 11 *Journal of Equity* 245, 267.

[66] *Akers* (n 34) [82].

[67] *Akers* (n 34) [82].

unknowing titleholder. The 'in rem' reference does not assert a liability on the whole world,[68] but as Lord Sumption says, only on those 'third parties into whose hands the property or its traceable proceeds may have come'.[69]

The orders made in response to the beneficiary's proprietary claim are not true in rem orders as the court does not declare ownership of property. The orders retain their in personam nature of being directed to a person, requiring them as the owner of the subject property to transfer it to the (possibly a replacement) trustee. The orders, once complied with, will have the effect of changing ownership, although they do not of themselves change that ownership directly. Nonetheless these in personam orders are still a significant imposition upon the recipient, and disruption to the continuity and stability of the underlying rules that define her title and according to which the recipient, as titleholder, has the exclusive authority to decide what she does with her title, as mentioned above. All this makes it important to be clear about when and why such orders are possible and equitable ownership, as seemingly stable and reliable as it seems, has some further problems.

Third, the rationale of equitable ownership fails to account for a range of cases in which the same claim is available to those who, in no way, can be understood to have equitable ownership (or any of the derivations of equitable title). One example is that a discretionary object (including a mere object or object of an open class of an exhaustive power)[70] can assert the same proprietary claim as can a beneficiary who has a present or future entitlement to the benefit of trust property. This is not simply a matter of a discretionary object, exceptionally, being granted standing to enforce the beneficiary's claim, and discretionary objects can assert this claim in their own right. As has been explained before, these objects do not have equitable ownership on an individual or collective basis and this makes the equitable ownership rationale inapplicable.

In relation to charitable trusts, the Attorney General,[71] or any person interested in the trust,[72] and in England, the Charity Commission for England and Wales,[73] can bring the proprietary claim.[74] An example is *A-G v Compton*[75] where the Attorney General, on the relation of members of the parish interested in the charitable trust, brought proceedings for recovery of misapplied property against the recipient.

[68] B McFarlane and R Stevens, 'What's Special About Equity? Rights About Rights' in D Klimchuk et al (eds), *Philosophical Foundations of the Law of Equity* (Oxford, Oxford University Press, 2021) 191, 197–98.

[69] *Akers* (n 34) [82].

[70] As recognised in: *Randall v Lubrano* (Supreme Court of New South Wales, Holland J, 31 October 1975), published as an annexure to *McDonald v Ellis* (2007) 72 NSWLR 605; *Lewis v Tamplin* [2018] EWHC 777 (Ch), [2018] WTLR 215 [39]; *Wright v Stevens* [2018] NSWSC 548 [56], [94], [235]–[246]; *The Serious Fraud Office v Litigation Capital Ltd* [2021] EWHC 1272 [203]–[205]. See further: C Mitchell, 'Commissioner of Stamp Duties (Queensland) v Livingston (1964)' in B Sloan (ed) *Landmark Cases in Succession Law* (Oxford, Hart Publishing, 2019) 273; J Hudson 'Mere and Other Discretionary Objects in Australia' in YK Liew and M Harding (eds) *Asia-Pacific Trusts Law*, vol 1 (Oxford, Hart Publishing, 2021) ch 2.

[71] *Wallis v Solicitor-General for New Zealand* [1903] AC 173 (PC) 181–82.

[72] Charities Act 2011, s 115, discussed in H Jing, 'Enforcing Charitable Trusts: A Study on the English Necessary Interest Rule' (2022) 42 *LS* 228.

[73] Charities Act 2011, s 15(1)(2) and s 114; Charitable Trusts Act 1993 (NSW), s 6; Trustee Act 1925 (ACT), s 94A(3).

[74] See eg *A-G v Earl of Chesterfield* (1854) 18 Beav 596, 599–600; 52 ER 234, 235.

[75] *A-G v Compton* (1842) 1 Y & C Ch Cas 417, 427; 62 ER 951, 955.

Neither the Attorney General nor the parish members could be understood to have an interest that makes equitable ownership a coherent rationale for the claim.

Added to this is that the claim is available to the trustee, who can bring the claim on behalf of beneficiaries,[76] or bring the claim in her own right,[77] and indeed may sometimes have a duty to do so.[78]

Fourth, the simple idea of a beneficiary asserting or vindicating their equitable title against the recipient does not make sense of the scope of the claim. A beneficiary cannot assert her equitable title against *any* recipient, notably when the transfer is one authorised by the trust terms. It is sometimes said that a beneficiary can only assert her equitable title if it persists and has not been *overreached* by the trustee,[79] where overreaching depends on whether the trustee's transfer is authorised by the trust terms[80] or applicable legislation. The continuing nature of B's interest, and the non-occurrence of overreaching, gets us closer to an account of the elements of the beneficiary's proprietary claim, specifically, that it will depend on the trustee's authority as defined by the trust terms. However, and for reasons to be discussed next, ultimately the premise that the beneficiary has a continuing 'proprietary' interest, which if not overreached can be asserted against the recipient, assumes the conclusion: the beneficiary's claim against the recipient. Equitable title might describe the availability of equitable relief against the third-party recipient in response to an unauthorised transfer but it does not help to make sense of why that relief is available. The determinative question is whether the trustee's exercise of power in transferring trust property to the recipient is authorised by the trust terms.

D. Equitable Title is Logically Impossible as a Justification

A further problem is that equitable title is logically impossible as justification. As mentioned already, equitable title (just) describes particular features of a beneficiary's legal entitlement(s) which can be analogised with those held by an owner.[81] The use of the proprietary metaphor has been criticised,[82] although cases persist in their reference to and reliance on it. Added to this, there are a range of statutory regimes that force us to characterise a beneficiary's, and sometimes a trustee's, legal entitlements under a trust as some form of a property interest. This means it is all the more important to be clear about when the metaphor or label of 'property' is being applied to a beneficiary's entitlement, and why. This is even the more so as 'property' can have

[76] See eg *Independent Trustee Services* (n 24) [76]–[77].

[77] See eg *Fouche v The Superannuation Fund Board* (1952) 88 CLR 609, 640; *Krnjulac* (n 25); *Presbyterian Church of Victoria Trusts Corp v Anstee* [2017] VSC 102 [14]–[20].

[78] *Young v Murphy* [1996] 1 VR 279, 281–83.

[79] See eg *Akers* (n 34) [51]–[52]; *Mortgage Express v Lambert* [2016] EWCA Civ 555, [2017] Ch 93 [21]–[39]; C Harpum, 'Overreaching, Trustees' Powers and the Reform of the 1925 Legislation' (1990) 49 *CLJ* 277.

[80] *Ali v Dinc* [2020] EWHC 3055 [318] (Sarah Worthington QC).

[81] As explained further in: SFC Milsom, *Historical Foundations of the Common Law*, 2nd edn (London, Butterworths 1981) 6; L Smith, 'Unravelling Proprietary Restitution' (2004) 40 *Canadian Business Law Journal* 317, 319–21; Worthington, *Equity* (n 5) 3.

[82] See n 59 and accompanying text above.

different meanings across different contexts[83] and '[i]t is not a "monolithic notion of standard content and invariable intensity"'.[84]

When it comes to characterising a beneficiary's legal entitlement(s) under a trust, the essential feature permitting the 'proprietary' characterisation is the 'right to exclude' or, more precisely, a prima facie duty of non-interference on third parties.[85] The proprietary characterisation of a beneficiary's entitlement thus depends on and describes the availability of the beneficiary's proprietary claim. This point has been made by Lord Sumption in *Akers v Samba Financial Group*, where he stated that a trust beneficiary's

> equitable interest possesses the essential hallmark of any right in rem, namely that it is good against third parties into whose hands the property or its traceable proceeds may have come.[86]

Indeed, even a discretionary object has been understood to have an interest that can be characterised as 'proprietary' in so far as the same claim is available to them.[87]

An equitable proprietary right or title is thus no more than an expression of the existence of the proprietary claim and consequent remedies in response.[88] Equitable title cannot logically justify the proprietary claim. Any justification for the claim that relies on equitable title is circuitous logic[89] as the premise – the proprietary characterisation of a beneficiary's interest – assumes the conclusion – the availability of the proprietary claim. This circuity has acknowledgement in the cases in relation to other equitable rules providing for proprietary relief against third parties.[90]

In calling out circuity of logic, I should not be understood as equating coherence with the rules of formal logic. As Oliver Wendell Holmes famously stated, the 'life of the law has not been logic: it has been experience'.[91] Judges call on other processes of reasoning and argument to elucidate and determine the organising principles according to which we can make sense of the law, and by which (often the hard) cases will be determined.[92] But whatever these processes are in reaching reasons for decision,[93] those reasons must provide a transparent and accessible

[83] See generally B McFarlane and S Douglas, 'Property, Analogy, and Variety' (2022) 42 *OJLS* 161.

[84] *Yanner v Eaton* (1999) 201 CLR 351 [19].

[85] A sample includes: *DKLR* (n 56) 518; *Akers* (n 34) [82]; R Nolan, 'Equitable Property' (2006) 122 *LQR* 232, 235; K Gray, 'Property in Thin Air' [1991] *CLJ* 252; Worthington, *Equity* (n 5) 65–67.

[86] *Akers* (n 34) [82].

[87] *Serious Fraud* (n 70) [205]; *Gartside v Inland Revenue Commissioners* [1968] AC 553 (HL) 617; *Commissioner of Stamp Duties (QLD) v Livingston* [1965] AC 694 (PC) 717; M Conaglen, 'Thinking about Proprietary Remedies for Breach of Confidence' (2008) 1 *Intellectual Property Quarterly* 82, 89 fn 57.

[88] The same point has been made as to the 'proprietary character' of a trustee's indemnity for properly incurred expenses in *Carter Holt* (n 38) [84]; *Equity Trust (Jersey) Ltd v Halabi* [2022] UKPC 36, [2023] 2 WLR 133.

[89] See further: Hudson, 'Equitable Ownership' (n 65); J Hudson, B McFarlane, C Mitchell, *Hayton, Mitchell and McFarlane on Equity and Trusts*, 15th edn (London, Sweet & Maxwell, 2022) [15–136].

[90] See eg *Colbeam Palmer Ltd v Stock Affiliates Pty Ltd* (1968) 122 CLR 25, 34; *Yanner* (n 84) [17]–[19]; *Zhu v The Treasurer of the State of New South Wales* [2004] HCA 56, (2004) 218 CLR 530 [125].

[91] O Holmes, *The Common Law* (London, Macmillan, 1881) 1.

[92] An example of which is *Harriton v Stephens* [2006] HCA 15, (2006) 226 CLR 52 [85]–[86].

[93] M McHugh, 'The Judicial Method', speech given at the Australian Bar Association Conference, London, 5 July 1998, available online at www.hcourt.gov.au/assets/publications/speeches/former-justices/mchughj/mchughj_london1 (accessed 10 June 2022). See also Lord MacMillan, 'The Writing of Judgments' (1948) 26 *Canadian Bar Review* 491, 491.

justification for the exercise of judicial power and according to which later cases will be predictably decided and made sense of as a whole. Despite Justice Holmes's anxieties about logic, there is a place for some sense of logic in achieving a minimum or basic standard of reasoning,[94] and as Lord Devlin pointed out in *Hedley Byrne & Co Ltd v Heller & Partners Ltd*,[95] 'no system of law can be workable if it has not got logic at the root of it'.

Along these lines, the same basic standard of reasoning should be satisfied when it comes to justifying orders requiring a (potentially innocent and unknowing) recipient to give up *her title* in response to the beneficiary's proprietary claim. As ingrained as 'equitable title' may be, it cannot provide a reasoned and rational, let alone coherent, justification as it tells us nothing about why the claim exists, other than that it does.

E. Achieving Coherence

Achieving coherence means we need to abandon reliance on equitable title to justify and make sense of the rule and the so-called beneficiary's proprietary claim it defines. Equitable title is (just) a description and 'should conform to, rather than dictate, the application of fundamental principles to "solving concrete legal problems"'.[96] The scope and operation of the rule, the availability of the claim and remedies in response should not be determined according to whether or not a claimant (trustee, object or beneficiary) has a complex of legal entitlements understood as equitable title. Equitable title, also, should not be dictating the availability of the claim in relation to property held on express trust, whether it extends beyond the express trust; whether the claim extends to traceable substitutes; the applicability of equitable discretionary bars to relief[97] and other defences; or how it coheres with other rules providing for further claims against recipients of trust property, such as those considered in Part IV. Finally, equitable title should not be the basis upon which the beneficiary's proprietary claim is made sense of in relation to other rules providing claims to legal titleholders.

Jettisoning reliance on equitable title removes any incoherence between equity and common law thought to arise from the beneficiary's proprietary claim. The claim is not responding to property, equitable or otherwise, and so should not be expected to cohere with other rules (common law or equity) that do. Achieving further coherence in relation to the claim depends on some other justification or organising principle, although space does not permit exploration of that here.[98]

It is acknowledged that in advocating for equitable title to be abandoned as a justification, some superficial sense of coherence will be sacrificed by departing from

[94] See eg O Dixon, 'Concerning Judicial Method' (1956) 29 *Australian Law Journal* 468, 469, 476; FW Maitland, 'Introduction' to *Seldon Society's Year Book Series*, vol 1, xviii.

[95] *Hedley Byrne & Co Ltd v Heller & Partners* [1964] AC 465 (HL) 516.

[96] *Carter Holt* (n 38) [84] speaking in relation to the 'proprietary' character of a trustee's indemnity for expenses, quoting *Livingston v Commissioner of Stamp Duties (Q)* (1960) 107 CLR 411, 448 (Kitto J).

[97] See further Hudson et al, *Hayton, McFarlane and Mitchell* (n 89) ch 22.

[98] See Hudson et al, *Hayton, McFarlane and Mitchell* (n 89) ch 15; Hudson, 'Equity's Gloss' (n 6).

the express reasoning in a body of cases that do rely on equitable title. Equitable title has gained such a degree of authoritative case support, and it is authoritative, as a matter of precedent, to explain the existence of the claim and availability of remedies in terms of equitable title and/or overreaching. Departure from this authority is not a move taken lightly, yet, it is respectfully submitted, it is one that is necessitated if a recipient's liability to the claim is to be made sense of and, ultimately, justified in a way that ensures the consistency and coherence of the common law (including equity) via the accepted processes of judicial reasoning.

IV. THE KNOWING RECEIPT CLAIM

A. Introduction

A coherence inquiry is complex when the operation of a rule and its supporting norms are both unsettled. Achieving coherence in such circumstances involves an iterative and interdependent consideration of the rule's operation and possible supporting norms. It may also involve an inquiry into, and have repercussions for, the coherence of other rules that overlap and interact with the rule in question. By way of illustration I consider the claim for knowing or unconscionable receipt of trust property (the 'knowing receipt rule' or 'knowing receipt').

B. The Unsettled Operation of the Knowing Receipt Rule

Coherence depends on having a stable and accurate understanding of a rule's operation. But the operation of knowing receipt is unclear in several respects. It is generally accepted that three elements must be proved:[99] first, a disposal of the claimant's assets in breach of fiduciary duty; second, the beneficial receipt by the defendant of assets which are traceable as representing the assets of the plaintiff; and third, knowledge on the part of the defendant that the assets he received are traceable to a breach of fiduciary duty.

However, each element in this statement of the law contains some ambiguity as to what precisely is required, and why. For example, the statement refers to 'assets' disposed of 'in breach of fiduciary duty', yet the seminal nineteenth-century case referred to property of an express trust and breach of express trust.[100] Despite this, it is generally assumed that trust property for the purposes of knowing receipt has an expansive meaning that includes property under the custodianship of a non-trustee fiduciary, who is subject to equitable obligations in relation to that property, and who has breached those obligations.[101] Trust property in this expansive sense includes, for example, company assets.[102] Yet, the High Court of Australia in 2007 noted that the

[99] *El Ajou v Dollar Land Holdings plc* [1994] 2 All ER 685 (CA) 700 (Hoffmann LJ).
[100] *Barnes v Addy* (1874) LR 9 Ch App 244 (CA) 251–52.
[101] See J Glister, 'Trust Property and Knowing Receipt' (2020) 34 *Trust Law International* 3.
[102] *Ultraframe (UK) Ltd v Fielding* [2005] EWHC 1638, [2006] FSR 17 [1487]; *Grimaldi* (n 28) [254].

expansive meaning of 'trust property' had been 'assumed, but rarely if at all decided', implying that the issue is not settled.[103] Furthermore, the practical relevance of a knowing receipt claim to scenarios involving receipt of company assets in breach of fiduciary obligation is now questioned.[104] A further issue concerns whether 'breach of fiduciary duty' or even 'breach of trust' is an accurate expression of the gravamen of the primary wrong, which appears from the case law scenarios to involve any unauthorised application of property to which equitable custodial obligations attach, whether or not such obligations are 'fiduciary' in the narrow sense of prohibitions on personal profit and conflict of interest.[105]

The second – beneficial receipt – element is the subject of current debate in Australia and, at the time of writing, consideration by the UK Supreme Court, as to what will constitute 'receipt' of trust property for the purposes of legislative registered title schemes.[106] And the third – mental – element of the rule is also controversial.[107] These and other questions concerning the operation of knowing receipt make it harder to discern the rule's supporting norms and are themselves a symptom of a lack of clarity as to those norms. Coherence here cannot be achieved by focusing simply on the rule or simply on its supporting norms; a dialogue must occur that takes into account the broader legal context in which knowing receipt operates.

C. Competing Understandings of the Norm(s) of Knowing Receipt

The nineteenth- and early twentieth-century knowing receipt cases are open to more than one interpretation regarding the claim's supporting norms and operation.[108] Hence, reliance on these authorities alone to divine the supporting norms of the knowing receipt claim is problematic. Accordingly, courts and commentators have sought to clarify the operation and supporting norms of knowing receipt by comparing it with seemingly alike common law and equitable rules. Famously, Professor Birks and others argued from the late 1980s onwards that knowing receipt could only be coherent within the common law as a whole if reformulated as a strict liability (subject to

[103] *Farah Constructions* (n 27) [113]. Ambiguous dicta in two earlier NSW Court of Appeal decisions were relied on. See *Consul Development Pty Ltd v DPC Estates Pty Ltd* (1975) 132 CLR 373, 396; *United States Surgical Corporation v Hospital Products International Pty Ltd* [1983] 2 NSWLR 157, 253. The dicta were considered and dismissed by RP Austin, 'Constructive Trusts' in PD Finn (ed), *Essays in Equity* (Sydney, Lawbook, 1985) 196, 217–23, but applied in *Rogers v Kabriel* [1999] NSWSC 368 [173]. See also *Bell Group Ltd (in liq) v Westpac Banking Corporation (No 9) and (No 10)* [2008] WASC 239, (2008) 39 WAR 1, 612–18 [4750]–[4778].

[104] *Criterion Properties plc v Stratford UK Properties LLC* [2004] UKHL 28, [2004] 1 WLR 1846; *Great Investments* (n 33).

[105] See *Breen v Williams* (1996) 186 CLR 71; *Howard v Commissioner of Taxation* [2014] HCA 21, (2014) 253 CLR 83 [56]–[57].

[106] See *Byers v Saudi National Bank* [2022] EWCA Civ 43, [2022] 4 WLR 22 (on appeal: *Byers v Saudi National Bank* UKSC 2022/0048); *Turner v O'Bryan-Turner* [2022] NSWCA 23, (2022) 107 NSWLR 171.

[107] See below text to nn 128–33.

[108] See eg the different interpretations of *Soar v Ashwell* (1893) 2 QB 390 (CA) and related cases and legislation taken in *Williams v Central Bank of Nigeria* [2014] UKSC 10, [2014] AC 1189. See Austin, 'Constructive Trusts' (n 103) 196, 204–07 for a detailed analysis of the inconsistencies in the nineteenth- and early twentieth-century cases concerning the application of limitation periods to ancillary claims, including knowing receipt.

defences) unjust enrichment claim, with the knowledge requirement removed.[109] This proposal and subsequent modifications of it were acknowledged by courts in England and Australia quite quickly,[110] but were rejected eventually in both jurisdictions in decisions affirming the fault-based nature of knowing receipt.[111] Other commentators, including Dame Sarah, have considered whether knowing receipt is the equitable equivalent of the tort of conversion.[112] Dame Sarah concluded that it is not, on the basis that the intangible equitable interests most commonly protected by the knowing receipt claim are fundamentally different in nature to common law rights to property protected by the tort of conversion.[113] It now appears uncontroversial that the supporting norms of common law claims involving receipt of non-trust property are unlikely to apply to knowing receipt because they do not resonate with the nature of equitable property.

Clarification of knowing receipt's supporting norms has also been sought through comparison with liabilities for procuring or assisting in a breach of trust or fiduciary duty.[114] Traditionally, these equitable accessory liabilities were grouped with a nascent form of the knowing receipt claim (against agents of trustees who 'receive and become chargeable with some part of the trust property'),[115] but they do not require the defendant to have received trust property, and their supporting norms are not necessarily directed to trust property.[116] They may, and often do, overlap with rules that respond to unauthorised receipt of trust property; but it does not follow that their supporting norms are identical. However, the same or similar pragmatic purposes (such as deterrence of third parties' facilitation of breaches of trust or fiduciary duty, and enhancing the claimant's protection by increasing the number of possible defendants) are relevant to both knowing receipt and equitable accessory liabilities, and demonstrate the importance attached by equity to trust and fiduciary obligations.[117] Furthermore, equitable accessory liabilities and recipient liability all

[109] See eg P Birks, 'Misdirected Funds: Restitution from the Recipient' [1989] *LMCLQ* 296; 'Misdirected Funds' (1989) 105 *LQR* 352; *Restitution – The Future* (Alexandria, NSW, Federation Press, 1992) ch 2. Birks later modified his position: 'Receipt' in Birks and Pretto (n 46) 213.

[110] In England, see *El Ajou* (n 99) 736; *Royal Brunei Airlines v Tan* [1995] 2 AC 378 (PC) 386; *Twinsectra Ltd v Yardley* [2002] UKHL 12; [2002] 2 AC 164, 194; *Criterion Properties* (n 104) 1849. In Australia, see *Koorootang Nominees Pty Ltd v Australia & New Zealand Banking Group Ltd* [1998] 3 VR 16, 100–05; *Say-Dee Pty Ltd v Farah Constructions Pty Ltd* [2005] NSWCA 309.

[111] In England, see *Bank of Credit and Commerce International (Overseas) Ltd v Akindele* [2001] Ch 437 (CA). In Australia, see *Farah Constructions* (n 27). See generally, *Investment Trust Companies v Revenue and Customs Commissioners* [2017] UKSC 29, [2018] AC 275, 295 [40]–[42].

[112] Worthington, *Equity* (n 5) 168–69.

[113] Worthington, *Equity* (n 5) 169. For an extended discussion of Worthington's conception of knowing receipt, see S Worthington, 'Exposing Third-Party Liability in Equity: Lessons from the Limitation Rules' in PS Davies and J Penner (eds), *Equity, Trusts and Commerce* (Oxford, Hart Publishing, 2017) 331.

[114] *Royal Brunei Airlines* (n 110); *Farah Constructions* (n 27).

[115] *Barnes v Addy* (n 100) 251–52.

[116] *Novoship (UK) Ltd v Mikhaylyuk* [2014] EWCA Civ 908, [2015] QB 499 [87]–[93]. See further J Dietrich and P Ridge, *Accessories in Private Law* (Cambridge, Cambridge University Press, 2015) para 8.3.1.3.

[117] P Ridge, 'Monetary Remedies for Equitable Participatory Liability: General Principles and Current Questions' in S Degeling and JNE Varuhas (eds), *Equitable Compensation and Disgorgement of Profit* (Oxford, Hart Publishing, 2017) 197, 201.

attach normative significance to the defendant's state of mind or knowledge, and in Australian law the same test of knowledge applies.[118]

There is some support in Australian case law for treating knowing receipt as a version of equitable 'participatory liability'.[119] On this approach, a principled rationale for knowing receipt and for equity's accessory liabilities concerns the defendant's knowing interference with the trust or fiduciary relationship. A similar approach can be seen in a line of English authorities, culminating in the UK Supreme Court's decision in *Williams v Central Bank of Nigeria*,[120] in which liability for dishonest assistance in breach of trust and liability for knowing receipt were described as 'ancillary liabilities' attaching to

> persons who never assumed and never intended to assume the status of a trustee, whether formally or informally, but have exposed themselves to equitable remedies by virtue of their participation in the unlawful misapplication of trust assets.[121]

The beneficiary's proprietary claim has also been used as a point of comparison for clarifying the supporting norms and operation of the knowing receipt rule. Much of the extensive discussion of the norms of knowing receipt that occurred in mid to late twentieth-century English cases grappling with the requisite mental element for liability concerned the relationship between these two claims.[122] One strand of cases saw knowing receipt as the personal companion to the beneficiary's proprietary claim and therefore as resting on the same normative foundations:

> Tracing claims and cases of 'knowing receipt' are both concerned with rights of priority in relation to property taken by a legal owner for his own benefit.[123]

On this view, knowing receipt protects a claimant's interest in the trust property or its traceable product. Hence, in this version of the two rules, a shared vindication of title norm is emphasised.[124] However, the same questions about vindication of title as a normative explanation for the beneficiary's proprietary claim, canvassed in Part III, also apply to knowing receipt. In addition, coupling the two claims in this way leads to the incorrect assumption that only personal rather than proprietary relief must be available for knowing receipt.[125] It is correct that knowing receipt comes into its

[118] *Farah Constructions* (n 27); *Grimaldi* (n 28) [267].

[119] In Australia, see *Farah Constructions* (n 27) in which the High Court retained the traditional *Barnes v Addy* liability framework of two limbs (knowing receipt of trust property and knowing assistance in a dishonest and fraudulent design by a trustee or fiduciary); *Grimaldi* (n 28) [247]. See generally Dietrich and Ridge, *Accessories* (n 116) 267–68.

[120] *Selangor United Rubber Estates Ltd v Cradock (No 3)* [1968] 1 WLR 1555 (Ch); *Paragon Finance v DB Thakerar & Co* [1999] 1 All ER 400 (CA); *Williams* (n 108).

[121] *Williams* (n 108) [9].

[122] See further *Re Montagu* (n 25); *Grimaldi* (n 28) 362 [263]–[264].

[123] *Agip (Africa) Ltd v Jackson* [1990] Ch 265 (Ch) 292 (Millett J).

[124] See eg M Conaglen and A Goymour, 'Knowing Receipt and Registered Land' in C Mitchell (ed) *Constructive and Resulting Trusts* (Oxford, Hart Publishing, 2010) 159, 172.

[125] For an example of this error, see Conaglen and Goymour, 'Knowing Receipt and Registered Land' (n 124) 161–62, 177. Although the Privy Council's citation of this work in *Arthur v Attorney General of the Turks & Caicos Islands* [2012] UKPC 30, [2012] All ER (D) 164 is sometimes taken to imply endorsement, the better view is that the question was left open: N Hopkins, 'Recipient Liability in the Privy Council' (2013) *Conv* 61.

own when the recipient no longer holds the trust property or its traceable proceeds, but as a matter of principle, proprietary relief is available if that property is retained by the recipient.[126] Where the claimant is not the beneficiary of a trust, proprietary relief via knowing receipt may be important, given that the beneficiary's proprietary claim does not extend to trust property in an extended sense.[127] This is not to say that a comparison of knowing receipt with the beneficiary's proprietary claim might not prove fruitful in some respects, but this depends on a more accurate understanding of the latter rule's supporting norms.

An alternative rationale for knowing receipt that emerged in a second strand of twentieth-century English cases also dealing with the mental element of knowing receipt was that the rule responded to the recipient's equitable fault.[128] On this approach it was said that:

> The recipient's state of knowledge [of the breach of trust or fiduciary duty] must be such as to make it unconscionable for him to retain the benefit of the receipt.[129]

The implication was that, generally, actual knowledge was required.[130] However, it seems that English judges are now reverting to comparison with the beneficiary's proprietary claim, by suggesting that, from an evidential perspective, and outside dealings in land, there is no difference in what is required to establish the mental element of knowing receipt on the one hand and the bona fide purchaser defence to the beneficiary's proprietary claim on the other.[131]

The Australian courts have also endorsed a fault-based normative explanation of knowing receipt that is founded on the recipient's knowledge, although the High Court preferred to categorise the requisite knowledge according to the so-called *Baden* scale of types or degrees of knowledge, rather than a general standard of unconscionability.[132] In Australia, actual knowledge, recklessness, or 'knowledge of circumstances which would indicate the facts to an honest and reasonable' person, is required.[133]

In summary, a common judicial method for ascertaining the supporting norm(s) of knowing receipt has been to compare and contrast the rule with seemingly alike rules, such as common law property-related liabilities, equitable accessory liabilities

[126] *Grimaldi* (n 28) [253]. D Hayton, 'Third-Party Liability of Recipients of Trust Property' in P Devonshire and R Havelock (eds), *The Impact of Equity and Restitution in Commerce* (Oxford, Hart Publishing, 2019) 236, 229 discussing *Akers* (n 34).

[127] *Grimaldi* (n 28) [254].The significance of proprietary relief for a knowing receipt claim in the context of unauthorised receipt of company assets is muted due to the limited scope for knowing receipt to apply on such facts and because the Federal Court of Australia has recognised a strict liability claim in equity, subject to defences, for specific restitution against a recipient of company assets transferred without authority: *Great Investments* (n 33).

[128] *Re Montagu* (n 25) 277 (Sir Robert Megarry VC); affirmed in *Akindele* (n 111) 452–54.

[129] *Akindele* (n 111) 455 (Nourse LJ).

[130] But see *Akindele* (n 111) 454.

[131] See eg *Papadimitriou v Crédit Agricole Corporation and Investment Bank* [2015] UKPC 13, [2015] 1 WLR 4265, 4281–82 [33]. See further Hayton, 'Third-Party Liability of Recipients of Trust Property' (n 126) 236; J Glister, 'Accounts of Profits and Third Parties' in Degeling and Varuhas (eds), *Equitable Compensation* (n 117) 175, 191 n 55.

[132] *Farah Constructions* (n 27).

[133] *Grimaldi* (n 28) [267]–[268].

and the trust beneficiary's proprietary claim, and then to analogise to the supporting norms of those rules. By early this century, a dominant view in the cases was that the principled rationale of knowing receipt was fault-based, the relevant fault being determined by the recipient's state of knowledge of a breach of trust or fiduciary duty. However, questions persist as to the precise normative significance of the recipient's state of knowledge, and this is reflected in uncertainty regarding the scope and operation of the knowing receipt rule.

D. Current Understandings of Knowing Receipt

At least two versions of the operation and fault-based supporting norms of knowing receipt can be seen in current English and Australian case law. They are not necessarily definitive as to the law in either England or Australia, which is in a state of flux, but they do represent alternative understandings of the law that might be endorsed by future courts. And they are useful vehicles for considering fundamental questions that beset this area of law.

(a) Version 1

As noted above, the English formulation of the knowing receipt rule at the time of writing requires that 'the recipient's state of knowledge must be such as to make it unconscionable for him to retain the benefit of the receipt' of the trust property.[134] Recently, the English Court of Appeal in *Byers v Saudi National Bank* emphasised that this requirement must be read in conjunction with a requirement that the claimant retain an equitable proprietary interest in the subject property in the recipient's hands.[135] Leaving aside the questions raised in Part III as to whether the claimant's interest can properly be described as an equitable proprietary interest, the gist of the Court's reasoning here is that the recipient must hold the trust property *with* knowledge. The Court concluded that the normatively significant fact justifying liability is that at the same point in time the recipient had control over trust property and knowledge that this was unauthorised.[136] The coincidence of control (referred to in the cases as 'possession') of trust property with knowledge renders the recipient a constructive trustee of the property from that moment. Consequently, according to the Court of Appeal in *Byers*, it is the subsequent knowing *retention* of the trust property contrary to the terms of the constructive trust, and not the initial knowing *receipt* of the trust property, that constitutes the relevant fault.[137] Equity does not respond to the knowing receipt itself, but to the trust that is now in place, by requiring the recipient to account and by providing remedies for breach of trust as appropriate to the facts.[138] In summary, the supporting norm of knowing receipt according

[134] *Akindele* (n 111) 455 (Nourse LJ).
[135] *Byers* (n 106) [69]–[75] (see also on appeal: *Byers v Saudi National Bank* UKSC 2022/0048).
[136] *Byers* (n 106) [76] ('possession and knowledge coincide').
[137] *Byers* (n 106) [76].
[138] *Byers* (n 106) [76]. cf C Mitchell and S Watterson, 'Remedies for Knowing Receipt' in C Mitchell (ed), *Constructive and Resulting Trusts* (Oxford, Hart Publishing, 2010) 115.

to this version of the rule is that the recipient's *retention* of trust property contrary to the terms of a constructive trust over that property is unconscionable. In essence, knowing receipt is a rule by which a trust is created. I will refer to this as 'version 1' of knowing receipt.

(b) Version 2

An alternative understanding of knowing receipt is implicit in Australian case law.[139] It is also consistent with an alternative reading of the English case law prior to the Court of Appeal's decision in *Byers* (as can be seen in its use by counsel for the appellants in those proceedings).[140] I will refer to this as 'version 2' of knowing receipt. Like the first version of knowing receipt, version 2 also treats the coincidence of knowledge and possession (control) of the property as normatively significant, but in addition attributes normative value to the point in time at which knowledge was acquired. More specifically, this version assumes that the presence of the requisite knowledge at the point of receipt of the trust property is itself a normatively significant event that justifies a remedial response. The knowing recipient is deemed to be a constructive trustee, meaning that she is liable to the same remedies as if she were in fact a trustee of the received property. Liability flows directly from the knowing receipt, not from a trust.

Two preliminary observations can be made regarding the implications for other rules of these two versions of knowing receipt. The first relates to the inconsistent dealing rule and the second to the liability of an innocent recipient of trust property who has not knowingly dealt with the property.

(c) The Inconsistent Dealing Rule

The first version of knowing receipt encompasses a scenario in which an unauthorised recipient for personal benefit acquires knowledge after receipt and then deals with the property. This understanding of knowing receipt reflects Millett J's influential judgment in *Agip (Africa) Ltd v Jackson*, which distinguished between unauthorised knowing 'receipt' of trust property (including scenarios where knowledge is acquired *after* the unauthorised receipt) and knowing/inconsistent dealing with trust property where the receipt was authorised and not for personal benefit (in other words, a ministerial receipt).[141] Conversely, a necessary implication of version 2 of knowing receipt (which emphasises that *receipt* is with knowledge) is that an inconsistent

[139] See eg *Farah Constructions* (n 27); *Grimaldi* (n 28); *Fistar* (n 17).

[140] *Byers* (n 106) [52]. Counsel relied on *Williams* (n 108) [31] (Lord Sumption JSC). *Dubai Aluminium Co Ltd v Salaam* [2002] UKHL 48, [2003] 2 AC 366 [141]; *Novoship* (n 116) [74]. See also *DD Growth Premium 2X Fund v RMF Market Neutral Strategies (Master) Ltd* [2017] UKPC 36, [2018] Bus LR 1595 [58] (as discussed in J Glister, 'Knowing Receipt' in W Day and S Worthington (eds), *Challenging Private Law: Lord Sumption on the Supreme Court* (Oxford, Hart Publishing, 2020) 217, 228.

[141] *Agip (Africa)* (n 123) 291–92.

dealing is normatively distinct from a knowing receipt. Liability for inconsistent dealing is said to be

> conceptually distinct [from the knowing receipt rule], because it is the *subsequent dealing*, rather than the *receipt of property*, that founds liability.[142]

However, it is unclear (in Australian law, at least) whether a further distinction should be drawn between inconsistent dealers who receive the trust property for personal benefit and inconsistent dealers who receive the trust property ministerially.[143]

(d) Innocent Recipients of Trust Property

The normative significance of an unauthorised recipient of trust property retaining the property with knowledge (unconscionable retention), which grounds version 1 of knowing receipt, *is* recognised in Australian law but not in relation to the knowing receipt rule and not as the basis for a trust to arise. Instead, the unconscionable retention rationale is used to explain a common law restitution claim for the value of stolen or fraudulently acquired property (a type of trust property), or its traceable proceeds, retained by an innocent recipient.[144] The common law claim has generated a body of modern cases in Australia and has been the subject of detailed judicial consideration as to its supporting norms.[145] It applies where receipt of the trust property was innocent and where there was no subsequent inconsistent/knowing dealing with the property. The claim is explained by Allsop P in *Heperu Pty Ltd v Belle* as follows:

> The equitable obligation arises from the later discovered position, not from wrongful conduct. Therefore, the extent of the personal equity involved, created by the circumstance in question, is the touching of the conscience of the volunteer recipient to deal with the property of another conformably with the interests of the owner, now discovered.[146]

That is, when the innocent recipient learns that their receipt of the trust property was unauthorised, their conscience is affected such that they can no longer deal with the property for their own benefit. Instead, they must account to the claimant for the value of the retained property. This explanation resonates with the 'unconscionable retention of trust property' norm in *Byers* that applies to *all* knowledge-based unauthorised receipt of trust property scenarios, but it does not lead to the interposition of

[142] *Fistar* (n 17) [45] (Leeming JA) (emphasis in original).

[143] Inconsistent dealing is distinguished from knowing receipt by Leeming JA in *Fistar* (n 17) [45]. However, the two English cases cited by his Honour differ in their formulations of the claim. cf *Agip (Africa)* (n 123) 291–92 (Millett J specifying that receipt is not for personal benefit); *Metall und Rohstoff AG v Donaldson Lufkin & Jenrette Inc* [1990] 1 QB 391 (CA) 474 (referring simply to receipt 'otherwise than as a purchaser for value without notice of the trust').

[144] In Australia, see *Heperu Pty Ltd v Belle* [2009] NSWCA 252, (2009) 76 NSWLR 230; *Break Fast Investments Pty Ltd v Perikles Giannopoulos (No 5)* [2011] NSWSC 1508; *Sze Tu v Lowe* [2014] NSWCA 462, (2014) 89 NSWLR 317; *Fistar* (n 17). See also *Smith v Leveraged Equities Ltd* [2020] WASCA 122 [58]. In England, see *Lipkin Gorman v Karpnale Ltd* [1991] 2 AC 548 (HL). See also *Agip (Africa)* (n 123) 287–88.

[145] See especially *Heperu* (n 144).

[146] *Heperu* (n 144) [154].

a constructive trust. Instead, the 'personal equity' is satisfied by an order for restitution of the value of the retained property or traceable proceeds.

E. Judging the Coherence of Knowing Receipt

So far, I have argued that there are two dominant versions of knowing receipt evident in English and Australian law, although neither version necessarily represents the definitive law in either jurisdiction. Which, if either, version is accepted has implications for the scope, elements and operation of knowing receipt and for the rules concerning inconsistent dealers and innocent recipients. On version 1, knowing receipt is a means by which a trust is created. Liability flows from the trust. On version 2, knowing receipt is a form of equitable wrongdoing that generates liability in and of itself. Version 1 of knowing receipt encompasses all scenarios of unauthorised receipt of trust property for personal benefit in which the recipient's control of the property coincides at some point in time with her knowledge of the unauthorised nature of its receipt. It thus encompasses scenarios of receipt, inconsistent dealing and innocent retention. It could be labelled more accurately as the 'unconscionable retention rule'. Version 2 is more limited in scope, applying only where the receipt itself is with knowledge. Scenarios of inconsistent dealing and innocent retention are dealt with by other rules. 'Knowing receipt' is an accurate label for version 2.

Support for either version of knowing receipt can be found in previous cases. Indeed, the version exemplified by the Court of Appeal decision in *Byers* may represent a natural progression from the more traditional understanding of knowing receipt and related claims that is embodied in version 2 of the rule, although it is also heavily influenced by academic theories of knowing receipt.[147] Both versions appear plausible. How, then, is coherence achieved? Can either version be said to be more or less coherent than the other, given that whichever normative account of knowing receipt prevails inevitably will shape the scope, operation and elements of the rule(s) in question? In this final section, I raise some questions to consider in settling on a preferred version of knowing receipt. They relate to the repercussions for the coherence of some of the other claims that respond to unauthorised receipt of trust property.

According to version 1 of knowing receipt, the recipient becomes a constructive trustee when possession of the trust property coincides with the requisite knowledge. There is no (relevant) unconscionability (fault) prior to that point.[148] Liability to account flows from subsequent breach of the recipient trustee's duty to restore the property to those rightfully entitled to it.[149] A concern here is that version 1 postpones any consideration of the culpability of the recipient's acts or omissions to the remedial stage and thereby lessens the expressive force of a finding of liability. It appears counterintuitive to say that a knowing *receipt* is not unconscionable in and of itself,

[147] See Alexander Georgiou, 'Knowing Receipt: Continuing Trusts and Conscionability: *Byers v Saudi National Bank*' (2023) 86(1) *MLR* 276–88.
[148] *Byers* (n 106) [76].
[149] *Byers* (n 106) [76]. cf Mitchell and Watterson, 'Remedies for Knowing Receipt' (n 138) 130, 153–54.

yet that is the logical consequence of explaining the rationale of receipt-based claims as unconscionable *retention* of benefit.[150]

Furthermore, this rationale does not distinguish between scenarios that might be thought to involve different degrees of culpability. For example, could an inconsistent dealing (that is, intentional conduct known to be contrary to the rights of those entitled to the property) be considered more culpable than a passive, albeit knowing, receipt of the trust property without more (ie an omission to disclaim the property)? And surely both inconsistent dealing and knowing receipt are quite different in terms of culpability to an innocent receipt alone? A counterargument might be that the recipient's culpability, or lack thereof, is addressed through the account procedures and other remedies that flow from breach of the constructive trust; however, this does not necessarily substitute for the expressive force and deterrence effect of holding that a knowing receipt and an inconsistent dealing are uniquely and distinctively wrongful in and of themselves.

Version 1 of knowing receipt has further implications for our understanding of the inconsistent dealing rule. An inconsistent dealing, as opposed to a knowing receipt or an innocent receipt without dealing, seems most amenable to conceptualisation as a wrong because there is intentional conduct contrary to the rights of those entitled to the property. This is so regardless of whether receipt was ministerial or for personal benefit. But is an inconsistent dealing following ministerial receipt really so unlike inconsistent dealing following receipt for personal benefit as to be treated as a normatively distinct rule (as is implied by the judgment of Millett J in *Agip (Africa) Ltd v Jackson*)?[151] Or does an inconsistent dealing by either an unauthorised or authorised recipient rest on the same supporting norms (namely, the wrongfulness in equity of inconsistent dealing with trust property)? A concern here is that the ministerial receipt cases typically involve agents of trustees[152] and raise unique policy considerations regarding an agent's obligation to follow their principal's instructions. Perhaps they should be distinguished from other instances of inconsistent dealing on that basis. A further consideration is that liability for inconsistent dealing by a ministerial recipient does not depend on there being a prior breach of trust or fiduciary duty; that is, it is not an ancillary liability. But is this a distinction without normative significance because liability is founded on the inconsistent dealing, rather than on the circumstances of receipt?[153] These questions suggest that the unconscionable retention of benefit rationale in version 1 of knowing receipt unduly simplifies what is a more complex network of (sometimes overlapping) claims with differing normative emphases.

The unconscionable retention of trust property rationale of version 1 of knowing receipt appears most persuasive in relation to an innocent recipient of trust property who has not dealt with the trust property since being apprised of the unauthorised

[150] *Byers* (n 106) [76].

[151] *Agip (Africa)* (n 123) 291–92.

[152] See eg *Williams v Williams* (1881) 17 Ch D 437 (Ch); *Carl Zeiss Siftung v Herbert Smith & Co (No 2)* [1969] 2 Ch 276 (CA) 304. See also *Agip (Africa)* (n 123) 291–92. In Australia, see *Adams v Bank of NSW* [1984] 1 NSWLR 285.

[153] Dietrich and Ridge, *Accessories* (n 116) 203–04.

nature of their receipt. Such a recipient has 'done nothing wrong' to the point of acquiring the requisite knowledge; however, to allow the recipient to retain the value of property still in their hands (or, indeed, the retained property itself) is clearly untenable given their current knowledge, and given the value placed by equity on trust and fiduciary obligations.[154] This has implications for understanding the strict liability claims that respond to unauthorised receipt of trust property. For example, the unconscionable retention rationale for version 1 of knowing receipt resonates with the operation of the common law restitution claim for the value of stolen or fraudulently acquired property or traceable proceeds retained by an innocent recipient discussed above.[155] It also resonates with the explicit rationale of that claim in Australian law.[156] So is the restitution claim simply a manifestation of version 1 of the knowing receipt claim? And what are the implications for the way in which either claim is pleaded, given that knowledge is not an element of the restitution claim (although relevant to defences)? The presence of more than one rule applying to a scenario of innocent retention of misapplied trust property is not a problem of itself, given the ways in which judge-made law develops in a common law system. But where rules appear identical in normative basis and operation, they surely cease to have independent existence.

It is also unclear whether the same rationale of unconscionable retention of benefit applies to the personal claim for restitution of property or its value against a recipient of company assets transferred without authority.[157] The claim is one of strict liability, subject to defences,' and can be made at common law (for the value of the property) or in equity (for specific relief).[158] The claim is formulated in terms of receipt of company assets, rather than applying to unauthorised receipt of trust property more generally. Yet the company-related cases discussed in the leading Australian authority provide only weak authority.[159] Support for the claim can be found in the House of Lords case of *Lipkin Gorman v Karpnale Ltd*, which is not so limited, but which is also a case relied on by courts as authority for the restitution claim for the value of stolen or fraudulently acquired property or its traceable proceeds retained by an innocent recipient.[160] It would be helpful to have some clarification from courts which endorse the first version of knowing receipt as to whether the unconscionable retention of trust property rationale applies also to strict liability claims involving trust property in either a narrow sense (such as stolen or fraudulently acquired property, for instance) or expansive sense (such as company assets) and, if so, what implications that has for the practical relevance of those claims.

The choice of supporting norms for knowing receipt is for the courts to decide based on principled and policy-based grounds. It is not unthinkable that English

[154] It appears that a change of position defence is available. See *Fistar* (n 17) [83].

[155] See text to nn 114–16.

[156] *Heperu* (n 144).

[157] See eg *Great Investments* (n 33).

[158] ibid [69], [70]–[76]. The Full Federal Court found it unnecessary to reach a conclusion on the normative basis on the claims for specific or personal relief.

[159] ibid (n 33). See further P Ridge, 'Modern Equity: Revolution or Renewal from Within?' in S Worthington, A Robertson and G Virgo, *Revolution and Evolution in Private Law* (Oxford, Hart Publishing, 2018) 251, 260–62.

[160] *Lipkin Gorman* (n 144).

and Australian courts might endorse different versions of knowing receipt, based on the predominance of one or other version in the particular jurisdiction's precedents and on other factors. The eventual choice may also represent a compromise between conflicting norms. Given the unsettled state of this area of law more generally (including in relation to the beneficiary's proprietary claim, which I have not discussed) it could be argued that either of the two versions of knowing receipt presented here will lead to greater coherence in the law, because the operation of the rule(s) can then be clarified in line with the chosen supporting norms. However, the questions raised above regarding version 1 suggest that that version has more profound implications for the existence and operation of other rules that respond to a third party's liability for unauthorised receipt of trust property, as well as for the scope and operation of the knowing receipt rule itself, than the second version of knowing receipt, which is more evident in Australian law.

V. CONCLUSION

Dame Sarah Worthington drew attention to the risk of incoherence in a dualist system of law through the simple and striking metaphor of a children's playground game. Since then, she has pursued the objective of coherence to great effect in her academic and judicial analysis of most, if not all, of equity's responses to breach of trust. In this chapter, we have engaged with only a small proportion of that body of law, but with a view to making out our arguments in Part II concerning coherence, why it matters and how it might be achieved. Our discussion has focussed on two of equity's responses to unauthorised third-party receipt of trust property, specifically, the beneficiary's proprietary claim and the knowing receipt claim. However, our arguments apply mutatis mutandis to making sense of any of equity's responses to breach of trust. Determining the coherence of these many rules depends on the same analytical processes of identifying and understanding the content and operation of a rule, its supporting norm(s) and its interconnections with other rules. As we have shown, these processes are iterative and interdependent, making coherence difficult to achieve when either or both of the rule and its norm(s) are uncertain. Nonetheless, having a clearer idea of a rule and its norm(s) is essential to making sense of an individual response, as well as equity's responses to breach of trust more broadly, and the interconnections between these rules and other equitable and common law rules.

11

Tracing and Payment Systems

JAMES PENNER*

I. INTRODUCTION

In 2006 Sarah Worthington wrote:

> [I]t is clear that the principles underpinning [claims to traceable proceeds] require urgent, rigorous analysis.[1]

It is fair to say, I think – just scan the citations in this chapter – that scholars have answered that call. In the first part, I shall begin with what are some theoretical observations on the nature of tracing. In doing so I shall largely endorse much of what was said by Lord Millett in *Foskett v McKeown*,[2] still the most important case on the law of tracing in the last century or more. I shall then argue that the standard explanation of 'tracing through payment systems' is founded on an error, though one easily corrected. The key to understanding tracing through payment systems turns simply upon taking seriously the legal concept of payment as it was developed in the laws of contract and agency. Doing so leads ineluctably to the conclusion that the only question relevant to whether a beneficiary of a trust has a claim to assets which were paid for by X is whether X's power to pay was in whole or in part *funded* with the trust assets. This analysis also shows that 'backwards' tracing is otiose; it is unnecessary for answering this essential question.

II. THE NATURE OF TRACING

An exchange is simply a transaction in which A transfers his title to some asset to B in return for B transferring her title to some asset to A.

* Thanks to Sandra Booysen, Michael Bridge, Rob Chambers, Timothy Chan, Christian Hofmann, Duncan Horne, Kelvin Low, Ben McFarlane, Charles Mitchell, Dora Neo, Lionel Smith, Rob Stevens, Bill Swadling, Tan Weiming, Marcus Teo and Sarah Worthington for helpful discussion. I owe especial thanks to Lusina Ho for her detailed comments on a first draft of this chapter.

[1] S Worthington, *Equity*, 2nd edn (Oxford, Oxford University Press, 2006) 110.

[2] *Foskett v McKeown* [2001] 1 AC 102 (HL).

As explained by Lord Millett in *Foskett*, following and tracing are evidentiary processes.[3] They are both ways of tracking what has occurred to assets initially subject to the beneficiary's equitable interest.[4] In the case of following, it tells us who is now the titleholder of the title once held by the trustee. That is, we track the title to a trust asset as it is transferred from one person to another. But the tracking does not by itself determine what sort of claim the beneficiary can or will have in relation to the followed or traced asset. To take the simplest example, T, a trustee, transfers a trust painting to a third-party recipient, TPR. The beneficiary, B, can certainly follow the title to the painting which is now held by TPR. But this alone does not establish that B has a claim. That depends upon whether or not TPR is a bona fide purchaser of the painting. If she is, then although B can follow the title to the painting into her hands, B will have no claim as TPR takes free of B's interest. B can continue following the title to the painting as it is transferred over the course of time from one owner to the next until the crack of doom if she wants, but this would be pointless, since she has lost her claim because of the first bona fide purchase.

The case of tracing is trickier.[5] Here we track the title to a trust asset into the title of what was received for it in an exchange. Continuing with the example, let us say TPR pays T £10,000 in cash for the painting. B will trace into the title to the cash. Now T pays that money into his bank account. B can follow the title to the cash into the bank's hands, but the bank is a bona fide purchaser of that cash, so B will have no claim against the bank, but B can trace into T's right in his bank account. As we will see regarding 'tracing through mixtures', depending on how T then deals with the money in the account, B will have a choice of claims against T, and which claim B chooses to press will not be determined by the tracing exercise, though of course it will depend upon it. But the point can be more simply made by taking the case of the bona fide purchaser TPR of the painting. Nothing stops the application of the

[3] ibid 127H–128G.

[4] More correctly, subject to the power of someone with standing to enforce the trust obligations against the trustee. This is of course true of a beneficiary with a fixed beneficial interest, and is also true of the Attorney General in the case of a charitable trust, and those entitled to a deceased's estate. Following the Privy Council decision in *Schmidt v Rosewood Trust Limited* [2003] UKPC 26, [2003] 2 AC 709, it seems to be the case that only some objects of discretionary trusts and powers of appointment will have such standing, roughly based on the court's determination of the likelihood that such an object will benefit from a distribution under the trust. For the sake of brevity I shall refer compendiously to this standing to enforce the trust as corresponding to a 'beneficiary's equitable interest'.

[5] MJ Hafeez-Baig and J English, *The Law of Tracing* (Alexandria, NSW, Federation Press, 2021) paras 1.83–1.89, deny that tracing is merely an evidential process. They say, at para 1.84, italics original:

> The proposition that tracing is neither a claim nor a remedy must be accepted. But to say that tracing does not determine substantive rights is misleading and rests on the fiction that when a claimant asserts equitable proprietary rights against a substitute right, he or she asserts *pre-existing* equitable proprietary rights. In fact, the equitable proprietary rights the claimant asserts against the substitute right are *new* rights conferred by tracing.

In one sense this is correct, as explained in the text accompanying this note – but for the tracing exercise the claimant could simply not have any claim to the substitute asset, aka the traceable proceeds of a disposition of trust property. But as also explained in the text accompanying this note, merely identifying the traceable proceeds does not determine whether the claimant has a valid claim to them. The authors seem to recognise this point at para 2.7 where they affirm that 'tracing is distinct from claiming'. See also Worthington, *Equity* (n 1) 89, 98–110.

tracing rules. B can trace into the money TPR receives if he sells the painting. B can trace into further subsitutions in TPR's hands until the crack of doom, but as with the case of following discussed at the end of the previous paragraph, this would be a pointless exercise.[6]

Now there is a sense in which tracing does more than merely track the evidence of asset substitutions. As we shall see immediately below when considering the justification for tracing, B is entitled to the traceable proceeds in those cases in that B's equitable interest binds the title to these assets immediately following the exchange. But this prima facie entitlement does not determine what claims B may make. As just mentioned above, B may have an election to choose one traceable asset rather than another. Moreover, the traceable proceeds may no longer exist. If B can trace into assets which by the time of the action have now been dissipated, eg into wine which TPR has drunk, B can have at most a personal claim against T or TPR for their value.

The next question we must ask is, 'Who may trace?' Beneficiaries of a trust[7] can of course follow and trace unauthorised dispositions of trust assets and make claims reliant upon following and tracing. But there is another important class of claimants: the principals of 'custodial fiduciaries',[8] typically company directors who act as agents of the company. A custodial fiduciary is much like a trustee because he has the authority or power to deal with the company's assets, in particular transfer title to them. The director must exercise his powers over the assets for, and only for, the benefit of the company.[9] Equity will treat a company director's unauthorised transfer of a company asset as equivalent to a breach of trust, and give the company the same sort of remedies as it would to a wronged beneficiary, allowing the company to follow and trace misapplied company assets.[10] For the sake of brevity, I shall henceforward speak about a trustee, T, misapplying trust assets, giving rise to claims by the beneficiary, B, against T and possibly a third-party recipient, TPR, although many cases will involve the misapplication of assets by custodial fiduciaries such as company directors who are not, strictly speaking, trustees, nor their companies, strictly speaking, beneficiaries.

Our next question is 'What is traced?' It is sometimes said (eg by Lord Millett in *Foskett*[11]) that one traces 'value', but this is misconceived.[12] What one traces are titles, or rights (including shares of rights, eg a co-ownership right). One traces one's

[6] Worthington, *Equity* (n 1) 102 presents a relevantly identical example concerning tracing against a thief.

[7] But see again n 4 above.

[8] The terminology of 'custodial fiduciaries' was used by the Singapore Court of Appeal in *Sim Poh Ping v Winsta Holding* [2020] SGCA 35 [87], [99]–[119].

[9] See also B McFarlane and R Stevens, 'What's Special about Equity? Rights about Rights' in D Klimchuk, I Samet and H Smith (eds), *Philosophical Foundations of the Law of Equity* (Oxford, Oxford University Press, 2020) 191–209, 204.

[10] See eg *John v Dodwell & Co* [1918] AC 563 (PC); *Re Duckwari* [1999] Ch 253 (CA); *JJ Harrison (Properties) Ltd v Harrison* [2001] EWCA Civ 1467, [2002] BCC 729. The classic statement of this position is by Kay LJ in *Re Lands Allotment Co* [1894] 1 Ch 616 (CA) 638.

[11] *Foskett* (n 2), 127C, 130G. Interestingly, Lord Millett seems to appreciate that what one really traces are rights or titles (when discussing mixtures of quantities at 141CF).

[12] J Penner, 'Value, Property, and Unjust Enrichment: Trusts of Traceable Proceeds' in R Chambers, C Mitchell and J Penner (eds), *Philosophical Foundations of the Law of Unjust Enrichment* (Oxford, Oxford University Press, 2009) 306–34.

equitable interest in the title to the cash into the title to the painting because it was given in exchange for the title to the £10,000 in cash. The mistaken 'tracing value' formulation is founded on the truism that titles (typically, though not necessarily) have value. In the case of things that can be used, there is both a use value, eg driving your car or living in your house, and an exchange value – you can hire or rent them out or sell them. In these ways, you can realise the value of your titles. Notice that the value of a right or title fluctuates all the time, but the title itself does not fluctuate. Your title to Blackacre is the same however much the market value of Blackacre fluctuates. Notice also that the exchange of titles upon which tracing is based makes no reference to the values of the titles exchanged. If T exchanged the £10,000 for a painting worth £1 million, B is perfectly entitled to trace into the title to the painting despite the fact that this would be an enormous windfall.

Our penultimate question is how we should explain what is known as tracing through mixtures where the mixture was caused by a wrongdoer.[13] As Hafeez-Baig and English establish in a careful review of the law, where a wrongdoer mixes trust funds with funds of her own, the wrongdoer's interests are subordinated to the interests of the innocent party or parties. Under this 'subordination principle':

> (1) Evidential uncertainties caused by mixing are resolved against the wrongdoer.
> (2) The wrongdoer is prevented from asserting that he or she holds a mixed fund, or any substitute rights derived from the mixed fund, beneficially unless and until the [innocent] claimant's claims are satisfied …[14]

This is just an application of the wider 'wrongdoer principle', which was explicitly adopted as the foundation for the subordination principle by Lord Millett in *Foskett*.[15] In particular, Lord Millett stated that '[t]he tracing rules are not the result of any presumption or principle peculiar to equity'.[16] Nor did he even refer to the alternative 'presumptions' in *Re Hallett's Estate*[17] and *Re Oatway*[18] which, prior to *Foskett*, were understood to be the doctrinal basis for the subordination principle, sometimes called the 'cherry-picking' rule. As Hafeez-Baig and English demonstrate,[19] these were never true presumptions, and the 'so-called rules' based upon these presumptions 'are simply inelegant ways of giving effect to a single principle: the subordination principle'.[20] It is therefore something of a puzzle and a disappointment to find that in the very recent decision in *ED & F Man Capital Markets Ltd v Come Harvest Holdings Ltd*,[21] the court, in setting out the law when a wrongdoer mixes funds of his own with those of an innocent party, regarded the issue as one of the correct

[13] Different rules concern tracing through mixtures where all the contributors to the mixture are innocent. I shall not go through those rules here, but I highly recommend the analysis by Audrey Lim J in *Pars Ram Brothers (Pte) Ltd v Australian & New Zealand Banking Group Ltd* [2018] SGHC 60; see also JE Penner, *The Law of Trusts*, 12th edn (Oxford, Oxford University Press, 2022) paras 12.19–12.25.

[14] Hafeez-Baig and English (n 5) para 6.22.

[15] *Foskett* (n 2) 132–33.

[16] ibid 132B.

[17] *Re Hallett's Estate* (1880) 13 Ch D 696 (CA).

[18] *Re Oatway* [1903] 2 Ch 356 (Ch).

[19] Hafeez-Baig and English (n 5) paras 6.39–6.44.

[20] ibid para 6.44.

[21] *ED & F Man Capital Markets Ltd v Come Harvest Holdings Ltd* [2022] EWHC 229 (Comm).

interpretation of *Re Hallett* and *Re Oatway*; although Hafeez-Baig and English's elaboration of the 'subordination principle' was considered, it was not endorsed; and *Foskett* was not mentioned by the court.[22]

Finally, we must explain *why* a beneficiary should be allowed to claim the traceable proceeds of misapplied assets. As Hafeez-Baig and English say,

> The 'dominant academic view' prior to the decision in *Foskett v McKeown*, and arguably even after, was that the equitable proprietary rights conferred against substitute assets 'always and necessarily [arise] as a response to the principle of unjust enrichment'.[23]

I have elsewhere explained why I believe the unjust enrichment analysis is unsustainable,[24] and I shall not reprise that here. In *Foskett* Lord Millett said:

> The transmission of a claimant's property rights from one asset to its traceable proceeds is part of our law of property, not of the law of unjust enrichment. There is no 'unjust factor' to justify restitution (unless 'want of title' be one, which makes the point). The claimant succeeds if at all by virtue of his own title, not to reverse unjust enrichment.[25]

Lord Millett's rejection of the unjust enrichment analysis was insufficiently elaborated but, it is submitted, the underlying justifying idea is that ownership not only comprises the right to use an asset, ie to realise its use-value, but also the power to exchange it for other property, to realise its exchange-value. But it is axiomatic that whilst T, having legal title to the property, has the power as legal owner to use it as consideration in exchange for other property, only B has any beneficial interest in the property. Thus, any realisation of the title to the property through the use of the power to exchange it must be a realisation for the benefit of B. In other words, T is not entitled to use his legal power to exchange the property otherwise than for the benefit of B; where T does use his power to exchange the trust property for some new asset, that asset is the proceeds of that power and thus belongs to B. Another way of putting this point is to say that but for T's use of his power to transfer title to an asset beneficially B's as consideration for his acquisition of the substitute asset, T would not have acquired it. How could it not then be considered the 'fruits' of the original title? A final way of putting the present point is to say that it would be inconceivable for equity to allow T to defeat B's interest by exercising, in his own favour, the very powers that go with title to the trust assets, by exchanging them for others. As McFarlane and Stevens say:

> Whatever the original reason for the duty to hold a right on trust, this reason is sufficient to require that the trustee holds unauthorized substitutions on the same basis. *The crucial point is that the new right was acquired by T's exercise of powers of title to the original right, and T was under a duty to B in relation to those powers.* No *fresh reason needs to be provided: it is the original reason for the original duty that requires the recognition of*

[22] ibid [658]–[685].

[23] Hafeez-Baig and English (n 5) para 2.21, footnotes omitted.

[24] See Penner (n 12); Penner (n 13) paras 16.36–16.39; JE Penner, 'The (True) Nature of a Beneficiary's Equitable Proprietary Interest Under a Trust' (2014) 27 *Canadian Journal of Law and Jurisprudence* 473–500; see also L Smith, 'Philosophical Foundations of Proprietary Remedies' in Chambers et al (n 12) 281–305.

[25] *Foskett* (n 2) 127E.

> *the new duty in relation to the substitute.* Just as T was under a duty to B in relation to the original right, T can now be under the same duty to B in relation to the substitute right. … *Once a trust has arisen, for whatever reason, that reason will suffice to capture substitute rights.* We do not need to invoke a new reason, such as unjust enrichment, to provide an explanation.[26]

This analysis applies with equal force to a non-bona-fide third-party recipient of trust property transferred in breach of trust. The property TPR receives is bound by the beneficiary's equitable beneficial interest. So bound, the entire beneficial interest in the property is B's. And so just as in the case of an express trustee, any use of the powers that go with his legal title to that property to exchange it for some other property, whether innocently or not, is just as much a realisation of B's interest in the exchange value of the property.

III. THE NATURE OF MONEY, THE ORIGINAL PAYMENT SYSTEM

The main claim I shall make is that what Lionel Smith has described as 'tracing in transit', in particular as this is applied to 'tracing' through payment systems, in particular bank payment systems, should not be regarded as a matter of tracing through exchanges as described in the examples above.[27] In short, the claim will be that there is no need to resort to an exchange analysis to determine that a payment to TPR has been made by T with funds which are beneficially B's.[28] Rather, the correct result is determined by the concept of 'payment', which is by and large a matter of contract and agency law. From this perspective, the exchange case is just the simplest example where T pays for an asset.[29] We can begin to understand the concept of payment by looking at the nature of money.

First, we must distinguish the idea of 'barter money' from what I shall call 'genuine money'. The 'barter' theory of money has been thoroughly discredited by Christine

[26] McFarlane and Stevens (n 7) 204, footnotes omitted, my italics; Hafeez-Baig and English (n 5) paras 2.47–2.50 (citing McFarlane and Stevens (n 7) and S Agnew and B McFarlane, 'The Paradox of the Equitable Proprietary Claim' in *Modern Studies in Property Law* (Oxford, Hart Publishing, 2019) vol 10, 303); and more recently R Stevens, *The Laws of Restitution* (Oxford, Oxford University Press, 2023) 243, claim that tracing on this non-unjust enrichment basis is an application of John Gardner's 'continuity thesis' (J Gardner, 'What Is Tort Law For? Part 1. The Place of Corrective Justice' (2011) 30 *Law and Philosophy* 1, 28–50). It is beyond the scope of this chapter to consider this claim, except to register my view that I do not think resorting to the continuity thesis genuinely augments the rationale for tracing given in the text.

[27] The consequence for me being that (channelling P Birks, *Unjust Enrichment*, 2nd edn (Oxford, Oxford University Press, 2005) xii) I must recall some of my prior writing for burning.

[28] Much of what I shall say about this was anticipated by T Cutts, 'Tracing, Value and Transactions' (2016) 79 *MLR* 381. In what I take to be something of a follow-up paper, T Cutts, 'Dummy Asset Tracing' (2019) 135 *LQR* 140, Cutts argues that in the case of payment systems, eg where T transfers money from a trust account to TPR's bank account, this should be seen as 'dummy asset tracing': 'The object of the tracing exercise in these cases – "the money paid" by T to X – is not a thing or right that actually moves from one to the other, but a *notional* money asset. The sum debited from the trust fund is treated as an independent right, which B pursues from T to X, to support B's claim against the latter' (ibid 147, italics original). It seems to me that this idea of 'notional money asset' tracing detracts from the points Cutts made in her earlier essay, and I shall not pursue this idea here.

[29] Or 'swaps' one asset for another, which would amount to a case of barter.

Desan in her magisterial *Making Money*.[30] The barter theory of money is essentially a 'numeraire' theory of money,[31] in which a certain amount of one commodity, whether a bushel of wheat or an ounce of silver, is used to price all other items that can be exchanged. Under the barter theory, a numeraire arises by conventional practice to avoid the problem of the 'double coincidence of wants', ie the unlikelihood that two producers under a division of labour will each seek exactly the same quantity of goods the other has to exchange. Instead, the presence of a numeraire allows more exchanges to take place because, being a universal unit of value by which other prices are determined, it can serve as a kind of money, facilitating exchange, assuming it is easily measurable, reasonably durable and reasonably portable. Precious metals are supposed to fill these requirements admirably.

Genuine money is different. Genuine money can be defined as a means of payment[32] (in particular for the settling of debts), denominated in units of account, a means which can pass from person to person without altering its ability to fulfil this function, and thus is also a store of value. Each feature is essential for something to be money.

Money does not arise primarily in response to the infelicities of barter, but in response to the infelicities of *credit*. Creditor–debtor relationships always precede the introduction of money.[33] Creditor–debtor relationships are the way that societies without money, or without sufficient money,[34] overcome the problem of on-the-spot barter, the double coincidence of wants. As Desan explains, money is constitutional or political because it only arises in communities with a *common creditor*,[35] the leader, whether king, lord or whatever, who has a right to demand tribute, typically

[30] C Desan, *Making Money: Coin, Currency, and the Coming of Capitalism* (Oxford, Oxford University Press, 2014). For a summary of the main points, see C Desan, 'Money as a Legal Institution' in D Fox and W Ernst (eds), *Money in the Western Legal Tradition: Middle Ages to Bretton Woods* (Oxford, Oxford University Press, 2016) 18–35. See also D Fox, FR Velde and W Ernst, 'Monetary History between Law and Economics' in Fox and Ernst, ibid 3–17; D Graeber, *Debt: The First 5,000 Years* (Brooklyn, NY, Melville House, 2011) ch 2.

[31] Desan, *Making Money* (n 30) 6, 430–31. AA Alchian, 'Why Money?' (1977) 9 *Journal of Money, Credit and Banking* 133 is the best attempt to defend a kind of 'numeraire' theory of money. Alchian argues that any good whose qualities can be assessed by non-experts can or will, on the general principles of market forces, spontaneously arise as a kind of money. At 139, he says, 'For example, chocolate candy and nylons became a near money during price controls in post-war Germany in the absence of other "money".' But although his argument is persuasive in the abstract, it supports, rather than undermines, Desan's theory. The kind of fiat, token money, issued by a common creditor is a perfect money on Alchian's account, for assessing its quality or value requires no expertise whatsoever in the community in which it circulates. And it is doubtful whether his spontaneously arising money ever reaches the standard of non-expert assessment he claims possible. 'Expert' assessment of quality applies pretty robustly to chocolate and nylons, which is why we have a tort of passing off.

[32] Money is commonly described or defined as a 'medium of exchange' but this is both inaccurate and confusing, since money *is exchanged* in consideration for what one's contractual counterparty provides; it is not the medium of exchange itself, which is the agreement or contract. Furthermore, money can be used to pay non-contractual debts (tax debts, judgment debts) which do not arise in virtue of a contract, and to make payments as gifts. It might well be that the chief 'agency' or causal impact of the institution of money is the *facilitation* of exchange, but that is a separate matter.

[33] Desan, *Making Money* (30) 24, 38–50, 58–62; see also Graeber (n 30) ch 2.

[34] See Desan, *Making Money* (n 30) ch 5 for an exploration of the way those at the lower rungs of the economic ladder in England formed extensive credit relationships in the absence of money of sufficiently low denominations to effect day-to-day exchanges. See also Graeber (n 30) 36–38.

[35] See eg Desan, *Making Money* (n 30) 43, 58.

paid in kind, as in agricultural products or forced labour or service. Desan refers to such a common creditor as a 'stakeholder', a somewhat misleading term given the common usage today in which a 'stakeholder' is thought of as anyone interested in a particular institution or enterprise. Two quotations will suffice:

> Money is created when a stakeholder uses its singular location at the hub of a community [its 'common creditor' status] to mark the disparate contributions of individuals in a common way. The moment occurs when the stakeholder takes contributions from people before they are due and gives out uniform receipts in return, each a token intended to document the early contribution. That token, turned in later at a time of reckoning, operates to convert goods and services that were not previously interchangeable or fungible – the variety of contributions due to the center – into matters counted in a standard unit. The initiative requires only one more twist to make money fully operational: if the stakeholder recognises the receipt and takes it from anyone's hand as an item that exonerates that person holding it from making a contribution otherwise due, the receipt can travel from hand to hand and maintain its worth as an item that pays off the center. The result is a token that fixes or entails value in a way that both the stakeholder and individuals can use, a novel accomplishment in a world without an agreed-upon way to measure and transfer resources.[36]

And:

> To produce money's basic structure, participants advance the time of resources owed to the center in return for that actor's singular ability to represent those resources in units that are countable and transferable. The units entail the fiscal value of the taxed resources, as it is enhanced by the cash quality they gain as countable, transferable markers. On the basis of money's fiscal infrastructure and in response to people's demand for cash services, societies can expand their money supplies beyond those made for public uses; they can sell money to individuals or license others to sell money to those people. Making money is therefore a material project: it proceeds by intervening in the way people relate to resources and it distributes profits and costs as it does so.[37]

Money has, then, both a 'fiscal value' and a 'cash value'. As to the first, it allows the state to spend in anticipation of future revenues. Secondly, and more importantly for individuals, in providing tokens in units of account to its subjects it creates liquidity, the ability of transactions to go forward immediately, as it were, without incurring the expenses of creating credit arrangements, recording, settlement, and ultimately, if necessary, resorting to legal enforcement of actions for debt.

It is not some independent value of precious metals, or some customary or conventional agreement about their value, that made them good material for money. Precious metal is relatively rare, difficult to imitate, very durable and requires skill to work. As Desan expresses the point:

> [C]oin solves an important problem that bedevils many monetary initiatives. To the extent that money circulates physically – and that property has been essential in many worlds, including our own – the tokens representing the unit of account must be both durable and

[36] ibid 43.
[37] ibid 24.

> difficult to imitate. … (While counterfeiting is the far more famous threat, note that the loss of tokens because of their fragility or decay would be just as destructive.)[38]

Finally, and most obviously, using precious metals to coin money itself creates a market for those precious metals, competing with other non-coinage uses and raising their price.[39]

In all these respects then, coin 'materialised' a debtor–creditor relationship in the form of tangible tokens. The token-holder is the creditor, and the credit it represents can be transferred to a third party. For this reason, coin became the first true means of *payment*, ie the provision of contractual consideration and the settling of debts measured by a universal unit of account.

The next significant step in the history of money was the introduction of banknotes, which in England, both in the case of Bank of England money and 'goldsmiths' notes', took the form of a promise to pay coin.[40] As a means of payment, banknotes passing in currency became subject to the same basic bona fide purchase rules as coins, as decided in *Miller v Race*.[41] But the most revolutionary step in the history of money occurred with the development of 'bank money'.[42]

Bank money is the 'money' that bank customers hold in 'demand deposits' or 'demand accounts'. As 'demand' indicates, money in these accounts can be withdrawn on demand in the form of cash, or more frequently, it can be 'transferred' to third parties by way of a payment system, in the past mostly by cheques, today mostly by way of electronic 'transfer'. 'Transfer' is put in quotation marks to indicate, as we shall see, that it is misguided to think of payments under payment systems as transfers from the payor to the payee. The demand aspect of these accounts means that money in a demand account is essentially equal to cash on hand in terms of its 'power' to pay others, which is why bank money is counted in determining (one measure) of the money supply.

Bank money has three sources. The balance in a demand account can be increased by the deposit of cash, or the receipt of a transfer of bank money from another bank account. In neither case is there an increase in the money supply. But the balance in a

[38] ibid 52.

[39] This was perhaps most farcically illustrated when Franklin Roosevelt, under pressure from senators from silver-producing states in the United States, decided to 'do something for silver'. The US mint bought up silver for coining (coins that never went into circulation). This drove up the world price of silver, precipitating an economic crisis in China whose money was on a silver standard, and China was forced to give up silver money, thus eliminating, of course, a major source of demand. The programme led to the almost complete worldwide demonetisation of silver. The tale is admirably told by M Friedman, *Money Mischief: Episodes in Monetary History* (New York, Harcourt Brace & Company, 1994) ch 5.

[40] See JS Rogers, 'Early English Law of Bank Notes' in Fox and Ernst (n 30) 535–55. Although these notes were made out to individual promisees they commonly also added 'or bearer', but 'the precise legal effect of the bearer clause remained in doubt until late in the eighteenth century' (ibid 553). There was also uncertainty whether the acceptance of a goldsmith's note as payment was conditional on the note being thereafter honoured (ibid 550–53).

[41] *Miller v Race* (1758) 1 Burr 452, 97 ER 398.

[42] More specifically 'commercial-bank money' to distinguish it from 'central-bank money'. See B Geva, 'Bank Money: The Rise, Fall and Metamorphosis of the "Transferable Deposit"' in Fox and Ernst (n 30) 359–86, 383–84.

demand account can also be increased when the bank issues credit, by lending money to its customer. It may thus increase the customer's 'power of withdrawal/power to pay' by crediting the demand account with the loaned amount, or by extending an overdraft facility. (Notice that the customer's power to demand, whether by withdrawal or by ordering payment to a third party, is equally enhanced whether this is by way of crediting the account or by extending an overdraft. This point will be important below.) This form of bank money is therefore sometimes called 'credit money'. This money, which is 'made' by banks in this way, constitutes most of the money in the system, on the order of 97 percent, cash making up the remainder.[43] For obvious reasons, this power of the banks to lend and increase the money supply is regulated, although as the 2008 financial crisis showed, perhaps not regulated enough.[44]

IV. PAYMENT AND PAYMENT SYSTEMS

The basic idea of payment derives from the law of contract. Contracting parties are generally free to determine their contractual obligations by agreement, and the parties can specify 'payment' for, say goods, in any form they wish; they can specify payment in the form of a quantity of coconuts if they so choose.[45] But, obviously, payment obligations are typically expressed as payment in money, and the parties can specify the form of payment in these cases as well,[46] for example, by cheque, or in cash, or via a bank deposit, or by credit or debit card.[47] But the notion of payment also extends to gifts. So, for example, in the case of a charity, the charity may specify the means by which it accepts donations. The lesson here is that whether a payment has been made depends entirely on the intentions of the transacting parties.[48]

Agency law also shows the determinative importance of the parties' intentions in understanding payment. It is trite law that an agent, A, may pay a third party, TPR, so as to discharge a liability of A's principal, P, or to make any other kind of payment to TPR on P's behalf.[49] In this case A is a 'paying agent'. A's ability to pay on P's behalf is a matter of A's actual or ostensive authority, and the source of the funds A uses to pay on P's behalf – what might be called their internal funding relationship – is irrelevant to the effect of the payment from A to TPR. P may put A in funds prior to the payment, or not. If P did, there is a second question of whether A receives those funds on trust to make the payment, or not – if not, A will simply have to account for those funds on a personal basis. It doesn't matter.

[43] See www.economicsnetwork.ac.uk/archive/starkey_banking (accessed 10 July 2022); see also Desan, 'Money as a Legal Institution' (n 30) 34.

[44] See eg Desan, 'Money as a Legal Institution' (n 30) 34–35; H Siekmann, 'Deposit Banking and the Use of Monetary Instruments' in Fox and Ernst (n 30) 489–531, 512–517.

[45] However, as Desan, 'Money as a Legal Institution' (n 30) 31, notes, 'By the High Middle Ages, the writ of "debt" was defined in a way that excluded all pleas but those claiming payment in the unit of account as currently decreed.'

[46] Where the form of money payment is not specified, the concept of 'legal tender' comes into its own.

[47] I notice that in England many pubs and shops are now 'card only'.

[48] Cutts makes this clear: see Cutts (n 28), 382, 391, 396–99.

[49] P Watts and F Reynolds, *Bowstead and Reynolds on Agency* (London, Sweet & Maxwell, 2018) paras 2-017 et seq.

We can now turn to the case of payments through banking payment systems, here understood to include interbank transfers and payments by way of credit cards. A bank is the clearest example of a paying agent. Take the following common fact situation. T has an account with Y Bank, and TPR has an account with Z Bank. T exercises a power under his banking account contract with Y Bank to order Y Bank to require Z Bank under Y Bank's contract with Z Bank to credit TPR's account with £1,000.[50] Colloquially, we say that T has 'transferred' £1,000 into TPR's account with Z Bank, although this is not a transfer in law.[51] The contractual relationship between Y Bank and Z Bank allows them to participate in a payment system with which they (for consideration of course) can facilitate payments for their respective account holder, in the sense of facilitating payments *by* their account holder. As between themselves, Y Bank and Z Bank are merely debtors or creditors inter se, depending upon whether at any one time their accounts[52] vis-à-vis each other show a positive balance for Y Bank or a positive balance for Z Bank. A similar analysis applies to payments by way of credit card. Where T pays TPR by credit card, the card issuer, CI, will expend its funds to pay TPR at the end of an accounting period (minus charges, and so on), and T will be required to reimburse CI, on whatever repayment terms (including charges, interest, and so on) are specified by their contract. Here, CI acts as T's paying agent.

V. PAYMENT VERSUS 'TRACING IN TRANSIT'

In his pathbreaking 1997 work *The Law of Tracing*,[53] Lionel Smith analysed bank transfers, credit card payments and so on, as cases of 'tracing in transit'. Because Smith relied upon the validity of 'backwards' tracing as a crucial element of the analysis, we must first consider that.

One 'backwards traces' when one traces into the title to property purchased by T where the title passes to T prior to his paying for it. As Smith explained:

> Suppose that D buys a car from C with some money. If we were tracing the value inherent in ownership of the money, we could trace it into ownership of the car. Now change the facts slightly, so that D buys the car on credit; he takes ownership of the car, but he is C's debtor in respect of the purchase price. A day later, D pays the debt with the money being traced. Can we trace from the money into the car as before? It is difficult to see why not. There is no substantial change in the transaction; the period of credit might be reduced to a minute or a second to better make this point. If that is right, then when money is used to pay a debt, it is traceable into what was acquired for the incurring of the debt.[54]

[50] Exceptional circumstance apart, Z Bank is not an agent or 'sub-agent' for T; see eg R Cranston, E Avgouleas, K van Zweiten and T van Sante, *Principals of Banking Law*, 3rd edn (Oxford, Oxford University Press, 2018) 232, 407.

[51] *R v Preddy* [1996] AC 815 (HL) 841; see also eg Geva (n 42) 384–85; perhaps the easiest way of seeing this is by noticing that a true transfer of the payor's right against his bank would be an assignment of that right to the payee which is not what happens.

[52] Either on a bilateral running account basis or via an account at a common correspondent bank; see LD Smith, *The Law of Tracing* (Oxford, Clarendon Press, 1997) 252–53.

[53] ibid.

[54] ibid 146.

I formerly (and recently) endorsed this analysis,[55] but I have changed my mind. We must consider two different cases of backwards tracing, which might be called two-party cases and three-party cases. The differences, and their consequences, were, as far as I know, first raised and analysed by Robert Chambers.[56] Take the simple two-party case first, of a sale of goods:

> When the payment of the purchase price follows shortly after the purchase, *the payment of that debt is part of the purchase transaction*. Money is paid to the vendor in exchange for the asset and the order of payment and transfer of title is irrelevant.[57]

Thus, following the analysis I have been defending, the only question is whether the purchaser is regarded as having paid under the contract of sale – nothing turns on whether payment is made before or after title passes to the purchaser. The Sale of Goods Act 1979, which is well known as a statutory embodiment for the most part of the pre-existing common law, treats the price paid by the buyer as consideration for title to the goods acquired whether or not the price is paid prior to or after title to the goods passes to the buyer.[58] This is why, for example, an 'unpaid seller', who has a lien over goods in his possession whether or not title has passed to the purchaser,[59] is *paid* under the contract by the purchaser when the latter does indeed make payment. I would only differ with Chambers on this point: it seems to me that it does not matter whether or not the purchase price follows 'shortly after the purchase'. Whether it counts as a payment is determined by the terms of the contract, and it is up to the parties to determine the timeframe for the making of those payments. I accept that in some contracts a provision for late payment may, on the proper construction of the contract, amount to an independent loan from the seller to the purchaser. As Chambers says:

> The distinction between purchase and loan is blurred when a vendor accepts delayed payment of the purchase price over an extended period of time. For example, if a vendor sells land under an agreement for sale over 25 years, this is essentially no different from a transfer of title at the outset with a mortgage back to the vendor for 25 years, which becomes no different from a mortgage to a bank for 25 years. At some point, the vendor ceases to be a vendor and becomes a secured lender.[60]

But whether the transaction is to be construed as something like a 'mortgage back' transaction is again dependent upon the intention of the parties. I can see no reason in principle for saying that an extended payment schedule is legally questionable,

[55] Penner (n 13) paras 12.26 et seq.

[56] R Chambers, 'Tracing and Unjust Enrichment' in J Neyers, M McInnes and S Pitel (eds), *Understanding Unjust Enrichment* (Oxford, Hart Publishing, 2004) 263–309, 298–99. See also Hafeez-Baig and English (n 5) paras 7.144–7.150.

[57] Chambers (n 56) 298 (emphasis added). See also Hafeez-Baig and English (n 5) paras 7.142–7.143. I previously considered the case of a sale of goods, still then under the rubric of 'backwards tracing', in J Penner, '"Sort of" Backwards Tracing' in PS Davies and J Penner, *Equity, Trusts, and Commerce* (Oxford, Hart Publishing, 2017) 123–49, 137–38.

[58] This seems to be the clear effect of s 2(1), which defines the 'price' as the money consideration for the goods, s 17, which would allow the property in the goods to pass prior to the price being paid, and s 39 (unpaid seller's rights), s 41 (seller's lien), s 49 (action for price) and s 57(2) (auction sales).

[59] Sale of Goods Act 1979, ss 41–43.

[60] Chambers (n 56) 299.

however lengthy the repayment term. Moreover, some contracts, like the contract of insurance in *Foskett* itself, are indeterminate regarding the length of time over which payments must be made, and Lord Millett was, it is submitted, correct in finding that later payments under the contract of insurance equally counted *as payments* under the policy.

If this is correct, then Smith's most intuitive example for the need to recognise backwards tracing is not really a backwards tracing case at all. It is a payment case, and determining whether the purchaser has paid for the goods turns on the terms of the contract which typically do not make relevant the timing of passing of title to the goods in determining *that* question.[61]

We can now turn to three-party cases, in which T pays for goods with funds borrowed from a third party, who T later pays with B's money. Chambers again:

> [W]hen the purchase price is borrowed from a third party, payment of that debt becomes a separate transaction. For example, when an asset is purchased by using a credit card, payment of the ensuing credit card debt is not part of the purchase transaction. Similarly, when a home is purchased with the aid of a mortgage to the bank, payment of the purchase price to the vendor and payment of that mortgage to the bank are different transactions. A claimant who pays these debts on behalf of a defendant is not contributing to the purchase price.[62]

Where a claimant can trace into the purchased asset through the repayment of the money borrowed from a third party to buy it, this is a genuine case of backwards tracing. It is unclear whether the law has ever recognised backwards tracing in such cases,[63] and as I shall go on to argue below, *Relfo v Varsani* and *Republic of Brazil v Durant* should not be regarded as backwards tracing cases at all, despite what Lord Toulson said in the latter.

Under the rubric of 'tracing in transit', Smith then considers interbank transfers and credit card purchases, an analysis that he rightly sees as depending upon backwards tracing, as the funding of the 'purchase' of rights created for the ultimate recipient, eg an augmented bank balance, may take place *following* the creation of those rights. The details are inessential here because what I wish to question is the force of the founding analogy Smith sets out.

There are two cases to consider:

> *Example 1*. T withdraws £25,000 from the trust bank account, then transfers this cash to a boat dealer to buy a boat; T then transfers title to the boat to TPR. Here the law is clear: B can trace from the right to withdraw funds from the bank into the title to the cash, and then trace into the title to the boat; B can follow the title to the boat on its transfer to TPR. If TPR is not a bona fide purchaser, B's beneficial interest will bind TPR's title to the boat.
>
> *Example 2*. T withdraws £25,000 from the trust bank account and then uses this cash to pay a boat dealer to transfer a boat to TPR; in other words, T buys a boat for TPR with £25,000 of trust money.

[61] If this is correct, then *Moffatt v Crawford* [1924] ST R Qd 241 (QSC) is wrongly decided, which I think it is.

[62] Chambers (n 56) 298–99. See also Hafeez-Baig and English (n 5) paras 7.144–7.150.

[63] Penner (n 13) paras 12.27 et seq; Hafeez-Baig and English (n 5) paras 7.96–7.126.

Example 2 is a case of what Smith calls 'tracing in transit'. The perceived problem for the law of tracing is that T never receives what is paid for, 'never sees the [boat]'.[64] The important intellectual move that Smith makes is to analogise Example 2 to Example 1, referring to the boat dealer as an 'intermediary'. He says:

> [That T never sees the boat] cannot change the substance of the matter; the boat received by TPR is the traceable product of the cash, and the boat can be followed to its receipt by TPR. The complication is that the substitution was not 'in T's hands' in the usual sense; he did not receive its proceeds. Nonetheless, if we are concerned with the value in the cash, as before we can either follow it to the boat dealer, or trace through into the boat, despite the fact that T does not get possession of the boat. There can be no substantive difference in the result when two transactions are rolled into one.[65]

As you will predict from what I have already said, I don't think there is any reason to analogise Example 2 to Example 1, nor is there any difficulty in holding that TPR's title to the boat is bound by B's interest, because *the boat was paid for with money in which B held the beneficial interest*. On this analysis, it is irrelevant *who* receives title to the boat, T or TPR, so long as it was paid for by exercising a power to pay which was funded by B.

In the interbank transfer case, the same lesson applies. If the multiparty contractual arrangements are such that T's instruction to his bank, Y Bank, is effective to credit TPR's account with Z Bank, then T *has paid* TPR. Thus, with Cutts,[66] I would submit that there is no reason to analyse interbank transfers, any more than the boat example, as cases where one needs to identify a chain of 'exchange substitutes', whether in T's hands or in the hands of 'intermediaries', followed by a transfer of the final substitute to TPR, to establish B's beneficial interest in TPR's title.

If all this is correct, then these cases require the answering of only two questions:

(1) Who exercised a power to make an effective payment?
(2) Who *funded*, or *payed for*, that power to make an effective payment? More specifically, with respect to following and tracing assets, the question is *whether T's power to direct A to pay TPR is one that is burdened by the beneficial interest of B.*

To recapitulate: a bank account just is a paying arrangement; when I withdraw funds, the bank pays me and my account is adjusted accordingly;[67] when I order it to pay funds to others, it acts as my agent to pay them and the account is adjusted accordingly. What I have, then, is a contractual legal power to order the bank to pay either me or a third party the totality of the funds I am entitled to pay, whether the account is in credit or in overdraft. As between my bank and me, whether I am in overdraft

[64] Smith (n 52) 244.
[65] ibid 244–45. I have changed the property and the names of the characters to align with my examples.
[66] Cutts (n 28).
[67] The power to withdraw money from a bank is not an 'exchange'. It is a power I have under a contract, true, but when I withdraw money I am just exercising a power I already have to provide myself with a different mechanism of payment, cash. I do not transfer anything to the bank when I withdraw funds; rather, my contract with the bank just entitles the bank to debit my account, reducing my power to withdraw more cash or order the bank to pay a third party.

simply determines whether I am paid interest (minimally, if at all) on the sum in the account if I am in credit or I pay the bank interest (always) when I am in overdraft. So, under the banker–customer contract, the customer's chose in action against the bank is the power of the customer to withdraw funds up to a certain amount or to order the bank to make payments to others of that amount. A payment by T to TPR's bank account augments[68] TPR's right to withdraw funds to a new limit or order the bank to transfer funds to a third party up to that new limit. It follows that when T pays trust money in breach of trust into T's personal bank account, or into the account of TPR (not being a bona fide purchaser), it matters not one whit whether T's or TPR's account is in overdraft or in credit when the payment is made for the purpose of B's tracing into the proceeds of T's or TPR's expenditures from the account thereafter.

This is best illustrated by examples in which TPR is not a bona fide purchaser of any payments he receives into his bank account.

> *Example 3.* On 1 June TPR's account, which has no overdraft facility, has a balance of £20,000. On 2 June T transfers £20,000 (money held on trust for B) into TPR's account, raising the balance to £40,000. On 3 June TPR buys a painting for £40,000.

It is orthodox that B can trace into TPR's expenditure from his account and claim a one-half (£20,000/£40,000) beneficial co-ownership interest in the painting. The result would be the same if T were the holder of the bank account: T would hold the painting on trust for T and B in equal shares.

> *Example 4.* On 1 June TPR's account has a £20,000 overdraft limit, and the balance in the account is at £0. On 2 June T transfers £20,000 (money held on trust for B) into TPR's account. This raises the balance to £20,000. On 3 June TPR buys a painting for £40,000.[69]

Although not a textbook case, it is hard to see how the result could differ from the previous example. The positive balance in the account is due to B's money, so B can trace into TPR's expenditure from his account and claim a one half (£20,000/£40,000) beneficial co-ownership interest in the painting. Notice, importantly, that TPR is exercising his own overdraft rights under the account to borrow from the bank. Nevertheless, he is entitled to his own half-share of the painting on 'mixed substitution' tracing principles – following the deposit of B's money, TPR's 'power to pay' has been enhanced in value by £20,000, raising TPR's power to pay to £40,000. He exhausts that power entirely by purchasing the painting for £40,000.

> *Example 5.* On 1 June TPR's account has a £20,000 overdraft limit, and it is £20,000 in overdraft. On that day T makes the same transfer of money held on

[68] The idea that the value of the right is augmented competes with the alternative analysis under which the old chose in action is replaced by a new one when money is deposited or withdrawn. For discussion, see Hafeez-Baig and English (n 5) paras 1.58–1.62. My analysis does not depend on which of these views is superior.

[69] As Kelvin Low pointed out to me, it does not matter whether or not T's account has a prearranged overdraft limit, so long as in the latter case the bank complies with the order to pay £40,000 to the painting dealer. In the latter case, T's contract with the bank will almost certainly allow the bank to impose charges on T of various kinds.

> trust for B, extinguishing the amount of the overdraft, raising the balance of the account to £0. On 2 June TPR transfers £20,000 into the account, raising the balance to £20,000. On 3 June TPR buys a painting for £40,000.

As I understand the orthodox position, B is entirely out of luck here because *her* £20,000 payment is untraceable because it was paid to discharge TPR's debt against its bank, and the painting cannot count as the traceable proceeds of TPR's payment.[70] With respect, not only is this entirely unjust, but it is so only on a misunderstanding of TPR's right to order its bank to make payments. If we correctly understand that TPR's chose in action against her bank is not a chose in action simply to withdraw funds or order the payment of funds when TPR's account is in credit, but also to do so when she is in overdraft (up to that limit of course), how is it the case that T's payment in Example 5 does not double the value of TPR's chose in action, her power to make the bank pay at her order? In colloquial terms, how did T's clearing of TPR's overdraft with trust money not 'buy' TPR double the money amount of her right to make her bank pay? Prior to T's payment TPR had a chose in action in virtue of which she could withdraw or order her bank to pay £0. Afterward, she had a chose in action in virtue of which she could withdraw or order her bank to pay £20,000. What these examples are meant to show is that, in principle, nothing is changed by the state of the account as between TPR and her bank, ie whether it is in overdraft or in credit at the time the money is paid, for the purpose of determining whether B can trace into an expenditure from the account into which T has paid moneys which are beneficially B's; the only question at issue is the extent to which the payment of trust money has increased TPR's power to make her bank pay.

We can complicate these examples by complicating TPR's expenditures and by adding a *Quistclose* trust element.

> *Example 6*. On 1 June T's personal account has a £20,000 overdraft limit, and it is £20,000 in overdraft. On that day T transfers into T's account £20,000 from a trust account held for B, extinguishing the amount of the overdraft, raising the balance of the account to £0. On 2 June T transfers £20,000 of his own money into his account, raising the balance to £20,000. On 3 June T spends £20,000 on shares which have increased in value. Thereafter T withdraws £ 20,000, up to his overdraft limit, and spends the funds on riotous living, giving rise to no traceable proceeds.

On the account set out here, on the subordination or wrongdoer principle, B can cherry-pick the expenditures from the account. Here B will obviously claim the entire beneficial interest in the shares.

> *Example 7A*. On 1 June T opens an account with Bank Q, in respect of which Bank Q extends an overdraft facility of £20,000; the overdraft facility is subject to a *Quistclose* trust obligation that T only spends the money to buy shares in a particular company. On 2 June, T transfers into the account £20,000 from a trust account held for B, raising the balance to £20,000. On 3 June, T withdraws £40,000 from the account and uses the cash to buy a boat.

[70] See eg Cutts (n 28) 38, and Hafeez-Baig and English (n 5) paras 7.96–7.126, and the cases cited therein.

Following the preceding analysis, B and Bank Q are each entitled to a beneficial half share in T's title to the boat.

> *Example 7B.*[71] T's account at Q Bank has an overdraft facility of £20,000, and it is £20,000 in overdraft. The overdraft facility is subject to a *Quistclose* trust obligation as set out in Example 7A. T deposits £20,000 trust funds into the account, raising the balance to £0. T then withdraws £20,000 to purchase a painting.

B can claim the painting, and Q Bank has no claim to it. Since T previously exercised his power under the overdraft, Q Bank no longer has any *Quistclose* restriction over the account. If T failed to comply with the *Quistclose* restriction in spending those funds, Q Bank has a breach of trust claim against T, including the right to trace into the proceeds of the misapplied funds.

The same analysis equally applies to credit cards.

> *Example 8.* T has a credit card with a credit card issuer, CI, with a credit limit of £10,000. At 1 June, the balance (what T must pay CI) stands at £5,000. Thus, on 1 June, T has a power to charge up to £5,000 worth of goods or services. On 2 June, T buys an antique table for £5,000, reaching his credit limit. On 3 June, T pays off his £10,000 balance by electronically transferring money to CI from a trust account held for B. On 4 June, T charges the purchase of a piano for £10,000.

On the analysis proffered here, B has funded T's card by paying off his balance, raising T's power to charge, his power to make CI liable to pay merchants for him, to £10,000. Thus B should be able to trace into any assets obtained by T's expenditures after 3 June, and so B should be able to claim the entire beneficial interest in the piano.

It is worth emphasising that none of the foregoing analysis invokes backwards tracing. Indeed, by properly characterising the chose in action a person has with a bank with an overdraft facility, or the chose in action held by a credit card holder against CI, one might say that Examples 5–8 are cases of tracing forwards through the payment of a debt because by paying that debt, that overdraft, a new more valuable chose in action – the account holder's power to make her bank make payments for her or her power to withdraw cash, or charge the credit card – has been created.

Consider two more examples which further illustrate the analysis.

> *Example 9.* T's personal account has a £20,000 overdraft limit, and it is £20,000 in overdraft. T transfers £20,000 of trust funds into the account, raising the balance of the account to £0.

As soon as this happens, T's power to withdraw funds or order payments from the account are held for the trust. T will be obliged to reverse the transfer. Prior to doing so, in having to account to B, this right to the bank account's 'power to withdraw/to order payments' must be brought into the trust account.

> *Example 10.* T has two personal accounts at N Bank, accounts 1 and 2. Account 1 has an overdraft facility of £10,000. T deposits £20,000 of trust funds into

[71] This example, as well as Examples 9 and 10, were suggested to me by Lusina Ho.

account 2, which improves T's credit record. In consequence N Bank increases the overdraft limit of account 1 to £20,000. T then withdraws £20,000 from account 1 to buy a painting.

On the analysis proffered here, B has no claim to the painting, since it is not the traceable proceeds of the trust money, which remains in account 2. The broader point is that following *Foskett*, tracing is *transactional not causal*. The fact that the trust money's deposit into account 2 led to, or caused, the augmented overdraft facility of account 1 is irrelevant to the tracing exercise.

It is beyond the scope of this chapter to consider the pros and cons of allowing B, where circumstances permit, to claim an asset identified via backwards tracing.[72] One may take different views of this. For example, in the cases of what I have called forwards tracing in Examples 5–8, this analysis is, I would argue, the logical application of the tracing principles we have regarding the making of payments. First B traces into T's power to pay, a genuine right T holds, and then into the traceable proceeds that arise upon the exercise of that power. In these cases, then, one might argue that there is no justified place for backwards tracing.

But a generous law might, in certain circumstances, give B an election whether to backwards trace. So, for example, in Example 8, the law might give B an election not to trace into T's enhanced power to charge, thus into the piano, but rather to apply a backwards tracing analysis, so that B could claim the antique table and whatever other proceeds T purchased so as to create the balance of £5,000 he had on 1 June. I register no opinion on that point.

But we must also notice that outside of payment systems in which credit is regularly extended, it is unlikely that this forwards tracing will be available to the Bs of this world. So take the standard case of a mortgage. If T uses trust money to discharge his mortgage loan, this will generally not augment, or create for T, any power against the mortgagee to make payments for him. The payment will just discharge T's liability to the mortgagee (or part of it). One might here, sympathizing with B, allow backwards tracing so as to generate an interest in the mortgaged land for B. Again, I register no opinion pro or con.

VI. INFORMAL AND 'ONE-OFF' PAYING AGENTS: *RELFO LTD v VARSANI*[73] AND *REPUBLIC OF BRAZIL v DURANT INTERNATIONAL*[74]

I have mentioned non-bank, non-credit-card issuer paying agents above, pointing out that A may pay TPR on P's behalf whether P has put A in funds prior to making the payment or whether A is utilising his own funds to do so, with a settlement of accounts between them occurring at some later time.[75] With this trite law under our

[72] For a recent helpful overview of the issues, see Hafeez-Baig and English (n 5) paras 7.151–7.178.
[73] *Relfo Ltd v Varsani* [2014] EWCA Civ 360, [2015] 1 BCLC 14.
[74] *Republic of Brazil v Durant International* [2015] UKPC 35, [2016] AC 297.
[75] See text to n 49.

belts, we can see why *Relfo v Varsani* and *Republic of Brazil* are not to be understood as backwards tracing cases at all. They can be resolved by answering the two questions set out above,[76] namely:

1. Who exercised a power to make an effective payment?
2. Who *funded*, or *payed for*, that power to make an effective payment? More specifically, with respect to following and tracing assets, the question is *whether X's power to direct A to pay TPR is one that is encumbered by the beneficial interest of B*.

In the case of an agent's payment, the second question is more clearly framed: whose money was it (beneficially) that was used to fund A's payment *in advance*, or was used to settle accounts between A and P in respect of that payment *afterwards*?

Schematically, both *Relfo* and *Brazil* involved payments with the following structure: A caused B to make a payment to C; A then afterwards paid B, which payment was equivalent to a payment of trust moneys; in both cases, the court held that the claimant could trace the second payment to B into the first, prior payment from B to C, so that C held those funds as a recipient of trust property.

In *Relfo*, a former director, G, fraudulently caused Relfo to transfer about US$900,000 to Mirren Ltd. On the same day a payment in like amount was made from Intertrade Group LLC to the defendant. On the facts it was clear that 'there was no transfer out of Mirren's account in advance of the Intertrade payment which could have funded it'.[77] Arden LJ held that the trial judge was right to infer that money from the Mirren account was subsequently paid over to Intertrade to fund, ex post facto, Intertrade's payment to the defendant.[78] In so holding, Arden J said:

> [62] … On the judge's findings, the Intertrade payment and the other payments made throughout the chain of substitutions was *made on the faith of the arrangement that Mirren would provide reimbursement*. By making that arrangement, Mirren exploited and used the value inherent in Relfo's money that had been paid into Mirren's account.
>
> [63] In my judgment, Mr Shaw is correct in his submission that Agip is authority for the proposition that monies held on trust can be traced into other assets even if those other assets are passed on before the trust monies are paid to the person transferring them, *provided that that person acted on the basis that he would receive reimbursement for the monies he transferred out of the trust funds*.[79]

As I read these passages, Arden LJ requires the claimant to establish two facts: the first is that where Y pays TPR, B will be able to trace if T promised to reimburse Y for the payment. I think that finding this is indeed essential to B's claim, because that arrangement essentially makes Y a paying agent for T. If T funds that payment either in advance of the payment or afterwards with money that is beneficially B's, then TPR's receipt will be burdened by B's beneficial interest. However, the italicised

[76] See paragraph following text to n 66.
[77] *Relfo* (n 73) [14].
[78] ibid [57]–[58].
[79] Emphasis added.

passage in [63] suggests that B will have to establish more: that not only did T intend to reimburse Y for Y's payment to TPR, but that it was part of T and Y's arrangement that T would reimburse Y with money beneficially belonging to B. It is submitted that this second fact need not be established by B for TPR's receipt to be burdened by B's interest.

This requirement seems to violate the general principle of tracing and payment to require that T intends in advance to use the trust property that was in fact misappropriated to pay for the asset to which TPR acquires title. All that is generally required is that he actually acquires the asset with the use of trust funds – his prior intentions are entirely irrelevant.[80] The requirement for proving this further intention of T, much less a requirement that this be a shared intention of T and Y, can be tested by a hypothetical. Assume Relfo's rogue director had merely promised to reimburse Intertrade, but did not disclose the source of the funds, or indeed gave no thought as to where he would source the funds to reimburse Intertrade. If this requirement is sound, then Relfo's claim would have failed, even though funds beneficially Relfo's were actually used to reimburse Intertrade. Or vary the facts again: assume that the director did intend to use Relfo's funds, but when the time came to reimburse Intertrade, he reimbursed Intertrade instead with money from another company, Delfo, of which he was also a director. Why should Delfo not have a claim in these circumstances? The director is still reimbursing his paying agent, A, for making the very payment the director authorised and instructed A to make. Another way of putting the objection to this requirement is that tracing and payment is normally regarded as *transactional*, not causal. As Lord Millett put it in *Foskett* in criticising the judgment in the Court of Appeal in that case:

> [That] argument is based on causation and as I have explained is a category mistake derived from the law of unjust enrichment. It is an example of the same fallacy that gives rise to the idea that the proceeds of an ordinary life policy belong to the party who paid the last premium without which the policy would have lapsed. But the question is one of attribution not causation.[81]

With respect, then, it is submitted that the first requirement of B's claim is sound, as that establishes that the payor of the fund to TPR is T's paying agent. But the second is not. Any B whose money was used to fund A's payment on T's behalf should have a claim against TPR.

Turning to *Brazil*, which explicitly adopted the terminology of backwards tracing, it is submitted that Arden LJ's reasoning is superior, for her first requirement does real work in establishing that Y was T's paying agent, whereas the Board's decision in *Brazil* is much more diffuse, and seems to identify no factors which would clearly bring the agency analysis into play. To summarise the gist of Lord Toulson's judgment,[82] the application of backwards tracing should be restricted to cases where the payor's debt and the payment with which it is discharged are in substance part of

[80] See L Smith, 'Tracing, "Swollen Assets" and the Lowest Intermediate Balance: *Bishopsgate Investment Management Ltd v Homan*' (1994) 8 *Trusts Law International* 102, 104.

[81] *Foskett* (n 2) 137G.

[82] Set out at *Brazil* (n 74) [38]–[40].

the same overall transaction, such that there is some sort of coordination between the depletion of the trust fund and the acquisition of the asset. But this requirement of coordination is very unspecified. In particular, it does not specifically identify either of the requirements set out by Arden LJ.

So, to summarise, my claim is that in cases of this kind, the first question is whether Y makes the payment to TPR on her own account, or on behalf of X that is, whether Y is acting as X's paying agent. The clearest indication that Y is X's paying agent is that Y makes the payment on the basis that X will fund that payment in advance or reimburse her later. The second question concerns the identity of the money that was *actually* used to fund that payment before or after the making of that payment. It should not matter whether X intended at the outset to use any particular fund, or any fund at all, to do so. What matters is what funds X actually used. If X exercised a power to pay Y and that power was one X held for the benefit of B, then TPR's receipt of the payment from Y is burdened by B's beneficial interest. In determining these questions, all reasonable inferences should be drawn from the proven facts.[83]

One final point on payments made by paying agents. There may be tricky issues of fact akin to the problems of tracing through mixtures, depending upon how the principal, P, and the agent, A, settle their accounts. To give just one hypothetical example, let us assume A is a paying agent for P, and the terms of their agency are that A will pay from her own funds on P's instructions, with A and P to settle up later. P instructs A to make three payments in June, £10,000 to Q, £20,000 to S, and £30,000 to R, all of whom are TPRs who are not bona fide purchasers of what they receive. P then settles with A by paying A £20,000 from B1's trust account, and £40,000 from B2's trust account. In determining the rights of B1 and B2, we shall have to deploy the rules on tracing through mixtures, and though this would appear to be an easy case since B1 and B2 are both innocent – it would seem right to attribute the payments to Q, S and R equally in the shares one-third in favour of B1, two-thirds in favour of B2 – the picture will obviously become more complicated if T, as a wrongdoer, settles with A using some money of his own as well as trust money, or if A's payments and B's settlements occur over time, so that the lowest intermediate balance principle[84] must be applied.

It is no necessary part of T's authorising A to make a payment on T's behalf in advance of T's settling accounts with A that A be informed what the source of funds for T's later settlement will be. Nor would T's later settlement using funds other than those he told A he would be sourcing normally make T's use of those funds to settle with A problematic, except in very exceptional circumstances. Normally the As of this world are interested only in reimbursement, not the source of T's funding in effecting that reimbursement. We should therefore leave those exceptional circumstances aside.

[83] See eg *El Ajou v Dollar Land Holdings* [1993] 3 All ER 717 (Ch) 734–36 (Millett J); *Relfo Ltd v Varsani* [2012] EWHC 2168 [77] (Sales J); *Relfo* (n 73) [58]–[62] (Arden LJ); *Brazil* (n 74) [40] (Lord Toulson). See also Hafeez-Baig and English (n 5) paras 1.52–1.54.

[84] Penner (n 13) para 12.16.

VII. CONCLUSION

In light of the preceding analysis, we see that tracing through payment systems is not some sort of fiction prompted by the law's aim to adhere to 'economic reality'. Rather, it is the legal reality of payment to which the law of tracing must, and does, necessarily defer in its protection of a beneficiary's interest in the trust assets.

12

Ownership, Personalty and Security Transactions

MICHAEL BRIDGE*

I. INTRODUCTION

THE ENGLISH LAW of security sharply divides security properly so called and devices (quasi-security) based upon the transfer or retention of ownership that serve the same economic purpose as security. That shared purpose is to support a right to repayment arising out of the grant of 'financial accommodation', an elastic, useful expression coined by the Consumer Credit Act 1974.[1]

Ownership is an elusive concept, waxing and waning according to context. It plays a fundamental role when, allied with the law's commitment to freedom of contract, it preserves the distinction between security and quasi-security. This distinction shields quasi-security from public scrutiny by exempting it from the requirement of registration demanded for security and allowing it to take place off a company's balance sheet. A further advantage is that it may avoid breaching a negative pledge clause in a previous security transaction.

Connected to the freedom given to individuals and contracting parties to find their own way through the law to best advantage is the resistance of English law to functional legislation such as Article 9 of the US Uniform Commercial Code (UCC). Article 9 defines security and security interests, not in accordance with the location of ownership and the direction in which proprietary rights are granted, but rather according to whether in economic terms a transaction dealing with 'collateral' does so in a way that adds proprietary support to a borrower's personal undertaking to repay a loan. Apart from the freedom given to pursue self-interest, the rejection of Article 9 in England may have something to do with an innate resistance to American cultural penetration and to the perceived need to be seen to be competing with New York law in the global battle for legal supremacy in international financial affairs.

* I have shared with Sarah Worthington a long-standing interest in personal property and security.

[1] Consumer Credit Act 1974, s1.

Ownership also enters the law of security and quasi-security to the extent that a debtor must have ownership rights in assets that are the subject of a mortgage or charge or other security interest to grant an effective security. This issue, which has a particular prominence in functional security systems, is also present in English law in attempts to carve security rights out of future and contingent property interests.

II. OWNERSHIP

The meaning of ownership must be determined before we can explore further English law's commitment to it. In particular, does ownership have a totemic quality transcending its practical importance so that the resistance of English law to a wholly functional definition of security is further explicable? This involves an excursion into the law of sale and personal property before the main subject of secured transactions is broached.

This question is particularly pertinent to property taking the form of tangible and intangible personalty.[2] A striking feature of the common law of property is the quite sharp division between real and personal property. The former consists of a sophisticated structure of interests defined over time in accordance with the doctrine of estates, and the latter an untidy domain, inhabited by both the archaic and the innovative, as it seeks to adapt itself to the proliferation of wealth outside landed interests in the modern world. Many issues are common to both sides of the real and personal property divide, but critical differences do exist. My claim of the elusive character of ownership is addressed particularly to personal property law.[3]

By ownership, I mean what is commonly referred to in US cases and literature as title. In proprietary transfers from seller to buyer in English sales law, ownership is expressed in somewhat oblique terms as the general property in goods,[4] which can be a mere residual husk after a lengthy possessory interest (or special property) has been carved out of it.[5] The word 'title' is sometimes loosely used in English law to signify ownership,[6] but its most common and orthodox use is to adjudicate between rival ownership claims.

Ownership in the world of personal property law has an almost impromptu and transient quality not associated with land. Whereas land is enduring, personal property, especially goods, is usually not. The ownership of land is recorded on a public register;[7] except for ships, aircraft and certain intellectual property rights, this is not

[2] The terminology of private international law is used to avoid some of the issues presented by terminology in domestic law – for example, whether intangible property is a class distinct from things (choses) in action.

[3] The importance of addressing differences between real and personal property is overlooked in J Gordley and U Mattei, 'Protecting Possession' (1996) 44 *American Journal of Comparative Law* 293.

[4] The Consumer Rights Act 2015, s 4, responding to the need for a lay understanding of legislation, explains general property as ownership.

[5] As in the case of a finance lease embracing the commercial life of equipment.

[6] One of the many examples is *Borealis AB v Stargas Ltd (The Berge Sisar)* [2001] UKHL 17, [2002] 2 AC 205 [7].

[7] The old process of establishing ownership by showing deeds of grant establishing a root of title going back so many decades is gradually being superseded by a registration system on a case-by-case basis as and when a particular parcel of land is conveyed.

so for personal property. Transfers of land are frequently complex, especially where the land is or is thought to be burdened by third-party encumbrances. Encumbrances, such as rights of way and use and restrictive covenants, do not burden and accompany personal property as it is transferred[8] and dealings are commonly of very short duration, even instantaneous. It is often far from easy to establish a clear root of title in the case of goods.[9]

Consequently, in the case of goods, ownership is not an absolute matter and is mediated through the concept of possession and comparative entitlement to possession, which 'largely usurp[s] not only the substance but the name of Property'.[10] Although possession overwhelms ownership itself in the means taken to protect ownership, the expression 'true owner' shows up regularly even in the world of relativity of title,[11] as though manifesting a yearning for an unattainable ideal state. The fragility of ownership is particularly marked in the case of intangible property, where English law sees no role for possession, outside the imported instance of dealings in financial collateral.[12] Unsurprisingly, there are some who would deny that rights to intangibles are property rights at all.[13] In the case of tangible items, a key characteristic of a property right is exigibility, the ability in fact to exercise the right against a thing. It is more than a little difficult to see how this works for intangible things.

In English law, judgments *in rem* concerning personal property will be met only where effect is sought for the enforcement of a foreign judgment *in rem*.[14] In English domestic law, a court invited to determine a case in favour of one litigant or the other merely determines which litigant has the superior right (or title).[15] Modern legislation does curb a little this application of the principle of bilateral, relative entitlement, since it calls for a claimant to identify any other person who to his knowledge has or claims an interest in the goods for joinder of that party in the proceedings.[16]

The importance attached to relative possessory entitlement is reinforced by the use of tort law, not property law, to protect ownership rights. An owner does not as such have standing to sue in the tort of conversion,[17] even though conversion is the primary means of protecting ownership rights. There is no proprietary remedy corresponding to the *vindicatio* of the civil law. If an owner does have standing to sue, it is because either he was in possession or had a right to immediate possession of goods at the

[8] See eg *Port Line Ltd v Ben Line Steamers Ltd* [1958] 2 QB 146 (QB); cf *De Mattos v Gibson* (1859) 4 De G & J 276, 282; 45 ER 108, 110.

[9] The art world is an obvious exception: the process of establishing provenance provides a narrative of the history of a work's ownership.

[10] F Pollock and R Wright, *An Essay on Possession in the Common Law* (Oxford, Clarendon Press, 1888) 5.

[11] See D Fox, 'Relativity of Title' [2006] *CLJ* 330, 340–51.

[12] Financial Collateral Arrangements (No 2) Regulations 2003, SI 2003/3226.

[13] See W Swadling, 'Property: General Principles' in A Burrows (ed), *English Private Law*, 3rd edn (Oxford, Oxford University Press, 2013) para 4.131: '[D]ebts or shares … are not property rights at all'.

[14] See eg *Pattni v Ali* [2006] UKPC 51, [2007] 2 AC 85; *Air Foyle Ltd v Center Capital Ltd* [2002] EWHC 2535 (Comm), [2003] 2 Lloyd's Rep 753.

[15] Strikingly demonstrated by *Costello v Chief Constable of Derbyshire* [2001] EWCA Civ 381, [2001] 1 WLR 1437, where a prior unlawful possessor trumped a later possessor with no continuing lawful right to retain possession.

[16] Torts (Interference with Goods) Act 1977, s 8.

[17] *Gordon v Harper* (1796) 7 TR 9, 101 ER 828; *Lord v Price* (1874) LR 9 Ex 54.

time of the defendant's challenge to his title.[18] This right to immediate possession is a translation of ownership into the language of possession in order to bend the tort to the necessary goal of protecting ownership. Even so, the category of persons with a right to immediate possession includes not just the so-called true owner but also any intermediate person in the holding chain whose possessory rights were interfered with. Consequently, the thief who steals from a thief is liable in conversion to that first thief. Moreover, the first thief can pursue the goods down a holding chain even to a good-faith purchaser, who is in no position to invoke one of the limited exceptions to the rule *nemo dat quod non habet*.[19]

The distorting effect of possession on the protection of ownership is seen in the award of damages. Contrary to normal rules of compensation, these are measured by the value of the goods at the date of the act of conversion and not by the extent or quality of the claimant's proprietary interest in the goods.[20] As between a person in possession and a wrongdoer, there is a 'presumption of law' that the person in possession has the property and is therefore entitled to recover in damages the full value of the thing converted.[21] As a further example of the indirect protection of ownership, however, any surplus in a damages recovery, over and above the interest of the successful claimant, is held on account for a third party with a superior title. The award of damages going beyond the bounds of the compensatory principle has experienced tremors in recent times[22] and there are a few exceptions.[23]

The common law by ramshackle means thus protects ownership whilst clinging on to possession. The statutory attempt to tilt the law towards a more open acceptance of ownership in the protection of property rights, contained in the Torts (Interference with Goods) Act 1977,[24] has not left any mark on the modern law[25] and so has not altered in any appreciable way the balance between possession and ownership.

III. OWNERSHIP AS A FUNDAMENTAL PRINCIPLE

With the location of ownership being identified in terms of relative possessory rights, and yet ownership being protected by tort in a way that denies standing to owners without the requisite possessory right, we come to the treatment of ownership's

[18] *The Winkfield* [1902] P 42 (CA).

[19] For example, the mercantile agency, seller in possession and buyer in possession exceptions to the rule: Factors Act 1889 ss 2, 8–9; Sale of Goods Act 1979 ss 24–25.

[20] *Kuwait Airways Corp v Iraqi Airways Co* [2002] UKHL 19, [2002] 2 AC 883.

[21] *The Winkfield* [1902] P 42, 55 (CA); *Jeffries v Great Western Railway Co* (1856) 5 El & Bl 802, 119 ER 680.

[22] Lord Nicholls asserts that conversion should not be an exception to the compensatory principle in *Kuwait Airways* (n 20) but then supports the award of damages in the usual way.

[23] Notably in hire purchase (*Wickham Holdings Ltd v Brook House Motors Ltd* [1967] 1 WLR 295 (CA)) and, less firmly established, other title-retention cases (*Clough Mill Ltd v Martin* [1985] 1 WLR 111 (CA), 117–18), both amounting to a limited acceptance of functional thinking.

[24] Torts (Interference with Goods) Act 1977, ss 8–9.

[25] In the one reported case where the provisions of the Act might have been applied, the Act received no mention: *O'Sullivan v Williams* [1992] 3 All ER 385 (CA).

fundamental importance in certain areas of the law, including security. I shall start with sale as an example before turning to security.

In assessing the role of ownership in sale contracts, a distinction has to be drawn between the quality of the title that a seller must invest in the buyer and the transfer to the buyer of the totality of the seller's property rights, however strong the title thus acquired by the buyer against third parties. This quality of title that the buyer is entitled to have is a vital element in the law of sale. It is distinct from the seller's transfer of the general property, which gives insolvency protection to the buyer and largely determines the seller's eligibility to sue for the price in the form of a debt action.[26] So fundamental is the quality of the seller's title[27] that a seller may not exclude its liability for a failure to pass a title good against the world to any buyer, commercial or consumer.[28] This gives rise to a tortured distinction between excluding liability and selling goods on a limited title basis.[29] Moreover, despite any factual benefit derived from goods by the buyer, the seller's failure to pass such a title is treated as a total failure of consideration. Consequently, the buyer may rescind the contract and recover the price in full even after prolonged use and enjoyment of the goods.[30] This right runs in parallel with, but independently of, the right to sue for breach of the statutory condition that the seller has the right to sell the goods. The two are often confounded, as appears strikingly in the leading case itself.[31]

Although not a case that turns on the quality of a supplier's[32] title, a decision of the UK Supreme Court has laid firm emphasis on the necessity for the supplier to pass the property in goods if the contract in question is to fall within the Sale of Goods Act.[33] The case concerned the supply of bunker fuel on credit terms with a so-called retention of title clause. The contract permitted the recipient to consume the fuel before payment and therefore before the property in the bunker fuel would pass. The mere contemplation of the parties that the goods might be consumed before the property could pass meant that the contract lacked a central feature of a sale of goods contract, namely, that the property should in all cases pass to a buyer. The court rejected the argument that the contract was conditionally one of sale and thus a contract of sale even if the condition never came to pass.[34] At first instance, the court refused the supplier leave to appeal from the ruling that the retention of title clause was extinguished at the time when the goods were consumed so as to permit the award of the price.[35]

[26] Sale of Goods Act 1979, ss 49, 51.

[27] As seen in *Rowland v Divall* [1923] 2 KB 500 (CA) and related cases.

[28] Unfair Contract Terms Act 1977, s 6(1).

[29] The latter being necessary to permit court enforcement officers and insolvency officers to carry out their statutory duties.

[30] *Butterworth v Kingsway Motors Ltd* [1954] 1 WLR 1286 (Assizes).

[31] *Rowland v Divall* (n 27).

[32] Supplier rather than seller, for reasons that will appear.

[33] *PST Energy 7 Shipping LLC v OW Bunker Malta Ltd (The Res Cogitans)* [2016] UKSC 23, [2016] AC 1034. For criticism of the case and the upheaval it brought about in sales law, see MG Bridge, 'The UK Supreme Court Decision in *The Res Cogitans* and the Cardinal Role of Property in Sales Law' [2017] *Singapore Journal of Legal Studies* 345.

[34] See A Tettenborn, 'Of Bunkers and Retention of Title' [2016] *LMCLQ* 24.

[35] *PST Energy 7 Shipping LLC v OW Bunker Malta Ltd (The Res Cogitans)* [2016] UKSC 23, [2016] AC 1034 [14].

IV. SECURITY

Of the various devices that amount to security (liens, pledges, charges and mortgages), by some distance the most significant in practice is the charge, a creature of equity, which may be fixed or floating. In either of these two forms, the charge has shown an admirable capacity for reaching into the future and capturing new assets as they come into existence, with an absence of fuss or additional forms.[36] The common law lacks this flexibility[37] as well as equity's ability to capture an entity pro rata, to the extent of any indebtedness incurred. The breadth and appetite of the charge is sufficient to rebut any accusation that English law is overly restrictive in recognising only a *numerus clausus* of security interests properly so called.

In tracking the characterisation of security and quasi-security in modern times, English courts have committed themselves to a search for the so-called substance of the agreement, an approach far removed from the way that equity intervened in its treatment of mortgages by subtracting an equity of redemption from the mortgagee's ownership. As thus labelled, this approach might tempt the reader to think that the English courts are governed by the same considerations that arise in the case of functionally driven legislation such as Article 9 UCC and its congeners. This, however, is far from being the case. When a financing agreement is construed by the English courts according to its substance, all that means is that the parties' characterisation of their agreement will be accepted as long as their actions under the agreement are consistent with this characterisation. They are free to determine the incidents of their agreement but are subject to whatever label the courts place upon their agreement.[38] Hence, artificial transactions are recognised for what they purport to be, but so-called shams, where the agreement is deceptively dressed up so as to be inconsistent with what the parties are in fact doing, are not.[39]

If, however, the English courts were to take a functional view of the boundaries of security, they would include within those boundaries the various ways in which ownership can be deployed in return for what the Consumer Credit Act calls financial accommodation. Ownership is exploited so as to produce the equivalent of, or even something superior to, a true security. In applying the substance-based approach and resisting the call of functionalism, English courts have sanctioned avoidance of the controls and limits imposed by the law governing security properly so called. Avoidance of this body of law can be accomplished in various ways. Taking first retention of title, a seller giving time to a buyer to pay for goods delivered may reserve the property in the goods until the price is paid. This can arise in a lump-sum transaction, where credit of 30–60 days is commonly granted, or it may occur under an instalment plan. An alternative to this type of transaction on conditional sale terms is the contract of hire purchase, whereby goods are delivered under the terms of an instalment payment plan, with the hirer exercising an option to purchase the goods once all the hire instalments have been paid.[40] Going beyond the conditional sale and

[36] See eg *Tailby v Official Receiver* (1888) 13 App Cas 523 (HL).
[37] *Lunn v Thornton* (1845) 1 CB 379, 135 ER 587.
[38] *Agnew v Commissioner of Inland Revenue* [2001] UKPC 28, [2001] AC 710.
[39] For example, *Snook v London and West Riding Investments Ltd* [1967] 2 QB 786 (CA).
[40] *Helby v Matthews* [1895] AC 471 (HL).

hire purchase is the finance lease,[41] akin to a hire purchase contract but lacking the option to purchase.

Ownership can also be manipulated by way of grant from the party seeking financial accommodation, thereby belying the appearance of a loan, which would be fatal to the aims of the contracting parties. There exist schemes for financing stock in trade involving sale and resale and agency, where any role for public policy or requirement that the interests of third parties be taken into account is firmly rejected.[42] Under block discounting schemes, the personal and proprietary rights of the supplier under instalment contracts of hire purchase and conditional sale can be assigned outright to a third-party financier. The supplier's future instalment rights are not charged; instead, they are discounted to present value, with other deductions also being made from the sum of future instalments to cover administration and the credit risk posed by the supplier's customers.[43]

Other ownership schemes also exist.[44] Goods may be sold to a financier and leased back or else repurchased. This type of arrangement is common in the case of land but such arrangements call for careful drafting. A sale and repurchase is particularly vulnerable to a recharacterisation risk, with the agreement being construed as giving rise to a charge with the consequences that follow from the failure to register it as such.[45] If the agreement is expressed in the language of credit and lending, it is likely to be recharacterised as a charge.[46] Even if such inappropriate language is excluded from the double-sale agreement, a court is likely to come to the conclusion that the transaction amounts to a charge. This is because the seller in the first leg, having both the right and the duty to recover the goods in the second leg, is seen as having an equity of redemption in the subject matter of the contract. There is a long-established, but perhaps overlooked, parallel for this conclusion of the court. At common law the mortgage consists of sale and resale. The sale leg is conditioned upon defeasance, taking the form of repayment of the advanced sum plus interest, in which event an automatic reconveyance takes effect. It was the intervention of equity with its equity of redemption that fixed the mortgage firmly as a type of security and effaced its double-sale character.

V. OWNERSHIP AND INTANGIBLES

Reference was made above to the contentious view that debts and contract rights are not proprietary at all.[47] It follows from this assertion, if correct, that they are

[41] Not a term of art in English law.

[42] See the ingenious example of *Welsh Development Agency v Export Finance Co Ltd* [1992] BCLC 148 (CA).

[43] See *Re George Inglefield Ltd* [1933] Ch 1 (CA); *Lloyds and Scottish Finance Ltd v Cyril Lord Carpet Sales* [1992] BCLC 609 (HL).

[44] Not discussed here are *Quistclose* trusts and 'repos' (the sale of securities and the repurchase of their fungible equivalents).

[45] An unregistered charge is void as against insolvency office holders and other secured creditors.

[46] See *Re Curtain Dream Ltd* [1990] BCLC 925 (Ch).

[47] Noting the diminishing 'divide' between property and obligation, see S Worthington, 'The Disappearing Divide between Property and Obligation: The Impact of Aligning Legal Analysis and Commercial Expectation' (2007) 42 *Texas International Law Journal* 917.

not susceptible to ownership rights. But debts and contract rights are, within quite relaxed limits, capable of being transferred, and transferability is an important if not indispensable indicator of property rights. The transferability of these rights, by means of assignment, therefore supposes that they are proprietary in character and susceptible to being owned. The abstract character of these intangibles, nevertheless, is bound to impose a strain on the meaning of ownership, if ownership is defined as the greatest possessory right, for the simple reason that these abstract rights cannot be possessed at common law.[48]

Intangibles do present a number of troublesome questions,[49] of which two in particular will be commented on here. The first of these is contractual rights qualified by non-assignment clauses; the second one concerns interests of a qualified nature.

Taking first non-assignment clauses, the effect of such clauses on the purported assignment of contract rights, as well as their effect on trusts of contract rights, has been the cause of much spilled judicial and academic ink. Taking the example of an outright bar on assignment, the supposed distinction between 'what I own' and 'what I am owed'[50] presents itself at this point. In a simple bilateral case of obligor and obligee involving no third parties, it might fairly be said that an *in personam* obligation to render contractual performance does not need to be elevated to a proprietary level. It is only upon the purported transfer of the right that the property feature of the contractual performance comes into play. The question, now, is whether the non-assignment clause sterilises the transfer at source so as to prevent the personal from becoming the proprietary. If this is so, then contractual rights subject to an outright bar on assignment are like other rights that are inherently non-assignable. The question whether contract or property prevails is apparently answered by English law in favour of contract,[51] but with exceptions[52] that expose the awkward location of assignment between the law of contract and the law of property.

A difficult question now concerns the fruits of performance in the hands of the assignor. If these fruits are the subject of a constructive trust in favour of the putative assignee, does this mean that the rights giving rise to them must themselves necessarily be proprietary in nature? An affirmative answer would treat as one both the right and the proceeds, which is a conclusion in effect reached in case law on fixed and floating charges, where the House of Lords[53] and the Privy Council[54] both ruled against an attempt to separate debts and their money proceeds in order that the former might

[48] But see the special statutory purpose served by a fictive notion of possession in the Financial Collateral Arrangements (No 2) Regulation 2003, SI 2003/3226. See also Law Commission, *Electronic Documents and Bill* (Law Com No 405, 2022).

[49] Cryptoassets, with their capability of being owned and transferred and used as security, are not discussed here.

[50] See E McKendrick, *Goode and McKendrick on Commercial Law*, 6th edn (London, LexisNexis, 2020) [2-012], citing in support *Bailey v Angove's Pty Ltd* [2016] UKSC 47, [2016] 1 WLR 1379.

[51] *Linden Gardens Trust Ltd v Lenesta Sludge Disposals Ltd* [1994] 1 AC 85 (HL).

[52] *Barbados Trust Co Ltd v Bank of Zambia* [2007] EWCA Civ 148, [2007] 2 All ER (Comm) 445; Small Business, Enterprise and Employment Act 2015.

[53] *Re Spectrum Plus Ltd* [2005] UKHL 41, [2005] 2 AC 680.

[54] *Agnew v Commissioner for Inland Revenue* (n 38).

be captured by the fixed charge and their proceeds by the residual floating charge.[55] Debts are like annuals, not perennials.

On the assumption that a failed assignment nevertheless gives rise to a constructive trust of the fruits of performance in the hands of the assignor, the distinction that remains is that between the collection process that can be launched unilaterally by an equitable assignee, where necessary joining the assignor in the proceedings, and the procedure by which a trust beneficiary may bring an action against an obligor in the name of a trustee who shrinks from taking this step, the so-called *Vandepitte* procedure.[56] The difference in practice between the two may not be great, especially if the assignor has to be joined as a co-defendant. If this indeed is correct, the so-called trust exception to non-assignment clauses[57] may not trench as much on contractual freedom as might be supposed. That said, the entire construct of assignment presents an irreconcilable clash between contract and property.[58]

The second question that brings into play the nature of ownership over intangibles concerns contingent and future interests and the difference between the two. Contingent and future interests can of course present themselves in connection with tangible personalty, but as a matter of practice they will do so more commonly in the case of intangibles.

Take the example of a charge over present and future book debts. For the purposes of both registration and priority, the charge is effective from the time of its execution for both present and future book debts.[59] Literally, however, book debts not yet in existence and that might never eventuate can hardly be the subject of a present charge. The ownership problem is skirted, not resolved, by the assertion that a charge, unlike a mortgage, does not amount to a proprietary transfer since it becomes complete only when on default it is enforced by the chargee. For charge and mortgage alike, the transaction is treated as giving rise to an enforceable promise to encumber or transfer assets as and when they come into existence.[60]

An arresting feature of the charge's capacity to reach into the future emerges when for the time being it is devoid of assets. On one view, charged assets are contained in an extant fund with shifting contents, the fund itself having a 'notional existence' apart from its contents.[61] This means that the empty fund is a fiction. The River Thames is cited as an example, with its constantly changing waters distinct from the river defined by its banks. If this idea of a fund is applied to intangible assets such as book debts, the banks of this fund being invisible means that in the absence of content we are looking at an invisible box with nothing in it. The connection, or rather the lack of it, thus made between ownership and security is striking.

[55] Successfully accomplished at the time in *Re New Bullas Trading Ltd* [1994] 1 BCLC 485 (CA).

[56] Named after *Vandepitte v Preferred Accident Insurance Corp of New York* [1933] AC 70 (PC).

[57] *Barbados Trust Co Ltd v Bank of Zambia* (n 52).

[58] MG Bridge, 'The Nature of Assignment and Non-assignment Clauses' (2016) 132 *LQR* 47.

[59] See further MG Bridge, 'Certainty, Identification and Intention in Personal Property Law' in J Penner and P Davies, *Equity, Trusts and Commerce* (Oxford, Hart Publishing, 2017) 87, 88–93.

[60] *Tailby v Official Receiver* (n 36).

[61] L Gullifer (ed), *Goode and Gullifer on Legal Problems of Credit and Security*, 6th edn (London, Sweet & Maxwell, 2017) para 4-04.

A vivid example of what might be called the fictitious proprietary effect of a vacant security is afforded by *Re Lind*,[62] where a debtor on two occasions mortgaged his future inheritance from his mother. When he became bankrupt, the mortgagees did not put in a proof. The debtor's mother died after he was discharged from bankruptcy and the mortgagees now claimed his inheritance. The debtor's argument was that the discharge freed him from his mortgage debts but the conclusion of the court was that the mortgages, though devoid of content prior to the death of the debtor's mother, burdened 'something more than a mere right in contract, something in the nature of an estate or interest'.[63] How slippery is the expression 'in the nature of'.

Now, there is something of the inevitable in active traders acquiring future book debts, answering to the universal description customary in such cases, as long as the traders remain in business. Inheritances, however, even in the most harmonious families, quite often fail to materialise. The power of capricious, ageing parents should not be underestimated. Mere expectancies are not recognised as existing things in action,[64] hence the object of a discretionary trust or of a power of appointment has nothing to assign.[65] The distinction between a future property right and a contingent right that might never materialise is therefore a very difficult one to draw.

VI. RETAINING THE DISTINCTION BETWEEN RETENTION OF TITLE AND SECURITY?

As regards the relationship between ownership (in particular, retention of title) and security, a financier's choice of an ownership device over security has significant legal consequences. First of all, the transaction is kept off a public register.[66] Secondly, the ability to repossess goods that are the subject of a title retention transaction creates the possibility of a retained surplus in the hands of the financier. Thirdly, there is the matter of priority as between a title-reserving financier and a financier claiming security rights over assets in the hands of the debtor.

Starting with registration, the resistance of the legal and financial communities to registration has been intense and prolonged. If registration serves a valuable publicity function for charges – which is apparently accepted without serious dissent – then why should this not also be the case for medium- to long-term title-retention transactions? If a charge over equipment has to be registered if it is to be opposable to designated third parties, why should the position not be the same for a finance lease? The City of London Law Society, in recently considering reform of the law of security, maintains its resistance to registration for title-based transactions.[67] This is despite the modest

[62] *Re Lind* [1915] 2 Ch 345 (CA).

[63] ibid 363.

[64] *Norman v Federal Commissioner of Taxation* (1963) 109 CLR 9. See also *Re Brooks' Settlement Trusts* [1939] Ch 993 (Ch); cf *Campbell Connolly & Co Ltd v Noble* [1963] 1 WLR 252 (Ch) 261.

[65] *Schmidt v Rosewood Trustee Co* [2003] UKPC 26, [2003] AC 709 [40]; *Gartside v Inland Revenue Commissioners* [1968] AC 553 (HL) 607.

[66] But exclusion may already have been effected under the widely drawn Financial Collateral Arrangements Regulations (No 2).

[67] Draft Secured Transactions Code (March 2020), ss 1.1 and 27, available at www.citysolicitors.org.uk/clls/committees/financial-law/ (accessed 30 September 2023).

cost of registering a charge.[68] A leading member of the City of London Law Society has defended the exemption from registration of title-based transactions on two principal grounds.[69] The first is that, if registration of title-based schemes were required, where would we draw the line between them and other transactions such as intellectual property licences? One answer is that lines always have to be drawn somewhere; each type of transaction should be considered on its own terms.

The second ground cited for non-registration of title-based schemes is that, in the event of a failure to register, the lessee is given an unencumbered asset and a property right that the parties never intended the lessee to have. The answer to this takes the form of a rebuttal. The lessor retains its ownership rights as against the lessee. It is only as against competing secured creditors and insolvency holders that the lessor is subordinated. The lessee does not acquire a proprietary windfall and the essential nature of the bargain between lessor and lessee remains unchanged. The treatment of a title-based instrument as security in respect of designated third parties does not compel the same approach to be taken between the immediate parties.[70]

When it comes to title-based transactions (eg, a five-year finance lease), any burden imposed by registration would be a minor one. It is hard to resist the conclusion that the resistance to registration in cases of this sort is linked to abhorrence of the expropriatory effect of legislation if registration is not effected. But a mortgagee's proprietary interest is equally confiscated if registration is not effected. Moreover, since the financier acquires the ownership of the equipment from a dealer for the purpose of effecting the lease, and may never have set its corporate eyes on the machinery, what might be called the sentimental sway of ownership is absent. The transaction might therefore be treated for publicity purposes as if the goods had been sold by the dealer to the user of the machinery and then immediately charged by the user in favour of the financier.[71]

The case of recurring small-scale transactions involving sellers on retention of title terms is a different one. A single act of registration for all possible future transactions may not be a practical matter. How large is the current transaction and how likely is it to be repeated in the future? If the economics of the affair justify it, the capacity of registration for accommodating future property and future advances should permit the avoidance of multiple registrations.[72] In effect, the act of registration would thus amount to the registration of a continuing relationship. If the burden of registration on suppliers under small-scale transactions were still thought to be oppressive, a temporary exemption from the registration requirement in the form of a grace period might be allowed to sellers reserving title in a particular transaction.[73] By the time the

[68] The present law allows for the registration of the security agreement itself, hence the costs of preparing documentation should not significantly differ as between, say, a charge over equipment and a finance lease.

[69] See R Calnan, 'What Makes a Good Law of Security' in F Dahan (ed), *Research Handbook on Secured Financing in Commercial Transactions* (Cheltenham, Edward Elgar, 2015) ch 17.

[70] Admittedly, UCC, Art 9 Part 6 (remedies) adopts a unitary approach to security of all kinds, with certain exceptions (notably consignment transactions), but there is no compelling reason for this to be the case.

[71] cf the priority case of *Re Connolly Bros Ltd (No 2)* [1912] 2 Ch 25 (CA).

[72] But there are priority issues presented by future advances.

[73] See the Art 9 discussion in section IX below.

period will have expired, it is highly likely that the goods will have lost their identity and the clause its utility.[74] Legislation distinguishing the two types of title retention, the ephemeral and the medium- to long-term, is thus feasible.

Unlike the position in Article 9 systems, registration in England does not create a priority position. Instead, it protects the priority position of a chargee that dates from the creation of the charge, provided that registration is effected within 21 days of the creation of the charge.[75] Since the chargor's future assets need be described for registration purposes only in general, albeit accurately descriptive, terms, a supplier of goods on retention of title terms could, if the incentive to do so were strong enough, register on a single occasion. Is there in such a case a risk of subordination to earlier charges also capturing future assets? An earlier chargee providing medium- or long-term finance can capture future assets in a single charge instrument and act of registration,[76] but not all is plain sailing. The security of that earlier chargee will amount to a floating charge, subject in priority terms to a later fixed charge and increasingly downgraded by subordination to the expenses of the insolvency process, preference creditors and unsecured creditors.[77] The problem for the small-scale supplier is that, if its reserved title were recharacterised as a charge, the necessary freedom given to the buyer to dispose of the goods supplied in the ordinary course of business would require the charge to be classed as a floating charge too.[78] This should not be so for equipment that is the subject of finance leases or similar title-based devices, given that a charge over them would be fixed in character. Consequently, any legislation requiring the registration of retention of title clauses should either continue recognising them as retention of title clauses, so that the supplier's legal interest in goods delivered from time to time would prevail over prior equitable charges, or, if treating the supplier's interest as amounting to a charge, treat it as having the special status of a purchase money security interest prevailing over earlier charges. The former approach recognises the continuing press of ownership. The latter is the approach of Article 9 systems. Having created the problem by assimilating charges and title-based devices under the neologist banner of security interests, Article 9 legislation is compelled by these means to recognise below the surface the immanent survival of ownership.[79]

VII. REMEDIES

The persistent character of ownership in the provision of financial accommodation is visible when it comes to remedies in the event of default. Starting with the remedies of

[74] English law is less accommodating than, say, German law when it comes to retention of title rights because attempts to extend the right to accounts receivable or new goods generated by the goods supplied will be re-characterised as charges.

[75] Companies Act 2006, ss 859A et seq.

[76] For future advances, English law is less accommodating to the financier than Art 9 systems in that, subject to limited exceptions, priority for the future advance ranks behind another creditor's intervening charge.

[77] See principally Insolvency Act 1986, ss 40, 175, 176A, 386 and Sched B1 para 65(2).

[78] *Agnew v Commissioner for Inland Revenue* (n 38); *Re Spectrum Plus Ltd* (n 53).

[79] Discussed in text to n 105 below.

a mortgagee, there is first of all the very rare remedy of foreclosure, which eradicates the mortgagor's equity of redemption and renders the initial transfer of ownership to the mortgagee unqualified. The very rarity of foreclosure bears witness to the long history of undermining the identity of mortgages as sale and resale. Another of the mortgagee's remedies is resale, with the mortgagee having to account to the mortgagor for any surplus arrived at, over and above the amount owed (a rare case). The same goes for chargees (except that foreclosure does not arise at all given that charges do not as such involve the *transfer* of a proprietary interest).[80] The freedom given by the law of security to expand remedies by contract in practice, as stated above, largely eradicates the distinction between mortgages and charges. In principle, a conditional seller or any other financier on title-retention terms should have no duty to account for any surplus if repossessing and retaining or disposing of goods. This is because the goods are the creditor's unencumbered property. Nevertheless, as stated above, a seller of goods on retention of title terms has been said unpersuasively to be under a duty to remit any surplus to the buyer upon repossession of the goods, either as a matter of restitution to avoid unjust enrichment or as a matter of implied contract.[81] It is easy enough to say that handing over a surplus is likely to be a rare event, apart from instances where a substantial part-payment has been made. The significant point is the inroad this move makes into the sanctity of ownership by its deviation from orthodoxy.

VIII. PRIORITY

The expression 'purchase money security interest', mentioned above, has no particular meaning in English law. There are isolated cases where a notion of this sort has been recognised so as to upset the normal first-in-time priority rule.[82] This has been done by consolidating two transactions as though they were one: first, the acquisition of assets by a debtor from a third-party supplier, and secondly, the charging or mortgaging of that asset in favour of the financier supplying the funds for the purchase. In this way, the rights of a prior financier with a charge over the debtor's future assets are overreached, even when the second financier has notice of the earlier security, since that prior chargee takes the future asset in question in its already charged state.

In an unstated way, title-based financing transactions, defeating as they do prior charges over a debtor's future assets, vindicate the purchase money interest of the later financier. This is because the prior charge attaches only to the debtor's own assets and does not capture assets owned by a third party. So, under the current law, besides being free from registration, the title-based financier takes priority over the earlier charge. Since the outcome of the priority contest is axiomatic – the debtor cannot charge an asset that it does not own – there is no need to justify the reversal

[80] *National Provincial and Union Bank of England v Charnley* [1924] 1 KB 431 (CA) 449–50.

[81] *Clough Mill Ltd v Martin* [1985] 1 WLR 111 (CA) 117–18.

[82] *Re Connolly Bros Ltd (No 2)* [1912] 2 Ch 25 (CA); *Abbey National Building Society v Cann* [1991] AC 56 (HL).

of the normal timeline in priority matters in the way that is done for purchase money interests in Article 9 systems.[83]

IX. ARTICLE 9 AND ITS CONGENERS

A. Functionalism and Ownership

That monumental display of the legislative achievements of US legal realism, Article 9 UCC, is a formidable challenge to anyone who is insistent on maintaining the division between title-based schemes and security properly so called. It has other defining features too, not least the suppression of any distinction between law and equity.[84] Another feature, less noticeable at first glance, is the way it builds upon existing US law on the protection of property interests and the scope of negotiability in the case of commercial documents.[85] When the Law Commission completed its work on company charges,[86] it had started with an ample commitment to functionalism, which had then over the course of two consultative documents and a report been substantially watered down. A point that was not reached in the process was the extent to which the English law of personal property would need to be modified if new functionalist legislation were to track the text of Article 9 without distorting the underlying legal base. For example, the bona fide purchaser of personalty dealing with a seller whose title is defective is more generously treated in the United States,[87] which treatment underlies a part of Article 9. Another way of putting this is to say that selective transplantation is dangerous if the instrument being transplanted is intimately linked to something that is not accompanying it in the transplantation journey.

In the world of security, Article 9 UCC and systems based upon it, inspired by functionalist thinking, represent the most extensive inroad into the principle that parties are free to structure their transactions in the way that best suits them. Consequently, a significant number of formerly title-based transactions are clustered together, alongside previously recognised security interests such as mortgages and charges, under a single statutory roof. The functionalist identity of these various transactions runs from the creation of the interest in question right through to the enforcement of the creditor's rights on default by the debtor. Yet, even functionalism has its limits. A sale of accounts receivable (book debts) and the consignment of goods on a prospective sale basis are not treated as security when it comes to the scheme of remedies upon the debtor's default.[88] Thus the legislation impliedly accepts that the purchaser of accounts receivable becomes their owner and that the supplier of inventory (stock in trade) on consignment terms remains the owner notwithstanding delivery until an on-sale by the debtor occurs.[89] It is as though these transactions were incorporated in

[83] See section IX below.

[84] See G Gilmore, *Security Interests in Personal Property* (Boston, MA, Little Brown, 1965) vol 1, [7.2].

[85] See Uniform Commercial Code Arts 1-201(16) and 2-503(4)(a).

[86] See Law Commission, *Company Security Interests* (Law Com No 296, 2005).

[87] Art 2-403 UCC. cf *Jerome v Bentley & Co* [1952] 2 All ER 114 (QB).

[88] Art 9-601(g) UCC.

[89] See M Bridge, R Macdonald, R Simmonds and C Walsh, 'Formalism, Functionalism and Understanding the Law of Secured Transaction' (1999) 44 *McGill Law Journal* 567, 581.

Article 9 for the sake of convenience, to bind them to a system of public notice and priority, without recognising them as security even in the functionalist sense. Default by the party receiving finance does not as such arise in these transactions since, in the case of consignments, the prospective buyer has only an option to purchase, and in the case of a sale of accounts, the seller performs as and when the accounts come into existence and are thus automatically acquired by the financier. The common inclusion of a recourse provision against the seller of accounts, in the event of a shortfall in receipts from account debtors, is not inconsistent with this assessment of the position for accounts receivable. Persisting with the sale characterisation for accounts receivable, the recourse provision may be seen as the equivalent of statutory warranties concerning the quality and fitness of goods sold.[90]

In pursuing its functional agenda, Article 9 and its progeny have to navigate between the two aspects of ownership mentioned in the introduction to this chapter. The first is the by now familiar matter of assimilating title-based transactions to security properly so called. The second concerns the question, discussed when considering future assets, whether the debtor has proprietary rights ('rights in the collateral') that may be encumbered in support of a payment obligation. How the existence of such rights and the demands of functionalism are to be reconciled now fall for consideration.

In the implementation of its functionalist agenda, Article 9 poses the following two questions. First, how does it override any intention of parties to create a genuine conditional sale agreement? The existence of any such intention is more conjectural than practical. From its inception, Article 9 never prevented parties from using old terminology, like conditional sale; instead, it subjected all transactions in a stated cluster to the same uniform legal treatment so that parties to security abandoned the old terminology, adopting instead the bland neologisms unburdened by legal cultural history, of security, security interest and so on. Secondly, how far did Article 9 go in expunging title (ownership) from the statutory scheme? It will be demonstrated that title lurks below the surface, rising from the depths when ordering priority with the aid of a super-priority rule in favour of the holder of a purchase money security interest.

Returning to the first question, a functional definition of security overriding the difference between title-based transactions and true security cuts across common law notions of property.[91] Grant Gilmore, the leading architect of Article 9, comparing conditional sales and chattel mortgages under the old law, observed:

> [T]he unpaid seller's rights against the goods … was not even remotely analogous to the right of a lender of money against his security; conditional sale and chattel mortgage were members of quite different families.[92]

Article 9, in dispensing with this sharp contrast, was integrated into a statutory scheme – the UCC – in a way that was designed to smooth the interface between it and the ancillary common law. It is probably true to say that this may have been

[90] Art 2-314, 2-315 UCC.

[91] See R Cuming, 'Internalizing Secured Financing Law' in R Cranston, *Making Commercial Law* (Clarendon Press, Oxford, 1997) 523.

[92] Gilmore (n 84) vol 1 para 3.2.

easier in the United States than it would have been in other common law jurisdictions. As stated above, Article 9 dispenses with the distinction between common law and equity, a distinction that for long has been significantly less pronounced in the United States than in other common law jurisdictions.

B. Article 9 and Conditional Sales

The treatment of conditional sales in Article 9 displays the same concerns about anchoring the new scheme of security interests in the underlying law of personal property. Article 9 applies, with stated exceptions, in the following terms: '[T]his Article applies to … a transaction, regardless of its form, that creates a security interest in personal property or fixtures by contract.'[93] Now, this provision should be read alongside Article 2-401(1) UCC: 'Any retention or reservation by the seller of the title (property) in goods shipped or delivered to the buyer is limited in effect to a reservation of a security interest.'[94] Article 2-401(1) therefore ensures that the debtor has rights in the collateral to which a security interest can be attached,[95] whether given in favour of the unpaid seller or a third-party secured creditor, which is a prerequisite of an effective security interest.[96] Saskatchewan legislation, for example, has no provision corresponding to Article 2-401(1). The Personal Property Security Act of Saskatchewan[97] applies to conditional sales because a conditional buyer has the relevant rights or power as a result of the Act applying to conditional sales; and conditional sales are governed by the Act because the Act applies to them. The debtor must be deemed to be the owner, regardless of what the contract of sale might say, in order for the goods supplied to be burdened with a security interest, whether in favour of the seller or of another creditor. The debtor has rights in the collateral because the legislation silently and fictitiously deems it to be so.

Article 2, in aid of promoting the workability of Article 9, thus imposes a limit on freedom of contract. The parties will not be able by contract to modify the application of Article 2-401 to remove the transaction from the reach of Article 9. In contrast with Articles 2 and 9, the English law of security is an emanation of the law of contract and attracts the same commitment to freedom of contract that exists outside the world of secured transactions. This is due at least in part to the intervention of equity and its insistence that a contract to give security is as good as security.[98]

[93] Art 9-109(a)(1) UCC.

[94] See also Art 1-201(35) UCC (definition of 'security interest').

[95] Hence, this is consistent with the Official Comment to Art 9-203: 'A debtor's limited rights in collateral, short of full ownership, are sufficient for a security interest to attach. However, in accordance with basic personal property conveyancing principles, the baseline rule is that a security interest attaches only to whatever rights a debtor may have, broad or limited as those rights may be.' Note that this reasoning does not apply to finance leases: there is no provision prohibiting a purported retention of ownership (see Art 1-203 UCC (lease distinguished from security interest)).

[96] Art 9-203(b)(2) UCC (or the power to transfer rights as an agent might have).

[97] Personal Property Security Act of Saskatchewan 1993, ch P-6.2.

[98] See eg *Tailby v Official Receiver* (n 36).

C. Remedies

A further point concerning Article 9 and its congeners is why true security and quasi-security needed to be assimilated for the purpose of remedies when and to the extent that there is no competing third-party involvement. It should have been sufficient to apply notice and priority rules to security and quasi-security alike.[99] The question of remedies between creditor and debtor is a bilateral matter that can be settled as a matter of contract between the two of them.[100] The imposition of a uniform scheme of remedies amounts to 'a profound interference with the contractual bargain between the parties'.[101]

D. The Purchase Money Security Interest

Article 9 and its congeners accord a super-priority to so-called purchase-money security interests, which are interests that secure a purchase-money obligation. Taking the Saskatchewan Act as an example, which is rather clearer than its Article 9 counterpart,[102] this interest arises in two cases: first, 'to the extent that [the security interest in collateral] secures all or part of its purchase price';[103] and secondly, where 'a person … gives value for the purpose of enabling the debtor to acquire rights in the collateral, to the extent that the value is applied to acquire those rights'.[104] The difference between the two relates to the directness of the connection between the credit advanced and the goods subsequently acquired. Consequently, using heritage language, a conditional sale and a finance lease would give rise to purchase money security interests of the former type. A bank loan advanced so as to give the debtor the means of acquiring an asset would be an example of the latter type. In granting a super-priority in the former case, outranking an earlier security interest in future assets, the legislation impliedly recognises the sway of ownership, accepting that the distinction between title and security cannot wholly be eliminated in a broad functional scheme of security.[105] This is underlined also by the priority position between the two purchase money security interests stated above: in a conflict, the former interest (accommodating the conditional seller and the finance lessor) prevails. Even in functional legislation, ownership still matters.[106]

[99] The approach of the Cape Town Convention on International Interests in Mobile Equipment (2001) demonstrates that this can perfectly well be done.

[100] Except that a second-ranking creditor might have a claim to the surplus that the conditional seller regards as its own when the goods are repossessed. It is axiomatic, or almost so, that third-party (or distributive) issues do not affect the bargain struck between debtor and creditor.

[101] Bridge et al (n 89) 590.

[102] Art 9-103 UCC.

[103] Saskatchewan Act (n 97), s 2(1)(jj)(i).

[104] ibid s 2(1)(jj)(ii).

[105] See R Macdonald, 'Article 9 Norm Entrepreneurship' (2006) 43 *Canadian Business Law Journal* 240, 283.

[106] Art 9-324(g)(1); Saskatchewan Act (n 97), s 34(5).

An oblique recognition of the special character of the purchase money security interest is also present in the rule that a purchase money security interest in consumer goods is perfected on attachment without any need for filing[107] and, to a lesser extent, in the rule that allows a grace period of up to 20 days for a filing to be made after the debtor receives possession of the goods.[108] The latter provision accommodates suppliers of goods with a short shelf-life. Apart from the totemic sway of ownership, another reason for recognising the primacy of the purchase money creditor is that the creditor adds value to the debtor's estate and is not detracting from the value of an earlier creditor's security. The advance made to the debtor is matched by the additional asset brought into the debtor's estate; the debtor is not using 'the new loan to roll over old debt'.[109] Recognising the superiority of the purchase money interest also avoids a debtor's subjection to a single creditor enjoying a situational monopoly[110] and avoids the transaction costs that would be incurred if two secured parties sat down together to enter into a priority agreement.

English law, while not yielding to the attractions of Article 2, recognises the purchase money security interest in a different way. First, a reserved title creditor will always prevail over a prior chargee since that prior charge is capable of attaching only to the property rights of the conditional buyer which do not arise until the purchase price of the goods has been paid in full. Again, English law goes further than Article 9 in exempting the conditional seller from having to fulfil a registration (or filing) requirement. Unlike US states and Canadian provinces, English law has never required conditional sales (or hire purchase contracts) to be registered.

X. OWNERSHIP AS A TOTEMIC SYMBOL?

We now return to the question that lies at the heart of this chapter. Are quasi-security and true security so different in kind as to justify the way they are treated so divergently in English law? Exceptional cases apart, goods are wasting things. They do not last forever and, like their owners, at some point return to the common soil. Their value declines over time and, as the doctrine of specific performance amply recognises, their character is not sufficiently distinctive to treat them in most instances as anything more than the monetary value ascribed to them. The law of sale and of personal property has displayed an uneven commitment to the importance of ownership. Exceptions exist. The ownership of a rare classic car is not to be equated to the ownership of a piece of construction equipment acquired unseen by a finance lessor from a dealer and then leased for a period approximating to its commercial lifespan. As for intangible property, it would be hard to find a common lawyer willing and able to see anything special about a debt that has been discounted in favour of a factor even if we accept the extensive conception of property by the common law

[107] Art 9-301(1) UCC.

[108] Art 9-324(a) UCC.

[109] D Baird and T Jackson, *Security Interests in Personal Property: Cases, Problems and Materials*, 2nd edn (St Paul, Minnesota, West Academic, 1987) 401.

[110] T Jackson and A Kronman, 'Secured Financing and Priorities Among Creditors' (1979) 88 *Yale Law Journal* 1141, 1171–78.

in a way that accommodates items such as debts and contract rights. In the case of mundane things, there is no sufficient difference between ownership and beneficial use of personalty as to justify the current state of the law concerning true security and quasi-security.

It is particularly in the case of registration of proprietary interests, whether of a non-possessory charge or of the ownership of a financier out of possession, that the case for assimilation is most vividly presented. To a lesser extent, a well worked out scheme of priority as between security and quasi-security based on ownership would benefit from seeing their conflict from an assimilationist point of view. This would, however, require some readjustment of the rule of *nemo dat quod non habet* and its various exceptions, an incoherent topic[111] that had better wait for another day. If registration, for example, serves a useful purpose, then it has to be wondered why the courts (and inactive legislators) are so tolerant of devices that are designed as measures of legal avoidance, frustrating what were considered to be desirable legislative goals. A substantial effort and considerable expense go into the legislative process, so why is it so easy to frustrate the legislative purpose with the aid of a quasi-security transaction such as a finance lease or a sale of accounts receivable (book debts)?[112] The parallels to be drawn in the matter of avoidance between the law of security and quasi-security and revenue law are striking. In the case of tax avoidance, too, we see ingenious schemes following offbeat paths to arrive at a goal beneficial for the tax avoider.[113]

Even those pursuing an assimilationist agenda, however, might have to give pause when dealing with one further aspect of the law. Assimilation is to be justified in a world of three parties and more. As between the provider and acquirer of financial accommodation, there is no good reason in a world of arm's length dealing to deny the basic bargain struck between the two parties. Freedom of contract makes a powerful case, subject to any controls imposed by the law relating to penalties and forfeiture, for respecting a bargain that allows an unpaid seller on title-retention terms, or a finance lessor, to recover the goods in the event of default without having to account for any surplus. If that is what the parties agreed, then so be it, even if it means that competing creditors obtain less. A party granted security, for instance, is not bound to consider the interests of the debtor's unsecured creditors. Distributive considerations do not come into play between two contracting parties unless they are dealing with each other in the run-up to bankruptcy or an insolvent winding-up.[114] Otherwise, a party providing financial accommodation is entitled to bargain for the position that best protects its interests without having to take account of any fall-out affecting third parties. Any requirement that a transaction be registered is not a denial of freedom of contract as between two contracting parties. It does not purport to alter the basic bargain between parties to a title-based transaction. The same can be said for a rationalisation of priority rules.

[111] See A Tettenborn, 'Transfer of Chattels by Non-owners: Still an Open Problem' [2018] *CLJ* 151.

[112] Even in the case of a sale of book debts, this is treated as a registrable bill of sale if the assignment is a general one and it is executed by an individual: Insolvency Act 1986, s 344.

[113] cf *Welsh Development Agency v Export Finance Co Ltd* [1992] BCLC 148 (CA).

[114] Unlawful preferences and undervalue transactions, for example. See Insolvency Act 1986, ss 238–45.

Provided freedom of contract were retained as far as remedies are concerned, a strong case exists for codifying the English law of security, sidelining ownership by assimilating true security and quasi-security for notice and priority purposes, in place of the existing piecemeal law. This would render the law more accessible: the density and dispersal of English law is a real barrier to understanding it. Given the extension of registration rules to at least some instances of quasi-security and a comprehensive statement of priority rules, such a codification would not be greatly different in outcomes from Article 9 and its congeners.[115] The style and language of the statute, however, would be a different matter.

[115] One outstanding difference, where the Art 9 systems are more protective of secured creditors, concerns future advances.

13

Netting Off Gains and Losses in the Law of Unjust Enrichment

CHARLES MITCHELL*

I. INTRODUCTION

THIS CHAPTER DISCUSSES a proposition that was recently accepted in principle by the Supreme Court, but has not yet developed into a rule with certain content, limits and rationale. The proposition is that a defendant to a claim in unjust enrichment is not enriched although she receives a benefit, to the extent that her receipt of the benefit causes her a loss. In such cases, it is said, the extent of the defendant's enrichment should be determined by netting off the defendant's gains and losses. The chapter begins by surveying some recent English cases which may bear on this topic. Some contain clear statements for or against the principle; others are harder to interpret, and whether they are relevant depends on how one conceives the principle and understands the judges' reasoning. The chapter then asks what a netting off rule might look like, and assuming that it goes to the question whether a defendant has been enriched, what this might tell us about the concept of enrichment, and whether it might be preferable to resolve cases of the relevant kind by allowing the defendant a change of position defence.

II. THE CASES

A. *Littlewoods Retail Ltd v HMRC (No 2)*

The claimant companies in *Littlewoods Retail Ltd v HMRC (No 2)*[1] paid money as VAT that was not due, then brought a claim in unjust enrichment for the value of the opportunity to use the money, quantified as interest – something that was possible at the time following *Sempra Metals Ltd v IRC*,[2] which had yet to be overruled by

* I thank Stephen Watterson and James Edelman for their comments on drafts of this chapter. However, the opinions expressed here – and any errors – are mine alone.

[1] *Littlewoods Retail Ltd v HMRC (No 2)* [2014] EWHC 868 (Ch), [2014] STC 1761.

[2] *Sempra Metals v IRC* [2007] UKHL 34, [2008] 1 AC 561.

Prudential Assurance Co Ltd v HMRC.[3] Among other answers which HMRC made to the claim, they argued that any liability they owed in unjust enrichment should be reduced to reflect the fact that if the claimants had not made the VAT payments, their profits would have been correspondingly larger and they would then have incurred and paid a larger corporation tax liability than that which they had actually incurred and paid. Henderson J rejected this argument, stating that:

> If the additional corporation tax were to be netted-off, it could only be on the basis of a general principle of considerable width and uncertainty which may have a place in the quantification of damages for wrongs, but seems to me to be at odds with the essentially subtractive nature of an unjust enrichment claim. The Government was undoubtedly enriched by the overpayments of VAT as and when they were received … [and] the presumption that the Government was thereby enriched by the full amount of the receipts must be a very strong one. That is the benefit which needs to be restored to the claimants, and the justice of the claim to restitution is not in my opinion affected by the probability that, but for the overpayments, the Government would subsequently have received larger amounts of corporation tax than it did in fact receive.[4]

This part of Henderson J's judgment was not considered on appeal. His conclusion can be justified on the basis that it would undermine the rule of law if public bodies were permitted to rely on counterfactual arguments to escape liability to repay money they are not legally authorised to receive.[5] However, this was not a justification on which the judge himself relied, and for present purposes, the reason he actually gave for rejecting HMRC's argument is the significant one. This was, essentially, that the law looks only at the benefits received by a defendant when assessing whether, and if so to what extent, enrichment has been established, and ignores any losses the defendant is caused to suffer by her receipt. Henderson J's comments, quoted above, suggest that his idea of "enrichment" was narrow enough to exclude the "netting off" of losses that have actually been caused by the defendant's receipt. However, this was not the argument made by HMRC in the case, which was only that they should not be liable to repay the sums received as VAT, to the extent that they would have lawfully received similar sums in a hypothetical world where the payments had not been made, where the claimants had made larger profits than they had made, and where they had incurred a corporation tax liability – although on the facts none of this had actually happened.

[3] *Prudential Assurance Co Ltd v HMRC* [2018] UKSC 39, [2019] AC 929. The court held that the opportunity to use money can never relevantly be acquired 'at the expense of' the payor and that the finding to the contrary previously made in *Sempra* was incorrect. This left open the separate question whether the opportunity to use money can relevantly be an 'enrichment', as the court had also held in *Sempra*. This means that analogous support can still be derived from *Sempra* for the view, also taken in other cases, that the opportunity to use land or goods can be an 'enrichment'. See further C Mitchell, P Mitchell and S Watterson (eds), *Goff & Jones on Unjust Enrichment*, 10th edn (London, Sweet & Maxwell 2022) paras 4.06–4.13.

[4] *Littlewoods (No 2)* (n 1) [434].

[5] C Mitchell, 'Counterfactual Arguments against *Woolwich* Liability' in A Dyson, J Goudkamp and F Wilmot-Smith (eds), *Defences in Unjust Enrichment* (Oxford, Hart Publishing, 2016). See now *Vodafone Ltd v Office of Communications* [2019] EWHC 1234 (Comm), [2020] QB 200; affirmed [2020] EWCA Civ 183, [2020] QB 857.

B. *Test Claimants in the FII Group Litigation v HMRC*

HMRC made a similar argument in *Test Claimants in the FII Group Litigation v HMRC*,[6] but this time they argued that the loss they had incurred as a result of receiving money from the claimants had actually taken place. The Supreme Court accepted HMRC's submission that as a matter of principle a defendant who has been paid money may not be enriched if she incurs 'liabilities … as a consequence of the receipt of the money'. More fully:

> [T]he court in ascertaining the defendant's enrichment cannot always conclude its enquiry by saying that because the claimant transferred £X to the defendant, the defendant's enrichment is £X. The court may, as the Revenue argues, have to have regard to liabilities which the defendant incurs as a consequence of the receipt of the money.[7]

The *FII* court found support for this proposition in several scholarly works,[8] including extra-judicial writing by Andrew Burrows to the effect that if a claimant pays £1,000 to a defendant by mistake with the result that 'a third party does not pay the defendant the £1,000 that she would otherwise have paid him, it would seem correct to say that the defendant has not been benefited at all'.[9] The court also noted Graham Virgo's statement that:

> In assessing whether the defendant has been enriched by the receipt of money it is necessary to have regard to the net transfer of value. So, … any consequent liabilities which might negate the enrichment also need to be taken into account.[10]

While the court endorsed these statements as a matter of general principle, however, it did not accept HMRC's further submission that the principle applied on the facts of the case to produce the conclusion that HMRC's liability should be reduced to zero.

Briefly summarised, the facts were as follows. The claimants sued HMRC in unjust enrichment for the value of the opportunity to use money paid as advanced corporation tax (ACT) under tax legislation that was contrary to the EU Treaty.[11] HMRC argued that although they had been paid money as ACT, these payments had triggered shareholder tax credits which HMRC had been bound to recognise under

[6] *Test Claimants in the FII Group Litigation v HMRC* [2021] UKSC 31, [2021] 1 WLR 4354. The FII Group Litigation has been long and complex and has featured three decisions of the Supreme Court so far. Under the GLO made at the start of the case, the issues were divided into two groups and a bipartite numbering system was used to distinguish them. The Supreme Court's first decision concerned some of the issues collected in the first group and was named *Test Claimants in the FII Group Litigation v HMRC (No 1)* [2012] UKSC 19, [2012] 2 AC 337. The issues from the second group that reached the Supreme Court were subdivided into two and so the court's second and third decisions are unnumbered: *Test Claimants in the FII Group Litigation v HMRC* [2020] UKSC 47, [2022] AC 1 and *Test Claimants in the FII Group Litigation v HMRC* [2021] UKSC 31. The third decision is the one discussed in the text.

[7] ibid [170].

[8] ibid [171].

[9] A Burrows, *The Law of Restitution*, 3rd edn (Oxford, Oxford University Press, 2010) 50.

[10] G Virgo, *Principles of the Law of Restitution* 3rd edn (Oxford, Oxford University Press, 2015) 73. The court also noted a similar statement in J Edelman and E Bant, *Unjust Enrichment*, 2nd edn (Oxford, Hart Publishing, 2016) 65.

[11] As was possible at the time: see text to nn 2 and 3.

section 231 of the Income and Corporation Taxes Act 1988. This meant that HMRC had suffered a loss, in the form of a liability to allow tax credits to shareholders, which should be netted off against HMRC's gain, producing the result that HMRC's enrichment was zero. To support this argument HMRC sought to establish that there had been an 'inextricable link' between the ACT payments and the shareholder tax credits.[12] HMRC contended that the House of Lords had previously held that such a link exists in its analysis of the relevant statutory scheme in *Pirelli Cable Holding NV v IRC*.[13] However, the Supreme Court disagreed with this reading of *Pirelli*, Lord Reed and Lord Hodge holding that the House of Lords' analysis was consistent with the opposite view taken by Park J at first instance, that 'it is not a precondition of the availability of a tax credit under [section 231] that there has been payment of, or a liability to pay ACT'.[14] Moreover, Lord Reed and Lord Hodge themselves considered this reading of the legislation to be correct, stating that:

> Where, in the circumstances which we are considering, the payment of the dividend is valid but ACT has unlawfully been levied on that distribution, it is the valid distribution that creates the entitlement to the tax credit. The unlawfulness of the levy of ACT has no bearing on the shareholder's entitlement to the tax credit. In our view, it follows that the tax credits paid to the ultimate shareholders should not as a matter of domestic law be taken into account in the calculation [of the amount for which the claimant is liable].[15]

This account of the *FII* case has deliberately omitted much technical detail because there are only two features of the judgment which matter for present purposes. First, it contains a clear statement of principle that a defendant may not be enriched where her receipt of a benefit causes her to incur a liability. Second, the judges held that this principle is not necessarily engaged in cases where a single event has occurred that itself results both in the defendant receiving a benefit and in the defendant incurring a liability (the relevant event in the *FII* case having been the distribution of dividends).

C. *United Biscuits (Pension Trustees) Ltd v HMRC*

Section 80(3) of the VAT Act 1994 gives HMRC a defence to statutory claims for the recovery of overpaid VAT under section 80 in situations where it would 'unjustly enrich' the taxpayer if HMRC were ordered to repay the taxpayer or allow her a credit. This wording once puzzled legal scholars because it seemed odd for the 1994 Act to say that a taxpayer's claim in unjust enrichment against HMRC would be disallowed if an award of restitution would lead to the taxpayer's unjust enrichment at HMRC's expense. However, this was persuasively explained by Monica Chowdry, who argued that the 'unjust enrichment' to which section 80(3) refers is gained not at *HMRC's* expense, but at the expense of *the customer* who has borne the economic burden of paying the VAT which has turned out not to be due.[16]

[12] *FII* (n 6) [2021] UKSC 31 [166] and [174].
[13] *Pirelli Cable Holding NV v IRC* [2006] UKHL 4, [2006] 1 WLR 400.
[14] *FII* (n 6) [2021] UKSC 31 [190].
[15] ibid [190].
[16] M Chowdry, 'Unjust Enrichment and Section 80(3) of the Value Added Tax Act 1994' [2004] *British Tax Review* 620.

Unpacking this, VAT is an indirect tax on consumers which is collected from traders who can choose to include a VAT element in the charges they make for their products or services. If a trader does so, and it transpires that the VAT was not due, allowing her to recover her payment from HMRC would often unjustly enrich her at the expense of her customers who effectively provided the money: she would be better off than she was before she paid HMRC because her payment would have been recouped both from HMRC and from the customers.[17] Furthermore, this would usually be an outcome to which the customers did not consent, their payments having been made either in the mistaken belief that equivalent sums were payable as tax to HMRC, or on the failed basis that these amounts were payable to HMRC.

There is, though, a situation where HMRC cannot make the section 80(3) argument, namely where the trader has put secure mechanisms in place to ensure that HMRC's repayment will be passed back to the customers.[18] In such cases, recovery from HMRC will not result in the trader's 'unjust enrichment' at the customers' expense; and the reason for this given by Warren J in *United Biscuits (Pension Trustees) Ltd v HMRC* was that:

> There will be no enrichment, let alone unjust enrichment, if the supplier makes arrangements under which any reimbursement obtained from HMRC is in turn reimbursed to the customer.[19]

The judge's thinking seems to have been that if the trader is legally bound to transfer the fruits of recovery to her customers, then although her receipt of money or a credit from HMRC appears at first sight to be an enrichment of a kind that would sustain a claim in unjust enrichment by the customers, it is not an enrichment if the effect of the trader's receipt is to trigger a legally enforceable liability to the customers for the same amount as a result of an agreement which the trader and customers have already made between themselves.

D. *Jeremy D Stone Consultants Ltd v National Westminster Bank Plc*

A further group of cases where it has been held that defendants are not enriched when they receive benefits for which they must account to another party concerns the receipt of benefits by agents. These are exemplified by *Jeremy D Stone Consultants Ltd v National Westminster Bank Plc*.[20] The defendant bank received a mistaken payment from the claimant, credited this to its customer's account, and later paid money out

[17] *Marks & Spencer plc v C&E Commissioners (No 5)* [2005] UKHL 53, [2005] STC 1254 [25]: 'reimbursement would amount to double recovery by, and unjust enrichment of, the trader'.

[18] *Lamdec Ltd v C&E Commissioners* [1991] VATTR 296; *C&E Commissioners v McMaster Stores (Scotland) Ltd* 1996 SLT 935 (IH); *C&E Commissioners v National Westminster Bank Plc* [2003] EWHC 1822, [2003] STC 1072; and cf *Lloyds Banking Group Plc v HMRC* [2019] EWCA Civ 485, [2020] 1 All ER 1045. The Value Added Tax Act 1994, s 80A empowers HMRC to make regulations governing reimbursement arrangements made by a claimant. This power has been exercised: Value Added Tax Regulations 1995, SI 1995/2518, regs 43A–43G.

[19] *United Biscuits (Pension Trustees) Ltd v HMRC* [2017] EWHC 2895 (Ch), [2018] 4 WLR 18 [208].

[20] *Jeremy D Stone Consultants Ltd v National Westminster Bank Plc* [2013] EWHC 208 (Ch). Cf *Portman Building Society v Hamlyn Taylor Neck (a firm)* [1998] 4 All ER 202 (CA).

of the account on its customer's instructions. Sales J said that even if the bank had not paid the money over, it would still have escaped liability to the claimants, because

> when the claimants paid sums to NatWest [the bank] for the account of SEWL [the customer], NatWest received those sums and added them to its stock of assets as monies to which it was beneficially entitled. However, the increase in its assets was matched by an immediate balancing liability, in the form of the debt which NatWest owed SEWL reflected in the increase in SEWL's bank balance as a result of the payments. This is how the relationship between bank and customer works. … Therefore, in my judgment, NatWest was not enriched by the payments made by the claimants into SEWL's bank accounts. … The claimants' proper unjust enrichment claim is against SEWL, whose assets were increased upon the making of the payments to its bank accounts by the increases in its balances on those accounts (representing the debt owed to it by NatWest).[21]

These dicta were accepted in *Sixteenth Ocean GmbH & Co KG v Société Générale*, where Peter MacDonald Eggars QC, sitting as a deputy High Court judge, observed that:

> Whether there was an enrichment is a question of fact. An enrichment is constituted by the receipt of a benefit, which can be money or a non-monetary benefit. The benefit must be a real one. Thus, if the receipt of a benefit is matched by a corresponding liability, the net gain to the defendant is zero, and the defendant will not have been enriched.[22]

Sales J's approach was also regarded as correct by the Supreme Court in the *FII* decision.[23] However, the judges' comments about this in *Sixteenth Ocean* and *FII* were obiter dicta.

In *High Commissioner for Pakistan v Prince Mukkaram Jah*,[24] Marcus Smith J declined to follow *Jeremy D Stone*, because he considered that an agent should not be entitled to escape liability in unjust enrichment unless she has paid over money received from a claimant to her principal or in line with her principal's directions. In other words, he thought that in principle a legally enforceable accounting liability owed by an agent to a principal should not count as a 'loss' that should be netted off against a benefit received by the agent for the purposes of deciding an unjust enrichment claim against the agent by the provider of the benefit.

Marcus Smith J gave several reasons for this. One was that the 'no enrichment' version of the defence of ministerial receipt (as opposed to the the 'payment over' version he preferred) was inconsistent with *Investment Trust Companies (In Liquidation) v HMRC*.[25] In that case, the Supreme Court held that claims in unjust enrichment are generally permitted only against direct recipients of benefits (such as agents) and are generally forbidden against indirect recipients (such as principals to whom agents are accountable). As the judge recognised, however, Lord Reed held that

[21] *Jeremy D Stone*, ibid [242]–[243].

[22] *Sixteenth Ocean GmbH & Co KG v Société Générale* [2018] EWHC 1731 (Comm), [2018] 2 Lloyd's Rep 465 [109].

[23] *FII* (n 6) [2021] UKSC 31 [172] (Lord Reed and Lord Hodge, with the agreement of the rest of the court, including Lord Sales).

[24] *High Commissioner for Pakistan v Prince Mukkaram Jah* [2019] EWHC 2551 (Ch), [2020] Ch 421 [286]–[291].

[25] *Investment Trust Companies (In Liquidation) v HMRC* [2017] UKSC 29, [2018] AC 275.

agency cases are an exception to the general rule which he stated in the *Investment Trust Companies* case.[26] Another reason given by Marcus Smith J was that recognition of the 'no enrichment' version would mean that there would be no need for the 'payment over' version, or of the change of position defence, in agency cases where the agent pays the money to a third party. That is true, but not a reason in itself for refusing to recognise the 'no enrichment' version, and there are policy reasons for favouring the latter version of the defence – essentially, that it supports the use of agents if they are enabled to 'drop out' of disputes between claimants who have paid them money and the principals to whom they have accounted for the money.[27]

E. *DD Growth Premium 2X Fund v RMF Market Neutral Strategies (Master) Ltd*

The Cayman Islands companies legislation, like the UK companies legislation, makes it unlawful for a company to pay money out of its share premium account to redeem shares unless the company is able to pay its debts as they fall due in the ordinary course of business immediately after the date of payment. In *DD Growth Premium 2X Fund v RMF Market Neutral Strategies (Master) Ltd*,[28] the claimant company made payments to a shareholder which infringed this rule. After the company went into insolvent liquidation, the liquidator caused it to sue the shareholder for the amount of the payments, making two alternative claims, one in unjust enrichment and one for knowing receipt of funds paid as a result of the directors' breach of fiduciary duty. The lower courts held that on the facts the payments had not been unlawful and so the question did not arise whether the company had any remedy. The majority of the Privy Council, whose advice was given by Lord Sumption and Lord Briggs, held that the payments had been unlawful, that as a matter of law no claim in unjust enrichment could lie, but that as a matter of law a claim in knowing receipt was possible. Hence, they ordered that the case should be returned to the Cayman Islands courts to determine whether the facts would support a knowing receipt claim.

The reasoning of Lord Sumption and Lord Briggs with respect to the unjust enrichment claim went as follows.[29] First, money paid 'under an ineffective (eg a void) transaction is recoverable' and 'the ground of recovery in these cases is failure of basis', the reason being that 'the transfer was not intended to be gratuitous, but the ineffectiveness of the transaction means that there never was any consideration for it'. Second, the 'same is in principle true if the reason why the transaction is ineffective is that it is illegal, although in this case the position is complicated by the public policy against the recovery of money paid for an illegal purpose'. Third, in the present case the basis for the payment did not fail because the money was paid in exchange for the debt owed by the company to the shareholder, and 'although the company acted illegally in making the payment, upon receipt it discharged a valid legal entitlement'.

[26] ibid [48].
[27] *Goff & Jones* (n 3) paras 28.01–28.06.
[28] *DD Growth Premium 2X Fund v RMF Market Neutral Strategies (Master) Ltd* [2017] UKPC 36, [2018] Bus LR 1595.
[29] ibid [60]–[64].

Fourth, the company could not rely on *Smith v Bromley*,[30] *Browning v Morris*[31] and *Kiriri Cotton Co Ltd v Dewani*[32] to argue that 'there was a right to restitution because the purpose of [the legislation] was the protection of the company's assets for the benefit of its creditors'. According to their Lordships, those cases assume

> a prima facie right to restitution and address the circumstances in which the illegality of the underlying transaction may afford a defence, whereas in the present case there is no prima facie right to restitution to call for such a defence. They go on to assume (as was in fact the case in all of them) that the party seeking restitution was party to the illegality, whereas in the present case the redeeming shareholder simply received payments which were due to him under lawful transactions. The purpose of the rule which made the transaction illegal may be relevant to defeat reliance on the principle of public policy *ex turpi causa non oritur actio*. But it cannot create a right of restitution which would not otherwise exist.[33]

This reasoning depends on the false premise that because claims to recover money paid as part of an illegal transaction can be grounded on failure of basis, that is the *only* way they can be pleaded, producing the conclusion that if the basis does not fail there can be no claim at all. According to the judges there was no failure of basis on the facts of *DD Growth* because the payment was made on the shared understanding that it would discharge the company's debt to the shareholder and that was accomplished. However, a more plausible reading of the facts is that the parties had a shared understanding *both* that the payments would discharge the company's debt *and* that the payments would be lawful – and this second condition for the defendant's enrichment failed completely. Moreover, claims to recover payments made as part of an illegal transaction can be made on grounds other than failure of basis, including mistake of law and arguably also illegality, where the policy of the rule rendering the transaction illegal would be supported by the making of a restitutionary award.[34] Lord Sumption and Lord Briggs did not accept the latter proposition, but did accept that the line of cases[35] cited by the company in its support 'needs to be revisited in the light of the decision of the Supreme Court in *Patel v Mirza*'.[36] Moreover, Lord Sumption's views in *Patel* on the effect of illegality on claims in unjust enrichment were not shared by the majority of the court and to the extent that they influenced his approach in *DD Growth*, there is further reason to doubt the soundness of this decision.

Putting these points to one side, the relevance of *DD Growth* for present purposes is that in connection with the third step in their analysis, Lord Sumption and Lord Briggs said that:

> It is fundamental that a payment cannot amount to enrichment if it was made for full consideration; and that it cannot be unjust to receive or retain it if it was made in satisfaction of a legal right.[37]

[30] *Smith v Bromley* (1760) 2 Doug KB 696n, 99 ER 441n.
[31] *Browning v Morris* (1778) 2 Cowp 790, 98 ER 1364.
[32] *Kiriri Cotton Co Ltd v Dewani* [1960] AC 192 (PC).
[33] *DD Growth* (n 28) [63].
[34] *Goff & Jones* (n 3) paras 25.07–25.17.
[35] See the cases cited in nn 30–32.
[36] *DD Growth* (n 28) [63], referring to *Patel v Mirza* [2016] UKSC 42, [2017] AC 467.
[37] ibid [60].

This statement is also problematic for several reasons. It is true that the defence of bona fide purchase is available to good faith defendants who give consideration in exchange for benefits (although the 'fullness' of the consideration is not tested).[38] However, it is unnecessary and confusing to treat this rule (or the defence of 'good consideration', which is the same) as a rule which goes to the question whether the retention of a defendant's enrichment is 'unjust'.[39] Liability in unjust enrichment does not depend on the 'retention' of benefits, as evidenced by the fact that claims generally lie from the date of receipt,[40] and the result produced by their Lordships' application of these principles to the facts of *DD Growth* was peculiar. But putting all that to one side as well, the statement that a defendant is not enriched if she receives payment in satisfaction of a legal right suggests another possible example of the 'netting off' principle: where money is paid to D to discharge a liability owed to D, D's gain is matched by D's loss of her legal right, and when they are netted off, D's enrichment is zero. The same idea was stated by Lord Templeman in *Lipkin Gorman (a firm) v Karpnale Ltd* where he said that:

> An innocent recipient of stolen money may not be enriched at all; if [a thief paid] £20,000 derived from the [victim] to a car dealer for a motor car priced at £20,000, the car dealer would not have been enriched. The car dealer would have received £20,000 for a car worth £20,000.[41]

F. *School Facility Management Ltd v Christ the King College*

In some cases, the counter-restitution of benefits received by a claimant from a defendant has been made a precondition for claims in unjust enrichment. There are two ways in which this rule has been understood. It has been seen as a rule that claim and counterclaim must be netted off, imposed with the pragmatic purpose of reducing multiplicity of suits. It has also been seen as a rule that benefits transferred and received in a process of exchange must be netted off, imposed to ensure that the reciprocity of the parties' performances is reflected in the unwinding process that follows failure of the basis for the parties' exchange. Neither version of the rule conceives it as being concerned with a netting off of the defendant's gains and losses, but the latter version of the rule might be reimagined in this way.

There are only a few English cases. One is *Kleinwort Benson Ltd v Sandwell BC*,[42] which concerned an interest rate swap contract that was performed for more than six years before the start of proceedings. The question arose whether the claimant

[38] *Goff & Jones* (n 3) ch 29.

[39] As Lord Sumption also did in *Fairfield Sentry Ltd (in liq) v Migani* [2014] UKPC 9, [2014] 1 CLC 611 [18]. Cf A Burrows, 'Is There a Defence of Good Consideration?' in C Mitchell and W Swadling (eds), *The Restatement Third, Restitution and Unjust Enrichment: Critical and Comparative Essays* (Oxford, Hart Publishing, 2013). The problems with this view are explained in H Scott, 'Defence, Denial or Cause of Action? "Enrichment Owed" and the Absence of a Legal Ground' in A Dyson et al (eds), *Defences in Unjust Enrichment* (Oxford, Hart Publishing, 2016).

[40] See further text to nn 61–65.

[41] *Lipkin Gorman (A Firm) v Karpnale Ltd* [1991] 2 AC 548 (HL) 563.

[42] *Kleinwort Benson Ltd v Sandwell BC* [1994] 4 All ER 890 (Com Ct).

bank should have to make counter-restitution of payments received more than six years previously, given that an independent claim by the defendant council to recover these payments would now be time-barred. Hobhouse J held that all payments both ways should be taken into account when quantifying the claim, proceeding on the basis that, as interest rates fluctuated and payments went back and forth between the parties, there was one single rolling enrichment consisting in the difference between the value of their performances. It followed that the bank's claim was only for the net amount that it was owed following the most recent payment under the contract (which had been made within the limitation period).[43]

Another case is *School Facility Management Ltd v Christ the King College*,[44] which concerned a supposed contract under which a firm would build a modular building to be hired by a school for at least fifteen years in exchange for an annual payment. After completion of the works, the school occupied the building and made four annual payments between 2013 and 2017. In 2018, the school stated that the contract was ultra vires and void and that it would no longer pay the hire charges; SFM, on whom ownership of the building and rights under the contract had devolved, denied that the hire contract was void but terminated for breach and issued proceedings. Between 2018 and 2020 (when the trial took place), the school continued to use the building and no hire charges were paid.

Foxton J held that the contract was ultra vires and void. In light of this decision, SFM made a claim in unjust enrichment for the school's occupation of the building between 2018 and 2020. The school counterclaimed for its payments between 2013 and 2017. In response to the counterclaim, SFM pleaded change of position, arguing that it had incurred building costs totalling £5.8 million in anticipation of the school's payments. The objective value of the benefit received by the school between 2013 and 2017 had been £1,024,000 and the sums paid by the school during the same period had amounted to £3,205,606. The value of the benefit received by the school between 2018 and 2020 had been £711,323.

The parties disputed the order in which the counter-restitution requirement and the change of position defence should be considered by the court when assessing the parties' liabilities. The school argued that the court should start by netting off the value of the school's occupation over all seven years (£1,735,323) against the value of the payments during the same period (£3,205,606); once that had been done, the firm's change of position defence should then be taken into account, producing the result that the firm's liability to make restitution of the net sum would be zero but that the school's liability to the firm would also be zero. In contrast, SFM argued that the court should start by reducing the firm's liability to repay the money received during the first period to zero by application of their change of position defence; only once that had been done should the court ask whether there was any counter-restitution

[43] ibid 941. See too his comments in *Kleinwort Benson Ltd v South Tyneside MBC* [1994] 4 All ER 972 (Com Ct) 978–79.

[44] *School Facility Management Ltd v Christ the King College* [2020] EWHC 1118 (Comm); supplementary proceedings [2020] EWHC 1477 (Comm), [2020] 1 WLR 4825; affirmed [2021] EWCA Civ 1053, [2021] 1 WLR 6129.

for the firm to make as a prerequisite for enforcing its claim respecting the school's occupation.

Foxton J preferred the latter approach, but he also held that the school was not liable for its occupation during the first period because it had paid SFM for this, and 'in circumstances in which the [school] cannot recover back the amounts paid by way of rent for this period because of [the firm's] change of position, the [school] has its own change of position defence to any claim in unjust enrichment by [the firm] for that period'.[45] This reasoning did not apply to SFM's claim for the school's occupation during the second period, however, and since there was no counter-restitution for the firm to make before enforcing this claim, Foxton J ordered the school to pay £711,323, this having been the value of the school's occupation.

In a supplementary judgment where he gave leave to appeal these findings, Foxton J explained at greater length why he thought his conclusions were justified and not inconsistent with the *Sandwell* case, which might have been thought to support the approach for which the school had argued, but which the judge had rejected.[46] He gave three reasons. First, even if it was appropriate on the facts of the case to apply the *Sandwell* approach, there were limits to the netting off process undertaken by Hobhouse J, as the judge had effectively recognised. This was because he had held that the payments under each of the five contracts had to be treated separately and had declined to aggregate all the payments made under all the contracts. The key question in every case where the court is asked to net off counter-benefits is therefore whether these are 'sufficiently distinct' to make it appropriate to consider them separately. On the facts of the present case, it was inappropriate to aggregate every year's worth of occupation benefit and to set all these off against the total amount of the payments because the value of each year's occupation had fluctuated with the market and the 'rent instalments paid by the [school] were referable to, and conditional on, the enjoyment of the use of the building during the contract years for which those payments were made'.[47]

Second, this was a case of anticipatory change of position: SFM had incurred substantial expenditure in advance of the school's payments with the result that the school had never been entitled to recover any of its payments, and this made it 'particularly unattractive' to calculate the firm's net benefit before taking the change of position defence into account.[48]

Third, the change of position relied on by SFM was not extraneous to the parties' dealings (as, for example, a payment to a third party would have been), but was closely linked to them, and there was 'nothing unconscionable in the [firm] refusing to [let the school occupy the building for free] to the extent that it had changed its position in anticipation of receipt of the payment, when it had done so for the purpose of providing a benefit to the [school]'.[49]

[45] ibid [2020] EWHC 1118 (Comm) [502], where the judge also suggested two other ways of analysing the situation which produced the same conclusion.

[46] *School Facility Management* [2020] EWHC 1477 (Comm) (n 44).

[47] ibid [24].

[48] ibid [25].

[49] ibid [26].

The Court of Appeal agreed with the judge's statement of the law governing the question of when the counter-restitution principle is engaged. Popplewell LJ formulated the test in a positive rather than a negative way as being whether the relevant benefits are 'sufficiently closely connected' to make it appropriate to aggregate them.[50] The appellate court also agreed with the judge's factual finding that the school's payments between 2013 and 2017 had not been made in exchange for the occupation of the building thereafter and it followed that his conclusions about the counter-restitution issue had also been correct. Popplewell LJ accepted that the language of 'sufficiently close connection' might be criticised as being 'unhelpfully broad' but was fortified by the fact that Lord Goff had used deliberately broad language in *Lipkin Gorman v Karpnale Ltd*[51] when describing the circumstances in which the change of position defence is available, as he thought that the law was at an early stage of development and that more detailed principles should be allowed to emerge on a case-by-case basis.

Earlier in his discussion of the limits of 'the counter-restitution principle', Popplewell LJ had proposed four possible ways in which it might 'conceptually be justified', the first being:

> *Enrichment*: benefits received by a claimant may prevent, or pro tanto reduce, the enrichment of the defendant, because the latter has paid or provided value to the claimant, in whole or in part, for the benefit he has received in exchange. Assume a void but executed contract under which A is to provide services worth £20,000 to B in return for a contract price of £15,000. The analysis may be that B has only been enriched by £5,000 representing the value of the services in excess of the price he has paid for them.[52]

Popplewell LJ did not express a preference for this or for one of the other possible explanations of the principle he identified, but he must have thought that at least one of them was correct, given that he upheld Foxton J's reasoning and conclusions.

III. ANALYSIS

The foregoing discussion suggests that the netting off principle recognised by the Supreme Court in *FII* has also made an appearance in other recent cases, but that significant questions remain about its content, scope and rationale. It is worth identifying some of these, both because this will help us gain a better understanding of how the principle might evolve in future cases, and because it will shed some light on our understanding of the law of unjust enrichment more generally.

A. Denial or Defence?

If a defendant's restitutionary liability is negated or diminished to the extent that her receipt of a benefit causes her a loss, then it must be determined how this argument

[50] *School Facility Management* (CA) (n 44) [83].
[51] *Lipkin Gorman* (n 41) 580.
[52] *School Facility Management* (CA) (n 44) [34].

fits within the existing conceptual framework of unjust enrichment claims. An important issue is whether the netting off principle operates as a 'denial' or a 'defence', ie as a means by which the defendant can show that the claimant has failed to establish an essential ingredient of her claim, or as a means by which the defendant can show that she should escape liability even though the claimant has established a cause of action so that she is prima facie entitled to restitution.[53]

The first possibility comes closest to the language used by the Supreme Court in *FII*, which suggests that the argument operates as a 'denial' because it denies that the claimant has succeeded in showing that the defendant was enriched to the extent pleaded. If this is correct then more work is needed to explain the circumstances in which a defendant's 'loss' should be relevant when determining whether, and if so to what extent, the defendant has been 'enriched' in a legally relevant sense. The alternative possibility, that the principle operates as a 'defence', proceeds on the assumption that the claimant has established that the defendant was enriched to the full extent of the benefit received, but that there is a countervailing reason why the defendant should nevertheless escape liability to repay the full amount. On this view, more work is needed to explain the relevant countervailing reason, and to understand how a defence framed in this way would relate to other recognised defences to unjust enrichment claims.

B. Netting Off Conceived as a Denial of Enrichment

Starting with the first possibility, a number of points can be made. First, it must be understood that enrichment is a term of art: what it means for the purposes of the law of unjust enrichment often corresponds to people's everyday ideas, but it does not always do so and it is a matter for the courts to decide what does and what does not count as an 'enrichment' in this context.[54] Henderson J's judgment in *Littlewoods (No 2)*[55] shows that a court might choose to define 'enrichment' in a way that excludes a defendant's (hypothetical and/or actual) losses from consideration.[56] Were a judicial consensus to form around such a definition, then in cases where a defendant's receipt actually causes her a loss and the court considers that her liability should be reduced to reflect this fact, it could not achieve this by saying that the defendant was not enriched: it could only produce this result by some other means, eg by allowing the defendant a change of position defence. This approach would have the merit of simplicity: the law's idea of enrichment would be easily understood and easily tested, wholly focused as it would be on benefits received. However, there are other cases,

[53] J Goudkamp and C Mitchell, 'Denials and Defences in the Law of Unjust Enrichment' in Mitchell and Swadling (n 39).

[54] *Goff & Jones* (n 3) paras 4.03–4.05.

[55] *Littlewoods (No 2)* (n 1), discussed above in the text to nn 1–5.

[56] cf *Community Savings Credit Union v Bodnar* [2022] BCCA 263 [13]–[18], rejecting the defendant's argument that it had not been enriched by the amount of illegally levied overdraft charges because it had used the sums received to benefit its members; the court held that this was inconsistent with the 'straightforward economic approach' that Canadian courts must take to the enrichment issue following *Peter v Beblow* [1993] 1 SCR 980, 990, and *Pacific National Investments Ltd v City of Victoria* [2004] SCC 75, [2004] 3 SCR 575 [15].

including *FII*,[57] which seem to favour a wider definition of enrichment that would enable the courts to take account of a defendant's causally connected losses when determining the extent to which she is enriched. This would make the law's idea of 'enrichment' more complex, but one that would correspond to the intuition shared by many people that defendants are not 'better off' if their acquisition of a benefit causes them to lose something of equal worth (as suggested by Burrows in the passage of his extra-judicial writing previously quoted[58]).

Second, if a netting off rule were to form part of the enrichment enquiry, the question would arise whether the rule was concerned with identification or valuation of the defendant's benefit. If the former view were taken, then this might suggest that English law was committed to a view, not clearly articulated in the existing authorities, that the subject-matter of a claim in unjust enrichment is the defendant's 'net benefit' rather than the value of what she 'received' from the claimant. If the latter view were preferred, then a further question would arise as to whether the value of the defendant's enrichment should be reduced as part of the 'objective' or 'subjective' stages of the valuation exercise identified by the majority of the Supreme Court in *Benedetti v Sawiris*.[59] In that case, all the members of the court agreed that the starting point is always to ask as an objective matter whether a defendant has been enriched, and that although the objective value of a benefit is generally represented by the market price, it is sometimes appropriate for the defendant's personal circumstances to be taken into account when assessing the objective value of benefits. In this connection, Lord Clarke said that the relevant question is what price a 'reasonable person in the defendant's position would have had to pay', and that the court could take note of 'conditions increasing or decreasing the objective value of the benefit to any reasonable position in the same (unusual) position' of the defendant.[60] Conceivably, a defendant might therefore argue that if her personal circumstances meant that she could not receive a particular benefit with a market value of £X without losing £X as a result, then the objective value of the benefit to her would be £0.

It is unclear, however, that this is the kind of 'personal circumstance' which the judges had in mind in *Benedetti*, since it seems that they were thinking of other kinds of personal characteristic, such as a defendant's unusually strong or weak buying power in a market. Alternatively, therefore, a court might prefer to say that the objective value of the benefit in the example given above is the same for the defendant as it is for everyone else, ie £X, but that the defendant would not have chosen to pay anything for it, given that its receipt would cause her a loss of the same amount. Taking the approach favoured by the majority in *Benedetti*, this would mean that the subjective value of the benefit to the defendant would then be zero and there would be no liability for that reason. The same outcome would also follow if one took the approach favoured by Lord Reed in the *Benedetti* minority, but he would have put this on the basis that injustice would follow if the defendant were forced to pay the

[57] *FII* (n 6) [2021] UKSC 31 discussed above in the text to nn 6–13.

[58] See text to n 9.

[59] *Benedetti v Sawiris* [2013] UKSC 50, [2014] AC 938.

[60] ibid [17] (Lord Clarke, endorsing Etherton LJ's analysis in *Benedetti v Sawiris* [2010] EWCA Civ 1427 [145]).

objective value of a benefit that she would not have chosen to acquire at that price, given her situation.

A third point is that the question of whether the defendant has been enriched, and if so, to what extent, are tested at the date of receipt.[61] This proposition may appear to be inconsistent with judicial dicta which say that restitution is awarded to prevent a defendant from 'retaining' an unjust enrichment,[62] but these should be understood to mean that the defendant's unjust enrichment creates a normative imbalance between the parties that must be corrected.[63] They do not mean that the defendant must still be enriched at the time when the parties are in court, since this would be inconsistent with the well-established rule that actions in unjust enrichment are generally complete at the moment of receipt,[64] ie success depends on the claimant establishing the 'receipt', but not the 'continued retention', of a benefit.[65] If that is correct, however, and if 'netting off' is a rule about enrichment, then the question arises whether the rule only applies in cases where the loss caused by a defendant's gain occurs at the same time as her receipt of the relevant benefit, or whether a version of the 'netting off' rule can be conceived that allows the defendant to bring subsequent losses into account?

C. Netting Off Conceived as a Defence

As noted earlier, the courts could choose to define 'enrichment' in a narrow way that focused only on benefits received by a defendant and excluded losses caused by the receipt from consideration. If that were done, and if it were thought desirable to reduce or eliminate the defendant's liability in cases where the receipt caused the defendant a loss, that would then have to be done by allowing a defence. Three advantages could be gained by proceeding in this way. First, it would enable the enrichment question posed at the start of all unjust enrichment claims to be kept simple. Second, it would mean that losses sustained by a defendant could all be treated in the same way, whether these occurred before, at the same time as, or after receipt of enrichment. Third, it would put the evidential burden of proving a relevant loss onto the defendant, rather than putting the onus of disproving loss onto the claimant, and this would be preferable because the defendant is the party with the best access to the information needed to establish the point.

If the netting off principle were characterised as a defence, then the most obvious possibility is that it could be understood as one aspect of the defence of change of position. However, this defence is currently understood to be available only in cases

[61] ibid [18] (Lord Clarke).

[62] See eg *Deutsche Morgan Grenfell Morgan Group Plc v IRC* [2006] UKHL 49, [2007] 1 AC 558 [21]; *Test Claimants in the FII Group Litigation v HMRC (No 1)* [2012] UKSC 19, [2012] 2 AC 337 [162]; *Patel v Mirza* [2016] UKSC 42, [2017] AC 467 [246].

[63] See eg *Kleinwort Benson Ltd v Birmingham CC* [1997] QB 380 (CA) 394 (Evans LJ): 'The principle of unjust enrichment … requires the recipient of money to repay it when the circumstances are such that it is contrary to "the ties of natural justice and equity" for him to retain it.'

[64] See cases cited in *Goff & Jones* (n 3) paras 33.16–33.17.

[65] *Portman Building Society v Hamlyn Taylor Neck (a firm)* [1998] 4 All ER 202 (CA) 207.

where the defendant can prove acts of detrimental reliance, and this requirement would have to be dropped to accommodate cases where a defendant's losses have been caused by her receipt of a benefit – no bad thing, many might think, since the existing rule already prevents defendants from invoking the defence in circumstances where it would be better to let them plead it, such as where a defendant is given cash that is stolen immediately afterwards.[66] And indeed, Lord Leggatt recently signalled that the time has come for the law to take this step in a Privy Council case, *Delta Petroleum (Caribbean) Ltd v British Virgin Islands Electricity Corp*, where he said that:

> [T]here is no reason why relevant changes in position should be restricted to those which have come about through decisions made and steps taken voluntarily in reliance on the receipt of a benefit. It is sufficient that receiving the benefit has caused the change of position.[67]

Adoption of a wider defence of change of position that included a netting off principle of the kind discussed in this chapter would prompt questions of the same kind as were triggered when the change of position defence was first recognised in *Lipkin Gorman*, about the relation between the defence and pre-existing defences. Following that decision, the questions arose (and indeed remain live) whether the change of position defence renders redundant defences such as estoppel, ministerial receipt, 'good consideration', and bona fide purchase.[68] Similarly, as discussed in part II, various cases where the netting off principle may have been in play have concerned situations where a defendant has suffered a loss, and where the elimination or reduction of the defendant's liability might conceivably be rationalised in terms of one or more other principles. These include: first, the defence of payment over or ministerial receipt (analysing the agent's liability to account to her principal as a 'loss' which negates her enrichment; second, the defence of receipt for 'good consideration' (analysing the discharge of a liability owed to the defendant as a 'loss' which negates her enrichment); and, third, the requirement that a claimant must make counter-restitution before she can be entitled to a remedy (analysing a liability to make counter-restitution as a 'loss' which negates her enrichment). Once again, therefore, the questions would arise whether an overlap between such defences and the netting off principle, conceived as an aspect of the change of position defence, would be tolerable, or whether expanding the change of position defence would undermine the justified parameters of these other defences in an unacceptable way?

D. Parameters of a Netting Off Principle

If the courts develop some version of a 'netting off' principle, either on the basis that it works as a denial of enrichment or on the basis that it is an aspect of the change of position defence, then some questions will need to be resolved regarding the operation and limits of the principle.

[66] See discussion in *Goff & Jones* (n 3) paras 27.38–27.40.

[67] *Delta Petroleum (Caribbean) Ltd v British Virgin Islands Electricity Corp* [2020] UKPC 23, [2021] 1 WLR 5741 [62] (although in this case the defence was not made out on the facts).

[68] *Goff & Jones* (n 3) paras 28.01–28.05, 29.12–29.17, 30.17–30.18.

For instance, it will need to be determined what counts as a 'loss' in this context. Possible examples include: first, D's incurring of a new liability, either to a third party (such as where D is an agent who incurs a liability to her principal) or to the claimant (such as where D is a contracting party who becomes liable to counter-perform to C); second, D's incurring of factually necessary new expenditure (such as where C transfers possession or ownership of an asset to D which must be looked after and/or insured, such as a racehorse); third, D's loss of a legal right against a third party (such as where D receives money which extinguishes a debt owed by X to D) or the claimant (such as where D receives money which extinguishes a debt owed by C to D); and, fourth, D's loss of a factual opportunity to make a gain (such as where D's friend, X, decides not to make a gift to D that she would otherwise have made). Should all of these be capable of qualifying as a 'loss', or is there a principled reason for distinguishing between them – with some categories or subcategories excluded?

It will also need to be decided what kind of link must exist between D's gain and D's loss to trigger application of rule? *FII* suggests that a 'but for' causal link between gain and loss must be established, and that it does not suffice for each of D's gain and loss to have been caused separately by some other event. However, it is evident from the account of the cases given in part II that their facts are various and it is predictable that as more cases unfold, different reasons will emerge for or against holding that a sufficient link exists between gain and loss as a result of which the principle will or will not be held to apply.

IV. FINAL THOUGHTS

At present, it is difficult to say with confidence that the English law of unjust enrichment accommodates a species of 'netting off' principle – the basis in authority is fragile and many of the materials are susceptible to alternative explanations. It also remains to be demonstrated that this is a step that the English courts are required to take. However, if English law contains such a principle at all, then it is in a very nascent state. The best testing ground for the questions highlighted here will be cases where the answers matter to the resolution of the parties' disputes. This prompts an observation about two other areas of unjust enrichment law that have been developing in the cases in recent times.

In *Lipkin Gorman*, Lord Goff held that change of position should be recognised as a defence in English law, and deliberately described the defence in broad and open-ended terms to leave room for case-by-case development.[69] The following three decades have gone in much the way that Lord Goff might have imagined. Subsequent judges have not tried to extrapolate the answer to questions arising in litigation from the words used in his judgment, nor have they criticised him for expressing himself in a broad way.

[69] *Lipkin Gorman* (n 41) 580: 'I am most anxious that, in recognising this defence to actions of restitution, nothing should be said at this stage to inhibit the development of the defence on a case by case basis, in the usual way.'

The development of the case law on the change of position defence can be contrasted with how an ingredient of unjust enrichment claims has been approached: the requirement that a defendant's enrichment must have been acquired 'at the claimant's expense'. Over the last decade or so, it has become clear that several difficult questions arise in connection with this rule – for example, whether, and if so when, unjust enrichment claims can lie against remote recipients. Some judges have expressed their answers to questions of this sort in broad terms – for example, allowing recovery on the ground that the 'economic reality' of the situation made it appropriate to treat the defendant's gain as having been acquired at the claimant's expense, or stating that there was a 'sufficiently close connection' between the two for this conclusion to be justifiable. Counsel seized on these words in subsequent cases to push the parameters of unjust enrichment claims until the Supreme Court put a stop to this in *Investment Trust Companies (In Liquidation) v HMRC*,[70] where Lord Reed denounced 'sufficiently close connection' as a helpful test because of its lack of precision.[71]

Paradoxically, in *Prudential Assurance Co Ltd v HMRC*,[72] the Supreme Court then used the 'direct transfer' test laid down in *Investment Trust Companies* to answer a different question (whether the value of the opportunity to use money is acquired at the expense of a payor), despite Lord Reed having recognised that the 'at the claimant's expense' inquiry concealed several different questions, and despite his having accepted that the 'expression "transfer of value" is … too general to serve as a legal test'.[73]

The lesson to be drawn from this comparison is that statements of law which are expressed in a deliberately open-ended away to allow for the law's future development should not be misread as being intended to lay down precisely stated legal tests with clear boundaries and content. They should be interpreted in the way that the court intended when formulating them and criticising judges for lack of precision when making such statements is to miss the point. Thus, if a judge uses language such as 'sufficiently close connection' to describe why she thinks 'netting off' is appropriate in a particular case,[74] then – whilst it is legitimate to ask that she explains the particular assumptions that underlie that conclusion – it may miss the point to denounce this use of language as 'imprecise' in later cases.

[70] *Investment Trust Companies* (n 25).
[71] ibid [37].
[72] *Prudential Assurance* (n 3).
[73] *Investment Trust Companies* (n 25) [43].
[74] cf *School Facility Management* (CA) (n 44) [83] (Popplewell LJ).

14

The Case for Cryptoassets as Property

PETER WATTS KC AND KELVIN FK LOW*

I. INTRODUCTION TO CRYPTOASSETS

CRYPTOASSETS AS A class are the invention of Satoshi Nakamoto, a pseudonym for a person(s) whose identity remains shrouded in mystery, in the aftermath of the global financial crisis. The original cryptoasset, Bitcoin, was introduced to the world as a concept on 31 October 2008, when Satoshi posted a white paper entitled 'Bitcoin: A Peer-to-Peer Electronic Cash System' to a cryptography mailing list. As the white paper reveals, Satoshi regarded the prevention of double spending – in which the owner of a digital asset could repeatedly spend the same asset[1] – as one of the key functions of financial intermediaries. This is unsurprising since this assumption has underpinned numerous visions of digital money since the 1990s.[2] In his white paper, Satoshi posited an elegant solution to this problem. But the problem was misdiagnosed. Wherein lies the misdiagnosis?

First, our trust in banks lies in the debtor–creditor relationship between banker and customer, not in double spending. Where our accounts are in credit, the relationship entails the customer performing its contractual obligation (extending a loan to the bank) before the bank counterperforms (repaying said loan). In other words, we trust that when we call upon our banks to perform their side of the bargain – whether by withdrawing cash at an ATM or directing them to make an interbank transfer to a particular payee – they are willing and able to perform. This trust is reversed when the bank extends credit to us since the order of contractual performance is here reversed.

Secondly, and perhaps surprisingly to many laypersons, we are not in principle concerned with whether or not a financial intermediary permits double payment of its customers' money. Today, it is not uncommon for financial intermediaries to encourage customers to make use of their services by way of so-called cashback schemes,

* The authors would like to thank Professor Megumi Hara for her comments on the section discussing Japanese law. All errors are ours alone.

[1] Since digital information can be perfectly replicated ad infinitum.

[2] S Levy, 'E-Money (That's What I Want)', *Wired*, 1 December 1994, www.wired.com/1994/12/emoney/ (accessed 29 December 2022).

in which a small percentage of payments are 'refunded' to the customer. Such cash-backs, in spirit if not precise form, offend the so-called double-payment principle. Because modern monetary theory assumes a flexible monetary supply, with private banks responsible for creating at least part of this supply,[3] double payments are not in principle objectionable. The key lies not in principle but in practical implementation: since private money is fundamentally a debt, the question is whether an intermediary is able to generate sufficient profits to cover such new money that it creates – whether through operating profits (eg merchant fees) or by large infusions of equity – so that it is able to meet its liabilities?

The confusion may have set in as a result of smart cards such as Transport for London's Oyster card or the Hong Kong MTR's Octopus[4] card. For smart cards, one security concern is the possibility that an end user can tamper with their card's record of the value of their credit. Whilst this may appear to be a problem of artificial inflation of monetary supply, the concern is actually more fundamental than that. No legal system allows private individuals to create claims against another without the latter's consent. Furthermore, because such digital money is fundamentally a claim against its issuer (here transport companies), there is no actual inflation of the monetary supply and the fraudulently 'created' money is booked as a loss to the issuer.[5] Nevertheless, owing to the nadir in trust in financial institutions that the global financial crisis brought, this spark of an idea based on double spending, absent any understanding of either law or economics, captured the zeitgeist of our times. Then theory was implemented in practice, when the genesis block of bitcoins was mined by Satoshi on 3 January 2009, and interest in the idea exploded.

Early cryptoassets were styled as crypto*currencies*, intended to replace fiat money. Many copycats of Bitcoin were birthed, christened 'altcoins'. Through the clever use of cryptography and the coding of game theory, the blockchain technology underlying Bitcoin and its ilk prevented the supposed problem of double spending. It did so by rendering the blockchain practically immutable except to a person(s) with control of at least 51 percent of the power to add to its ledger. As the Bitcoin blockchain employs a proof of work (PoW) consensus algorithm in which the parties who add to the ledger – dubbed miners – compete to solve a cryptographic hash, an attacker who wished to engage in a double-spending attack would need to control 51 percent of the network's hashing capacity. Although this may sound daunting, and in the early days such attacks were dismissed as academic in the pejorative sense of the word, it is not actually as challenging as it appears, at least for smaller networks. Because the Bitcoin blockchain and many of its copycats operate in a permissionless fashion, the attacker need not actually compromise any particular computer in order to launch an attack. All the attacker would need to do is to rent the requisite computing power, download the permissionless blockchain's software, and he or she will be up and running. Although the largest permissionless blockchains such as Bitcoin and

[3] M McLeay, A Radia and R Thomas, 'Money Creation in the Modern Economy' [2014, Q1] *Bank of England Quarterly Bulletin* 14.

[4] cf PYK Chau and S Poon, 'Octopus: An E-Cash Payment System Success Story' (2003) 46 *Communications of the ACM* 129.

[5] cf *HKSAR v Lau Chi Chiu* [2013] HKDC 967 [42].

Ethereum remain unaffected to date, some major networks such as Ethereum Classic have been successfully targeted. In January 2019, Ethereum Classic was successfully subjected to a 51 percent attack and in August 2020, it was successfully so attacked three times. Today, alternative consensus algorithms such as proof of stake (PoS) and proof of authority (PoA) have emerged, but each is susceptible to variations of the 51 percent and other attacks, as demonstrated in the Solana[6] (PoS) and Axie Infinity[7] (PoA) exploits.

Although no crypto*currency* has ever attained currency,[8] this has not inhibited growth in the varieties of cryptoassets that have emerged as cryptomania swept the world. So, the initial coin offering (ICO) boom of 2017 saw the explosion of cryptoassets that were either securities in tokenised form or utility tokens, ie tokens that entitled their holders to goods or services from the issuer. Tokenisation is a poorly understood concept. The expression originated in the context of data security, in which sensitive data (eg credit card numbers) is substituted by a non-sensitive equivalent, commonly referred to as a token. In this context, tokenisation is eminently sensible. Information is non-rivalrous[9] and some information (eg credit card details) are intended to be repeatedly used in multiple transactions. By tokenising the sensitive data and transmitting its non-sensitive equivalent, we ensure that an intercept of the transmitted data does not enable the perpetration of fraud in the future. Where the token represents a legal right, whether in the form of a security or a right to goods or services, the only security that tokenisation provides is that provided by the blockchain on which the token resides since the legal right is, unlike information, rivalrous. This means that tokenised assets are exposed to 51 percent attacks as well as attacks targeting the end user. No foolproof way of eliminating the vulnerability of the end user exists. After all, there may be 'an undisputable, mathematical link between the private and public key, but there is no similar link between a private key and its user'.[10]

Another development has been the stablecoin – cryptoassets whose values are pegged to traditional assets, most commonly fiat currencies but occasionally commodities. These fundamentally serve to enable investors to enter and exit markets for other cryptoassets. Stablecoins may be backed by real-world assets such as fiat currencies or other cryptoassets or a combination of the two. They may also seek to maintain stability merely through the use of algorithms, a means that has been

[6] D Nelson, 'Solana Goes Dark for 7 Hours as Bots Swarm "Candy Machine" NFT Minting Tool', *Coindesk*, 1 May 2022, www.coindesk.com/tech/2022/05/01/solana-goes-dark-for-7-hours-as-bots-swarm-candy-machine-nft-minting-tool/ (accessed 29 December 2022).

[7] M White, 'The Axie Infinity Hack, What Happened, and Why People Keep Talking About Bridges', *Molly White Blog*, 30 March 2022, https://blog.mollywhite.net/axie-hack/ (accessed 29 December 2022).

[8] Despite El Salvador declaring bitcoin to be legal tender, the cryptoasset faces resistance to adoption: see FE Alvarez, D Argente and D Van Patten, 'Are Cryptocurrencies Currencies? Bitcoin as Legal Tender in El Salvador', National Bureau of Economic Research Working Paper 29968 (April 2022) doi: 10.3386/w29968.

[9] Non-exclusive, so that possession of information by A does not automatically imply the exclusion of possession of the same by B or other persons.

[10] KFK Low and E Mik, 'Pause the Blockchain Legal Revolution' (2020) 69 *International and Comparative Law Quarterly* 135, 158.

heavily criticised[11] and recently ended in disaster.[12] A yet further development are non-fungible tokens (NFTs), which burst into the public imagination with the record-setting auction by Christie's of Beeple's *Everydays: The First 5,000 Days.* NFTs supposedly differ from their fungible brethren in that each token is unique, often supposedly representing ownership of digital art. The nomenclature, however, demonstrates a fundamental misunderstanding of fungibility. It is perhaps more accurate to describe them as representing ownership of a digital certificate of authenticity of commonly available digital art rather than as providing ownership of art per se. At around the same time, the idea of decentralised finance (DeFi) also became popularised, promoting what has been criticised as effectively shadow banking.[13]

Despite their multifarious variety, so far as the law is concerned, cryptoassets may be broadly broken down into two categories. They may be exogenous, whereby the cryptoasset is simply a token of some off-chain property that has value, or they may be endogenous, whereby the cryptoasset is valuable in and of itself. Broadly speaking, most tokenised assets would be exogenous although it is arguable that some NFTs are actually endogenous since digital art per se is, as pure information, incapable of ownership. The former category is straightforward since the blockchain simply operates as a ledger[14] so that it is the off-chain asset that determines whether any particular exogenous cryptoasset merits the property label and if so what precise meaning that label entails.[15] It is the latter category that has proven challenging for the law to accommodate. In the absence of legislation, the question is how the courts should seek to accommodate cryptoassets within private law? Should they be accommodated as part of the law of property, which is how users of cryptoassets appear to regard them? Or should they be denied property status in the absence of parliamentary fiat? If so, how might disputes over cryptoassets be resolved?

II. PROPERTY: A PRIMER

Like many concepts, the related concepts of property and ownership have a core surrounded by broad penumbra. At property's core are tangible things, land and chattels. In relation to these, the concept of ownership, which in common law systems is premised on possession, pre-dates the law. It is often said that there can be no ownership without a legal system, but in relation to tangible property the legal concept of ownership, rather than being the founding idea, was a quid pro quo for imposing controls on private means of maintaining ownership (in particular the outlawing of private armies).[16] Without the additional protection offered by a legal system,

[11] R Clements, 'Built to Fail: The Inherent Fragility of Algorithmic Stablecoins' (2021) 11 *Wake Forest Law Review* 131.

[12] C Davies and J-A Song, '$40bn Crypto Collapse Turns South Korea Against the "Lunatic" Leader', *Financial Times*, 24 May 2022, www.ft.com/content/c46f767c-c8e3-47cf-b0a3-46d3b84498c3 (accessed 29 December 2022).

[13] HJ Allen, 'DeFi: Shadow Banking 2.0?' (2023) 64(4) *William & Mary Law Review* 919.

[14] H Liu, 'The Legal Nature of Blockchain Securities' [2021] *LMCLQ* 476.

[15] UK Jurisdiction Taskforce, *Legal Statement on Cryptoassets and Smart Contracts* (2019) para 33.

[16] See the discussion in *Anthony v Haney* (1832) 8 Bing 187 (CP) 191–92, 131 ER 372, 374; and *R v Jones* [2006] UKHL 16, [2007] 1 AC 136 [77]–[78]. In relation to chattels, see C Hawes, 'Recaption of Chattels: The Use of Force Against the Person' (2006) 12 *Canterbury Law Review* 253.

possession and hence ownership would be precarious and all owners would have to be prepared to maintain (or recapture) possession by force, to the detriment of the whole of society. This legal safeguarding of an extra-legal social norm is beneficial not only for the weak but society as a whole. Such legal reinforcement of extra-legal social norms is not just some historic artefact. Cryptoassets themselves are a modern example of the law adding flesh to extra-legal bones.

Implicit in the reference to private armies is that at the core of the concept of ownership, extra-legal or legal, is the assertion of rights to exclude others from having access to something where it can be anticipated that others might like to have such access. Prominent in Commonwealth discourse on property and ownership has been Professor Gray's, definition, albeit state-centred:

> Property is a power-relation constituted by the state's endorsement of private claims to regulate the access of strangers to the benefits of particular resources.[17]

If the core classes of the concept of property are extra-legal in origin, lawmakers have deployed the concept for a variety of purposes that are internal to the legal system. These borrowings have been diverse and in some cases loose. Context is everything.[18] Some usages have been intended to empower, others to disable.

On the empowering side, the very recognition by a legal system of a right in one person to sue another can generate in third parties an economic interest in 'having a piece of the action'. In enabling and controlling third-party access to such claims, courts of equity have drawn on, but not duplicated, the concepts of property and ownership used to govern access to tangible assets. The right to sue is deemed a 'thing' or 'chose' over which there can be competition for control. Such reification of a bare in personam claim mimics but does not replicate all the features of tangible property. Quite obviously, reification does not in itself make the resulting in personam claims effective erga omnes, ie against the world. Whereas ownership of tangible property entails legal protection of exclusive rights *over* things, reification of the right to sue sees the law treat bare rights *as* things. Reification eventually enabled an in personam right-holder to externalise the right – by permitting its assignment – in spite of a right's deeply personal nature, as borne out by the rule of privity for contractual rights. This again entails the legal reinforcement of extra-legal social norms. Choses in action were originally conceived by the common law to be non-transferable[19] in spite of the social practices of the time. This historical instinct survives today in various forms, including the law of champerty, today akin to a form of legal skeumorphism.[20] Over time, however, as a result of changing perceptions of balance between benefits and drawbacks of permitting assignment, the law – specifically equity – came to facilitate and reinforce extra-legal social norms. Propertisation of contractual rights does not, therefore, confer upon them

[17] K Gray, 'Property in Thin Air' (1991) 50 *CLJ* 252, 294.

[18] See *Hocking v Director-General of the National Archives of Australia* [2020] HCA 19, (2020) 271 CLR 1 [89] and [201].

[19] W Holdsworth, 'The History of the Treatment of "Choses" in Action by the Common Law' (1920) 33 *Harvard Law Review* 997.

[20] cf D Capper, 'Access to Justice and the Assignment of Rights to Litigate' (2022) 41 *Civil Justice Quarterly* 274.

any erga omnes effect but merely permits the externalisation of that which would otherwise be considered personal. This is not to say that intangible property cannot embody erga omnes rights. So, legislatures have drawn on property concepts to confer marketable rights in 'intellectual property', mostly by circumscribing certain instances of the innate capacity of humans to copy or engage in some other non-rivalrous activity, thereby creating erga omnes rights to prohibit the relevant activity. That prohibition then enables the relevant act (eg copying) to be licensed. Intangible rights can also fall in the middle of the spectrum between being in personam and erga omnes. This is the case with company shares, which are enforceable by all members and the company inter se. Nevertheless, regardless of their exigibility, intangible assets remain mere metaphorical cousins inspired by their tangible cousins. Insofar as they are regarded as part of the law of property, they embody rights *as* things,[21] not rights *over* things.

On the disabling side, concepts of property have had a major role in limiting the law's response to disputes that arise out of the fact that in our daily interactions we can both disenrich and enrich others. Causation is present in such cases but no cause of action may arise. Hence, the absence of a possessory or ownership interest in property (tangible property in particular) is in many legal systems one of the bars to mounting a claim for careless damage caused by one party to another's economic position.[22] We all owe a duty not negligently to damage the property of others, at least tangible property, but we do not owe a such a duty in relation to a third party's purely economic interests. Those legal systems that have abandoned the key of property have had great difficulty defining and containing the types of claims that should be sanctioned.[23] Equally, legal systems that have untied actions for restitution from receipts of property in favour of mere increases in wealth have had difficulties controlling the scope of liability for having been benefited by another's actions.[24] Not much more need be said here on these topics, since this chapter is concerned with the enabling side of the property equation.[25]

III. CRYPTOASSETS AS PROPERTY?

A. An Analytical Framework

As noted, cryptoassets, products of the computer age, have generated their own demand for access without the help of the legal system – control of access to cryptoassets is

[21] J Crossley-Vaines, *Personal Property*, 4th edn (London, Butterworths, 1967) 14: 'choses in action … are not rights over intangibles; the intangible thing or *res incorporalis* is the right itself'.

[22] See eg *Leigh and Sillivan Ltd v Aliakmon Shipping Co Ltd* [1986] AC 785 (HL). Cf R Cooke, 'An Impossible Distinction' (1991) 107 *LQR* 46.

[23] See, in particular, New Zealand, where the test is simply whether it is 'fair, just and equitable' to impose a duty of care: *Carter Holt Harvey Ltd v Ministry of Education* [2016] NZSC 95, [2017] 1 NZLR 78 [14].

[24] P Watts, 'Unjust Enrichment: The Potion that Induces Well-meaning Sloppiness of Thought' [2016] *Current Legal Problems* 289. See too *Investment Trust Companies v HM Commissioners for Revenue v Customs* [2017] UKSC 29, [2018] AC 275 [51] (Lord Reed).

[25] But for a contrasting view, see S Worthington, 'The Disappearing Divide Between Property and Obligation: The Impact of Aligning Legal Analysis and Commercial Expectation' in S Degeling and J Edelman (eds), *Equity in Commercial Law* (Sydney, Lawbook, 2005).

initially assured through cryptography built upon game theory. However, for reasons too numerous to address, the idea that cryptoassets could operate in an extra-legal world was always quite unrealistic.[26] Quite apart from the frailties and limitations of the blockchain systems and technologies that lie behind most cryptoassets,[27] where demand for access to something exceeds supply, there will always be a role for the law. In the absence of perfect security, owners of scarce cryptoassets risk being deprived of them in much the same way as owners of chattels, through force or guile, even though their means of extra-legal security differ – possession in the case of chattels, cryptography in the case of cryptoassets.

Accordingly, it is plausible for the law to supplement extra-legal control of cryptoassets as it did extra-legal possession, albeit it should be noted that the extra-legal control of cryptoassets via private keys is, unlike extra-legal possession which is rivalrous, non-rivalrous since private keys, as information, are non-rivalrous. The Law Commission's suggestion that cryptoassets enjoy some sort of 'fragile rivalrousness'[28] is conceptually unsound. Rivalrousness is by definition an absolute concept, and in property law terms relates not to an object per se, but to control of the said object. Possession is rivalrous because A's possession of an object ipso facto means B is not in possession and vice versa. That it is the form of control that is protected rather than the object per se can be seen from the absence of any conception of trespass by merely viewing something.[29] All forms of control are imperfect – A may be dispossessed by B – but their imperfection has no impact on the rivalrousness of possession as a form of control. When so dispossessed, B is in possession of the object and by definition A is not. The Law Commission appears to have fallen into the mistake of concluding that just because possession is an imperfect *and* rivalrous form of control that other imperfect forms of control (such as via a private key in a decentralised system) can also be regarded as rivalrous.

Nor is possession a form of rivalrous control that means consumption of the subject matter entails destruction.[30] The consumption of a book does not entail its destruction in the way that the consumption of an ice-cream does, but the possession of both is equally rivalrous. Neither is it desirable to conceive of cryptoassets as transactional power.[31] Transactional power, or transmissibility, is an incident of ownership,[32] *not* its object. Where, it is submitted, the Law Commission is mistaken is in assuming that just because cryptoassets exist outside the law and have value, they must exist as property. However, both natural and legal persons engage in all manner of value exchanges on a daily basis, some involving property (eg sales), others not (eg the provision of services). It is by the legal recognition of cryptoassets as property

[26] For a summary, see KFK Low, 'Confronting Cryptomania: Can Equity Tame the Blockchain?' (2020) 14 *Journal of Equity* 240.

[27] For example, limitations in accessibility have meant that most small players have needed to use intermediaries to invest in cryptoassets.

[28] Law Commission, *Digital Assets* (Law Com CP 256, 2022) paras 10.100–10.114.

[29] See *Victoria Park Racing and Recreation Grounds Co Ltd v Taylor* (1937) 58 CLR 479.

[30] Law Commission, *Digital Assets* (Law Com CP 256, 2022) paras 2.62–2.69.

[31] D Fox, 'Digital Assets as Transactional Power' (2022) 1 *Journal of International Banking and Financial Law* 3.

[32] A Honoré, 'Ownership' in AG Guest (ed), *Oxford Essays in Jurisprudence* (Oxford, Oxford University Press, 1961) 120–21.

that legal rivalrousness is conferred upon the power relation between a subject and his cryptoassets. Until and unless the law does so, such a holder simply enjoys an imperfect and non-rivalrous form of control over the object. Whatever else it may be, it cannot be an object of property. Like other things in action, the object is the right itself (since it is the right that is legally rivalrous), not some other abstraction, whether conceived in purely technical terms or in sociotechnical terms (since, however conceived, such control is non-rivalrous). This does not detract, however, from the Law Commission's wider aim to reify cryptoassets. Such legal reification of cryptoassets would enable the law to apply simple, readily available solutions to the manifold problems that disputes over this novel class of property could present.

One everyday problem, death, suffices to demonstrate the inevitability of intervention by the legal system. Suppose Alice sells her house and acquires from the proceeds 20 bitcoin. She dies naming Bob as the executor of her will. She writes the private key for her bitcoin wallet on a piece of paper and tells Bob where he can find it when she dies. In the will she leaves all her bitcoin to her nephew Carlos. Alice then dies. Bob does not accept the role of executor and, using a photograph of the paper containing the private key, sells the bitcoin. Did Alice succeed in her desire for what should happen to her bitcoin after her death? Is Bob accountable to Carlos, and for what? Variations to the hypothetical can multiply the difficulties. Say Bob engages in transactions that result in his spouse, Daksha, 'holding' 10 bitcoin derived from the initial 20. Is Daskha accountable to Alice's estate or to Carlos? The donee of a gift that is causatively connected to a wrong is not usually accountable to the victim, merely by receiving, except through the rules that allow the following and tracing of 'property'.

B. The Case for Cryptoassets as Property

Returning to the main hypothetical, prima facie, only property is devisable by will.[33] A will that does nothing other than stipulate who is to make funeral arrangements is not a will and the expressed wishes are not by themselves legally effective.[34] It is possible, however, to string together from authority, mostly old, support for the proposition that trade secrets and perhaps some other forms of confidential information can be bequeathed by will, and otherwise assigned.[35] If that proposition holds water, then it would make sense at least to treat the private key enabling the disposition of cryptoassets as confidential information that can be bequeathed.

How much simpler it would be, however, to conclude that cryptoassets are a species of property. It should be accepted that the incidents of that conclusion might take some working out,[36] and one would reserve the possibility that some types of

[33] See *Re Berger* [1990] Ch 118 (CA) 129. The Wills Act 1837, s 3 provides for it to be lawful 'to devise, bequeath, or dispose of, by his will … all real estate and all personal estate which he shall be entitled to'.

[34] See *X v Y* [2018] EWHC 4026 (Ch) [50].

[35] See T Aplin, L Bently, P Johnson and S Malynicz, *Gurry on Breach of Confidence*, 2nd edn (Oxford, Oxford University Press, 2012) paras 8.105–8.119.

[36] For general discussion of the different incidents that might attach to intangible property compared to tangible, see B McFarlane and S Douglas, 'Property, Analogy and Variety' (2022) 42 *OJLS* 161.

cryptoasset might fall short of having the characteristics that warrant the status of property. Such a conclusion would trigger restitutionary responses, dispositions of property being restitution's core business.[37] In all events, we might regard as mildly catastrophic someone in the position of Bob in the above example being free to run off with the cryptoassets. Statute law would be a satisfactory solution only if it was made retrospective.

Necessity as the mother of invention is a cliché not unknown to property lawyers. One well-known example is Lord Bridge of Harwich's dictum in *Att-Gen of HK v Nai-Keung*:

> It would be strange indeed if something which is freely bought and sold and which may clearly be the subject of dishonest dealing which deprives the owner of the benefit it confers were not capable of being stolen. Their Lordships have no hesitation in concluding that export quotas in Hong Kong although not 'choses in action' are a form of 'other intangible property'.[38]

Other examples of the law adapting its concepts to meet market practices can be found. A joke of Gordon Pollock QC famously helped to persuade the Court of Appeal that the International Tin Council had legal personality, when he submitted: 'debeo ergo sum' (I owe therefore I am).[39]

No embarrassment arises, it is suggested, from the fact that the law follows practice rather than the other way round. Indeed, as commercial law (in particular, London's Commercial Court) demonstrates, that is often the case. The very fact that parties are purporting to grant and obtain access to something intangible raises the possibility of the law invoking property principles to resolve disputes that arise out of such dealing. This is not to say that one should stop short of further analysis. So, if (as is frequently said) confidential information is not usually property,[40] one needs to address what it is about cryptoassets that could justify a court declaring it a species of property when one essential, at least practical, aspect of its being the subject of market demand is the secrecy of the private key, itself just a combination of letters and numbers.

At least part of the answer is that the private key is only one component of a data system with many components. Not only does one need to add the concept of

[37] See n 23.

[38] *Att-Gen of HK v Nai-Keung* [1987] 1 WLR 1339 (PC) 1342. See too *New Era Printers and Publishers Ltd v Commissioner of Stamp Duties* [1927] NZLR 438 (SC) 444 (plea that trade secrets were property): 'it seems to me to be a contradiction in terms to assert that anything which is owned by one person and can be sold and transferred to another is not property, both within the legal and the popular understanding of that term'.

[39] See *JH Rayner (Mincing Lane) Ltd v Department of Trade and Industry* [1989] Ch 72 (CA) 173, affirmed [1990] AC 418 (HL). See also *Nightingale v Devisme* (1770) 5 Burr 2589, 2592; 98 ER 361, 363 (KB) (Lord Mansfield), in relation to shares in the East India Company: 'This is a new species of property, arisen within the compass of a few years.'

[40] See *Boardman v Phipps* [1967] 2 AC 46 (HL) 127 (Lord Upjohn); *Your Response Ltd v Datateam Business Media Ltd* [2014] EWCA Civ 281, [2015] QB 41. But cf *Lloyd v Google Inc* [2019] EWCA Civ 1599, [2020] QB 747 [46] (Vos C), reversed on appeal on other points: [2021] UKSC 50, [2022] AC 1217. For a detailed criticism of *Your Response*, see submissions for the account holders in *Ruscoe v Cryptopia Ltd*, available at www.grantthornton.co.nz/globalassets/1.-member-firms/new-zealand/pdfs/cryptopia/2020/c.submissions-of-counsel-for-account-holders-13-january-2020.pdf (accessed 29 December 2022).

the public key (another string of characters that enables open access to information from which one can determine the extent of the coinholder's stake in the totality of the, usually equal, units created by the system to which the private key is related) but there are also the cryptographic protocol-based system (usually deploying blockchain technology) and the many players who participate in its operation through the 'distributed ledger'.[41]

Collectively these elements are designed to promote every transaction on the system being definite, unique on the database and immutable. The fact that many types of cryptoasset do not achieve those ideals across every transaction would not be fatal to the system giving sufficient confidence to parties to want to trade using it. The data system as a whole demonstrates that we are concerned with much more than confidential information.[42] That is not to say that the law of breach of confidence could not also apply to the private key whilst it remained private.

However immune to suit the creators and operators of the data system may be to legal suit,[43] it seems fairly obvious that a legal system with jurisdiction should conclude of a functioning cryptoasset system that each holder of the cryptoasset defined by a public key has the legal right as against all parties outside the system to use the corresponding private key in order to cause the data system to recognise a new transaction involving the cryptoasset. That right is a species of intangible property.

This is so whether or not the private key remains secret; it is the right to cause the system to operate, not the key, that is the property. If the private key gets into the public domain, the right retains its value despite the loss of confidentiality.[44] It is simply that the value attached to the private key's use can be realised only once, by the first person to use it to give directions to the data system. If the party who uses the private key does so without the consent of the holder (or a party claiming through him or her) a legal wrong will have been committed. In contrast, with mere confidential information once the information is in the public domain legal protection generally ceases. Modern privacy law has modified that position somewhat, but then the subject-matter of privacy was never intended to be the subject of access, and hence the potential subject of property law, in the first place.[45]

[41] For a broad overview of the technicalities, see Low and Mik (n 10). See too J Sarra and L Gullifer, 'Crypto-Claimants and Bitcoin Bankruptcy: Challenges for Recognition and Realization' (2019) 28 *International Insolvency Review* 233; and D Fox, 'Cryptocurrencies in the Common Law of Property' in D Fox and S Green (eds), *Cryptocurrencies in Public and Private Law* (Oxford, Oxford University Press, 2019).

[42] See also UK Jurisdiction Taskforce, *Legal Statement on Cryptoassets and Smart Contracts* (2019) para 65: a cryptoasset is 'a conglomeration of public data, private key and system rules'.

[43] See *Tulip Trading Ltd v Bitcoin Association for BSV* [2022] EWHC 667 (Ch), [2022] 2 All ER (Comm) 624.

[44] In theory, the testator, or the estate, may still own the cryptocoins even if the private key is permanently lost, although there may be insurmountable difficulties in realising the property: see M Bridge, L Gullifer, K Low and G McMeel, *The Law of Personal Property*, 3rd edn (London, Sweet & Maxwell, 2021) para 8-057.

[45] See, however, the recognition of the possibility of licence-fee damages in *Gulati v MGN Ltd* [2015] EWCA Civ 1291, [2017] QB 149 [45]; and *Lloyd v Google LLC* (n 40) [142]. In *Dixon v R* [2015] NZSC 147, [2016] 1 NZLR 678 where the making of an unauthorised digital copy of CCTV footage was held, for the purposes of the Crimes Act 1961, to involve an invasion of property rights. For criticism, however, of this case, see Bridge et al (n 44) paras 8-016–8-017.

If the plight of the testator and her intended beneficiary in the hypothetical given above were not enough to convince one that property law needs to attach itself to cryptoassets, then the enormous amounts of fiat currency that have been invested in them around the world should prove compelling on that score. At its peak, the market capitalisation for cryptoassets reached US$3.2 trillion.[46] Those investments may yet prove a house of cards, and the use of market capitalisation to estimate the value of cryptoasset markets is highly dubious,[47] but in the meanwhile they cannot be ignored by the legal system. Regardless of their true value, real people have invested large sums of money – sometimes their life savings[48] – into these markets, and while the legal system is unable to protect them from poor investment decisions, they should not be simply cast aside where their losses stem from exploitation by others. Exacerbating the concerns is that the vast majority of investors do not engage directly with the currency but only through intermediaries in the form of cryptoasset exchanges. That in itself creates what economists call agency problems. Otherwise, investors in cryptoassets can be, and have been, the victims of frauds and misappropriations by third parties.[49] Investors can also become insolvent, raising a host of questions, including as to the rights of their secured and unsecured creditors, and where the investor is itself a cryptoasset exchange whether it held the cryptocoins on trust for its own subscribers. Property law has an important role to play in all such eventualities and treating cryptoassets as property greatly simplifies their resolution. Those are the honest parties. Property law is also a key part of the pursuit of dishonest investors,[50] including rogue states.

In these circumstances it is scarcely surprising that a growing body of case law around the Commonwealth shows that courts have been prepared to accept that cryptoassets, at least those before the court, are a form of property.[51] In most of the cases the issue was either conceded or determined as meeting the threshold necessary for pre-judgment remedies. In the New Zealand case *Ruscoe v Cryptopia Ltd (in Liq)*,[52]

[46] J Oliver and G Silverman, 'Bitcoin Tumble Leaves the Average Buyer in the Red', *Financial Times*, 16 June 2022, www.ft.com/content/27cd8e4b-8be4-4efc-875d-bf7671727e9c (accessed 29 December 2022).

[47] A Back, 'Why Market Cap Is a Meaningless & Dangerous Valuation Metric in Crypto Markets', *Medium*, 17 December 2018) https://medium.com/blockchain-review/why-market-cap-is-a-meaningless-dangerous-valuation-metric-in-crypto-markets-8deb78c50995 (accessed 29 December 2022).

[48] S Kale, '"I Put My Life Savings in Crypto": How a Generation of Amateurs Got Hooked on High-risk Trading', *The Guardian*, 19 June 2021, www.theguardian.com/lifeandstyle/2021/jun/19/life-savings-in-crypto-generation-of-amateurs-hooked-on-high-risk-trading (accessed 29 December 2022).

[49] Some investors have been coerced into buying cryptoassets by blackmailers: see *AA v Persons Unknown* [2019] EWHC 3556 (Comm), [2020] 4 WLR 35.

[50] cf R Anderson, I Shumailov and M Ahmed, 'Making Bitcoin Legal' in V Matyáš et al (eds), *Security Protocols XXVI. Security Protocols 2018. Lecture Notes in Computer Science*, vol 11286 (Cham, Springer, 2018).

[51] See *Vorotyntseva v Money-4 Ltd* [2018] EWHC 2596 (Ch) [13]; *Shair.Com Global Digital Services Ltd v Arnold* 2018 BCSC 1512 [15]; *B2C2 Ltd v Quione Pte Ltd* [2019] SGHC(I) 03 [142], but the issue was left open on appeal: [2020] SGCA(I) 02 [144]; *AA v Persons Unknown* (n 49); *Ion Science Ltd v Persons Unknown* (unreported EWHC (Ch), 21 December 2020, Butcher J) [11]; *Fetch.AI Ltd v Persons Unknown Category A* [2021] EWHC 2254 (Comm), 24 ITELR 566 [9]; *Mr Dollar Bill Ltd v Persons Unknown* [2021] EWHC 2718 (Ch) [10]; *Wang v Darby* [2021] EWHC 3054 (Comm), [2022] Bus LR 121 [55]; *Danisz v Persons Unknown* [2022] EWHC 280 (QB) [13]; *CLM v CLN* [2022] SGHC 46 [46].

[52] *Ruscoe v Cryptopia Ltd (in Liq)* [2020] NZHC 728, [2020] 2 NZLR 809. For discussion, see M Solinas, 'Investors' Rights in (Crypto) Custodial Holdings: *Ruscoe v Cryptopia Ltd*' (2020) 84 *MLR* 155; and KFK Low, 'Trusts of Cryptocurrency' (2021) 34 *Trust Law International* 191.

however, the issue was fully contested between investors in a failed cryptoasset exchange and the unsecured creditors of the company running the exchange. At its height the exchange had over 900,000 simultaneous account holders around the world and was hosting some 900 different types of cryptoasset. On the property issue, no attempt was made by the liquidators or counsel appointed to represent the unsecured creditors to differentiate amongst the types of asset the exchange was hosting.[53]

In *Cryptopia*, a much wider range of arguments for and against cryptoassets being regarded as a species of equitable property were canvassed than there is space for here.[54] One can note that the judgment attempts to explain how the criteria suggested by Lord Wilberforce in *National Provincial Bank Ltd v Ainsworth*[55] for testing the existence of a new species of property claim might be applied to cryptoassets. These criteria have been much criticised,[56] and it might be doubted whether Lord Wilberforce was intending to say anything profound, but it is suggested that with some necessary elaboration they are not without utility.[57] Gendall J also rejected an argument that cryptoassets of the type before him are neither tangible property nor a chose in action and accordingly fail to fit into the two exclusive categories of property suggested by Fry LJ in *Colonial Bank v Whinney*.[58] The Judge stated:

> On this, I am satisfied the argument here is in fact a red-herring. This is because cases which might be perceived to be problematic in this area are not about the limits of what can be recognised as 'property' but simply about the number of categories of 'property' one needs.[59]

In other words, the most that Fry LJ can be taken as saying is that the category of chose in action is broader than its litigation-oriented label might suggest. It can be inferred that if necessary the Judge would have concluded that the idea that there were only two basic categories of property was wrong. He stated:

> Indeed, it would be ironic that something that might be said to have more proprietary features than a simple debt is deemed not to be property at all when a simple debt qualifies.[60]

Gendall J went on to instance circumstances where courts have found a property interest to exist that is at least as difficult to categorise as cryptoassets. Prominent

[53] This is not explicit in the judgment but it is implicit.

[54] Many of the arguments are recorded in the judgment, and the written submissions of the parties are available at www.grantthornton.co.nz/update-for-cryptopia-account-holders-10-february-2020/ (accessed 29 December 2022). NB: Peter Watts was counsel appointed by the Court to represent the account holders. At the hearing, counsel for the unsecured creditors adopted a stronger stance against cryptoassets being property than had been taken in the written submissions.

[55] *National Provincial Bank Ltd v Ainsworth* [1965] AC 1175 (HL) 1247–48.

[56] See eg Gray (n 17); Low (n 62) 193–94.

[57] The criterion of 'permanence or stability', in particular, is not without content but it does not amount to much. One could own a butterfly that lived only for a day, or the snow on a mountain, such was held to be property in *State Insurance Ltd v Ruapehu Alpine Lifts Ltd* (1998) 10 ANZ Insurance Cases 74,434 (HC) (affirmed (1999) 10 ANZ Insurance Cases 74,946 (CA)).

[58] *Colonial Bank v Whinney* (1885) 30 Ch D 261 (CA) 285, noted in KFK Low, 'Bitcoins as Property: Welcome Clarity?' (2020) 136 *LQR* 345.

[59] *Ruscoe v Cryptopia Ltd (in Liq)* (n 52) [123]. See also *Dempsey v Traders' Finance Corp Ltd* [1933] NZLR 1258 (CA) 1296.

[60] *Ruscoe v Cryptopia Ltd (in Liq)* (n 52) [124].

amongst these was *Gwinnutt v George*,[61] where the England and Wales Court of Appeal held that a barrister's claim for fees for services which had been performed under the old legal regime where barristers had no contract with either solicitor or client was a property 'right'. It should be emphasised that the claim was not just unenforceable, there was no contract at all. It appears that the claim was more than moral but not actionable. The Judge also noted that a whole body of cases has held that exemptions from statutory bans can in principle be recognised as a form of property, even though the exemptions provide a *defence* to legal liability rather than a right to make a legal claim.[62] Ordinarily, it is the transferability of the rights to exemption that is key, but in other contexts even non-transferable rights have been found to be a species of property.[63] Certainly, it will not matter that the process of transfer involves the relevant regulatory authority cancelling the seller's right and granting the buyer a replacement right.[64]

It is useful to compare and contrast the relatively straightforward resolution of *Cryptopia* in New Zealand with the convoluted and confusing insolvency proceedings involving Mt Gox in Japan. Once the world's largest crypto exchange, Mt Gox lost some US$460 million in cryptoassets to hackers in the then largest crypto-heist of all time and became insolvent.[65] Despite this insolvency occurring some six years before that of Cryptopia's, the fallout from Mt Gox's insolvency appears only now to be reaching final resolution. Numerous legal actions arose in response to Mt Gox's insolvency. The first one was the well-known Tokyo District Court judgment on 5 August 2015, No 2014(wa)33320,[66] in which the Tokyo District Court held that bitcoins were not capable of being the object of ownership (or *shoyuuken* 所有権) because the Japanese Civil Code, modelled after the German Pandecten model,[67] had a strict definition of things (or *mono* 物). Where ownership is concerned, only corporeal things qualified as things. Since bitcoins lacked corporeality, they could not be owned in the sense of being the object of *shoyuuken* (所有権). Property as wealth, unlike the common law, is referred to by a different vocabulary, specifically *zaisan* (財産) or wealth. This meant that the customers of Mt Gox could not claim the

[61] *Gwinnutt v George* [2019] EWCA Civ 656, [2019] Ch 471.

[62] See *Att-Gen of HK v Nai-Keung* [1987] 1 WLR 1339 (PC) 1342 (export quotas); *Swift v Dairywise Farms Ltd* [2000] 1 WLR 1177 (Ch) 1185 (milk quota); *Commonwealth of Australia v WMC Resources Ltd* (1998) 194 CLR 1 (petroleum exploration licences, not being an interest in land); *Re Celtic Extraction* [2001] Ch 475 (CA) (waste disposal licences); and *Armstrong DLW GmbH v Winnington Networks Ltd* [2012] EWHC 10 (Ch), [2013] Ch 156 (carbon credits).

[63] See *Yanner v Eaton* [1999] HCA 53, (1999) 201 CLR 351 [85]. See also *Zim Properties Ltd v Procter* (1984) 58 Tax Cases 371 (Ch) (non-assignable chose an asset but perhaps not property); *Swift v Dairywise Farms Ltd* (n 62) 1185 (milk quota).

[64] See *Re Celtic Extraction Ltd* [2001] Ch 475 (CA) [33].

[65] R MacMillan 'The Inside Story of Mt Gox, Bitcoin's $460 Million Disaster', *Wired*, 3 March 2014, www.wired.com/2014/03/bitcoin-exchange/ (accessed 29 December 2022).

[66] A translation is available at www.law.ox.ac.uk/sites/files/oxlaw/mtgox_judgment_final.pdf (accessed 29 December 2022). See also KFK Low and Y-C Wu, 'The Characterization of Cryptocurrencies in East Asia' in Fox and Green (n 41) 215–18 and L Gullifer, M Hara and CW Mooney Jr, 'English Translation of the Mt Gox Judgment on the Legal Status of Bitcoin Prepared by the Digital Assets Project', *Oxford Business Law Blogs*, 11 February 2019, www.law.ox.ac.uk/business-law-blog/blog/2019/02/english-translation-mt-gox-judgment-legal-status-bitcoin-prepared (accessed 29 December 2022).

[67] cf G Gretton, 'Ownership and its Objects' (2007) 71 *Rabel Journal of Comparative and International Private Law* 802.

bitcoins held by the exchange on their behalf as their property and in so doing shield themselves from Mt Gox's insolvency. This led to another action which resulted in the perplexing Tokyo District Court judgment on 31 January 2018, No 2017(wa)10977. According to this later judgment, the right of a bitcoin holder was a 'personal right, that is not a monetary claim but a claim to demand a payment similar to a monetary claim … without specifying who this claim is against'.[68] The dispute was eventually resolved between the parties when, owing to the volatility of bitcoin's pricing, the hitherto insolvent Mt Gox found itself suddenly to be solvent after all.[69] The parallel bankruptcy proceedings came to be superseded by a civil rehabilitation plan proposed by the court-appointed trustee. The plan, first mooted in January 2021, and filed on 15 February 2021,[70] was approved by 99 percent of the rehabilitation creditors and a notice to that effect was published on 20 October 2021.[71] By this time, bitcoin was less than a month away from its all-time high price of US$67,567, which it reached on 8 November 2021, though the proposed distributions have not in fact been made at the time of writing.[72] Meanwhile, the crypto market convulsions of 2022 have caused bitcoin prices to plunge to US$16,500 at the time of writing[73] so it is unclear how satisfied the rehabilitation creditors remain with the concluded civil rehabilitation plan.

Interestingly, prior to this surprising development, yet another action had been filed on 19 February 2018 in the Tokyo District Court arguing that Mt Gox held its customers' bitcoins on trust for them. Although it seems to be accepted that bitcoins *can* be held on trust under Japanese law,[74] the concept being introduced in 1922,[75] it was less obvious that the trust argument would succeed under Japanese law in the absence of clear language to that effect in the contracts between Mt Gox and its customers and any segregation of assets. Although it is possible to *infer* a trust, given the general hostility to the idea of constructive trusts under Japanese trust law[76] and the ease with which inference can shade into construction/imputation,[77]

[68] KFK Low and M Hara, 'Cryptoassets and Property' in S van Erp and K Zimmermann (eds), *Edward Elgar Research Handbook on EU Property Law* (Cheltenham, Edward Elgar, forthcoming).

[69] A Jeffries, 'Inside the Bizarre Upside-Down Bankruptcy of Mt Gox', *The Verge*, 22 March 2018, www.theverge.com/2018/3/22/17151430/bankruptcy-mt-gox-liabilities-bitcoin (accessed 29 December 2022).

[70] T Franjkovic, 'Mt Gox Rehab Plan of Returning 141,686 BTC Gets Approved', *Yahoo! Finance*, 17 November 2021, https://finance.yahoo.com/news/mt-gox-rehab-plan-returning-152305328.html (accessed 29 December 2022).

[71] English translation of Notice of Confirmation Order of Rehabilitation Plan, available at www.mtgox.com/img/pdf/20211020_announcement_en.pdf (accessed 29 December 2022).

[72] W Pessarlay, 'Are the Missing Mt Gox BTC Billions on Their Way Home?', *be[in]crypto*, 28 March 2022, https://beincrypto.com/are-the-missing-mt-gox-billions-on-their-way-home/ (accessed 29 December 2022).

[73] J Rubin, 'First Mover Asia: Bitcoin Retreats Further Into the Gloom', *Coindesk*, 29 December 2022, www.coindesk.com/markets/2022/12/29/first-mover-asia-bitcoin-retreats-further-into-the-gloom/ (accessed 29 December 2022).

[74] K Takahashi, 'Cryptocurrencies Entrusted to an Exchange Provider: Shielded from the Provider's Bankruptcy?' in C Hugo (ed) *Annual Banking Law Update 2018: Recent Legal Developments of Special Interest to Banks* (Juta, 2018) 9.

[75] M Tamaruya, 'Japanese Law and the Global Diffusion of Trust and Fiduciary Law' (2018) 103 *Iowa Law Review* 2229; Y-C Wu, 'Trusts Reimagined: The Transplantation and Evolution of Trust Law in Northeast Asia' (2020) 68 *American Journal of Comparative Law* 441.

[76] Y-C Wu, 'Constructive Trusts in the Civil Law Tradition' (2018) 12 *Journal of Equity* 319.

[77] cf *Jones v Kernott* [2011] UKSC 53, [2012] 1 AC 776.

it was difficult to be confident of the outcome in the absence of precedent. The viability of this argument remains untested in relation to the Mt Gox insolvency due to the proposal and eventual conclusion of the civil rehabilitation plan. In the absence of clarity, in order to safeguard crypto exchange customers' interests, the Japanese National Diet amended the Payment Services Act to include a new Article 63-19-2(1), which provides:

> A person who has concluded a contract for the management of crypto-assets with a crypto-asset exchange service provider has the right to receive, in preference over other creditors, payments with regard to a claim for the transfer of crypto-assets that the person holds against the crypto-asset exchange service provider, for the return of the regulated crypto-assets (meaning the crypto-assets of the users of the crypto-asset exchange services that the crypto-asset exchange service provider manages separately from its own crypto-assets pursuant to the provisions of Article 63-11, paragraph (2) and the performance-guarantee crypto-assets).[78]

Despite the travails of Mt Gox's customers, it appears clear that bitcoins and other cryptoassets are property in the wider wealth or *zaisan* (財産) sense based on case developments in South Korea[79] and China,[80] whose civil codes share the Pandectist structure. Thus, as the South Korean case demonstrates, cryptoassets can be the subject of criminal confiscation. Such a classification is likely to provide a satisfactory resolution of some disputes relating to cryptoassets such as our example involving Alice, Bob, Carlos and Daksha, but not perhaps the insolvency context, which required parliamentary intervention in the form of amendment of the Payment Services Act.

C. The Case against Cryptoassets as Property

Absent a compelling reason, a legal solution that is consistent with how laypersons regard and treat an asset should be preferred over one that is not so consistent. This may not, however, always be possible or desirable. For example, although many laypersons envisage inter-bank transfers as transferring 'bank money' so that a recipient receives the 'money' transferred by the transferor, such a conception contradicts important legal rules and so cannot be so understood. This is because, in an *inter*-bank transfer, since bank money is simply a debt claim against a bank, one ends up with a different claim against a different bank than one started with. As Fox so elegantly explained, '[t]he chose in action representing the money transferred to the recipient's bank account is a distinct item of property from the chose in action representing the funds which were originally in the payer's account'.[81] What is transferred

[78] This unofficial translation is provided by the Japanese Law Translation Database System at www.japaneselawtranslation.go.jp/en/laws/view/3965#je_ch4sc4at1 (accessed 29 December 2022).

[79] Low and Wu (n 66) 212–14.

[80] ibid 228. See also 蓝鲸财经, '上海高院：比特币作为虚拟财产具有财产属性，受财产权法律规范的调', *Sina*, 5 May 2022, https://finance.sina.com.cn/money/lczx/2022-05-05/doc-imcwiwst5740140.shtml (accessed 29 December 2022).

[81] D Fox, *Property Rights in Money* (Oxford, Oxford University Press, 2008) para 5.05.

is value, not property,[82] as 'in fact nothing tangible or intangible is transferred'.[83] Another scenario in which it is not desirable to accommodate lay conceptions of transfer involve computer file transfers because lay conceptions do not accord with how computers actually work. As Bridge et al explain:

> What computer users perceive as a transfer of a digital file from one medium to another (or indeed one computer to another, accompanied as it sometimes is by an icon suggesting that something is being transferred) actually involves a two stage process: the first of which creates a duplicate of the file on the new medium, followed by the second, that deletes the file from the original medium.[84]

Indeed, deletion typically simply means 'transferring' the file to a different folder location, often the computer system's recycle bin. Even emptying a file from a computer system's recycle bin does not delete the actual data itself but simply rather removes the reference to the file from the computer system's master file table, the computer equivalent of a book's table of contents, which is what allows for data recovery even thereafter. Technically, it is only when this freed up space is written over with new data that the deleted data is irrecoverable and can truly be regarded as deleted. The metaphorical nature of file transfers is perhaps most obvious when we consider file transfers within the same medium. Assuming the medium has not been partitioned, it would comprise a single volume, which is '[a] logical unit of data storage'. A 'transfer' between two folders within the same volume entails no copying or deletion of data at all, which is why such 'transfers' are practically instantaneous. Such 'transfers' merely effect a change to the logical path location of the file.

Neither objection – inconsistency with other established legal conceptions or with operational facts – applies to the law's conceptualisation of cryptoassets as property in a manner consistent with lay conception and usage. Although on-chain transfers superficially resemble inter-bank transfers, particularly on account crypto-ledgers such as Ethereum (as opposed to transactional ledgers such as Bitcoin), it is not imperative (albeit admittedly possible[85]) to conceive of cryptoasset transfers in the same way as inter-bank transfers as entailing an extinction and regrant of separate and distinct assets. Cryptoassets not only need not be conceived of as claims against particular persons, they cannot be so conceived. Accordingly, it is unnecessary for the law to conceive of distinct ledger entries as distinct assets. Rather, it is entirely possible to conceptualise the right as one to maintain one's control over particular abstract value within a distributed ledger. Since control is effectively transferred upon a cryptoasset transfer, the law can simply conceive of what has been transferred as the right of control, which is not distinct but one and the same. Doing so greatly simplifies the resolution of disputes because it is consistent with the expectations of the majority of lay participants.

[82] ibid paras 5.25–5.32.

[83] B Geva, '"Bank Money": The Rise, Fall, and Metamorphosis of the "Transferable Deposit"' in D Fox and W Ernst (eds), *Money in the Western Legal Tradition: Middle Ages to Bretton Woods* (Oxford, Oxford University Press, 2016) 360.

[84] Bridge et al (n 44) para 8-011.

[85] See eg Fox (n 41) para 6.53.

This leaves objection on the grounds of public policy, in a manner not perhaps unlike why the courts are resistant to recognising property in human tissue. Although a case can perhaps be made in theory for similarly refusing proprietary status to cryptoassets,[86] we consider that it would be inappropriate for the judiciary to take the lead in doing so without any legislative action. Without Parliament acting to outlaw cryptoasset transactions, as for example China has done, it is inappropriate for the courts to deny them property status of their own accord on their own independent assessment of the public policy considerations. Indeed, this is a fortiori given the numerous pronouncements from various branches of the executive suggesting that cryptoassets have a significant role to play in the future of the British economy.[87] However wrongheaded this may be, it is not the role of the judiciary to contradict the other branches of government.

IV. CONCLUSION

Following the spectacular events of 2022, where one crypto participant after another imploded in quick succession,[88] cryptoasset markets have lost more than three-quarters of their capitalisation from their peak only half a year ago. At the time of writing, the cryptoasset market capitalisation had fallen below US$795 billion according to data from CoinMarketCap,[89] or more than 75 percent off its peak of more than US$3.2 trillion not so long ago. It remains to be seen if the recent collapse marks the death knell for a novel asset class. Cryptoassets have survived apparently catastrophic collapses before, most notably following the Mt Gox hack and the post-ICO boom in 2017. On each occasion, there has been a resurgence, sometimes following a long crypto winter, as was the case following the late 2017 crash. However, on each of the previous occasions, the macroeconomic conditions were different from that which the cryptoasset market faces today. Currently, major economies are facing quantitative tightening rather than quantitative easing and rising interest rates in the face of the worst inflation the world has seen in forty years. Regardless of whether cryptoassets prove to be a flash in the pan or the revolutionary innovation promised by enthusiasts, the courts will have to resolve disputes relating to them. Some early cases have already found their way to the courts and no doubt more will follow. These early cases treat cryptoassets as property because that is how their holders regard them and doing so allows the courts to resolve disputes in a manner as consistent with their expectations as possible. The recent collapse in the DeFi markets[90] also portend

[86] See J Grower, 'Better Left to the Legislature? Notes on a Nagging Doubt as to Whether Cryptoassets Are Property' in chapter 15 of this volume.

[87] J Oliver and P Stafford, 'Why the UK Joined the Race to Woo the Crypto Industry', *Financial Times*, 28 April 2022, www.ft.com/content/65eb9636-d253-42af-8526-50d70c41a19b (accessed 29 December 2022).

[88] E Nicole et al, 'All the Ways that Crypto Broke in 2022', *Bloomberg*, 22 December 2022, www.bloomberg.com/graphics/2022-crypto-contagion-from-bitcoin-to-FTX/ (accessed 29 December 2022).

[89] https://coinmarketcap.com/ (accessed 29 December 2022).

[90] A Samson et al, 'Bitcoin Tumbles After Crypto Lender Celsius Blocks All Redemptions', *Financial Times*, 14 June 2022, www.ft.com/content/25ac1667-9f50-4f16-b553-448ea4582613 (accessed 29 December 2022).

legal disputes that a property classification is well placed to aid in resolution. The only plausible objection to doing so is public policy, but in the absence of a ban on cryptoassets by Parliament, we suggest that it should not be open to the courts to deny cryptoassets property status, especially when the other branches of government have espoused enthusiasm for such assets.[91] Doing so will unnecessarily complicate the resolution of simple disputes such as that set out in this chapter or of the many disputes that arise out of the hacking and theft of cryptoassets, for which the law of property is uniquely suited. Even so, the pseudonymity[92] that is a feature of cryptoasset transactions means that the efficacy of the law is much diminished as tracing misappropriated cryptoassets often requires the use of professional services.[93] Should traced funds/assets under the control of a third party, usually an exchange, be insufficient to compensate a claimant for their losses, the matching of a pseudonym to an actual person is a painstaking process that is today mostly reserved for the worst abuses of cryptoassets such as the operation of an illegal marketplace for drugs and murder[94] or the trafficking of child pornography.[95] Nevertheless, the courts must do what they can to uphold the legitimate expectations of lawful (if misguided) users of cryptoassets until they are banned. It may not be sufficient but it is, if not quite necessary, at least expedient to recognise cryptoassets as property.

V. POSTSCRIPT

On 28 June 2023, the Law Commission published its Final Report in which it concluded, contrary to our analysis, that there was a need for a 'third' category of personal property.[96] In the Report, it disagreed with our criticism in this chapter of the Consultation Paper's discussion of fragile rivalrousness but without explaining how our analysis is mistaken.[97] The Law Commission insists that rivalrousness is a binary concept but that cryptoassets' rivalrousness is contingent on the existence of robust technical authentication and validation mechanisms as well as the continued active operation of the system by a network of participants.[98] If this is true, then surely cryptoassets are not absolutely rivalrous but only conditionally so? A key reason for the Law Commission's conclusion that a 'third' category of personal property was necessary for English law to accommodate cryptoassets was that 'crypto-tokens cannot be conceived of as rights or claims in themselves'[99] but it is not clear why this

[91] See n 86 above.

[92] Many cases are brought against 'persons unknown'.

[93] cf *AA v Persons Unknown* (n 49) [13].

[94] A Greenberg, 'Prosecutors Trace $13.4m in Bitcoins from the Silk Road to Ulbricht's Laptop', *Wired*, 29 January 2015, www.wired.com/2015/01/prosecutors-trace-13-4-million-bitcoins-silk-road-ulbrichts-laptop/ (accessed 29 December 2022).

[95] A Greenberg, 'Inside the Bitcoin Bust that Took Down the Web's Biggest Child Abuse Site', *Wired*, 7 April 2022, www.wired.com/story/tracers-in-the-dark-welcome-to-video-crypto-anonymity-myth/ (accessed 29 December 2022).

[96] Law Commission, *Digital Assets: Final Report* (Law Com No 412, 2023).

[97] ibid para 4.34.

[98] ibid para 4.33.

[99] ibid paras 3.32, 3.34.

is so. So long as the law does not recognise them as property, this is certainly true,[100] but if the law chooses to accommodate them *as* property, it must do so through the creation of rights. The Law Commission's search for a patchwork of causes of action[101] to protect these apparently non-rights-based properties necessarily entails the creation of rights, albeit viewed in reverse as wrongs and with any emergent rights obscured from view. It is also unfortunate that the Law Commission's Final Report does not consider any of the policy criticisms to accommodating cryptoassets as property,[102] especially in light of the catastrophic events of 2022, which curiously also go unmentioned.

[100] cf R Stevens, 'Crypto Is Not Property' (2023) 139 *LQR* 615.
[101] Law Commission, *Digital Assets* (n 96) Chapter 9.
[102] cf Stevens (n 100) and Grower (n 86).

15

Better Left to the Legislature? Notes on a Nagging Doubt Over the Legal Recognition of Cryptoassets

JULIUS AW GROWER*

I. INTRODUCTION – QUESTIONS OF 'CAN', 'SHOULD' AND 'IS'

In this jurisdiction, if something is *capable* of being property ('can'), and if it *should* be property ('should'), then at least in the sense that its 'owner' will be afforded the benefit of what Harris termed 'legal trespassory rules',[1] it *will* be recognised as property ('is'). Applying this syllogism to the subject at hand, then, one might say that, to determine whether cryptoassets *are* property ('is'), it is first necessary to answer in the affirmative each of the two logically prior questions of whether they are *capable* of being property ('can') and whether they *should* be property ('should'). Indeed, it follows from this that, even if cryptoassets are *capable* of being property,[2] were it determined that they should *not* be, then it is certain that they would *not* be recognised as such.

The specific focus of this chapter is on what has just been called the 'should' question. More specifically, it will examine the important preliminary issue of which branch of our government is entitled to provide an answer to it, at least in relation to cryptoassets. Its conclusion will be unequivocal and in favour of the legislature. Now, for the avoidance of doubt, I am essentially ambivalent as to whether or not cryptoassets *should* be recognised as property. Consequently, what is to come should not be read as disclosing any particular view on that matter either way. My aim is solely to argue that that debate is one which can only be resolved by Parliament.

* Thanks are due to David Fox, Peter Watts, Kelvin Low, Martin Dixon, Alexander Waghorn, Rory Gregson, Poorna Mysoor, and Robert Stevens. Any errors are solely my own.

[1] JW Harris, *Property and Justice* (Oxford, Oxford University Press, 1996) 5.

[2] A matter upon which there appears to be much agreement. See eg M Solinas, 'Bitcoiners in Wonderland Lessons from the Cheshire Cat' [2019] *LMCLQ* 433; UK Jurisdictional Taskforce, 'Legal statement on Cryptoassets and Smart Contracts' (November 2019); Law Commission, *Digital Assets* (Law Com CP No 256, 2022); H Liu, 'Title, Control and Possession in the Digital Asset World' [2022] *LMCLQ* 597; R Goode 'What Is Property?' (2023) 139 *LQR* 1; and P Watts and KF Low, 'The Case for Cryptoassets as Property' in chapter 14 of this volume.

Moreover, I believe this is something of an urgent point to make. After all, although there is always a risk of exaggerating the impact of interlocutory decisions, it is undeniable that in recent years there have been cases in which judges have decided, or at least taken it as read, that it *is* within their power to decide whether or not cryptoassets *should* be property. This is because, without more, the courts have started to treat cryptoassets *as* property and, consistently with this chapter's opening syllogism, the only way in which that could have occurred is if they had previously (if only implicitly) answered the 'should' question favourably. It therefore seems that a significant transgression of the normal constitutional allocation of powers is in progress. What is more, for once, it is being effected by the judiciary.[3]

In addition to raising a public law storm cone, this chapter is intended to serve a second useful purpose. Regardless of one's views on the legal status of cryptoassets, what is to come should be of interest to any private lawyer seeking to understand the hitherto self-declared limits of the courts' law-making abilities. Those hard edges, which must be ever-present in the minds of both judges and litigants, reflect a range of concerns deriving from the nature and function of our adversarial courts system and its place within the wider structure of English and Welsh government. Indeed, for that reason, they also provide an important set of insights into the judicial mind.

II. THE BASIS OF MY CONCERN – A QUESTION OF COMPETENCE

I must begin with the cases. After all, they are the proximate cause for my concern over the legal recognition of cryptoassets. The most prominent of the interlocutory decisions referred to above is that of Bryan J in *AA v Persons Unknown*.[4] He held that, at least for the purpose of granting an interim proprietary injunction, 'crypto currencies *are* a form of property capable of being the subject of [such an order]'.[5] Another impactful judgment has been that of HHJ Pelling QC (sitting as a Deputy Judge of the High Court) in *Fetch.AI Ltd v Persons Unknown*.[6] When considering whether or not to grant permission for the claimant to serve outside the jurisdiction, his Lordship held that the contention that cryptoassets '*are* to be regarded as property for the purposes of English law'[7] involved a serious issue to be tried. It is true, of course, that these are not the most radical statements of law it is possible to imagine. However, in their own way each tends towards a distinct wider conclusion.

[3] A classic example of attempted *legislative* overreach can be found in *Anisminic Ltd v Foreign Compensation Commission* [1969] 2 AC 147 (HL). A more modern example comes from *R (Privacy International) v Investigatory Powers Tribunal* [2019] UKSC 22, [2020] AC 491.

[4] *AA v Persons Unknown* [2019] EWHC 3556 (Comm), [2020] 4 WLR 36. See, alternatively, *Vorotyntseva v Money-4 Ltd* [2018] EWHC 2598 (Ch); *Robertson v Persons Unknown* (unreported), 15 July 2019 (Commercial Court); *Toma v Murray* [2020] EWHC 2295 (Ch); *Ion Science Ltd v Persons Unknown* (unreported), 21 December 2020 (Commercial Court); *Mr Dollar Bill Ltd v Persons Unknown* [2021] EWHC 2718 (Ch); *Danisz v Persons Unknown* [2022] EWHC 280 (QB).

[5] *AA* (n 4) [61] (emphasis added).

[6] *Fetch.AI Ltd v Persons Unknown* [2021] EWHC 2254 (Comm), 24 ITELR 566. See, alternatively, *Tulip Trading Ltd v Bitcoin Association For BSV* [2022] EWHC 667 (Ch), [141], [2022] 2 All ER (Comm) 624.

[7] *Fetch.AI* (n 6) [9] (emphasis added).

Indeed, for this reason it is worth noting that the courts in other common law jurisdictions have gone further still on this issue. In the New Zealand case of *Ruscoe v Cryptopia Ltd*,[8] for example, Gendall J concluded that all of the various cryptocurrencies which formed the subject matter of the dispute before him were '"property" within the definition outlined in s 2 of the [New Zealand] Companies Act and … probably more generally'.[9] He also said that, 'being property', those digital assets were 'capable of forming the subject matter of a trust'.[10] To his credit, his Honour *did* identify that various 'public policy arguments' could be raised in objection to his holding, including the fact that 'at least some types of cryptocurrency are used by criminals for the transmission of funds across borders in order to pursue criminal activity and as a means of laundering the proceeds of past criminal activity'.[11] Yet strikingly he also made clear that he thought himself competent to evaluate the weight of such arguments. He thus stated:

> Any failure by the general law to recognise cryptocurrencies as property, as I see it, would have little effect in reducing potential criminal activity.[12]

For a variety of reasons, I am deeply uneasy about conclusions such as this. I do not believe that the judges of England and Wales have the competence to reach them, and that, as and when they do (or, at least, as and when they purport to), they engage in activity which is beyond the scope of their offices. This means they should not behave in that way.[13]

A. Two Types of Competence

If one considers what competence could mean in the judicial context, two alternative definitions come to mind. The first relates to the question of whether the courts possess the appropriate procedures and expertise to make a particular decision. For clarity's sake, I will call this *skills competence*. The second relates to the idea that, in this jurisdiction, it is constitutionally apposite for the courts (rather than the legislature or the executive) to make a particular decision. This can be labelled *institutional competence*. Ultimately, it is not hard to find examples of the Supreme Court/House of Lords refusing to decide cases in a certain way on the basis that they lacked either

[8] *Ruscoe v Cryptopia Ltd* [2020] NZHC 728, [2020] 2 NZLR 209.

[9] ibid [133].

[10] ibid [133]. Of course, insofar as this holding involves an implicit assertion that property rights are the only type of right which is capable of being held on a trust, it should be rejected. It is plain that at least some personal rights can also form the subject matter of a trust. See, eg, *Tomlinson v Gill* (1756) Amb 330, 27 ER 221.

[11] *Ruscoe* (n 8) [129].

[12] ibid [129].

[13] For a less conservative view on judicial activism, albeit one not expressed in relation to the question of whether cryptoassets should be recognised as property, see A Burrows, 'Challenges for Private Law in the Twenty-First Century' in K Barker, K Fairweather and R Grantham (eds), *Private Law in the 21st Century* (Oxford, Hart Publishing, 2017) 30–32, repeating points made in A Burrows, 'The Relationship between Common Law and Statute in the Law of Obligations' (2012) 128 *LQR* 232, 247–48.

the skills competence or the institutional competence to do so. Indeed, on some occasions the judges have concluded that they lack both.

Beginning with skills competence, consider the refusal of the Supreme Court in *Berrisford v Mexfield Housing Co-operative Ltd*[14] to abolish the rule which requires that a lease exists for a certain term. One reason it provided was that such a change would affect a range of different people with a range of different interests, none of whom were before the court, and who ought to be consulted before such a step was taken. In other words, the court recognised that it did not have the ability to do that itself. Here is an illustrative part of Lord Dyson's judgment:

> There is much to be said in favour of getting rid of the rule. But I think that, rather than the court introducing a change to such a fundamental tenet of the law of landlord and tenant, it would be better if this were done by Parliament after full consultation of interested parties of the kind that is routinely undertaken by the Law Commission.[15]

A similar point was made by Lord Mance in *Cavendish Square Holding BV v Makdessi*.[16] In that case, his Lordship refused to abolish the much-criticised penalties doctrine on the basis that doing so would involve acting 'without the benefit of the sort of research into the consequences and merits of such a step, which the Law Commission or Parliament would undertake before venturing upon it'.[17] As indicated by Lord Hoffmann in *OBG Ltd v Allan*,[18] the concern underlying such reasoning seems to be that, without such information being available to the relevant decision-maker, the risk of them making a choice which imports unforeseen and undesirable consequences is too high.[19] Indeed, this point was echoed by Lord Neuberger in *R (on the application of Prudential plc) v Special Commissioner of Income Tax*,[20] in which the Supreme Court refused to extend legal advice privilege from lawyers to accountants who provide legal advice to their clients. He stated:

> The general implications of extending the generally understood limits of [legal advice privilege] could clearly have significant implications, which, at least in my view, would be very difficult to identify, let alone to assess. [It] may well have significant consequences which should be considered through the legislative process, with its wide powers of inquiry and consultation.[21]

At base, the problem stems from the fact that the courts of England and Wales employ an adversarial procedure and, although the presence of interveners is at least in some

[14] *Berrisford v Mexfield Housing Co-operative Ltd* [2011] UKSC 52, [2012] 1 AC 955. See, alternatively, *Launchbury v Morgans* [1973] AC 127 (HL) 151 (refusing to adopt Lord Denning MR's so-called 'family car' doctrine); *Rhone v Stephens* [1994] 2 AC 310 (HL) 321 (refusing to overrule *Austerberry v Oldham Corporation* (1885) 29 Ch D 750 (CA)); *Morris-Garner v One Step (Support) Ltd* [2018] UKSC 20, [2019] AC 649 [139]–[142] (refusing to depart from the decision in *Wrotham Park Settled Estates v Hertsmere Borough Council* [1993] 2 EGLR 15 (CA)).

[15] *Berrisford* (n 14) [115].

[16] *Cavendish Square Holding BV v Makdessi* [2015] UKSC 67, [2016] AC 1172.

[17] ibid [163].

[18] *OBG Ltd v Allan* [2007] UKHL 21, [2008] 1 AC 1.

[19] ibid [99].

[20] *R (on the application of Prudential plc) v Special Commissioner of Income Tax* [2013] UKSC 1, [2013] 2 AC 185.

[21] ibid [63].

contexts on the rise, they usually hear only from the actual parties to the cases they are seized of. No one in particular is arguing specifically for any wider interests, let alone the so-called public interest. They are thus fundamentally unsuited to being the place where decisions that require the expression of a range of different views and ideas in advance of them being taken are made.[22] In contrast, Parliament, with its two chambers and the benefit of the various stages of consultation and scrutiny which proposed legislation necessarily goes through, 'is better suited … to [weighing] up competing interests'.[23]

A second form of skills competence concern can also be found in the cases. This relates to the nature of the rules of law generated by the courts in the course of the judicial process compared to those created by the legislature. Generally speaking, the judges recognise that while on a case-to-case basis they *are* able to produce fine-grained legal standards, more widely they can only really provide broad-brush guidance. In contrast, through the medium of a statute, Parliament can produce large blocks of consistently detailed regulation. There are therefore cases in which the courts refuse either to create a new law or to develop an old law on the basis that the sort of rules required to address a particular legal problem are those they are incapable of promulgating.[24] A good example of this habit in action comes from Lord Hoffmann's speech in *Wainwright v Home Office*.[25] In it, his Lordship refused to introduce 'a general tort of invasion of privacy' on the basis that the task of satisfactorily articulating the scope of an individual's 'right' to privacy required 'a detailed approach which [could] be achieved only by legislation rather than the broad brush of common law principle'.[26] Similar sentiments were expressed by Lord Goff in *Cambridge Water Co Ltd v Eastern Counties Leather plc*.[27] There, in the course of partially collapsing the rule in *Rylands v Fletcher* into the law of private nuisance, he stated:

> As a general rule, it is more appropriate for strict liability in respect of operations of high risk to be imposed by Parliament, than by the courts. If such liability is imposed by statute, the relevant activities can be identified, and those concerned can know where they stand. Furthermore, statute can where appropriate lay down precise criteria establishing the incidence and scope of such liability.
>
> … Given that so much well-informed and carefully structured legislation is now being put in place for this purpose, there is less need for the courts to develop a common law principle to achieve the same end, and indeed it may well be undesirable that they should do so.[28]

[22] See also the dissent of Brandeis J in the United States Supreme Court case of *International News Service v Associated Press*, 248 US 215 (1918), 262–67. I am grateful to Ben McFarlane for bringing this judgment to my attention.

[23] *Fearn v Board of Trustees of the Tate Gallery* [2020] EWCA Civ 104, [2020] Ch 621 [84]. See also Lord Reed in *R (on the application of Prudential plc)* (n 20) [102], noting that Parliament has powers of 'consultation and consideration *of a wider character*' than the courts (emphasis added).

[24] See, again, the dissent of Brandeis J in *International News* (n 22) 262–67.

[25] *Wainwright v Home Office* [2003] UKHL 53, [2004] 2 AC 406. See, alternatively, *R (on the application of Prudential plc)* (n 20) [66] (refusing to extend legal advice privilege from lawyers to accountants); and note also *Radmacher v Granatino* [2010] UKSC 42, [2011] 1 AC 534 [133]–[137], where Baroness Hale said that, for the same reason, she would refuse to make various changes to the law on prenuptial agreements.

[26] *Wainwright* (n 25) [33].

[27] *Cambridge Water Co Ltd v Eastern Counties Leather plc* [1994] 2 AC 264 (HL).

[28] ibid 305.

Turning to institutional competence, it is necessary to bear in mind the often-unexpressed but entirely fundamental point that while the legislature is elected, the judiciary are not. This means that the rules created by Parliament have direct democratic legitimacy, while those promulgated by the courts lack it.[29] It also means that judges are not as free as parliamentarians to make certain policy choices which are rightly the preeminent domain of *elected* officials.[30] The legislature is therefore justified in taking a wider range of decisions over what the law should be than the judiciary.[31]

It is true, of course, that the doctrine of parliamentary sovereignty means that the legislature can, if it wishes, overturn any particular judicial decision (or part of such a decision) it wants to.[32] What is more, for that reason, its enduring acquiescence with the vast majority of judge-made law might provide those rules with some indirect democratic legitimacy. Nevertheless, it is still the case that on a day-to-day basis a judge might well develop the law in such a way that alters the legal rights and obligations of every citizen, without ever having been vested with any popular authority to do so.[33]

Perhaps the most obvious instance of cases in which the courts recognise and respond to their limitations as rule creators, namely, their lack of institutional competence, are those in which they identify that a certain proposed legal development would have a substantial macroeconomic impact within the jurisdiction. In those circumstances, judges consistently say that, regardless of how beneficial any particular change in the law could be, it is for Parliament to set the mood music and for them to dance along. In *Cavendish Square Holding BV v Makdessi*,[34] for example, several members of the Supreme Court declined to extend the scope of the penalties doctrine to cover clauses which apply even in the absence of a breach of contract on the basis that to do so would involve affecting a substantial change to our settled economic

[29] As Baroness Hale has put it, extra-judicially, 'judges lack the seal of approval from the people that elected politicians enjoy'. See B Hale, 'Fifty Years of the Law Commissions: The Dynamics of Law Reform Now, Then and Next' in M Dyson, J Lee and SW Stark (eds), *Fifty Years of the Law Commissions* (Oxford, Hart Publishing, 2016) 23.

[30] Note, though, that I do not agree with Lord Hope's remark, made in *R (on the application of Prudential plc)* (n 20), [82], that 'if there are reasons of public policy for making [a certain] change, the matter should be left to Parliament'. There will inevitably be *some* public-policy-based reason either for or against every single potential legal development which a court might be asked to affect. Likewise, there *are* some public policy choices which judges *are* competent to make. Consider, for example, that involved in deciding whether a tortious duty of care should be recognised in a novel situation, on which see *Home Office v Dorset Yacht Co Ltd* [1970] AC 1004 (HL) 1059. The question is therefore as to where to draw the line.

[31] See also J Stapleton, *Three Essays on Torts* (Oxford, Oxford University Press, 2021) 16: 'One strength of legislative lawmaking … is the legitimacy flowing from its electoral mandate, which is especially valuable in the context of highly controversial issues.'

[32] See eg Compensation Act 2006, s 3, overturning part of the decision in *Barker v Corus (UK) plc* [2006] UKHL 20, [2006] 2 AC 572, at least with respect to mesothelioma claims, or Dissolution and Calling of Parliament Act 2022, s 3, overturning part of the decision in *R (on the application of Miller) v Prime Minister* [2019] UKSC 41, [2020] AC 373.

[33] As Lord Reed noted in *R (on the application of UNISON) v Lord Chancellor* [2017] UKSC 51, [2020] AC 689 [69]: 'To say that [*Donoghue v Stevenson*] was of no value to anyone other than Mrs Donoghue and the lawyers and judges involved in the case would be absurd.'

[34] *Cavendish Square Holding BV* (n 16).

order. Quoting from Hoffmann LJ's judgment in *Else (1982) Ltd v Parkland Holdings Ltd*,[35] Lords Neuberger and Sumption stated:

> We agree … that, while it is true that the question [of] whether the penalty rule applies may sometimes turn on 'somewhat formal distinction[s]', this can be justified by the fact that the rule[,] 'being an inroad upon freedom of contract which is inflexible[,] … ought not to be extended', at least by judicial, as opposed to legislative, decision-making.[36]

A similar point was made by Lord Hodge.[37] Indeed, in the recent case of *Pakistan International Airline Corp v Times Travel (UK) Ltd*,[38] the same judge returned to this idea to reject any suggestion that the Supreme Court should introduce a general doctrine of inequality of bargaining power.[39]

A final illustration of this sort of judicial reasoning comes from *OBG Ltd v Allan*.[40] There, several of the judges accepted that they had no business in attempting to draw a line 'between fair and unfair trade competition' and that 'such things are better left to Parliament'.[41] Baroness Hale provided a clear explanation as to why. Such decisions, she observed, 'can involve major economic and social questions which are often politically sensitive and require more complicated answers than the courts can devise'.[42]

A second type of decision the courts are persistently reluctant to take are those that would have a major impact on public finances. They understand that they do not have the popular authority to interfere so deeply in the workings of public services that they end up making spending decisions which are rightly those of elected officials. They are thus sensitive to the risk of 'bankrupting' the police or the National Health Service 'overnight'. As Lord Hoffmann observed in *Stovin v Wise*,[43] 'the law must recognise the need to protect the public exchequer as well as private interests'.[44] In addition, in *Gregg v Scott*,[45] one of the reasons the same judge gave for refusing to recognise the actionability of a so-called 'loss of a chance' (at least in cases involving medical negligence) was that 'it would have enormous consequences for insurance companies *and the National Health Service*'.[46] 'Any such change [in the law]', he added, 'should be left to Parliament.'[47] Although parts of it have since been criticised,[48] another good example of this sort of reasoning comes from Lord Keith's speech in *Hill v Chief Constable of West Yorkshire*.[49] There, his Lordship spoke

[35] *Else (1982) Ltd v Parkland Holdings Ltd* [1994] 1 BCLC 130 (CA) 145.
[36] *Cavendish Square Holding BV* (n 16) [43].
[37] ibid [241].
[38] *Pakistan International Airline Corp v Times Travel (UK) Ltd* [2021] UKSC 40, [2023] AC 101.
[39] ibid [26].
[40] *OBG Ltd* (n 18) 21.
[41] ibid [306]. See also [56] (Lord Hoffmann).
[42] ibid [306].
[43] *Stovin v Wise* [1996] AC 923 (HL).
[44] ibid 934.
[45] *Gregg v Scott* [2005] UKHL 2, [2005] 2 AC 176.
[46] ibid [90] (emphasis added).
[47] ibid.
[48] See eg *Michael v Chief Constable of South Wales* [2015] UKSC 2, [2015] AC 1732 [36]–[44].
[49] *Hill v Chief Constable of West Yorkshire* [1989] AC 53 (HL).

against imposing a duty of care on the police with respect to their investigation of crimes on the basis that, amongst other things:

> A great deal of police time, trouble and expense might be expected … to be put into the preparation of [a] defence to [any new] action [brought against them] and [the] result would be a significant diversion of police manpower and attention from their most important function, that of the suppression of crime.[50]

A second constitutional fundamental pertinent to the question of whether or not a court has institutional competence to make a certain decision is connected to the fact that, although it is subject to important qualifications, the doctrine of precedent requires that the courts have regard to previous judicial decisions. As Cross and Harris explain: '[a] judge [in any particular] case may be obliged to decide it in the same way as that in which [a relevant] previous case was decided, *even if he can give a good reason for not doing so*'.[51] In general, then, it is not open to the judiciary to make truly fundamental changes to the law, even if it wishes to. Further, it is not surprising that there are cases in which the courts have declined to make a proposed change on the basis that it would involve too big an alteration to existing doctrine and so was one for which they did not have the capacity. Recognising and responding to their limitations as rule creators, they identify that such developments are properly the province of Parliament. Here, once again, is part of Lord Hoffmann's speech in *Gregg v Scott*:

> A wholesale adoption of possible rather than probable causation as the criterion of liability would be so radical a change in our law as to amount to a legislative act.[52]

Further examples come from *White v Chief Constable of South Yorkshire*[53] and *Launchbury v Morgans*.[54] In *White*, although unhappy with the state of the law on the recovery of damages for pure psychiatric harm suffered by the secondary victims of negligence, Lord Steyn refused either 'to wipe out [any possible] recovery' or 'to abolish all the special limiting rules applicable to [it]' on the basis that to do so 'would be contrary to precedent'.[55] 'It must be left to Parliament to undertake the task of radical law reform',[56] he added. In *Launchbury*, Lord Salmon refused hold that 'the owner of a family car should be held responsible for the negligent driving of any member of [his] household whom he allows to drive it'. This was because, while his Lordship acknowledged that 'it is an important function of [the courts] to develop and adapt the common law to meet the changing needs of time', the proposed development before him constituted 'such a radical and far-reaching departure from accepted principle that it [seemed] to smack of naked legislation'.[57]

[50] ibid 63.
[51] R Cross and JW Harris, *Precedent in English Law*, 4th edn (Oxford, Oxford University Press, 1991) 4 (emphasis added).
[52] *Gregg* (n 45) [90].
[53] *White v Chief Constable of South Yorkshire* [1999] 2 AC 455 (HL).
[54] *Launchbury v Morgans* [1973] AC 127 (HL).
[55] *White* (n 53) 500.
[56] ibid 500.
[57] *Launchbury* (n 54) 151.

B. The Debate Over Cryptoassets

In light of the above, my concern over whether it is for the courts, rather than a different branch of the state, to recognise that cryptoassets *should* be property may well be coming into focus. If, in order to satisfactorily answer the 'should' question in relation to any particular thing, a decision-maker will need to consider factors or produce rules they do not have the skills to properly analyse or create, or if the result of their decision would be to bring about a change in the law that it is not constitutionally appropriate for them to affect, *then they should not do so*. Judges should only take those decisions that they are genuinely competent to take. Furthermore, it seems to me that this is entirely true for the courts vis-à-vis cryptoassets. Along with being new and complex, they are controversial and too many aspects of that controversy require the legislature's consideration in order to satisfactorily resolve.

As noted, above, in his decision in the New Zealand case of *Ruscoe v Cryptopia Ltd*,[58] Gendall J identified that various 'public policy arguments' could be raised in objection to his holding that all of the cryptocurrencies which formed the subject matter of the dispute before him were '"property" within the definition outlined in s 2 of the [New Zealand] Companies Act and … probably more generally'.[59] Yet it is also true that his Honour only cared to consider one of them, stating:

> It is widely known that at least some types of cryptocurrency are used by criminals for the transmission of funds across borders in order to pursue criminal activity and as a means of laundering the proceeds of past criminal activity.[60]

Unfortunately, there are at least two problems with this. The first is the fact that the judge thought that he was competent to evaluate this point's weight at all. The second is the fact that he engaged in such an evaluation without recourse to any properly curated evidence. His Honour appears to have taken judicial notice of various facts surrounding cryptoassets[61] and did not hear any serious argument over them.[62] In my view, it would be entirely inappropriate for a judge in this jurisdiction to act in the same way.

It must be true that cryptoassets are not *exclusively* the domain of criminals. Moreover, this means that Gendall J was surely correct to observe that 'cryptocurrencies have also become popular with honest people as a method of effecting payments and of investing'.[63] However, there is clearly *some* nefarious use also going on.[64]

[58] *Ruscoe* (n 8).
[59] ibid [133].
[60] ibid.
[61] See ibid [133]: 'The traditional banking sector is itself widely reported to be already using block chain technology and to be planning to create trading platforms for cryptocurrencies.' He then cited an article on bloomberg.com.
[62] See ibid [131].
[63] ibid [133].
[64] Chainanalysis's 2022 *Crypto Crime Report* (available online at go.chainalysis.com/2022-Crypto-Crime-Report.html (accessed 26 August 2023)) indicates that in 2021 approximately US$24bn of cryptoassets were transferred for criminal purposes. This figure can be obtained by multiplying the total value of all the cryptoasset transactions done in that period (approximately $15.8trillion) with the proportion of those transactions which Chainanalysis identified as involving illicit addresses (0.15%). Note, however, that other

As a result, where the balance of convenience lies in relation to their legal recognition is a political and economic question which will require a range of submissions from different and potentially competing perspectives to properly determine. Deterring and/or preventing crime *is* a legitimate reason for shaping the rules of private law as they apply to financial instruments. For example, the reason why under the Bills of Exchange Act 1882 a cheque must be signed by its would-be transferor in order for it to be effectively endorsed is to discourage theft or fraud. Plainly this formality requirement comes with a cost: it reduces the transferability of cheques. But the legislature has decided that this is a price worth paying.

In the end, hard data as to the financial and social impact of crimes connected to or underpinned by the use of cryptoassets need to be collated and properly scrutinised before a decision as to whether or not cryptoassets *should* be property is taken. Submissions from the Ministry of Justice and/or various law enforcement agencies (such as the National Crime Agency) also need to be obtained, as do analyses from the Bank of England and/or various other national and international economic institutions. What is more, the body competent to assess this information and make major economic and social choices about the economy and the risk of crime is surely the legislature not the judiciary. The courts have no real mechanisms for procuring information of the kind just described and, crucially, they have no way of recreating the opportunities for input which the parliamentary process involves, not least given the major role that government plays in it. Instead, they rely on the narrowly self-interested and often tactically focused submissions of the parties before them to determine issues. This may be fine for deciding between two competing interpretations of a contract, but not for at least some more impactful choices. At one point in his judgment in *Cryptopia*, Gendall J stated: 'In my view, honest commercial developments may very well be hindered by a failure of the general law to recognise cryptoassets as property.'[65] Yet it seems to me that for a judge to take such a decision as his Honour did on this sort of basis is entirely unacceptable. It is, in essence, for him to fly blind.

Along with their growing popularity amongst criminals, another deeply significant feature of cryptoassets – and in particular those, such as Bitcoin, which are based on so-called proof-of-work blockchains – is their environmental impact. It is, to say the least, considerable. Although it was not noted at all in *Cryptopia*, the 'mining' of cryptoassets is a hugely energy-intensive activity.[66] In its 2021 *Global Financial*

sources suggest that this second figure could well be substantially higher. See eg S Foley, JR Karlsen, and TJ Putniņš, 'Sex, Drugs, and Bitcoin: How Much Illegal Activity Is Financed through Cryptocurrencies?' (2019) 32 *Review of Financial Studies* 1798, 1800, which suggests that approximately 23% of the total dollar value of all cryptoasset transactions have related to illegal activity. For an explanation as to why estimates on this topic vary so wildly, see www.coindesk.com/policy/2022/05/09/how-big-is-crypto-crime-really/ (accessed 26 August 2023).

[65] *Ruscoe* (n 8) [130].

[66] The process of adding to a proof-of-work blockchain is called 'mining'. The process of adding to a so-called proof-of-stake blockchain is called 'forging'. 'Forging' is apparently a materially less energy intensive activity than mining. Nevertheless, it is certainly not an energy-insignificant exercise: see M Platt et al, 'The Energy Footprint of Blockchain Consensus Mechanisms Beyond Proof-of-Work', *2021 IEEE 21st International Conference on Software Quality, Reliability and Security Companion (QRS-C)* (2021) 1135–1144 (available at ieeexplore.ieee.org/document/9741872 (accessed 26 August 2023)).

Stability Report, the International Monetary Fund was prepared to endorse the estimate that Bitcoin production alone uses up to 0.36 percent of the word's electricity, an amount comparable to the total energy consumption of Belgium or Chile.[67] Likewise, others have concluded that, 'based on average emission factors … and the Bitcoin network's estimated electric load demand … Bitcoin mining may be responsible for [generating] 65.4 megatonnes of CO_2 … per year'.[68] That is comparable to country-level emissions in Greece and represents 0.19 percent of global CO_2 output. The environmental cost of recognising cryptoassets as property must therefore be taken into account when deciding whether to give the green light to their increased usage that their recognition as property would surely bring.

In addition, given how considerable the environmental impact of cryptoasset production might be *if things were to go wrong*, there needs to be real accountability underpinning any such decision. The United Kingdom, of which England and Wales is a constituent part, has many obligations under international law (and the government has many domestic law targets) with respect to reducing our fossil fuel consumption. Assuming, then, that we cannot magically increase the amount of renewable energy in our national grid by the requisite amount – which we cannot – it is the legislature which needs to decide what to do. This country's place in the world and its ambitions and views on climate change are not just of widespread public interest but are also of considerable political importance. Our elected representatives, and the people who vote for them, are deeply concerned with environmental matters, and this means that how we go forward with respect to cryptoassets is and ought to be a macro-level policy choice for us all, through Parliament, to partake in. The appropriate accountability mechanisms are surely also mainly political/democratic rather than legal.

A third major factor, which again Gendall J did not consider, is the political and governmental impact of recognising cryptoassets as property. Because doing so would inevitably green-light their increased use, we have to think hard about whether, as a political matter, that is something we want to happen. In short, there is a reason why politicians such as Ted Cruz like cryptoassets so much. They take money outside both governmental control and oversight. They decentralise the flow of capital and conceal it from authority. Now one may very well think that this would be a good thing. Nevertheless, it is also clearly an intensely political point, with huge implications for how our country and in particular our government will function in the future. It is therefore one which cannot legitimately be decided by a judge or panel of judges. A large part of our government's power rests on its financial authority over the economy, and its ability to raise revenue depends on its ability to collect taxes. As a consequence, any loss of control, or any increase in tax evasion, could constitute a major threat to the state's present nature and function. To make this point in a different way, consider the fact that, if one would agree with the proposition that the

[67] The report is accessible online at www.imf.org/en/Publications/GFSR/Issues/2021/10/12/global-financial-stability-report-october-2021 (accessed 26 August 2023) and the relevant figure (and the comparisons) can be found on p 53.

[68] de Vries et al, 'Revisiting Bitcoin's Carbon Footprint', *Joule* (2022), https://doi.org/10.1016/j.joule.2022.02.005 (accessed 26 August 2023).

judiciary cannot decide to abolish the Bank of England, His Majesty's Revenue and Customs, or the Royal Mint, then by parity of reasoning one should not accept that those institutions' respective authority could or should be eroded by judicial fiat.

III. CONCLUSION

This chapter began with the proposition that, as a matter of law, if something is *capable* of being property ('can'), and if it *should* be property ('should'), then all other things being equal it *will* be recognised as property ('is'). It thus drew out the existence of two separate but equally important conditions which need to be satisfied in relation to any particular thing before that thing can be said to be property in a legal sense. Of course, if this is so, it is not enough for the courts to decide that, because a particular thing has met the law's minimum necessary conditions for *being* property (assuming there are any),[69] there is without more sufficient reason for them to recognise that thing *as* property. Something further – a positive answer to the *should* question – is required.

This chapter focused on the *should* question and, in particular, the issue of which branch of our government ought to answer it, at least when it comes to cryptoassets. It argued unequivocally in favour of the legislature. It looked at a variety of cases in which judges from this jurisdiction have refused to change various aspects of our private law and attempted to categorise the reasoning put forward within them. It then applied a number of those reasons to cryptoassets and found that they were directly applicable. In other words, this chapter has argued that the question of whether or not cryptoassets *should* be recognised as property is one the judiciary lacks the competence to answer. The result of this is that any move by the courts either to skip the *should* question as it applies to cryptoassets, or to answer it themselves in the affirmative, would be one made without the appropriate expertise and involve unacceptable constitutional overreach on their part. It should not be allowed to happen.

Is the position espoused in this chapter too conservative? Does it fail to give enough weight to the incremental rule-making power of our judges? It is, after all, undeniable that the courts have regularly updated the common law, and when appropriate introduced new rules, in light of economic and technological developments.[70] What is more, most of these changes have not been (and should not be) seen as seriously controversial.

Nevertheless, I am not convinced that cryptoassets are things which, even in the context of the digital revolution of the past thirty years, are particularly ordinary. I am also not sure that all of the legal questions their increasing use has begun to raise fall within the usual scope of the property and financial puzzles with which

[69] For doubts on this point, see eg R Stevens, *Torts and Rights* (Oxford, Oxford University Press, 2009) 5–7.

[70] Consider, for example, the rule of law which allows the owner of a negotiable instrument to sue someone guilty of converting it for the value of the right to which the instrument related, not just the value of the instrument itself, which is presumably pennies. That rule is discussed in *OBG Ltd* (n 18) [102]–[106]. As Lord Hoffmann explained, it was introduced to fill a gap in the law caused by the use of cheques.

practitioners and judges are used to engaging. Indeed, it therefore seems to me to be important that even the Law Commission, a body in favour of the increased legal recognition of cryptoassets, is proposing that they are categorised (whether by the courts or the legislature) as some form of *tertium quid*.[71] In cryptoassets, we have come across a phenomenon which is, in substance, of a very different type or kind to electronic documents, computer software or wireless communication. This means we are not playing anything like a normal game when we consider whether or not (and, if so, how) to bring them within the fold of our legal system. In his poem 'An Essay on Criticism', Alexander Pope suggested that 'fools rush in where angels fear to tread'.[72] I think that it would be good for the judiciary, the general public and the UK's economy, if our judges were to avoid doing anything else as regards cryptoassets which risks proving him correct.

[71] Law Commission, *Digital Assets* (n 2) paras 4.68–4.99.
[72] A Pope, 'An Essay on Criticism' (London, William Lewis, 1711) line 628.

Index

www.ingramcontent.com/pod-product-compliance
Ingram Content Group UK Ltd.
Pitfield, Milton Keynes, MK11 3LW, UK
UKHW020234290926
15470UKWH00002B/537

9 781509 965151